The Modern American Metropolis

Uncovering the Past: Documentary Readers in American History
Series Editors: Steven Lawson and Nancy Hewitt

The books in this series introduce students in American history courses to two important dimensions of historical analysis. They enable students to engage actively in historical interpretation, and they further students' understanding of the interplay between social and political forces in historical developments.

Consisting of primary sources and an introductory essay, these readers are aimed at the major courses in the American history curriculum, as outlined further below. Each book in the series will be approximately 250–300 pages, including a 15–20 page introduction addressing key issues and questions about the subject under consideration, a discussion of sources and methodology, and a bibliography of suggested secondary readings.

Published

Paul G. E. Clemens
The Colonial Era: A Documentary Reader

Sean Patrick Adams
The Early American Republic: A Documentary Reader

Stanley Harrold
The Civil War and Reconstruction: A Documentary Reader

Steven Mintz
African American Voices: A Documentary Reader, 1619–1877

Robert P. Ingalls and David K. Johnson
The United States Since 1945: A Documentary Reader

Camilla Townsend
American Indian History: A Documentary Reader

Steven Mintz
Mexican American Voices: A Documentary Reader

Brian Ward
The 1960s: A Documentary Reader

Nancy Rosenbloom
Women in American History Since 1880: A Documentary Reader

Jeremi Suri
American Foreign Relations Since 1898: A Documentary Reader

Carol Faulkner
Women in American History to 1880: A Documentary Reader

David Welky
America Between the Wars, 1919–1941: A Documentary Reader

William A. Link and Susannah J. Link
The Gilded Age and Progressive Era: A Documentary Reader

G. Kurt Piehler
The United States in World War II: A Documentary Reader

Leslie Brown
African American Voices: A Documentary Reader from Emancipation to the Present

David M. P. Freund
The Modern American Metropolis: A Documentary Reader

In preparation

Edward Miller
The Vietnam War: A Documentary Reader

Joseph Cullon
The Era of the American Revolution: A Documentary Reader

John A. Kirk
The Civil Rights Movement: A Documentary Reader

James C. Giesen & Bryant Simon
Food and Eating in America: A Documentary Reader

The Modern American Metropolis

A Documentary Reader

Edited by David M. P. Freund

WILEY Blackwell

This edition first published 2015

Registered Office
John Wiley & Sons, Ltd, The Atrium, Southern Gate, Chichester, West Sussex, PO19 8SQ, UK

Editorial Offices
350 Main Street, Malden, MA 02148-5020, USA
9600 Garsington Road, Oxford, OX4 2DQ, UK
The Atrium, Southern Gate, Chichester, West Sussex, PO19 8SQ, UK

For details of our global editorial offices, for customer services, and for information about how to apply for permission to reuse the copyright material in this book please see our website at www.wiley.com/wiley-blackwell.

Library of Congress Cataloging-in-Publication Data

The modern American metropolis : a documentary reader / edited by David M.P. Freund.
pages cm.
Includes bibliographical references and index.
ISBN 978-1-4443-3901-7 (cloth) – ISBN 978-1-4443-3900-0 (pbk.)
1. Urbanization–United States–History. 2. Urban policy–United States–History. 3. City planning–United States–History. 4. City and town life–United States–History. I. Freund, David M. P.
HT123.M577 2015
307.760973–dc23

2014018420

A catalogue record for this book is available from the British Library.

Cover image: Brooklyn Bridge and Manhattan reflected in the East River, New York, 1934.
© Keystone-France/Getty Images
Cover design by Simon Levy

Set in 10/12.5pt Sabon by SPi Publisher Services, Pondicherry, India
Printed and bound in Malaysia by Vivar Printing Sdn Bhd

1 2015

For the teachers who always asked questions and let the sources have their say.

Contents

List of Illustrations xii
Series Editors' Preface xiv
Acknowledgments xvi
Source Acknowledgments xvii

Introduction Or, What Can a Wet Basement Tell Us about Metropolitan History? 1

Part I Cities and Hinterlands in Mid-Nineteenth-Century America 27

Chapter 1 Transforming the Landscape and Its Functions 29

1 Chicago's *Daily Democrat* Measures the Impact of the Transport Revolution, 1852 29
2 Cyrus McCormick Markets the Virginia Reaper to the Nation's Farmers, 1850 and 1851 36
3 Texans Appeal for the Removal of Native Peoples, 1858–1859 40
4 *Hunt's Merchants' Magazine* Discusses the Value of Slave Labor, 1855–1858 45

Chapter 2 Snapshots of Urban Life on the Eve of the Civil War 50

1 An Irish Immigrant Writes Home about Life in the United States, 1850 50
2 Frederick Law Olmsted Compares Northern and Southern Cities along the Atlantic Seaboard, 1856 53
3 The *New York Times* Reports on a Millworker Strike in Lynn and Marblehead, 1859 60
4 Reverend Albert Williams Describes San Francisco's Fires 63

Part II From Walking City to Industrial Metropolis, 1860–1920 69

Chapter 3 Commerce and the Metropolis 71

1 The Pacific Railway Act of 1862 Connects the Nation 71
2 William Dean Howells Describes Suburban Boston, 1872 75
3 August Spies Addresses Workers about Their Conditions, 1886 80
4 An Engineer Describes the Work Required to Make Seattle Competitive, 1908 84
5 New York City Retailers Organize to Protect a Fifth Avenue Shopping District, 1916 87

Chapter 4 "Natives," Migrants, and Immigrants 90

1 A Polish Immigrant Describes Life and Work in New York City, 1902 90
2 Unions Call for Boycott of Chinese and Their Patrons, 1891–1892 96
3 *La Crónica* Reports on Challenges Facing the Texan Mexican Community, 1910–1911 97
4 *Good Housekeeping* Counsels "The Commuter's Wife," 1909 106
5 Black Southerners Write the *Chicago Defender* for Information about Employment, 1916–1918 110

Chapter 5 Big City Life 118

1 Urban Imagery, 1889–1913 118
2 A Young Governess Discusses Her New Freedoms, 1903 122
3 A Columnist Describes the Pleasures and Perils of Coney Island, 1915 125
4 A *Harper's Weekly* Columnist Worries about Garbage, 1891 129

Chapter 6 Local Politics in the Gilded Age 135

1 George Washington Plunkitt Defends Patronage Politics in New York City, 1905 135
2 Dallas City Commissioner Advocates Running a City Like a Business, 1909 139
3 Jane Addams Describes the Goals of Hull House, 1893 141
4 An Economist Investigates Employers' Response to Labor Unions 147

Part III City and Suburb Ascendant, 1920–1945 155

Chapter 7 Commerce, Consumption, and the Suburban Trend 157

1 An Investment Banker Insists that "Everyone Ought to Be Rich," 1929 157
2 Commerce and the Good Life 159
3 Former Employees Describe Finding Work and Building Cars for Ford Motor Company 160
4 Alfred Kazin Recalls New York City's Ethnic Boundaries Before World War II 170
5 A Social Scientist Explains the "Suburban Trend," 1925 175
6 Suburban Speculation Creates Empty Subdivisions, 1925 179

Chapter 8 Economic Collapse and Metropolitan Crisis 182

1 The New Deal Rebuilds the Metropolis during the Great Depression 182
2 Jane Yoder Describes Living through the Depression in a Central Illinois Mining Town 185
3 Langston Hughes Remembers Rent Parties in Harlem 187
4 Jose Yglesias Describes the 1930s in Tampa and New York City 190

Chapter 9 The Metropolis at War 194

1 The LA Chamber of Commerce Coordinates the Region's War Production Efforts, 1942–1943 194
2 Henry Cervantes Describes His Journey from Migrant Farm Worker to World War II Hero 199
3 White Transit Workers Walk Off the Job in Philadelphia, 1944 206
4 Jeanne Wakatsuki Houston Recounts Her Family's Forced Relocation from Santa Monica, California 208

Part IV Creating a Suburban Nation, 1945–1970s 215

Chapter 10 "The Affluent Society" 217

1 Veterans Line Up for Homes in Long Island, 1949 217
2 *Sunset* Magazine Markets a Suburban Way of Living, 1946 and 1958 219
3 *Ebony* Discusses Homeownership and Domestic Life for a Steelworker's Family in Gary, Indiana, 1957 223
4 Catherine Marshall Defends a Woman's Right to Work, 1954 226

Chapter 11 Public Policy and "Best Use" in American Neighborhoods **229**

1 The Federal Housing Administration Defines Value in Single-Family Suburban Housing 229
2 A US Senator Argues That Military Spending Is Producing Inequality, 1962 232
3 Herbert Gans Critiques Federal Urban Renewal Programs, 1959 236
4 *U.S. News and World Report* Warns of Contaminated Suburban Water Supplies, 1963 240

Chapter 12 Metropolitan Contests over Citizenship, Rights, and Access **244**

1 Local Activists Organize a Boycott in Montgomery, Alabama, 1954 244
2 Suburban Homeowners Mobilize to Exclude "Incompatible" Development, 1950–1951 250
3 Residents of a Memphis Neighborhood Block Construction of the Interstate, 1967 253
4 Activists Define Black Power, 1967 257
5 Gays and Lesbians in New York City Organize to Combat Discrimination, 1969 263
6 A Photograph Captures Divisions in Boston over Court-Ordered Busing, 1976 264

Part V What Makes a City? The "Postindustrial" Metropolis **269**

Chapter 13 Redefining "Urban" and "Suburban" **271**

1 U.S. Steel Demolishes Its Plant in Youngstown, Ohio, 1983 271
2 Hoboken Residents Debate the "Yuppie" Invasion, 1984–1987 273
3 Jersey City Markets Itself to a New Demographic, 2003 and 2006 278
4 A Professor Explains How Urban Redevelopment Has Impacted Los Angeles's Minority Communities, 1987/1988 281
5 Planners Assess an Experiment in "New Urbanism" (Before the Great Recession), 1999 286

Chapter 14 Growth and Its Challenges **292**

1 The Global Economy and Global Politics Create New Challenges in the Twin Cities Region, 2012 292
2 College Students in Merced Rent Empty McMansions, 2011 295
3 The *Great Wall of Los Angeles* Pictures the Region's Development History, 1974 to the Present 298
4 City Building in Kansas: An Immigrant's Perspective, 2007 300
5 Developers in Los Angeles County Spark a Twenty-First-Century Debate over City Building and Environmental Protection, 2009 305

Further Reading 313
Index 319

List of Illustrations

1.2	McCormick's Patent Virginia Reaper, 1850	37
4.2	Flyers distributed by Silver Bow Trades and Labor Assembly and Butte Miners' Union, 1891–1892	98
5.1(a)	Traffic jam on Dearborn Street, Chicago, 1909	119
5.1(b)	MetLife's Industrial Audit and Policy Division, New York City, 1896	120
5.1(c)	Lewis Hine, "A Little Spinner in Globe Cotton Mill," 1909	120
5.1(d)	Boardwalk at Rockaway Beach, NY, postcard, 1913	121
5.1(e)	J. A. Riis, "Lodgers in Bayard Street Tenement, Five Cents a Spot," 1889	121
7.2(a)	"For the Young Business Man," advertisement for 1925 Ford Model T Runabout, 1924	161
7.2(b)	Advertisement for Clara Smith's "Percolatin' Blues," 1927	162
7.2(c)	"Tobacco at its best – in a pipe!" Edgeworth advertisement, 1920s	163
7.2(d)	"It cannot be found in cook books," advertisement for Aunt Jemima Pancake Flour, 1924	164
7.2(e)	"Everything is Hot-tentotsy now," *Life* magazine cover, 1926	165
7.2(f)	A. N. Scurlock, Young women at outdoor sports event, *c.* 1920–1930	166
7.2(g)	Fourth of July at Venice Beach, photograph, 1931	167
7.6	Aerial view of Dearborn, Michigan, 1925	180
8.1(a)	The New Deal rebuilds the metropolis, Tuskegee, Alabama, 1936	183

8.1(b)	WPA road grading project, Pennsylvania	184
8.1(c)	WPA sewer project, San Diego. Photo by Russell Lee, 1941	184
10.3	Photo of Denver Lee and family, 1957	225
12.5	Mattachine Society of New York, "Where Were You during the Christopher St. Riots?" 1969	265
12.6	Stanley Forman, *The Soiling of Old Glory, Boston, April 5, 1976*	266
13.1	The demolition of Ohio Works, Youngstown, 1983	272
13.3	The Majestic Theatre Condominiums sales brochure	279
14.3(a)	Judith F. Baca, "Farewell to Rosie the Riveter," 1983	299
14.3(b)	Judith F. Baca, "Division of the Barrios," 1983	300
14.3(c)	Judith F. Baca, "Asians Gain Citizenship and Property," 1983	300

Series Editors' Preface

Primary sources have become an essential component in the teaching of history to undergraduates. They engage students in the process of historical interpretation and analysis and help them understand that facts do not speak for themselves. Rather, students see how historians construct narratives that recreate the past. Most students assume that the pursuit of knowledge is a solitary endeavor; yet historians constantly interact with their peers, building on previous research and arguing among themselves over the interpretation of documents and their larger meaning. The documentary readers in this series highlight the value of this collaborative creative process and encourage students to participate in it.

Each book in the series introduces students in American history courses to two important dimensions of historical analysis. They enable students to engage actively in historical interpretation, and they further students' understanding of the interplay between social, cultural, economic, and political forces in historical developments. In pursuit of these goals, the documents in each text embrace a broad range of sources, including such items as illustrations of material artifacts, letters and diaries, sermons, maps, photographs, song lyrics, selections from fiction and memoirs, legal statutes, court decisions, presidential orders, speeches, and political cartoons.

Each volume in the series is edited by a specialist in the field who is concerned with undergraduate teaching. The goal is not to offer a comprehensive selection of material but to provide items that reflect major themes and debates; that illustrate significant social, cultural, political, and economic dimensions of an era or subject; and that inform, intrigue, and inspire undergraduate students. The editor of each volume has written an introduction that discusses the central questions that have occupied historians in this field and the ways historians have used primary sources to answer them. In addition, each introductory essay contains an explanation of the kinds of materials available to investigate a particular subject, the methods by which scholars analyze them, and the considerations that go into interpreting them. Each source selection is introduced by a short headnote that gives students the necessary information and a context for understanding the document. Also, each section of the volume includes questions to guide student reading and stimulate classroom discussion.

David Freund's *The Modern American Metropolis: A Documentary Reader* provides a fresh and extended perspective on the growth of the United States from a predominantly rural to a largely urban and metropolitan nation. Freund traces this development from the eve of the Civil War through the first decades of the twenty-first century. Although events unfold chronologically, Freund organizes chapters around themes that provide students with a sense of the larger issues raised by increased urbanization and the resulting reconfiguration of public and private spaces. He pays particular attention to how the growth of cities and suburbs altered the environment, as well as to the variety of people and groups that built and inhabited urban America. In addition, Freund traces urban development within the context of immigration, industrialization, local and national politics, wars, and depression, while also showing the influence of social and cultural forces related to race, gender, and consumption.

The primary sources Freund includes in this volume document the construction of metropolitan America from diverse perspectives. We hear from businessmen, workers, government officials, urban planners, architects, engineers, academics, writers, clergy, housewives, military veterans, women, African Americans, Hispanics, and gays and lesbians, all of whom participated in and influenced the shape of the metropolitan United States. They do this through speeches, letters, brochures, newspaper and magazine articles, advertisements, photographs, legal statutes, memoirs, interviews, and public reports. In introducing and presenting these documents, Freund guides students toward a better understanding of the complexities and challenges of the metropolitan society most of us live in today.

Steven F. Lawson and Nancy A. Hewitt
Series Editors

Acknowledgments

Thank you to Peter Coveney of Wiley-Blackwell, and Nancy Hewitt and Steven Lawson of Rutgers University. I was fortunate enough to receive their invitation to design this volume and have appreciated their support and constructive criticism throughout the writing and production process. I am very grateful to Elizabeth Saucier, Georgina Coleby, Tom Bates, Leanda Shrimpton, Sarah Dancy, and Jacqueline Harvey for their fine work turning the manuscript into this book. We are all thankful for editorial software and email.

A legion of scholars, librarians, archivists, public historians, and students contributed to this volume's design and completion, through their own research and by generously offering assistance, ideas, and materials. A very small sample of their work is cited in the suggested readings and several contributing institutions are cited in the Source Acknowledgments. Special thanks are in order to Peter Baldwin, Susan Burneson, Pilar Castillo, Lee Grady, Gladys Hansen, Kelly Kerbow Hudson, Matthew Klingle, Maggie Rivas-Rodriguez, Chris Romero, Priam Saywack, Dace Taube, Sarah Traugott, Cezar Del Valle, Karen Wisniewski, to the staffs of the Ohio Historical Society and the Texas State Library and Archives Commission, and finally to the students who have engaged me in discussions about metropolitan sources and issues for nearly two decades. I am indebted to colleagues and friends who read parts or all of the manuscript at various stages and whose critical responses and suggestions have made this a much better book. Thanks to Michael Berk, Adina Popescu Berk, Willow Lung-Amam, Raymond Mohl, Robert Self, Andrew Wiese, and the anonymous readers for Wiley Blackwell. Karen Caplan, Nathan Connolly, and Matthew Lassiter performed heavy and extremely helpful lifting during the revision process. Time spent in metropolitan places with Jonah, Benjamin, and Karen made this project possible.

Source Acknowledgments

The editor and publisher gratefully acknowledge the permission granted to reproduce the copyright material in this book:

1.2 Courtesy of the Wisconsin Historical Society.

4.3 "En Pro de la Raza Mexicana del Estado de Texas," *La Crónica*, November 26, 1910, p. 1; "A El Imparcial de Texas," *La Crónica*, December 10, 1910, p. 4; "Tanto los Niños Mexicanos como los Mexico-Americanos son exluidos de las Escuelas Oficiales – ¿ya se Olividaron los Tratados de Guadalupe?" *La Crónica*, December 24, 1910, p. 1; "La Exclusión en el Condado de Guadalupe" and "Los Mexicanos de San Angelo Demandan a Los Síndicos de las Escuelas Públicas," *La Crónica*, December 31, 1910, p. 1; "Cobarde Infame e Inhumano Lynchamiento de un Jovencito Mexicano en Thor[n]dale, Milam Co., Texas," *La Crónica*, June 29, 1911; "Nuestro Deber en Este País: Solidaridad y Altruismo," *La Crónica*, December 24, 1910. Courtesy of the Dolph Briscoe Center for American History, University of Texas, Austin. Translation by Karen D. Caplan.

7.1 Samuel Crowther, "Everybody Ought to Be Rich: An Interview with John J. Raskob," *Ladies' Home Journal*. Copyright © 1929, Meredith Corporation. All rights reserved. Used with permission of Ladies' Home Journal.

7.3 Judith Stepan-Norris and Maurice Zeitlin, *Talking Union* (Urbana: University of Illiniois Press, 1996), pp. 27–32, 48–49. Reproduced by permission of the University of Illinois Press.

7.4 Alfred Kazin, *A Walker in the City* (New York: Harcourt, Brace, 1951), pp. 8–12, 17–20, 39–41, 15–17. Copyright © 1951 and renewed 1979 by Alfred Kazin. Reprinted by permission of Houghton Mifflin Harcourt Publishing Company. All rights reserved.

8.3 Langston Hughes, "House Rent Parties Are Again Returning to Harlem," *Chicago Defender*, March 9, 1957. Reproduced by permission of Real Times Media.

9.2 Henry "Hank" Cervantes, interviewed by Maggie Rivas-Rodriguez and Bruce Ashcroft, Washington, DC, May 30, 2004, videotape recording, U.S. Latino and Latina World War II Oral History Project. Reproduced with permission from VOCES Oral History Project, the University of Texas at Austin.

9.4 Jeanne Wakatsuki Houston and James D. Houston, *Farewell to Manzanar* (New York: Bantam, 1973), pp. 3–18. Copyright © 1973 by James D. Houston, renewed 2001 by Jeanne Wakatsuki Houston and James D. Houston. Reprinted by permission of Houghton Mifflin Harcourt Publishing Company. All rights reserved.

10.1 "Line Forms Early in Sale of Houses," *New York Times*, March 7, 1949, p. 21. Reproduced by permission of The New York Times Company.

11.3 Herbert J. Gans, "The Human Implications of Current Redevelopment and Relocation Planning," *Journal of the American Institute of Planners*, 25(1), February 1959, pp. 15–19, 22. Reproduced by permission from Taylor & Francis and H. J. Gans.

11.4 "Just How Safe Is Your Drinking Water?" *U.S. News and World Report*, 55(3), July 15, 1963. Reproduced by permission of U.S. News and World Report LLC.

12.1 Henry Hampton and Steve Fayer (eds.), *Voices of Freedom: An Oral History of the Civil Rights Movement from the 1950s through the 1980s* (New York: Bantam Books, 1990), pp. 17–24, 26–27, 29–31. Copyright © 1990 by Blackside, Inc. Used by permission of Bantam Books, an imprint of The Random House Publishing Group, a division of Random House LLC. All rights reserved.

12.2 *Southwest Dearborn Civic Association* (newsletter), October 1950 and April 1951. Dearborn Historical Museum, Dearborn, Michigan. Reproduced by permission of the Dearborn Historical Museum.

12.3 (Mrs.) Anona Stoner, Secretary, Citizens to Preserve Overton Park to President Lyndon B. Johnson, January 5, 1967. Tennessee Department of Highways and Public Works, Record Group 84, Box 26, Folder 3,

Tennessee State Library and Archives, Nashville. Courtesy of the Tennessee State Library and Archives.

12.4 Kwame Ture and Charles V. Hamilton, *Black Power: The Politics of Liberation in America* (1967; New York: Vintage, 1992), pp. 147–149, 152, 155–156, 160–162; 9–10, 18–19, 22–23, 34, 39–40, 44, 46–49, 52–54. © 1967 by Stokely Carmichael and Charles Hamilton. Used by permission of Alfred A. Knopf, an imprint of the Knopf Doubleday Publishing Group, a division of Random House LLC. All rights reserved.

13.2 Joseph Barry and John Derevlany (eds.), *Yuppies Invade My House at Dinnertime: A Tale of Brunch, Bombs, and Gentrification in an American City* (Hoboken, NJ: Big River Publishing, 1987), pp. ix–xiii, 9–11, 26, 77–80, 125–126. Reproduced with permission from J. Derevlany and the *Hudson Reporter*.

13.3 Christopher Zinzli, "Sugar House Lofts: A Bit of History Restored for Fine Living," *Jersey City Magazine*, Spring/Summer 2006, pp. 32–33. Reproduced by permission of Hudson Reporter Association, L.P.

13.5 Brian Wolshon and James Wahl, "Novi's Main Street: Neotraditional Neighborhood Planning and Design," *Journal of Urban Planning and Development*, 125(1) (March 1999), pp. 2–7, 13, 16. Reproduced by permission of the American Society of Civil Engineers.

14.1 Maya Rao, "Immigrants Draw Lines for Change in Minneapolis," *Star Tribune*, February 14, 2012. Reproduced by permission of Star Tribune.

14.2 Patricia Leigh Brown, "Animal McMansion: Students Trade Dorm for Suburban Luxury," *New York Times*, November 13, 2011, p. A1. Reproduced by permission of The New York Times Company.

14.4 "El Mojado," in Peter Orner (ed.), *Underground America: Narratives of Undocumented Lives* (San Francisco: McSweeney's, 2008), pp. 205–216. Reproduced by permission.

14.5 Edward Humes, "The Last Frontier," *Los Angeles Magazine*, 54(6) (June 2009), pp. 94–97, 124. Reproduced by permission of Emmis Publishing Company. Reproduced by permission of Edward Humes.

Every effort has been made to trace copyright holders and to obtain permission for the use of copyright material. The publisher apologizes for any errors or omissions in the above list and would be grateful if notified of any corrections that should be incorporated in future reprints or editions of this book.

Introduction Or, What Can a Wet Basement Tell Us about Metropolitan History?

As I began working on this book in the summer of 2010, the basement of my house flooded on five separate occasions when a series of intense thunderstorms struck the Washington, DC, metropolitan area. I live just north of the DC border in Silver Spring, Maryland, and have an office in that basement. In fact my desk sits between two of the windows – the kind built partially below ground level, within window wells – that were breached during the storms. Repeatedly in late July and August our family discovered water underfoot in saturated carpeting or trickling down a basement wall and then battled against the elements. The problem was the frequency of severe weather and the sheer volume of rain. Water from the downpours pooled in the yard so rapidly that it spilled into and filled the window wells, then gradually seeped into the basement from what seemed like every angle. In two especially dramatic episodes the pressure was so great that water streamed steadily through window frames, as if pouring from a faucet, into the office and a nearby utility room. Our first responses were stopgap measures, digging trenches in the yard to draw water away from the house and positioning sandbags to redirect lingering runoff, all the while fighting back growing puddles on the basement floor with a shop vacuum. Then, after each threat passed, we cleared out the damage and fortified against the next storm as well as we could. But our fixes were never sufficient. Water kept finding a way in. Eventually we turned to a contractor, who removed drywall to identify hidden points of entry in the foundation and engineered

The Modern American Metropolis: A Documentary Reader, First Edition.
Edited by David M. P. Freund.

a drainage system in the yard to divert runoff and groundwater away from the house. By summer's end we had sealed the basement, at least for now, against errant water.

Of course, it is not uncommon in American cities and suburbs for the water from heavy rains to accumulate in yards and intersections or to find its way into buildings. Land can absorb and drain only so much water at a time, and buildings leak. But that summer's fierce and unrelenting storms repeatedly left the DC region to deal with an unusual amount of water. With the land constantly saturated, each new downpour soaked residential subdivisions and commercial districts, overpowering the drainage system designed to channel runoff to the Chesapeake Bay. Rainwater simply had nowhere to go, and so instead it filled up and lingered in unaccustomed places: sidewalks and streets, parking lots and plazas, window wells and basements. One roadway in Washington's Rock Creek Park was transformed into a rushing river; compelling video footage of the scene was a staple of local and national news coverage of the region's weather-related woes. Meanwhile strong winds brought down scores of trees and power lines, blocking streets and cutting off electricity to thousands of businesses and households, often for days at a time. Water saturates anything permeable in its path, and that season the leaky basements of our metropolitan area were in its way. Evidence of its power and persistence was constantly on display in the piles of discarded carpeting, storage boxes, and furnishings that appeared on sidewalks and yards throughout DC and nearby sections of Virginia and Maryland.

Given nature's long tradition of wreaking havoc on cities, I was not surprised when the metropolitan area and our house were damaged by torrential rains. But that summer I learned firsthand the difficulty of *controlling* water, especially for amateurs fumbling about in a muddy yard and in a soggy, darkened basement. And witnessing the weather disrupt the region's normal routines while repeatedly battling groundwater in that basement had the unanticipated effect of helping me organize my thoughts for this introduction and book. It helped me articulate three broad themes that I encourage you to consider while using the volume, and that I will introduce by raising some of the issues that came to mind as we watched our neighborhood and the greater metropolitan region negotiate a summer of unusually severe weather.

*

The first theme concerns what cities are made of, literally. *Metropolitan structures and landscapes are artificial, human-made things that exist in delicate balance with the natural environment. And for this reason considerable effort is required to build and maintain them.*

While this point might seem obvious, I encourage you to think carefully about what metropolitan places are and the work involved in fashioning them, both materially and as systems of organization. Of course, the American experience is part of a centuries-long history of city building, as humans have strived to create ordered and lasting settlements in a variety of "disorderly" environments. Nature never stands still, but this has not stopped people from building shelter and complex social, economic, and political systems with the intention, or at least hope, that they will remain stable and safe. And these efforts to bend nature to our will have grown especially ambitious over the last two centuries, thanks to innovation, industrial technologies, and new scales of bureaucratic organization. We regularly create habitable places through massive manipulations of the environment: much of Lower Manhattan is built on landfill; Miami's expansion required draining its adjacent wetlands; and Las Vegas relies on water from a distant reservoir created by damning the Colorado River. We are building far *more* structures than in the past, many of them quite elaborate and imposing – think of skyscrapers, the Interstate System, or sports stadiums – and all at increasingly lower costs. Finally, we carefully manage developed areas, by restricting properties to specific residential, commercial, and public uses and then linking them together with a high-maintenance infrastructure that coordinates flows of people, water, goods, energy, information, and waste. Through this array of technically sophisticated, labor-intensive, and expensive interventions we have imposed more and more human preferences on the land and thus created new kinds of useful and economically valuable property.

Taken together, this collection of structures, landscapes, and human-made systems makes up what scholars call "the built environment." The term refers, basically, to the stuff that people have constructed and changes that they have made to the land. In the modern era – certainly in the United States – we tend to expect that our built environment, if properly maintained, will withstand most of nature's challenges. But then, again and again, extreme weather or gradual environmental change or human error illustrates the limits of our control. For me, that summer of flooding provided a humble reminder that the nonhuman world is indifferent to our preferences (dry rooms and passable streets, for example) and that keeping habitats comfortable and safe requires enormous effort. Protecting and repairing a 700-square-foot basement was exhausting, expensive, and repeatedly left me wet and caked in mud. But, in light of the storms' regional impacts, it was clear that the challenges faced by households like ours were comparatively modest. Local officials scrambled to provide emergency services, repair roads and bridges, replace power lines (2,000 came down in just the first storm), rebuild electrical substations, and clear away hundreds of fallen trees. Businesses, public offices, and hospitals dealt with extensive structural damage while struggling to resume normal operations. These emergency efforts got me thinking in turn about the complex work required to maintain a city under "normal" conditions: to build and manage businesses, services, utilities, and transport networks; to access and control water, secure sources of energy, and then monitor waste and other hazards; to provide police and fire protection, run schools and libraries, and maintain public spaces and parks. Witnessing the storms' disruption in light of our efforts to keep a basement dry underscored a point that even an urban historian can, at times, take for granted. Keeping a vast metropolitan region up and running is complicated, labor-intensive, and costly work. Cities are artificial things and difficult to maintain.

*

Closely related but distinct is a second theme, which concerns the social and political complexity of this city-building process. *Constructing and sustaining the metropolis – its buildings, landscapes, and the intricate systems of which they form a part – is a product of constant negotiation and often conflict between numerous public and private interests.* American metropolitan life has always been a contested political process demanding that people settle, in some fashion, their differences.

Maintaining the built environment would be hard enough if there were agreement about what should be built and how resources should be distributed, but this is rarely the case. Consider the negotiations required to repair storm damage to just one building – for materials, labor, permits, inspections, and paying for the work – and then consider the infinitely more complicated and conflict-ridden task of responding to a metropolitan-wide emergency. In metropolitan DC that summer there were a lot of problems to solve, yet constant disagreement between municipal authorities, contractors, landlords, employers, renters, homeowners, service providers, and insurance companies, all while millions of people navigated disruptions to their commuting patterns and normal delivery schedules. Meanwhile local officials and utilities companies faced daunting emergency and reconstruction challenges with limited resources, which forced them to make unpopular decisions about service provision and to prioritize certain repairs over others. Some neighborhoods waited days or even weeks for crews to clear streets or restore power. Again my thoughts turned to the everyday process of city building, this time its politics. To pay for routine repairs and operating costs, local governments must levy and collect fees and taxes, secure federal funding, and manage disbursement. At the same time, coordinating development requires constant negotiations over the design, placement, and maintenance of every structure and landscape. Each project must respect zoning and building codes or, alternatively, local ordinances must be amended. Invariably there is disagreement about what should be built, who should have access, the impacts of private investment, and who should pay for and benefit from the public contribution. Corruption regularly influences the bargaining process and some rules are enforced while others are ignored. Rarely is construction or maintenance undertaken without conflict and some groups fare better than others, leaving one or more parties unhappy with the results.

A famous and far more destructive flood illustrates the point. When Hurricane Katrina barreled through the Gulf Coast region in 2005 and overwhelmed New Orleans' levees, water rapidly filled nearly 80 percent of that city and caused incalculable devastation. Within its municipal borders alone the storm killed well over 1,000 people (the precise figure is unknown), stranded and displaced thousands, and destroyed private property and infrastructure valued at billions of dollars. Katrina's impact on New Orleans demonstrates why resource distribution and public policy – the social and political negotiations essential to making and sustaining urbanized places – are so consequential. Years of neglect by local and federal levee authorities left sections of the city vulnerable to catastrophic flooding. Then the ensuing crisis, broadcast worldwide in the 24-hour news cycle, illuminated New Orleans' racial and class divisions. The affluent generally escaped harm's way or, if caught off guard, were likely to receive aid promptly, while less privileged residents, disproportionately African American, were ill-equipped to deal with the crisis and often abandoned or even hindered by public officials. The result was considerable human suffering. Residents retreated to their rooftops to wait for the volunteer rescue crews that stepped in to fill the vacuum left by municipal, state, and federal leadership. City and state officials abandoned inmates at the Orleans Parish Prison as their cells filled with sewage-tainted water. Meanwhile officials corralled poor and displaced New Orleans residents into the Louisiana Superdome, leaving thousands in horrendous conditions for days. In several instances law enforcement helped white residents cordon off neighborhoods to keep out blacks seeking refuge from uninhabitable sections of the city. When attention turned to recovery, the affluent and well-connected were more likely to receive compensation for lost property and prompt help from crews that rebuilt basic infrastructure. By contrast, the city's poorer parishes, mostly on the east side, have struggled to rebuild and attract investment, and the public housing authority has destroyed more residential units than it has repaired. Tens of thousands of residents have had little choice but to abandon their neighborhoods and their city, with the result that communities of New Orleans "expatriates" have taken root in cities nationwide, the largest concentrations in Houston, Dallas, and Atlanta.

An environmental event need not be as catastrophic as Katrina, in terms of lives lost or social dislocation, to highlight the complicated and often strife-filled negotiations involved in the city-building process. Consider any severe storm, flood, fire, drought, or earthquake that has harmed people or property in your region. Since I began writing this book, tornadoes have devastated Greater Oklahoma City and Central Illinois, massive wildfires twice have swept through residential neighborhoods in Colorado, and "Superstorm Sandy" ravaged the eastern seaboard. In any such case, the emergency response and reconstruction effort spark disagreements over resource allocation. Then legislative chambers and media coverage are filled with debates over who should pay for recovery, who will gain from public investment, and whose preferences will shape the reconstruction effort. The point is that these high-profile, "newsworthy" events shine a light on the kinds of mundane negotiations and conflicts that are always underway in the American metropolis, concerning issues ranging from infrastructure maintenance and new development to education and police practices. They reveal that the condition and uses of built environments result from ongoing contests over the exercise of public and private powers. Every American place is the product, in one way or another, of a political process.

*

This political give-and-take is key to understanding the third theme, which is the most encompassing and, admittedly, often a source of frustration for students of the subject. *People's experiences and expectations of metropolitan life have varied considerably throughout US history. Urbanized places have always meant different things to different people and, because of this, there is no singular or definitive history of the American metropolis to tell.*

When you stop and think about the social complexity of urbanized places familiar to you, today, it is probably not surprising to learn that the history of the metropolitan experience is equally complex. Consider people in a variety of American cities, towns, and regions, and the range of needs and motivations that shape their decisions about where to live and how to use built environments. Perhaps they want to find employment or build wealth, keep a family together, protect or assert basic rights, or gain more living space. Perhaps they are escaping poverty or other dangers, or attending school, or simply seeking a peer group and a way to express themselves, essentially claiming a space as their own. Think of how you and your peers use public or private locales to gather and spend free time. Again, access to resources is a crucial variable. Many people have flexibility when deciding where to live; for example, some can easily afford to relocate in order to take a different job, move to a different neighborhood, or attend college. Others find themselves with few or no alternatives; consider the options facing political refugees, dependent children, or anyone who must relocate, no matter the cost, simply to *find* a source of income. And, of course, some people have more freedom than others to use metropolitan spaces. A homeless person, carrying all of his or her possessions, will not be welcomed in most retail stores or hotel lobbies, nor in many public places.

Meanwhile Americans with different needs and priorities use built environments in different, at times conflicting, ways. The modern metropolis is both multiuse and a site of constant reinvention, where individuals and communities develop a variety of ways to live, work, socialize, organize, play, and express themselves. Thus the same stretch of urban or suburban thoroughfare viewed by one person as little more than part of a daily commute – simply a way from Point A to Point B – is often a place of business, or the site of a home or organizational center, or a place of leisure for others. More concretely, one person's public square or outdoor stairwell is another's skate park. A neighborhood viewed as modest or even "rundown" by one person might offer considerable opportunity or solace to another. These and other variables that help explain the complexity of contemporary places can help us think about cities' complex histories. Because the metropolis has always been home to a variety of uses, possibilities, and outcomes, Americans' responses to urban change have always been shaped by their relationship to and their stake in particular built environments.

With this in mind, consider how different people might respond if a storm damaged their home. Naturally anyone in metropolitan DC who watched her or his basement fill up with water in the summer of 2010 was concerned and frustrated. But context matters. Because my wife and I own our home, have steady, well-paying jobs and health insurance, and live in a county with a secure tax base, we were fairly confident that we could handle the expense and that neighborhood infrastructure would be repaired in a timely fashion. Having such resources and expectations is far from universal. For the countless people who rely on meager wages or irregular employment, making expensive home repairs or relocating on short notice would pose a considerable financial burden, and in many lines of work missing a couple days on the job means losing that job. Many municipal and county governments lack sufficient resources to maintain local infrastructure, with the result that some people wait much longer than others for basic repairs. And, of course, millions of people rent their homes, often from landlords who lack incentives to maintain the properties. Flooded basement apartments often displace families of renters – as they did in the DC region that summer – forcing on them a desperate search for shelter. An impoverished family might have to resort to sleeping in a car or on the streets. Finally, property damage or forced relocation might look different, still, to someone who had settled in one of the region's cities or suburbs to escape other threats, such as political persecution or violence. An array of opportunities, challenges, and even outright dangers have long influenced people's relationships to American places. People's pasts shape how they see those places in the present, how they react in the face of adversity, and how they respond to urban change.

The larger point might seem self-evident but deserves special consideration. Americans' experiences, expectations, and views of the modern metropolis have always ranged widely and they can shift over time. Thus, to make sense of urban history requires remaining attentive to both the multiplicity of perspectives and the fact that they change. One of the greatest challenges is making sense of how and why the urbanization process and the varieties of metropolitan development have meant different things to different people.

Sources, Interpretation, and Big Questions

Keep in mind these broad themes – the complexity of the built environment, the contested politics that create and sustain it, and the wide variety of metropolitan experiences – as you examine the sources collected in this volume. These sources sample the kinds of materials that historians turn to regularly, including interviews, government documents, photographs, journalism, correspondence, autobiography, political speeches, and popular advertising. While no single document can adequately tell the story, each provides insights that will help you reconstruct metropolitan history and each introduces topics, perspectives, and questions that scholars continue to debate.

Each source also poses an interpretive challenge for anyone who wants to reconstruct and make sense of the past. Thus it is important to consider how we use documents and how our interpretations of them are shaped by existing knowledge and assumptions. We never come to a source without preconceptions. I did not became an urban historian by locking myself in a room with primary sources – maps, planning documents, oral histories, political broadsides, and the like – and then simply drawing conclusions from the evidence before me. By the time that I decided to do this for a living

I had powerful assumptions about the topic, informed by years of living in the United States surrounded by actual, real-life urbanized environments and by countless images and stories about metropolitan places. Growing up in a predominantly white, upper-middle-class suburb of Los Angeles, I was reminded daily of the distinctions – some real, some imagined – between various landscapes, structures, neighborhoods, and the people that used them. This learning process continued when I moved to the East Coast and then to the Midwest. Then testing those assumptions was part of the task when I did what all graduate students and professional scholars do: study what is known about a subject. In effect I entered into a dialogue with generations of scholars and nonacademic observers engaged in reconstructing urban history. Their work has helped me recognize broad patterns of change, interpret individual primary sources, and focus on particular issues and themes. Indeed their work has had a significant influence on this book's organization and the selection of materials. As any historian will tell you, those decisions are quite difficult, and different scholars would make different choices.

Part of the challenge is sorting through an enormous amount of accumulated knowledge. Writers in many fields have long examined cities, suburbs, and their relationships to what are often called "hinterlands" – the less developed areas outside of metropolitan regions devoted primarily to agricultural production, resource extraction, and recreational use. Scholarship on the built environment has proliferated in recent years due to specialization in disciplines including history, sociology, economics, political science, planning, geography, and anthropology. Meanwhile generations of journalists, activists, artists, and others have contributed valuable materials. As a result, we simply know a lot more than we used to, as more of the documentary record has been uncovered and explored in publications, artistic production, and a variety of public forums. We also have access to more perspectives on that past, in part because the scholarly community has embraced a broader range of people and analytical approaches. The coverage and interpretations that you encounter in course readings and lectures reflect that range. To take one example, for years the study of urban politics focused primarily on elections, elite power brokers, formal organizations, and problems of government administration. In recent decades, by contrast, scholars have devoted considerable attention to other sites of political power and change, such as grassroots organizing, popular protest, and informal or extralegal systems of rule. You would be hard-pressed to find an urbanist who denied the importance of elections to understanding the modern metropolis. But many argue, in addition, that informal kinship and workplace networks or forms of cultural expression ranging from country music and hip hop to street parades and humor are equally significant for understanding urban politics and power. The expansion of approaches has occurred in most urban studies subfields, be it work focusing on law, environmental change, gender, public policy, technology, immigration, or intellectual life.

The flip side of this proliferation of work is that there are too many books, articles, exhibits, and blogs to take in. Even experts struggle to keep up with the steady stream of new scholarship and commentary. And this creates a special challenge for people who are new to the subject and trying to navigate their way through sources and introductory materials. No one is expecting a student new to this field to be familiar with the vast array of available materials and perspectives. More important is that you use primary sources, like those collected here, to explore the *kinds of issues and questions* that scholars and other observers have been examining for generations. If particular topics pique your interest, there are numerous places to go for more material, commentary, and introductions to analytical approaches. In addition, you might identify questions about these sources that scholars have not explored in great detail. A document might reveal things to you that have escaped previous observers.

The study of American metropolitan history is an interdisciplinary endeavor, heir to multiple scholarly traditions and ongoing debates between practitioners over priorities and methodologies. I have not attempted here to introduce those traditions and debates in systematic fashion. Instead, in the discussion that follows I pose and then begin to answer two seemingly straightforward questions about the subject. First, what distinguishes *modern* metropolitan places in the United States from the urban forms that had existed for centuries? Second, what distinguishes the component *parts* of the modern American metropolis – its urban centers, suburban areas, and hinterlands – from each other. It turns out that the answers are complex, and raise complicated issues about geography, power, progress, identity, the forces driving urban change, and even about basic definitions. Considering these two questions will serve as a brief introduction to a number of topics that animate contemporary debates about the urban past and about the subject's importance for understanding the urban present.

What exactly is a *modern* metropolis?

People have built cities for centuries. In North America, indigenous and early colonial urban forms predated the British settlements, and together these helped give rise to the towns and cities, new and old, that grew steadily after the American Revolution. What does it mean, then, to talk about the *modern* metropolis? What makes it different from its predecessors and a distinct subject of study? We can say with some confidence what the modern metropolis is *not*. It is not a visibly distinct or easily definable category of built environment, one that "appeared," fully formed, at a particular moment. Rather the term describes an evolving urban form that took shape gradually, unevenly, but decisively over the course of the nineteenth century. And by the 1850s – when the story documented in this volume begins – both the shape and functions of the modern metropolis were increasingly recognizable and exerting considerable influence over development patterns, politics, economic growth, and intellectual and cultural life in the United States.

Of course its most famous characteristic *was* visible and widely celebrated: the appearance of industry and its products. In the United States, the first industrial cities took shape in the 1840s and 1850s – mid-century Chicago is an iconic example – as managerial and technological innovation revolutionized urban life as well as cities' influence on nonurban places. Engines, interchangeable parts, new construction and production methods, new means of transport – these were among the forces that transformed the size, scale, work environments, social relations, and day-to-day operations of metropolitan regions. For example, the advent of the omnibus and eventually the trolley quickly made the compact "walking city" of the early nineteenth century obsolete. Factory production and the mechanization of farming transformed how goods were made, processed, and distributed. The Bessemer process revolutionized steel production and reduced its costs, which translated into more train service, taller buildings, and even changes in American kitchens, when reliable and affordable stoves helped transform family diets and the responsibilities of the (primarily) women who prepared the food (sources 1.1–2; 2.2–3; and 4.4).

But the industrial city – site of managerial and technological innovation, and a visible symbol of modern urban life – was only one component of a wide-ranging modernization process. Again, defining the modern metropolis requires acceptance of some imprecision, because it developed gradually and impacted different places in different ways. To get a sense of its evolution and dynamics, we need to consider the relationship between the appearance of the industrial city and four other transformations – less visible but equally significant – that were drawing people throughout the United States and well beyond its borders into a modern metropolitan world.

First, the nation's cities, suburbs, and hinterlands were transformed in the nineteenth century by new kinds of economic organization. Most important was the concentration of landed property and productive resources in fewer hands, as wealthy individuals and eventually corporations came to control an increasing share of the country's manufacturing and agricultural sectors. Put simply, the development of American places grew increasingly dependent on powerful investors. Combined with innovation – indeed the two trends were often inseparable – this concentration of wealth transformed the built environment. Investment paid for the expensive machines and new scales of organization that revolutionized how goods were made, processed, and exchanged, in turn dramatically reducing costs and increasing profits. The material life that more and more Americans came to take for granted – its products, efficiencies, and comforts – was made possible in large measure by this new concentration of resources and by the contributions of entrepreneurs, industrialists, and managers who thrived in this environment. At the same time, economic concentration meant that an increasing share of the nation's labor was performed by wage workers or, until 1865, slaves, and that their jobs required fewer skills and posed new dangers. Of course, laboring Americans, both free and enslaved, had always been especially vulnerable and led difficult lives. But, prior to the commercial and industrial revolutions, they were far more likely to work in craft production, or receive wages from family-owned businesses, or labor on small farms and plantations, traditions that were steadily undermined by the growth of the capital-intensive economy. Factory work contrasted sharply with artisanal labor, and wage labor became the norm for free people working in agricultural production and ranching. Meanwhile the slave economy expanded rapidly and the conditions of enslaved people deteriorated even further in the plantation belt, the growth of which was essential to the urban revolution. In short, by mid-century both the advantages and disadvantages of new levels of economic concentration were shaping virtually every settled region in the United States (sources 1.1–2, 4; 2.3; and 3.1).

Second, and closely related, the American metropolis was transformed by the new scale, speed, and ease of movement and exchange. The revolutions in transport, communications, and production integrated American places into dynamic national and international networks of people, goods, wealth, and ideas, all of which circulated more reliably and efficiently than ever before. With these changes came both spectacular opportunities and unprecedented risks. Integrated and expansive markets thrived on growing cities and encouraged them to grow further. Canals, railroads, and other transport technologies accelerated existing trade and migration and linked far *more* places to these fast-growing networks. In urban and rural regions alike, daily life was quickly transformed by the introduction of inventions and new goods, such as the mechanical reaper, the steam engine, canned food, and short-staple cotton. Meanwhile migrants were drawn to places and into relationships formerly unimaginable, revolutionizing settlement patterns, commerce, and politics throughout the United States and well beyond. Consider the constant movement of people both within and across the nation's borders. For example, the East Coasters who joined the California Gold Rush after 1848 were more likely to travel by sea, with a short overland trip across the Isthmus of Panama, than to follow the slower and more arduous route of the Oregon Trail. Thus, at the same time that San Francisco was reinvented by the influx of migrants, so was New Granada's (later Colombia's) politics, development, and relationship to the United States transformed. Likewise, following the Civil War, cities and towns throughout the American Southwest and Northern Mexico were transformed when railroad development accelerated the flow of goods and people throughout the region. Finally, throughout North America this new mobility gave investors greater access to natural resources such as lumber, coal, arable land, and pasture, together with the means to build new production centers and communities deep in undeveloped areas or on the periphery of existing cities. In short, all parts of the metropolis, from city center to distant hinterlands, rapidly came to depend on a steady and reliable flow of capital, people, information, and goods, and all of these places were changed by these new connections (sources 1.1–4; 2.1–3; 3.1–4; and 4.1–3, 5).

Indeed, the scale of exchange and integration could be a mixed blessing because, in the context of economic concentration, it also meant that the terms of development and the nature of opportunity in any one place were often dictated by a small number of investors and public officials. To be sure, local people generally benefited by gaining access to new goods, technologies, and jobs. But their well-being often came to depend on actors – manufacturers, transport companies, commodities traders, policy-makers – with little personal or emotional investment in the place. Thus many of the forces that made the modern metropolis so vibrant also introduced new kinds of instability and vulnerability. Wage laborers might find options for employment, but usually in low-paying, insecure, and often dangerous jobs. Because cities and regions had to compete for their share of private investment and public resources, some regions prospered while others struggled. And, while communities flourished by focusing on the production or processing of a single commodity, such as wheat, or steel, or cattle, to do so required reliance on distant investors, rapid expansion of a low-wage labor force (factory workers, cowboys), and, quite often, abandonment of other kinds of production or economic activity. Specialization came with a trade-off, for if the wheat crop failed or commodity prices plunged, the region and many of its residents had little to fall back on, as well as mounting debts to pay. Wage laborers struggled to keep steady employment, while the family-owned farms and businesses that borrowed heavily to keep up with the capital-intensive requirements of production and exchange were especially vulnerable to market disruptions or rising costs. Thus people regularly lost their property and with it their economic independence, not for lack of effort but rather because the changing terms of production and profit-making put them at a disadvantage. Over the course of the nineteenth century, these trends created comparable dilemmas in virtually every corner of the American economy. The modern metropolis created great wealth and opportunity, but left most Americans dependent on and vulnerable to forces over which they had very limited, if any, influence (sources 1.1–2, 4; 2.1–3; 3.1–4).

The third characteristic of modern metropolitan development challenges powerful myths and countless popular renderings of the nation's dynamic urban growth, for over the course of the nineteenth century that growth came to depend heavily on government power and resources. By the 1850s, municipal, state, and federal authorities were growing more and more involved in the expansion and management of the built environment and they have remained deeply involved ever since. At the local level, the increasing density and complexity of cities demanded a new level of government responsibility. Because adequate infrastructure and services were needed to make communities livable and attractive to investors, municipal and state authorities granted charters to utility, transport, and other providers or, in some cases, managed service provision directly. The rise of novel urban land uses and hazards drew local officials into debates over regulation, forced them to police development and enforce nuisance laws, and ultimately led to widespread adoption of the municipal zoning power. Finally, to compete for development resources and revenues, local governments offered incentives to investors, such as preferential treatment in the franchising process. Local authorities subsidized private business interests in order to ensure the vitality of their city or region. All told, municipal and state actions increasingly blurred the lines between the private and public sectors, lines that have blurred further ever since (sources 3.4–5 and 5.4).

Federal involvement in metropolitan development has been even more wide-ranging and has taken forms, again, that make the boundaries between public and private difficult to discern. While the US government had always promoted economic growth, its early interventions focused not on cities per se but on development and governing projects that happened to promote urbanization. The federal state fought wars, encouraged exploration and trade, and purchased and platted land, in the process establishing rules for the sale and settlement of newly acquired territories. But by mid-century the federal role had evolved considerably, as strategic considerations, commercial pressures, and controversy over slavery's expansion drew the state deeply into development politics and, specifically, into realms inseparable from the expanding influence of cities. Federal budget priorities are indicative:

between 1840 and 1860, as much as a third of federal spending in any given year was devoted to settlement and investment in the American West, processes inextricably linked to the nation's urban growth. The government published reports on discoveries in the new territories, sponsored an Army Corps of Engineers survey of the transcontinental railroad, and funded both Indian removal and a military presence along migration routes. Meanwhile the case for a direct federal role in infrastructure development gained considerable traction, so that, by the 1840s, officials were granting land to states for the purpose and, in the 1850s, Congress attempted to expand rail networks through the legislative process. The Civil War then opened the way for aggressive federal promotion of commercial expansion that relied on and actively promoted cities' centrality in American life. The meteoric growth and increasing influence of the metropolis has been a characteristic of the American experience ever since, with the federal government serving, in different degrees, as a full-fledged partner in the development process (sources 1.3; 3.1, 3–5; 4.2–3; 6.4; 7.4; and Chapters 8–14).

The final characteristic of the modern American metropolis was the emergence of a paradox for its residents: life in the rapidly urbanizing nation presented unprecedented challenges while also offering unprecedented opportunities. As cities grew in size, complexity, and technological sophistication; as regions grew materially richer and more dependent on private and public investment; and as urbanized areas developed increasingly complex and reliable links to networks of people, goods, and capital, most American places became more difficult to navigate but also open to new possibilities. Life in urbanized places and even in the countryside grew increasingly hectic and often burdensome, yet it was simultaneously full of opportunities for reinvention.

The increasing complexity of American cities is no doubt familiar from novels, films, and documentary treatments of nineteenth-century urban life. Urbanized places grew more congested; they got dirtier; and they were filled with dangers, such as accumulated garbage and the threat of disease, crime, and fire. There were simply more people with more things to negotiate, be it securing work and decent housing, finding fresh food, or dodging traffic on busy streets. In addition, the constant stream of new arrivals, both migrants and immigrants, brought together people with divergent experiences and expectations, often creating new sources of competition and conflict. American cities had always been characterized by class, ethnic, racial, and gender divisions, but now these divisions continued and new conflicts arose in increasingly crowded, challenging, geographically decentralized, and anonymous places. One response was a new spatial separation of neighborhoods and activities, as people of different class and ethnic backgrounds, as well as men and women, tended to work, live, and socialize in discrete and sometimes distant places. Meanwhile the economy's complexity bred considerable instability – falling commodity prices, uncertain wages, unemployment – which only added to the insecurity for most Americans. The comparatively modest, walking cities of the early nineteenth century became sprawling and intensely competitive multiethnic centers of production and trade, serviced by railroads and trolleys, susceptible to more fires and public health problems, and repeatedly struck by economic crises (sources 1.3–4; 2.1–4; 3.2–5; 4.1–3, 5; and 5.4).

Yet these unpredictable places also presented Americans with new opportunities and ideas to pursue. Of course they offered jobs and, for some, the chance to strike it rich, but many benefits are more difficult to measure. For example, the separation between home and work created new spaces where people could congregate and exchange ideas. As manufacturers grew dependent on wage laborers, those laborers gained some leverage to organize for better conditions and wages. And as a growing middle class grew dependent on paid domestic servants, the men and women who provided those services developed new strategies for political self-assertion. Meanwhile the constant flow of people and ideas created contacts and contrasts that enabled people to challenge conventions and to fashion, gradually, new norms in American society – concerning work, citizenship, gender roles, racial equality, domesticity, leisure, even courtship. The unique combination of affluence, technology, scale, options, and juxtapositions seemed to constantly create new openings for political, cultural, and economic change (sources 2.1, 3; 3.2–3; 4.1–5; 5.1–3; and 6.1–4).

Perhaps most consequential, the modern metropolis enabled Americans to further test and gradually transform conventions about opportunity and rights. The United States was a nation rhetorically committed to the merit system and to broad ideals about political and economic freedom, yet it afforded those freedoms to only a small percentage of its residents. And metropolitan growth in some ways aggravated these inequities, as the powerful responded to modernizing trends that challenged their privileges by creating *new* tools of restriction, such as Jim Crow laws, strict land use codes, and new methods for policing certain populations. Yet, at the same time, urban growth and its conspicuous benefits created material and cultural resources that the less powerful could leverage in their fight for access and inclusion. It became increasingly problematic for men and whites to restrict the franchise, for example, or for the state to promote or sanction discrimination, in light of the visible, palpable advantages of "progress" and "modernity" showcased in the nation's fast-growing metropolitan centers. Thus it is not surprising that protests over rights and inclusion were increasingly centered in urban spaces, both public and commercial, like downtown business districts and trolley cars, or eventually in buses and restaurants. On one level, American cities promised their inhabitants all things "modern" – including access to opportunity and full citizenship – and people used urban places, resources, and *ideas* to make a claim on those rights.

Of course the nineteenth-century metropolis remained for most people a restrictive and often dehumanizing place; consider the narrow franchise, slavery and the sharecropping economy, and the work and living conditions of most Americans, be they urban or rural dwellers. Yet at the same time its new forms, its material abundance, and its central place in dynamic national and international networks helped to energize existing political movements and give rise to new ones that would eventually produce more democratic and equitable outcomes. The labor, abolitionist, women's, LGBT, and civil rights movements, as well as the municipal and federal reforms that would dramatically transform American life in the twentieth and twenty-first centuries, have deep roots in the modern metropolitan revolution itself.

*

Again, there is no precise "start" date for the modern American metropolis. Nor can we identify it with data points such as population growth or density, or with physical markers such as streetcars or skyscrapers. Rather it has been an evolving form, a product of changing relationships between people, technologies, institutions, the built environment, and the natural environment. Indeed it is best to understand the modern metropolis not simply as a particular *place* per se but also as a *process* that gave rise to new urban forms (including the industrial and, eventually, "postindustrial" city); that transformed patterns of work, residence, and leisure; and that rapidly altered development patterns in nonurban locales. Its emergence also helped to revolutionize American politics, institutions, expectations, and cultural norms. The modern metropolis represented – and still represents – a complicated and unwieldy urban form, one increasingly difficult to build and maintain because of its dependence on technology and investment, one responsible to countless competing interests, and one filled with people who often have few if any easily recognizable connections to one another. It fast became a place filled with possibilities for redefining citizenship, opportunity, and belonging on the one hand, while its new geographies, institutions, and technologies also gave people new means to reassert and misuse their power on the other. The metropolis became a central locale for Americans' ongoing struggles to find new political, economic, and cultural solutions. With the emergence of the modern metropolitan form, city building became inseparable from the basic distribution of resources in the United States, from the defining of private rights and public powers, and ultimately from setting the terms of American citizenship.

What makes a place "urban," "suburban," or "rural"?

How do we distinguish between the component parts of the modern metropolis? Have "cities" functioned differently than "suburbs" or "exurbs," and what relationships have they had to their "hinterlands"? These seemingly straightforward questions do not lend themselves to simple answers. Indeed there has never been agreement among scholars, public officials, or average Americans about how to define or categorize these places and their uses. This fact reveals a great deal about metropolitan history's complexity and introduces key debates that have long engaged those interested in the topic. Here, rather than offer fixed definitions of urban, suburban, or rural, I ask you to consider some of the variables that have always made agreement about these terms so difficult.

A good way to approach this sprawling historical subject is by beginning in the present and scrutinizing assumptions about familiar terminology. For most Americans, calling a place "urban" invokes a set of familiar characteristics; it is a built-up and densely populated place, with concentrated areas of commercial activity, perhaps a downtown with skyscrapers, and residential neighborhoods adjacent to or mixed with commercial uses. With space at a premium, people live in attached dwellings (townhouses, row houses) or multiple-unit buildings of apartments or condominiums. New York City and Chicago usually come to mind, or the older central city neighborhoods of, say, Boston, St. Louis, Cleveland, or San Francisco. By contrast, most people think of American "suburban" places as very different environments: spread out, car-dependent, and dominated by stretches of large-lot, single family homes on winding streets. Their residents are expected to shop in neighborhood strip malls or large, centralized retail complexes accessible only by car or bus. Urban and suburban environments have also long been associated with specific populations and ways of life. Many Americans see the city as home to a broad mix of people, including immigrants, racial minorities, the working poor, and more recently young middle-class professionals. And cities' diversity, coupled with their compact form and mix of uses, is seen as making them more engaging and interesting – places where people interact with strangers and have new experiences. Standing in sharp contrast is the supposedly homogeneous and dull American suburb, home primarily to the middle class and affluent, to families, and especially to whites. So, while many view the city as a place to visit a museum or a club or to eat "ethnic" food, free time in the suburbs is commonly associated with a trip to the mall, an indoor sportsplex, or a national chain restaurant. The suburbs of Kansas City are presumed to be more or less indistinguishable from those of Seattle or Los Angeles or Baltimore.

Are these accurate characterizations? We know that they were born out of real trends in US history that took hold in the nineteenth century and were solidified in the twentieth. Yet they have never adequately described the range of environments characteristic of the modern metropolis. It is true that American suburbs have long been home to middle-class and affluent whites, with the most exclusive areas celebrated as a "refuge" from the congestion, racial or ethnic diversity, and poverty of central cities. But, since the nineteenth century, suburbs have also been home to racial minorities, working-class and poor families of all backgrounds, recent immigrants, and even extensive industrial development (sources 3.2; 7.5; and 14.1). Central city forms have also varied. American downtowns have long hosted concentrations of racial minorities and immigrants, disproportionately working class and sometimes impoverished, as well as commercial and manufacturing districts. But they have also featured neighborhoods of million-dollar homes, business and financial centers, fashionable shopping districts, and new upper middle-class enclaves (sources 3.5; 5.1–2; and 7.1–2).

Arguably the distinctions between urban and suburban have grown especially murky in the last half century, as important shifts in American politics, including a series of rights revolutions and immigration reform, coupled with seismic technological and economic changes, have further undermined popular assumptions about metropolitan locales. The redevelopment of American central cities is a telling example. Since the 1950s, cities have competed for investment dollars to clear land, refurbish infrastructure, and rebuild older neighborhoods. But the new, revitalized districts that have taken shape usually have little in common with the urban forms that they aspire to replace. Consider the change in social composition. Throughout the nineteenth and much of the twentieth centuries, American cities were shared by a wide variety of people, ranging from elites to middle-class professionals to the working poor. Longtime residents worked and lived near recent migrants and immigrants. Nostalgia for those cities can be misplaced, for these were hardly laboratories of equal opportunity. Class, gender, and racial boundaries were strictly enforced and economic inequality extreme. Nonetheless, a wide range of Americans interacted with one another and benefited, albeit in different ways, from a city's resources. Thus it is striking that most urban renewal areas, by sharp contrast, cater primarily to the well-off. Redevelopment usually displaces working- and even middle-class residents, as real estate interests and city officials go to great lengths to attract affluent homeowners, renters, and consumers. Meanwhile much of the labor that sustains these communities is performed by low-wage workers who cannot afford to live there and must commute from other urban areas or even distant suburbs. Cities have always attracted the affluent, but urban redevelopment increasingly does so to the exclusion of middle- and working-class Americans (sources 11.3; 12.3; and 13.2–4).

The nature of urban commerce has also changed. When American cities were dominated by small, family-owned businesses, much of the commercial activity in any one place supported entrepreneurs who lived locally or at least nearby. Even bankers used to lend primarily, and some lent exclusively, to people in their area, because they *knew* their customers and felt confident judging whether or not they would repay their loans. By sharp contrast, the day-to-day commercial activity in revitalized urban neighborhoods is dominated by large corporations and by national chains and franchises of restaurants, groceries, drugstores, office supply and hardware outlets, movie complexes, and retailers of clothing and home furnishings. CVS has replaced the local pharmacist, while The Gap or the remarkably named Urban Outfitters might occupy several storefronts previously leased to family-owned retailers. Needless to say, the owners of national or multinational corporations rarely live in the neighborhood, let alone the region, and most of the profits generated by local sales are not circulated directly back into the locality. Typical residents in America's "new" downtowns are white-collar professionals who are employed by and spend much of their discretionary income at institutions with few, if any, local ties. Most make their mortgage payment to a bank based in another state or pay rent to a corporate developer or property management company with minimal attachment to the particular city. Even much of the tourist dollar goes to national chain hotels and restaurants. Hard Rock Cafe – long a fixture in urban revitalization areas – has its corporate headquarters in Orlando, Florida (sources 13.2–4).

Familiar expectations about American places are often challenged in the suburbs or in small towns and cities, as well. Many of the "inner ring" suburbs in major metropolitan regions, for example, depart dramatically from the supposedly classic postwar suburban form, by including extensive commercial development and manufacturing, large sections of multiunit rentals and condominiums, enclaves of recent immigrants, working-class communities, and the working poor, or in some cases an increasing share of the nation's homeless. The skid rows long associated with American downtowns are now often found in its suburbs. Meanwhile, these supposedly nontraditional suburban neighborhoods tend to alternate with the supposedly iconic version. Indeed most suburban regions are patchworks, alternating between subdivisions of detached homes, stretches of townhouses and apartment buildings (often along major thoroughfares and highways), intensive commercial development, mixed use projects designed to mimic traditional urban forms, and, increasingly, enclaves dominated by ethnic and racial minorities. What do we call these places? The stretch of Route 128 forming a semicircle around Boston runs through dense commercial hubs and residential neighborhoods dominated by single-family structures. Are the areas with concentrated commercial development "urban" – for example, between Burlington and Reading or the pockets of manufacturing near the Cambridge Reservoir? Are the stretches of single-family homes and wooded areas "suburban"? How should we label the section of Woburn, Massachusetts, where a Panera Bread and a Sports Authority anchor a shopping mall just across railroad tracks from the warehouses and light manufacturing plants on Industrial Parkway (sources 13.5 and 14.1–2, 4–5)?

Comparable patchworks of development are visible in most metropolitan regions: look at satellite views of Los Angeles's San Fernando Valley, or the near suburbs of Nashville, Tennessee, or the development corridor southwest of Cincinnati, Ohio, along Interstate 75. Or consider one final paradox. Strip malls in many suburban communities, particularly the inner ring suburbs, have become sites of a robust revival of independently owned businesses, including hair salons, restaurants, groceries, discount stores, and financial services. Quite often they are run by entrepreneurs linked to local minority and immigrant communities established in affordable sections of the metropolis. In these areas, commercial activity supports local businesspeople and helps sustain local communities as well as extended family networks living elsewhere in the United States or abroad. Here is one of many cases in which suburban neighborhoods are acting as cities used to, whereas many urban areas are growing relatively homogeneous – at least socioeconomically – and are dominated by the corporate forces once blamed for making suburbs so dull.

Of course the large-lot, single family home is alive and well in America's suburbs, and the affluent still tend to opt for suburban zip codes that are rich in resources and distant from neighborhoods viewed as "marginal" or "bad." Meanwhile, suburban commerce is still dominated by big-box stores and chains, so much so that major corporations often work hard to market themselves as *connected* to the local community. Appleby's has nearly 2,000 restaurants in 49 states and a corporate headquarters in Kansas City, Missouri, yet advertises itself as a "Neighborhood Grill and Bar." The larger point is that using shorthands like "urban" and "suburban" to describe locales can often obscure as much as it reveals. Arguably there are no clearly defined "rural" or "wilderness" areas in the United States either, even deep in the interior of its national parks, as all American places are now decisively shaped by the actions of private parties and public authorities. This is important to remember when trying to make sense of metropolitan history as well as contemporary environments. Consider how and why these definitions are used differently, in different contexts. What kinds of development, activities, and people are associated with a "city" or a "suburb" or a "rural" area at different moments? Why do these categories change?

And rest assured that scholars and other experts have no monopoly on defining urban forms. Evidence of this can be found in the long history of confusion, documented in the sources collected in this volume, about what to call these places and how to characterize them. Or consider the dilemma faced by the US Bureau of the Census after World War II in response to metropolitan sprawl. With increasing commercial and industrial development in the suburbs (many corporations began to relocate urban manufacturing plants immediately after World War II) and the fantastic growth of suburban homeownership, new nodes of residential and economic life began to take shape outside of traditional downtowns. Census officials thought that it made little sense to designate the "city" and its "suburban" regions as disconnected entities, thus in 1950 they created a new spatial category, the Standard Metropolitan Area, for the purposes of collecting and reporting data about population, housing construction, and employment. This new designation described, in the bureau's words, "the metropolitan extent around large cities," conceived of as a "function zone of economic and social integration around a central place or places."[1] The agency's decision highlighted a recurring theme in modern American development. For at the moment that the bureau acknowledged the continual blurring of boundaries and functions between city and suburb, most contemporaries and popular culture representations were insisting on the sharp differences between city and suburb and depicting them as inherently different kinds of places (see the sources in Parts IV and V).

Urban scholars continue to wrestle with the problem of definition. Compare texts in urban history, sociology, politics, planning, and economics for a snapshot of the ongoing debates over terminology and over the meanings and implications of the urbanization process.

What then, in the final analysis, makes a place "urban" or "suburban," and what distinguishes either from the countryside? Have urban renewal and neighborhood gentrification brought the "suburb" to the "city," and has the appearance in suburbs of more corporate headquarters or immigrant gateway communities or impoverished working-class communities "urbanized" these places? Does something change when you step across the boundary line between a stretch of forest or farmland and a new subdivision of suburban homes built in their midst? (Remember that even the *oldest* suburban districts in most metropolitan regions once bordered similar undeveloped hinterlands.) And do designations such as "urban" and "suburban" even apply to the proliferation of gated communities that privatize services such as security, garbage collection, and infrastructure maintenance? Or perhaps these traditional categories are insufficient to describe development in the modern era. Perhaps contemporary cities and suburbs represent a new kind of built environment, and thus require new analytical tools and a new vocabulary to describe the metropolis, its functions, and how residents understand its component parts.

I'll leave you with a hypothesis to explore and test. Basically I'll suggest a common denominator, a characteristic that all American places have shared in the modern metropolitan era. But, first, a qualifier is necessary. Cities, suburbs, and their hinterlands have always been and continue to be differentiated and multifaceted locales. And every local history is unique, a fact, it should be noted, that makes organizing an urban history course or sourcebook quite challenging. In short, place continues to matter, American places differ dramatically in form and function, and these differences are very consequential for understanding the American experience. Nonetheless – and here is my hypothesis – *what unites all American built environments in the modern era has been the steady blurring of distinctions between urban, suburban, and rural locales, despite widespread popular investment in the idea that they remain distinct kinds of places.* We may be attached to ideas about cities, suburbs, and hinterlands, and convinced of their supposedly discrete characteristics and functions. Yet, in reality, their functions and distinctions have been slowly but steadily redistributed *across* regions. And for some time they have been redistributed around the world, a process greatly accelerated in the age of the Internet, Skype, supply chain management, and electronic currency transfers. If you disagree with this hypothesis, use these and other sources to make a counterargument. If you think that this argument has merit, use those sources to think about its implications for understanding the metropolis and the process of urban change.

*

One final word about studying this subject is in order. If you have lived in an American metropolitan region or simply spent a good deal of time in one, then you have already collected evidence that will help you study its history. Your experience of American places offers a starting point for thinking about the processes and relationships that have characterized metropolitan life in the modern era. Of course there are limits to this strategy, since our contemporary settings are strikingly different from those that took shape in the nineteenth century. We now have electricity and modern medicine, automobiles and digital communications, drywall and reinforced concrete. Slavery has been abolished, the franchise expanded, the nation's demographic composition transformed, ideas about equity and opportunity revolutionized, and the government's role in everything from shaping world events to protecting its citizens' rights vastly expanded. Nonetheless, the *processes* that shape today's metropolis are extensions of those that converged in the nineteenth century to create new kinds of urbanized environments and relationships. Innovation and mechanization; economic consolidation and the rising importance of finance; the accelerated flow of people, goods, and ideas; an active and growing public sector; anonymity, possibility, and the constant transformation of ideas about rights and opportunities – these continue to be defining characteristics of metropolitan life and help explain why urban change continues to have such a stunning impact on every person living in the United States, indeed on people throughout the world.

Thus, despite the striking differences between nineteenth-century America and our own, you can use your relationship to contemporary places as a point of departure for thinking about this history. Start by considering your place in the built environment and how you relate to it. Where do you live, work, study, and spend free time? How and why have these places taken their current forms, who built and maintains them, and who covers the costs? And how does your experience of specific spaces differ from that of people with different backgrounds, life histories, or access to resources? Indeed, why might people you encounter on a regular basis – perhaps in class, at work, or while commuting – have radically different relationships to the places that you both use regularly? An easy starting point is to consider locales where people feel at ease or safe, and how a place's status can change over the course of a 24-hour period. Or simply stop the next time that you pass a construction site. Who is building it, who will use it, who is paying for it, and how might development change the nature of its neighborhood? Why might some passersby see it as a mark of "renewal" or "progress," while others consider it a far more complicated remaking of the environment with disparate and perhaps inequitable impacts? Finally, how might your experience of places differ, perhaps dramatically, from that of someone living in a region of the country with a very different developmental and political history?

In short, you can begin to approach the story of the urban past in the United States by considering the urban present and your place within it. For me, winding up the work on this book coincided with another episode of extreme weather, this time in the form of "Superstorm Sandy." This was a 1,000-mile-wide hurricane, later an unusually strong overland formation, that bore across the Mid-Atlantic and Northeast in the fall of 2012. Maryland was spared the worst of it and our basement, thankfully, remained dry. But countless people in New Jersey, New York, and elsewhere along the Atlantic seaboard were not so fortunate, and are still struggling to rebuild, redesign, pay for the work, and sort out who, in the end, will get what. Like all metropolitan histories, it is a work in progress.

Note

1 US Department of Commerce, Economics and Statistical Administration, Bureau of the Census, *Geographic Areas Reference Manual*, November 1994, ch. 13, p. 4.

Part I Cities and Hinterlands in Mid-Nineteenth-Century America

Chapter 1 Transforming the Landscape and Its Functions

1 Chicago's *Daily Democrat* Measures the Impact of the Transport Revolution, 1852

Canals and railroads were centerpieces of a nineteenth-century transportation revolution that transformed the US economy, fueled territorial expansion, and remade North America's metropolitan landscape. Between the 1820s and 1840s, canal construction linked existing waterfront cities, created bustling new urban centers, and connected much of the nation to ports in New York, Philadelphia, and New Orleans. In 1830 the first American rail line – the Baltimore and Ohio – opened for operation, and by 1850 the nation boasted 9,000 miles of track. Thanks to the railroad's many advantages – not least its ability to defy inclement weather – by mid-century it surpassed water transport as the primary means for moving people and goods, with Chicago emerging as a booming gateway city linking the nation's eastern and western lines. Railroads did more than provide reliable and affordable access to faraway places. They also attracted considerable investment, mostly from New York City and Europe, to the regions they ran through. This in turn accelerated growth and further integrated American cities and their hinterlands with national and international markets. Alongside the new railway routes arose lucrative markets for real estate, goods, and services as well as the first "railroad suburbs." In sparsely settled western states and territories, the railroad's arrival often helped determine where businesses, settlers, and even farmers would congregate.

The Modern American Metropolis: A Documentary Reader, First Edition.
Edited by David M. P. Freund.

The railroad's rapid advance was the product of innovation, entrepreneurship, countless hours of hard labor, and generous public policies (see source 3.1). But equally important was the persistence of boosters – in Chicago especially – who recruited investors into the railroad business by advertising their city's strategic advantages. The first rail link between Chicago and its western hinterlands, the Chicago–Galena line, opened in 1848 thanks to an aggressive campaign selling shares to businesspeople and farmers along the proposed route. Four years later the new line figured prominently in this account by local newspapermen of how Chicago's gateway status was transforming the city's size, shape, and functions. Also documented here is the railroad's impact on Chicago's hinterlands and other urban centers. By 1852 trunk and branch lines totaling about 3,700 miles had a terminus in Chicago.

We lay before our readers to-day our first Annual Review of the business of the city ... The past has been, a year of unexampled prosperity, and our city has shared largely in the general progress of the country. In no former year has so much been done to place its business upon a permanent basis, and extend its commerce. By the extension of the Galena Railroad to Rockford, we have drawn to this city the trade of portions of Wisconsin, Iowa and Minnesota, that hitherto sought other markets; and when our roads reach the Father of Waters, as two of them will within the present year, we may expect an avalanche of business, for which we fear all our wholesale houses will not be prepared ...

The opening of the Rock Island Railroad, Oct. 18th to Joliet, Jan. 5th to Morris, Feb. 14th to Ottawa, and to La Salle March 10th, has brought customers during the winter from a different direction, and made an unusually lively winter for our business men ...

We subjoin a table of the value of imports and exports from 1836 to 1848 inclusive.

	Imports	Exports
1836	$325,203.90	$1,000.64
1837	373,677.12	11,665.00
1838	579,174.61	16,044.75
1839	630,980.26	33,843.00
1840	562,106.20	228,635.74
1841	564,347.88	348,862.24
1842	664,347.88	659,305.20
1843	971,849.75	682,210.85
1844	1,686,416.00	785,504.23

1845	2,043,445.73	1,543,519.85
1846	2,027,150.00	1,813,468.00
1847	2,641,852.52	2,296,299.00
1848	8,338,639.86	10,709,333.40

... The internal commerce of Chicago is conducted through twelve Bankers and Dealers in Exchange, one hundred and twenty-two wholesale, forwarding, commission and produce houses, and fifty-two lumber dealers.

FLOUR.

The total amount of Flour handled, during 1852, was 124,316 barrels, and was received from the following sources:

Chicago–Galena Railroad 44,316 bbls.
Lake 2,875
Canal 1,846
Eastern Railroads 4,300
Manufactured in city 70,979

... During the early part of [1850], the market was not animated, and prices ruled low. Toward the latter part of the season, however, there was an advance, occasioned partly by the large home demand, and the general upward tendency of the Eastern market.

CORN.

There is no feature of our trade that presents a more gratifying aspect than that of corn. Previous to 1847, the receipts at this point were but little greater than the then small local demand, and not one-half as great as the present consumption of the city distilleries. Our prairies were thought to be unfavorable to the culture of corn, not, however, for want of success in it so far as it had been attempted, but because of the general impression that it was too far north. Our farmers are mainly from New England, where corn is not grown much, and it was difficult for them to overcome a belief in which they had been educated, that it could only be made a profitable crop in a more southerly latitude. Nevertheless, the failure of the wheat crop in 1850 and 1851, and the more profitable business of growing hogs, stimulated the production of corn, and the misapprehension in relation to its adaptation to our soil and climate is fast giving way to correct views on this subject. As a consequence, the receipts by railroad and teams have largely augmented during the past year, and the coming one, we doubt not, will show a still further increase. During the past year the total receipts at this point were 2,991,011 bushels, which were derived from the following sources:

Illinois and Michigan Cadan	1,810,830 bushels
Chicago and Galena Railroad	671,961
From teams	508,220
Total	2,991,011

This shows a large increase by railroad, compared with the previous year, of nearly 400,000 bushels, and a decrease [of] 180,000 bushels by teams, and 540,000 bushels by canal. The decrease of receipts by teams is unquestionably in a measure the result of the extension of the railroad, while the falling off in the receipts by canal is entirely owing to the suspension of navigation on the Illinois river, during over three months of last year ...

OATS.

The increase of the oats trade for 1852 over 1851, was nearly 300 percent, and more than doubly compensated for the falling off in corn ... The shipments for the last seven years show an increase almost unequalled in the history of commerce ... The soil and climate of Northern-Illinois is eminently adapted to the growth of oats, and we are confident that our exports, during the ensuing four years will be increased to many millions of bushels. The rapidly increasing consumption over production, of this staple in the Eastern and Middle States, impresses us with the conviction that our market will continue to have many more advantages than any one south of this, and that the bulk of the surplus of the Mississippi valley will seek this channel as the most direct route to the ultimate market ...

HOGS AND PORK.

Since our farmers commenced a more general cultivation of corn, the Pork-packing business of Chicago has steadily increased, and now promises to grow to an extent second in importance to no other production ... The hog-packing season commences in November, and runs through the winter ... [T]he advantages of the Chicago and Galena Railroad to our city, have been manifest in the pork business during the past season. Four-fifths of all the hogs sold here, come in on that thoroughfare a large proportion of them from Rock river, and many of them from Iowa. Had the weather been favorable to hauling during the winter, it is thought we would have received from the latter State over 20,000. It is not unfair to suppose that if the farmers of Iowa can afford to carry their pork, in wagons, from 80 to 150 miles to reach our market, they will send all their surplus here when the railroad shall be completed to the Mississippi river …

[BEEF]

… In the article of BEEF we think it will be conceded that Chicago now stands pre-eminent. There is no city in the Union that pretends to compete with us … The beef-packing business, it must be remembered, has all grown up within the last six or eight years. We are not yet able to form a correct judgment as to what effect the opening of our Railroads to the sea board, and, therefore, the greater facilities that we are soon to have to ship live stock to Eastern markets, is to have upon the packing business in our City; but we are entirely certain that our rich prairies have only commenced to yield us their rich treasures … [W]e may justly anticipate the commercial position that our City will occupy in a very few years, with feelings of honest pride. When contemplating such facts in regard to the growth and prosperity of our City, we always feel like going back to the time when Chicago was "no where." She is still in her "teens," not having arrived at the full age of even twenty years. Long [before] that period, every barrel of beef and almost every other article of food was imported from New York and Ohio.

LUMBER.

LUMBER forms one of the most important elements of our commercial prosperity. The position of Chicago gives her the control of an extensive and lucrative lumber trade. Owing to the rapid settlement of the country to the south and west of us for the past few years, the amount of lumber brought to this market has very rapidly increased, as a comparative statement of the receipts will show …

The large number of railroads now centering in this city will greatly augment this business. To the south and west of us there is no pine lumber, and only a limited supply of oak and other kinds of timber, that can measurably be used in the place of pine. That whole region looks to Chicago for its supply of this important article, and no other city can compete with us for this trade. Within the next three years more than two thousand miles of railroad will be opened to this city, and the people who dwell upon the immense fertile prairies through which they will pass, will all look to Chicago for their building materials ...

The incidental advantages of the Lumber business to our city, are varied and expensive. It affords a market for a large amount of our surplus products, at a much better profit than shipments East will afford. Pork, beef, flour, coarse grain of all kinds, groceries and provisions of every description, are shipped in large quantities to the lumber regions. The carrying trade furnishes employment to a great many vessels, and business for hundreds and thousands of laboring men. This trade is in the hands of far-seeing, intelligent merchants, who know its importance to our city, and most of them are reaping a rich reward for their energy and enterprise ...

CITY IMPROVEMENTS.

Our time and limits will not permit us to enter into a detailed statement of the improvements made for the past year. Suffice it to say, that more progress has been made than at any former period. Elegant residences have been built in all parts of the city, splendid blocks of stores have been erected on our principal streets, and the limits of the inhabited part of the city have been greatly extended. On the 20th of February, 1852, the Michigan Southern Railroad was opened to this city. The Depot is located near Gurnee's Tannery, on the South Branch. The Rock Island Railroad have built their Depot directly opposite. A year [earlier], there were only a few old buildings in that neighborhood, and it was considered far "out of town." Now nearly the whole of Clark street is built up as far south as the depot, and there has an important addition been made to the city where, a year since, it was open prairie ... The Michigan Central Railroad was opened to Chicago on Friday, May 21st ...

In the summer season, both these lines furnish a direct steam communication with the cities on the seaboard. About the 1st of January last, all the railroad lines along the south shore of Lake Erie were completed, and these, with the Erie Railroad and the Michigan Southern, give us a direct railroad line to New York ... Our merchants who, in the depth of winter, were obliged to consume some two weeks in staging through Canada mud "up to the hub," in order to purchase their goods for the spring trade, can now go through, and enjoy the luxury of a comfortable railroad car, in two days ...

MANUFACTORIES.

During the past few months, two extensive car manufacturing establishments have been put in active operation. One is located near the Rock Island Depot, and is owned by two distinct companies. G. W. Sizer & Co. cast the wheels and do all the iron work connected with the manufacture of cars. They have a large establishment and are doing a heavy business. They are now using eight tons of iron per day, brought mostly from Ohio and New York. A. B. Stone & Co. do the wood work and the upholstery and finishing of the cars. The two companies are building ten cars per week, and employ nearly two hundred men ... The AMERICAN CAR COMPANY have erected their works about half a mile north of Myrick's on the lake shore, and will have, when completed in all respects, one of the most perfectly appointed manufactories that can be found in the western states. They have in their enclosure thirteen acres. The buildings now completed have an aggregate length of 1250 by an average width of 60 feet. The capital of the Company is $200,000, and they have already expended some $130,000. Three thousand five hundred tons of pig iron are used per year, in the manufacture of car wheels and the other car castings, and 2,000 tons of coal are consumed ... The completion of these extensive manufactories in the short space of a few months is a fair specimen of western enterprise. At the West, whatever we take hold of, "is bound to go ahead" not at an old fogy pace, but with railroad speed.

CONCLUSION.

... The facts above given, we think, will convince the most skeptical, that the march of improvement at the West is *onward*. They show an increase in population, wealth and resources, which must prove exceedingly gratifying to all our citizens. They will serve to extend the conviction, now almost universal, that Chicago is destined to become the great commercial centre of the Northwest, and among the first, if not the first, city in the Mississippi Valley. Her position at the head of a thousand miles of lake navigation gives her a commanding influence. She has no levee to be inundated causing the destruction of millions of property. Neither is she situated upon a river, whose navigable capacity the clearing up of the country will be liable to affect. She is subject to no floods nor inundations. To the north, west and south, almost boundless prairies and groves are inviting the toil of the husbandman to develop their treasures and yield a rich reward to honest industry. In all the elements of wealth, their resources are exhaustless. The mineral treasures of Lake Superior will soon pay tribute to Chicago; and our railroads in a few months will have reached the lead regions of the Galena district. The Rock Island and the Illinois Central Railroads will soon penetrate the most extensive coal field in the United States, and in fact in the world, and our commerce, and more especially our manufactures must increase in a ratio far beyond what has hitherto been realized.

Within the next five years the railroads that will be completed and centre in this city will extend more than three thousand miles. If we should add the extensions of these trunk lines to their ultimate limits, their aggregate lengths would amount to tens of thousands. Within five years we expect to be in railroad connexion with Milwaukee and Madison, Wis., with Dubuque and Council Bluffs, Rock Island, St. Louis, Cairo, New Orleans, Mobile, Savannah, Ga., Charleston, S.C., Richmond, Va., Washington, Baltimore, Philadelphia, New York, Boston, Portland, and "the rest of mankind." A bright future is therefore before the "GARDEN CITY." Let our merchants and mechanics, our artisans and business men generally, understand the advantages which our commanding commercial position affords. Let them with becoming prudence, but with far-seeing, intelligent views as to what the spirit of the age and the stirring times in which we live demand, gird themselves for the work of making Chicago the great commercial emporium of the Mississippi Valley. The prize is within their grasp; let them show the world that they are worthy, and the rich commerce of the prairies and of the lakes will most certainly crown their efforts with success.

Source: *Chicago: Her Commerce and Railroads: Two Articles Published in the Daily Democratic Press* (Chicago: Democrat Press Book and Job Print Office, 1853).

2 Cyrus McCormick Markets the Virginia Reaper to the Nation's Farmers, 1850 and 1851

The rise of the modern metropolis required extensive use of natural resources from nonurban environments, including farmland and pasture, forests and deserts, riverways and coastlines. Innovation has been essential to the process, by providing easier and cheaper access to raw materials and forging dynamic new relationships between city and hinterland. In the agricultural sector, for example, the mechanical reaper revolutionized farming practices by more efficiently harvesting grain. Cyrus McCormick was the first to patent and effectively market the device, first from his base in Virginia and then, beginning in 1847, from a manufacturing plant in Chicago. The Chicago business was wildly successful, thanks to effective marketing and the timely expansion of rail connections that facilitated shipment of its "Virginia

McCORMICK'S
PATENT
VIRGINIA REAPER.

The above cut represents one of M'CORMICK'S PATENT VIRGINIA REAPERS, as built for the harvest of 1848. It has been greatly improved since that time, by the addition of a seat for the driver; by a change in the position of the crank, so as to effect a direct connection between it and the sickle, (thereby very much lessening the friction and wear of the machinery, by dispensing altogether with the lever and its fixtures;) by board ribs on the reel, (which operates more gently on the grain than the round ones;) by a sheet of zinc on the platform, (which very much lessens the labor of raking;) by an increase of the size, weight and strength of the wheels of the machine, and by improvement made on the cutting apparatus.

D. W. BROWN,
OF ASHLAND, OHIO,

Having been duly appointed Agent for the sale of the above valuable labor-saving machine (manufactured by C. H. McCormick & Co., in Chicago, Ill.,) for the Counties of Seneca, Sandusky, Erie, Huron, Richland, Ashland and Wayne, would respectfully inform the farmers of those counties, that he is prepared to furnish them with the above Reapers on very liberal terms.

The Wheat portions of the above territory will be visited, and the Agent will be ready to give any information relative to said Reaper, by addressing him at Ashland, Ashland County, Ohio.

Ashland, March, 1850.

Figure 1.2 Broadside advertising McCormick's Patent Virginia Reaper, manufactured by what was then known as C. H. McCormick & Co. Features an illustration of the reaper in use. This early model required a person to ride on the machine and rake the grain from the platform. The local distributor listed on the advertisement is D. W. Brown of Ashland, Ohio.

Source: Wisconsin Historical Society, WHS-40417.

reaper" to farmers nationwide. McCormick's operations eventually gave rise to the International Harvester Corporation in 1902.

Beginning in the 1840s, the company distributed promotional brochures for the reaper widely. The two sampled here – one pictured, from 1850, the other excerpted, from 1851 – highlight the developing interdependence between city and countryside in the nineteenth century. Urban centers like Chicago were sites of trade, industrial production, and service provision that relied heavily on rural hinterlands for supplies of food and raw materials. Rural townspeople and farmers came to depend, in turn, on urban manufactured and processed goods. Even more important, they needed access to urban-based transport networks, middlemen, investors, and creditors in order to remain competitive in the new industrialized markets for agricultural products. Few families farmed simply to sustain themselves and their local community, but instead participated in regional, national, and international markets for raw materials and finished goods. What do these marketing publications tell us about the people, technologies, and new commercial networks that were transforming the nation's cities and its countryside? How might dependence on the reaper and other costly equipment alter farming practices and farmers' relationship to urban America? Would you consider the Virginia reaper to be an "urban" or a "rural" invention?

McCORMICK'S PATENT VIRGINIA REAPER.

NOTICE. All persons friendly to Agricultural interests receiving this Bill, are respectfully requested to post it in a conspicuous place.

Below will be found two blank orders, which being filled out by responsible men and returned, will be promptly attended to.

Chicago, April 1, 1851

With my acknowledgments to Farmers and others for the very liberal patronage heretofore extended to me, I have now to say, that by a thorough course of practical experiments in cutting grain and grass in bad condition, and after an actual test side by side of all the different forms and shapes of cutting apparatus, including the Hussey principle, the zig-zag edge used by Seymour & Morgan (on which they are sued), and those used by others in Illinois, the straight edge, and my *last* improvement – after carefully testing them all, I have now adopted, as can safely be said, the best possible arrangement and combination for cutting grain and grass and yet the simplest and most durable ...

In view of the continued encouragement of the Farming community, I design to have 1500 to 1800 Reapers for the next harvest, and a good number of the Mowers in connection with the Reaper. And Farmers will bear in mind, that I shall afford them an opportunity of *seeing* my Improved Machine as early as possible after the opening of navigation, as I shall have one on exhibition in each of the different sections of the country where the Reaper may be wanted, throughout New York and the West. Farmers and others coming to Chicago are respectfully requested to call and see.

THE IMPROVEMENT MADE ON THE REAPER SINCE THE LAST HARVEST, which is in the Cutting Apparatus ... consists of a combination of the Shoulder or back angle of the Finger (as patented and used in my Machine), with a slightly indented or zig-zag edged Sickle, by which arrangement, as seen from the cut, the angle in the Sickle edge is made so obtuse, as, together with the angle of the Finger for *holding the grain to the Sickle*, to effect the most perfect philosophical principle of cutting, by using just the right slope for cutting with the *least resistance*, and in the most perfect manner ... This is understood by every boy who knows how to draw a knife in cutting a stick, and needs only to be stated to be understood by all ...

From my long experience in the Reaper business, having been engaged exclusively in the business of improving and manufacturing Reapers; having sold in the West more than 4,000 of them – I have, with great care and expense, secured and adopted the simplest, best and most substantial wheels and geering ... [T]he Farmer ... may reasonably conclude, that in ordering my Machine, he runs no risk of being in any way disappointed; while the terms upon which I offer my Machine, as will appear below ... must be a sufficient guarantee.

... I may say that I received the Gold Medal of the American Institute, in 1849, and the Certified Diploma of the same Institute in the year 1850, for my Reaper, one of which has been exhibited at their late Fair, preparatory to its exhibition at the great World's Fair in London, in May next, and its immediate introduction into Great Britain, where it has been patented. It has been introduced into Austria, and arrangements are being made for its introduction into South American and other Countries ...

Having been the first to introduce successfully, cutting grain by Horse Power, much imposition has been in practice upon me, and also upon the Farmers, by the sale of my Machine, altered to EVADE my patents, and thrown out upon the country as *new* and *better* Machines. Seymour & Morgan, Baker & Love, Baker, Glagg & Ewing, and others, are already sued for infringements ... One of these parties [has intimated] that HIS customers would have to pay the penalty of his misdeeds – whether others will play the same game remains to be seen.

... Those interested can see how this whole matter stands for themselves, as I shall have agents appointed in time, in all the different sections of the country in New York and the West, who will be furnished with all the papers, and specimens of my improved Machine, and will with pleasure furnish such information as will enable the Farmer to judge for himself, and in acknowledging our obligations for past favors, we only ask an impartial examination of our claims to continued public patronage.

It is true that he who uses a Machine *unlawfully* made, infringes the rights of the Patentee, and is equally as liable as the manufactures. This is the Law, and it matters not what S. & M. may say upon this point ...

In conclusion I will add, that the only difference in price, (if any) charged for my Machine, will be in the amount of my patent fee, which S. & M. and others try to swindle me out of, and which is a small matter at most to the Farmer, compared to getting a good Machine, with a *perfect right to use it.*

All orders addressed to me at Chicago, Ill., will be promptly attended to.

C. H. McCormick

Mr. C. H. McCORMICK will please manufacture for the undersigned, and deliver at the Warehouse of _____ in _____ on or before the _____ day _____, 1851, one of McCormick's last *Improved* Patent Virginia Reapers (including three Fingers, three sections of the Sickle, and the Pinion extra), for which the undersigned agrees to pay thirty dollars, and freight (and Warehouse charges, if any), on delivery of said machine as aforesaid, and the further sum of ninety dollars on the first of December thereafter, with interest from the first day of July, 1851: Provided that said Reaper will cut one and half acres of wheat or other small grain, in an hour; that it will save at least three-fourths of all the wheat scattered by ordinary cradling; that it is well made, of good material and durable with proper care; and that the raking of the wheat can be well done by a man riding upon it.

If, upon a fair trial, to be made next harvest, said Reaper cannot perform as above specified ... the undersigned will ... store it safely and re-deliver it to C. H. McCormick, subject to refunding the thirty dollars paid as above ...

Source: Wisconsin Historical Society

3 Texans Appeal for the Removal of Native Peoples, 1858–1859

The nation's nineteenth-century westward expansion is usually imagined as proceeding behind a rural and agricultural frontier. Popular histories and even video games like The Oregon Trail *depict explorers, traders, and adventurous pioneer families paving the way for waves of settlement, thriving markets, and ultimately the towns and cities that followed. In fact, though, urban outposts and considerable investment from Eastern and European cities preceded the extensive settlement of the Trans-Appalachian West. Then rapid urban development in Western regions was a prerequisite for the robust expansion of agriculture, ranching, and extractive industries that would come to define them (source 1.1). Essential to every step of this process were actions of the federal government. It acquired territory (through purchase, war, and treaties), established rules for land sales and use (beginning with passage of the Northwest Ordinance), distributed resources (by selling and granting territory), and provided military forces to police the region. And central to both acquisition and policing was the removal of indigenous populations. Beginning in the mid-eighteenth century, indigenous peoples living west of the Appalachian range lost considerable ground to the British and then to Americans. Government-sponsored punitive expeditions, coupled with the floodtide of settlement and expansion of trade, accelerated urban growth and the rural economic activities that depended on cities. In case after case, Native Americans were driven from lands that they had used for very different purposes, in some cases for centuries.*

This exchange of letters between Texan officials provides a rare, "on the ground" glimpse into the relationship between Indian removal, economic development, and urbanization. Twice in January 1858 Thomas Harrison – a lawyer, soldier, and local legislator – wrote to State Senator George Bernard Erath to request protection from Indian incursions in Bosque County, just southwest of present-day Dallas–Fort Worth. Erath was a veteran of both Indian removal and city building. Born in Austria, he migrated in 1833 to the Republic of Texas, where he served as a land surveyor (he designed towns and cities including Meridian and Waco), a soldier in the Indian wars, and a legislator in the new state of Texas. When he received the letters reproduced here, Erath was pressing Governor Hardin R. Runnells to recruit a militia for policing the state's border against Indian incursions. Runnells did so later that month. In 1859 Erath wrote two letters to Runnells describing the border situation and calling for more action to protect local settlers, many of them recent arrivals from Norway. This handwritten correspondence captures some of the conversations that justified military actions against Native Americans, and reveals settlers' assumptions about "productive" uses of the land and the links between urban and rural development. When you reach sources 4.3 and 6.2, consider how Mexican Americans and Anglos engaged the region's changing landscape just five decades later, following extensive railroad development, considerable demographic growth, and the emergence of powerful local industries.

Meridian January 2nd 1858

Capt. Geo. B. Erath

My Dear Sir.

The citizens of Bosque County herewith enclose a petition to be laid before the Governor.

Their grievances are real not imaginary. I saw myself today the body of Johnson ... with five wounds inflicted with arrows. The host of Indians that killed Johnson, carried away a large drove of the most valuable horses in the country – other invasions are expected, the country is in a state of insecurity and alarm – men dare not leave their families unprotected at night. This condition of things is [ruinous] to the country. Emigration will cease those here will wish to leave, there will be no improvements. It is not supposed that these repeated incursions are commenced and carried on by a few young and rash warriors of the tribes, but that they are [seen] as of a coming hostility which [will be] general and destructive of the frontier, unless efficient protection is [provided by] the State. Can you not serve ... the cause of humanity by increasing the frontier protection

Thos. Harrison

Waco Texas
January 4th 1858

Capn. Geo. B. Erath

Dear Sir

I have just received intelligence from Bosque (I left home four days ago), that the Indians have made another [descent] and killed one man certainly and it is thought two others carried off a little boy and shot a Negro who they left for dead but it is said he will recover. This occurred it is said within six or seven miles of Meridian. They also carried off some 30 head of Horses. Some of the citizens have gone in pursuit I fear from the want of experience they will ride their horses down the first day or two and have to abandon the pursuit. I shall start home in the morning and if I can raise horses and men will make an effort to find some of the [impudent] marauders. But our people are in a bad condition to leave home their horses poor and their arms very deficient. Can't you ... get the state to order out fifty men from Bosque for protection of that section to act in congregation with ... 20 men in Erath and from the country between The [Leon] and Bosque. That seems to be the [direction] which they all come in from and 20 men cannot guard it as is evident from this affair. The people immediately [concurrent] as you know are too poor to make a campaign on their own account it is true that at this season of the year and the resources of this country but little more than defensive operations can be considered practicable but if I had fifty men I would make a determined effort to chastise the [??] and I shall do it at all the hazzards if I can get the men, if authorized by the state I could get them from this and [??] counties in three days. Let me hear [??] immediately.

From the distance given from Meridian [??] my own on Dn. [??] Negro that was that the man who brought the news was a stranger and could not remember names except the man who was found killed and whose little son they carried off. That he gave as Walker and I greatly fear it is our old friend and my neighbor Dixon Walker if so retribution and that tenfold shall be had if I live.

In haste [??]
[??]

Brasos Agency
10 January 1859

To his Excellency H. R. Runnells
Governor of the State of Texas

Honoured Sir

By Request of the Citizens of the upper County wich i have the honour to represent in the state Senate i proceeded to the frontier and the principle scene of excitement caused by late indian Depredations and the unfortunate occurrence of part of the men in pursuit of hostile indians and other hors thiefs whom those fired on a camp of friendly Indians

i regret that my prediction of similar occurrences have become true

the Indians of the lower reserve have been hunting and passing over the territory where hostile indians where making continual incursions and the population excited suspicions

those indians concerned as a natural consequence they not being able to distinguish difference tribes

and as it is costumary with indians doing mischief to retreat by the camps of friendly indians on whom they equally depredate

trails of the enemy where frequently found to the camps of our allys on the lower reserve wich to men not acquainted with customs and war fare of Indians was an easy source of suspicion

the citizens have demanded continually that friendly indians be kept from among us

it created equally a continual interruption and successive false alarms while in the mean time those friendly indians took many libertys not consistent with the customs of the white man it was on this ground that the attack on those indians who had been warned a day or two previous to leave was perhaps excusable if not justifiable

the [means] in which it was done was not approved of by the citizens of the country generally but nevertheless meets with partial approbation as a necessity to enforce the demand for the indians to remain without the limits of settled county

where the hostile indians where so frequently committing outrages and where there is but little doubt that a certain class of a [??] white men where also on the credit of indians creating disturbances of the country

some 200 men having assembled on the palopinto from the countys of Coryell, Bosque, and [Erath] and others for the purpose of protecting the country from retaliation by the reserve indians among whom a disposition prevailed in the excitement of the times to [breach] on the lower reserve

but this was not the desire of a majority if it could be prevented and the indians came to terms and let the law take its course.

Being deputized by the citizens in [??] to proceed with Mr. J.M [Vorris] and Dixon Walker the former of Coryell the latter of Bosque county we went to the agency where capt. [Rojs] was absent we had [??] councils with the Chiefs who promised to remain friendly and keep hereafter the indians on the reserve.

[Geo. B. Erath]

Stephenville 13 Jan 59
To his excellency the governor

the former lines where written at Brazos agency being interrupted in course of business i close the communication here on the 12 we arrived in camp reported the result of our mission and the men dispersed

I would now beg leave to suggest what i think will be a necessary policy

it is impossible to convince the settlers at least a respectable minority of the differences of Disposition and friendly relations of the lower reserve indians and the upper reserve and hostile indians [??] where now there is every evidence necessary to convince and proof to the world that the indians of the upper reserve are doing mischief and harbour and assist the enemy

and immediate steps ought to be taken to destroy its existence at least it ought to be removed

the suspicions and feelings excited against the lower will leave the matter in such a condition that it will be impossible for the population of this section of country to be neighbours with those indians

whatever may be done by Comanches will be charged on the lower reserve and it will be impossible for to confine the indians of the lower reserve within their limits as the range is insufficient for their stock nor are they sufficiently provided by the U.S. to subsist within its limits as the country is not productive enough for new land and bad seasons

wich is a local failure in this post for this number and i am informed that already the U.S. government has under consideration a project of this removal across the river

now i would beg leave to recommend that your Excellency assist and urge this project and represent to the federal government the great necessity in furthering her friendly policy to accomplish an entire removal of said indians beyond our state as the consequences of different course are beyond our control and am your obdt. servant

G.B. Erath

the above is written in haste if published please have copied

Sources: Harrison to Erath, January 2, 1858, and Harrison to Erath, January 4, 1858, in Texas State Archives, Governor's Papers: Hardin Richard RUNNELS, Folder 2: January 1858. Erath to Runnells, January 10, 1859, and Erath to Runnells, January 13, 1859, in Texas State Archives, Governor's Papers: Hardin Richard RUNNELS, Folder 14: January 1859.

4 *Hunt's Merchants' Magazine* Discusses the Value of Slave Labor, 1855–1858

The urban–rural linkages that fueled metropolitan growth in the nineteenth century depended on an institution seldom associated with the "modern," namely, chattel slavery. The North American slave economy flourished after the Revolutionary War, as the plantation system's geographic base expanded enormously and the racial ideology on which it depended grew more entrenched. Essential to slavery's expansion were conditions in the American South, where climate, soil, and access to steamboat transport on the Mississippi river created an ideal environment for growing and marketing short-staple cotton, a commodity in high demand by Northern and European textile producers. Meanwhile slave labor was essential to other Southern agricultural sectors, mining, and construction. As a result, the enslaved population in the United States increased from 1.5 million persons in 1820 to 4 million persons on the eve of the Civil War, making it the largest in the Western Hemisphere. By mid-century, 60 percent of the world's cotton supply came from the vast region of short-staple production stretching from South Carolina to Texas, some of it former Native American land auctioned to northeastern investors seeking speculative profits (source 1.3). Most of the South's richest men owned their wealth not in factories or mills but in land and slaves.

Northern and Southern cities flourished from the slave economy. Baltimore's antebellum growth and prosperity depended heavily on trade in slave-produced goods. Atlanta had its origins in a railroad hub built in 1842, and just two decades later served as commercial center of the Confederacy. Meanwhile, up to 40 percent of the nation's cotton revenues went to New York City, where businesses provided services to Southern planters, including shipping, finance, insurance, and the sale of finished goods. The economics and politics of slavery thus factor prominently into the decision-making of the nation's urban economic elites – investors, merchants, manufacturers, and the traders on the floor of the New York Stock Exchange. These excerpts from Hunt's Merchants' Magazine and Commercial Review, *an influential business monthly founded in 1839 and based in New York, provide a glimpse into the world of American business leaders during the decade that saw metropolitan growth and sectional divisions fracture national politics and ultimately lead to Civil War. How would you characterize Northern merchants' views toward the institution of slavery in the 1850s? How did they reconcile slavery's spread with their vision of the United States as a modern, urbanizing, and opportunity-filled nation?*

Slavery and Commerce

Right or wrong, there is more truth than poetry in the following statement from the Richmond (Va.) *Dispatch*:

> The whole Commerce of the world turns upon the product of slave labor. What would Commerce be without cotton, sugar, tobacco, coffee, rice, and naval stores? All these are the products of slave labor. It is a settled fact that free labor cannot produce them in sufficient quantity to supply the demands of mankind. It has been said that one free laborer is equal to five slaves. If this be so, why has not free labor been employed in the production of the above staples? It has been attempted, and in every case in which it has been introduced, has failed. The world follows its interests, and if free labor was more valuable than slave, it would be employed at this moment in the United States, Cuba, and Brazil, which are all open to free labor. And herein note the greater liberality and self-reliant strength of the slave over the free States. The former freely permit the Northern capitalist to come in with his free labor and compete with slave labor. The latter pass laws prohibiting the Southern capitalist from coming in with his slaves to compete with Northern labor. Their prohibitory laws are passed, because they are afraid of slave competition; whereas the South, in the face of the pretense ... that one white laborer is equal in value to five slaves, throws her doors wide open and invites the free labor to walk in

> and try its hand, and it dare not come. What would become of England, the arch agitator of abolitionism, but for cotton, by the manufacture of which she has waxed fat and strong, while she curses the system by which it is produced! By the way, will some one inform us why the English conscience has never suffered as much from slavery in Brazil as slavery in the United States?

Source: *Hunt's Merchants' Magazine*, 32 (1855), p. 264.

Value of Slave Labor

The value of slave labor in the South – particularly upon the sugar plantations of Louisiana – is well illustrated in a recent article in the New Orleans *Picayune*. That journal gives some interesting statistics concerning the Parish of St. Mary's, in Louisiana, which show not only an extraordinary productiveness of soil, but perhaps a larger net return from the labor of slaves than can be found in any other portion of the Southern country. The Parish of St. Mary's is situated in the swamp district of Louisiana, immediately upon the gulf coast. To enable our agricultural friends to make a comparison of the value of slave labor in Louisiana and Virginia, we subjoin the interesting figures of the *Picayune*:

> The population of St. Mary's ... consists of 4,021 whites of all ages and sexes, and 12,019 slaves ... The slave property is assessed at $6,433,250, averaging $535.25 as the value of each slave, and about $1,600 a head of slave property for every white man, woman, and child in the parish.
>
> The total assessed valuation of all the taxable property in the parish is $13,978,169, or within a trifle of $3,500 a head for every white inhabitant ... The number of plantations in the parish is 171, and the number of acres cultivated and in swamp lands is 279,547, of which the assessed value is $5,948,100 ... The average deduced from all the circumstances is, that the cultivated land in St. Mary's is to be valued at $65.62 per acre ... The figures ... show ... an extraordinary state of prosperity.
>
> The products of these 171 plantations for the year ending with the crops of 1857, are estimated by the prices furnished in New Orleans, viz., sugar at $55 net per hogshead, molasses at 6¼ net, corn at 70 cents, and cotton at $40 per bale, although only forty bales were raised in the parish ... The total value of the products raised ... is put down at $2,316,553.50. The average production is, therefore, $39 and a small fraction per acre of the cultivated lands ... [Thus] the production of every slave on the plantation – men, women, and children – exceed $231 a head ... Net profit [on each plantation] amounted to $1,755,325. Each slave, therefore, netted his master $175 a year, or nearly 33 per cent on his assessed value.

Source: *Hunt's Merchants' Magazine*, 39 (October 1858), p. 523.

New York Cotton Market for Month Ending December 22 ("Prepared for the *Merchants' Magazine* by Uhlhorn & Frederickson, Brokers, New York")

... The sales for the week ending December 15th were 4,000 bales, the largest portion being for export. Prices paid showed a still further decline for the week of ¼ cent per pound. Even this reduction failed to impart any confidence in the article, and a lower range of figures is anticipated. Owing to the monetary difficulties throughout the country, and the low stage of the Southern rivers, the receipts at the ports are somewhat retarded, and in consequence our imports are extremely small. Our own spinners for the past month have purchased sparingly ...

Crop. – Crop estimates attract but little attention – the favorite figures are, however, 3,150,000 [or] 3,250,000 bales. Either amount is sufficient, in the present deranged state of foreign affairs, to warrant low prices.

Source: *Hunt's Merchants' Magazine*, 32 (1855), pp. 91–92.

New York Cotton Market for Month Ending January 19

Our last monthly report closed December 22d, since which prices have advanced a half and five-eights of a cent per pound on all grades of cotton from store ...

The improvement in our market is owing mainly to our extremely small stock, and the demand from continental buyers, and for the home trade. There has also been a delay (which continues) in the receipts at the South, owing to the low stage of the rivers, which has prevented an increase of stock here. Our own spinners have bought to a larger extent during the past than the previous month, although there is no disposition to stock themselves at the present high prices – their purchases being only for immediate wants. We are sorry to hear that many of our small mills are working short time, and that some of the largest mills in the country have stopped running. The opinion, on both sides of the Atlantic, is quite strong in favor of lower prices – even should the crop not exceed 3,000,000 bales, it would be a sufficient quantity for the wants of the world, in the present deranged state of affairs, both political and monetary. The effect of the present war between England and Russia is nowhere more forcibly illustrated – in its bearings upon cotton – than that shown by the returns of the British trade for the month of November, 1854, presenting a decrease of nearly two millions of pounds sterling, of which, half a million was of cotton manufactures ... These facts, together with the vast loans required by England and France to carry on the war, must necessarily curtail the operations of trade – limit confidence – and cheapen fabrics and the raw material.

Source: *Hunt's Merchants' Magazine*, 32 (1855), p. 219.

New York Cotton Market for Month Ending March 23

The sales for the month greatly exceed that of the month previous – large transaction, and a rapid advance of nearly one cent per pound having taken place during the last two weeks of the month, owing to the intelligence received ... of the *reported* death of the Russian Emperor, Nicholas, on the 2nd of March. This announcement at once caused an active demand from those who see in the Emperor's death the return of the dove and olive branch to the belligerent courts of Europe, and an immediate renewal of confidence and improvement in trade as a consequence ... Should ... the intelligence at hand prove true, there is no doubt that the above advance will be sustained ...

... The market for the week ended March 16th closed with an advance ... on all grades, with sales of 15,000 bales. The [news by telegraph] of the death of the Russian emperor reached here on the 15th, and the peace prospects being much strengthened by such an event, our market immediately advanced, with large sales for export and on speculation.

Source: *Hunt's Merchants' Magazine*, 32 (1855), pp. 467–468.

New York Cotton Market for Month Ending April 20

Since our last monthly report (March 23rd) a large business has been transacted in cotton ... [A] favorable termination to European difficulties is also anticipated, and has tended materially to advance rates beyond a shipping point. The consumption of cotton in England continues on a large scale, and is no doubt to be attributed to the peculiar wants of the government *at the present time*, and which a state of peace would not require. It needs but a glance at the condition of the state of manufacturing, at a time of peace, in this country, to warrant the above conclusion – if not, what element does England possess that gives her power to increase her manufacturing over that of the last two years ... at a time when she is carrying on a war with one of the most powerful nations of Europe [which is also one of] her own, as well as one of continental Europe's best customers.

Source: *Hunt's Merchants' Magazine*, 32 (1855), p. 598.

Chapter 2 Snapshots of Urban Life on the Eve of the Civil War

1 An Irish Immigrant Writes Home about Life in the United States, 1850

It is difficult for historians to access the voices of average Americans in the nineteenth century, particularly voices of the working poor. Few had the time, resources, or inclination to record their thoughts. But the documents that do exist – here, a letter sent in 1850 by a young Irish immigrant in New York to her family in Ireland – capture views of Americans who benefited tremendously from urban growth, yet were also quite vulnerable to its instability and harsh conditions.

Irish migration to the United States was long-standing and, beginning in the 1840s especially, provided a safety valve for a nation enduring famine as well as a boon for American cities desperate for a cheap, unskilled workforce. Yet while "natives" welcomed immigrants' labor, they remained wary of newcomers like the Irish, whom they viewed as unassimilable, indeed as racially inferior. Most immigrants lived in overcrowded and impoverished neighborhoods, and performed the hardest and poorest-paid work. However, these conditions did not prevent recent arrivals from celebrating the promise represented by life in the United States, as this letter from Margaret McCarthy to her distant family members reveals. This optimism is especially telling in light of the fact that chances of climbing the social ladder were slim at best. Most immigrants remained poor, unable to establish economic independence either in the cities or in the

The Modern American Metropolis: A Documentary Reader, First Edition.
Edited by David M. P. Freund.

countryside. As McCarthy explains to her family, going "west" was prohibitively expensive. What she could not know was that even those who managed to make the journey seldom saw a dramatic improvement in their conditions. Most of the families that would later take advantage of the Homestead Act, for example, became landless wage workers, often deep in debt. What does this letter suggest about a young immigrant's priorities and her impressions of the American experience, its opportunities, and its limitations?

New York September 22nd 1850

My D[ea]r Father and Mother, Brothers and Sisters,

I write these few lines to you hoping that these few lines may find you all in as good State of health as I am in at present, thank God. I Received your welcome letter to me Dated 22nd of May which was a Credit to me for the style and Elligance of its Fluent Language, but I must say rather Flattering. My D[ea]r father, I must only that this [is] a good place and a good Country for if one place does not suit a Man he can go to Another and can very easy please himself. But there is one thing that's Ruining this place especially the Frontier towns and Cities where the Flow of Emmigration is most. The Emmigrants has not money Enough to take them to the Interior of the Country which oblidges them to remain here in [New] York and the like places for which Reason causes the less demand for Labour and also the great Reduction in wages. For this reason I would advise no one to come to America that would not have Some Money after landing here that would enable them to go west in case they would get no work to do here. But any man or woman without a family are fools that would not venture and come to this plentiful country where no man or woman ever hungered or ever will and where you will not be Seen Naked, but I can asure you there are Dangers upon Dangers Attending coming here, but my friends nothing venture nothing have. Fortune will favour the brave. Have courage and prepare yourself for the next time that that worthy man Mr. Boyan is sending out the next lot; and come you all together courageously and bid adieu to that lovely place the land of our Birth. That place where the young and old joined together in our Common union both night and day Engaged in Innocent Amusement.

But alas I am now told – it's the Gulf of Misery, oppression, Degradation, and ruin of every Description which I am sorry to hear of so Doleful a History to be told of our D[ea]r Country. This my D[ea]r Father induces me to Remit to you in this Letter 20 dollars, that is four pounds, thinking it might be some acquisition to you until you might be Clearing away from that place all together and the Sooner the Better, for Believe me, I could not Express how great would be my joy at our seeing you all here together where you would never want or be at a loss for a good Breakfast and Dinner. So prepare as soon as possible for this will be my last Remittance until I see you all here.

Bring with you as much Tools as you can as it will cost you nothing to Bring them and as for your Clothing you need not care much. But that I would like that yourself would bring one good shoot [suit] of cloth that you would spare until you come here. And as for Mary, she need not mind much as I will have for her a Silk Dress, a Bonnet and Viel according, and Ellen I need not mention what I will have for her. I can fit her well. You are to Bring Enough of Flannels and do not form it at home as the way the[y] wear Flannel at home and here is quite different ...

... Thade Houlehan wrote to me saying that if I wished to go up the country that he would send me money, but I declined so doing until you come and there after your coming if you think it may be Better for us to Remain here or go west it will be for you to judge, but until then I will Remain here.

Dan Keliher tells me that you knew more of the House Carpentry than he did himself and he can earn from twelve to fourteen shilling a day, that is seven shilling British. And he also tells me that Florence will do very well and that Michael can get a place right off as you will not be the second day when you can Bind him to any Trade you wish. And as for John, he will be very shortly able to be Bound too, so that I have every reason to believe that we will all do well Together So as that I am sure it's not for slavery I want you to come here. No, it's for affording my brothers and sisters and I an opportunity of Showing our Kindness and Gratitude and Coming on your seniour days that we would be placed in that possision that you, my D[ea]r Father and Mother could walk about Leisurely and Independently without Requiring your Labour, an object which I am Sure will not fail even by myself if I was obliged to do it without the assistance of Brother or Sister for, my D[ea]r Father and Mother.

I am proud and happy to be away from where the County Charges man or the Poor Rates Man or any other Rates Man would have the Satisfaction of once Impounding my cow or any other article of mine. Oh how happy I feel and am sure to have looke[d] as [at?] the Lord had not it destined for [me] to get married to Some Loammun or another at home that after a few months he and I may be an Incumberance upon you or perhaps in the Poor House by this [time] ...

Well I have only to tell my D[ea]r Mother to Bring all her bed Close and also to bring the Kittle and an oven and have handles to them and do not forget the Smoothing Irons and Beware when you are on Board to Bring Some good floor [flour] and Ingage with the Captain['s] Cook and he will do it Better for you for very little and also Bring some whiskey and give them [to] the Cook and Some Sailors that you may think would do you any good to give them a glass once in a time and it may be no harm ...

... [A]nd when you are coming do not be frightened. Take courage and be Determined and bold in your undertaking as the first two or three days will be the worst to you and mind whatever happens on board. Keep your own temper. Do not speak angry to any, nor harshly. The Mildest Man has the best chance on board ... [A]s soon as you Receive this letter write to me and let me Know About everything, when are to come and what time and state the particulars of evry thing to me ...

No More at present But that you will give Mr. and Mrs. Boyen my best love and hope and let me know how they and family are as they would or will not be every better than I would wish them to be. [A]lso Mrs. Milton and Charles, Mr. and Mrs. Roche and family, Mr. and Mrs. Day and family, Mr. Walsh and as for his family, I [am] sure are all well. Mr. and Mrs. Sullivan and family, Mrs. O'Brien, Con Sheehan, wife and family, all the Hearlihys and family, Tim Leahy and family, Owen Sullivan of Caragan and family, Darby Guinee and family, John Calleghan and family, Timothy Calleghan and family, Timothy Sheehan and Mother. So No More at present from your Ever Dear and Loveing Child,

Source: PRO, Dublin, QRO file 11821, Margaret McCarthy to her parents, September 22, 1850.

2 Frederick Law Olmsted Compares Northern and Southern Cities along the Atlantic Seaboard, 1856

In the early 1850s Connecticut-born journalist and landscape architect Frederick Law Olmsted was commissioned by a New York newspaper to travel through the American South. His dispatches were then published in three volumes, including A Journey in the Seaboard Slave States: With Remarks on Their Economy *(1856). Olmsted's travelogue provides a firsthand account of Southern development on the eve of the Civil War and introduces a prominent white Northerner's perspectives on the nature of "progress" in an urbanizing and industrializing nation.*

Metropolitan development had followed notably different paths in the nation's slaveholding and free states. Large-scale production was transforming most regions of the Northeast and Midwest, as factories fueled by water and later by coal-powered steam engines reorganized local

geographies, work conditions, and residential patterns in cities and the countryside. By 1860, as much as 30 percent of the population in New England was employed in the manufacturing sector, and agriculturalists throughout the North and West depended on national, capital-intensive markets for raw materials and finished goods (sources 1.2 and 2.3). Slaveholding states were also linked to those markets, as they profited handsomely by producing goods for industries centered in the Northeast and in England (source 1.4). But slave states relied primarily on a captive black labor force, most of it engaged in agricultural production. The centrality of slavery to Southern life is evident in Olmsted's descriptions of cities and rural settings. In this excerpt, he details the beginning of his travels through the Upper South, including his visit to Washington, DC, and parts of Virginia. What, in Olmsted's view, was the function of cities and the most appropriate use of land? How did he reconcile economic growth and slavery? Notably he would later become a vocal critic of slavery, arguing that it made the region's economy and its white residents less productive.

Food and Shelter. Therewith should a man be content. It will enable me to accomplish my purpose in coming to Washington. But my perverse nature will not be content: will be wishing things were otherwise. They say this uneasiness – this passion for change – is a peculiarity of our diseased Northern nature. The Southern man finds Providence in all that is: Satan in all that might be ...

The population of [Washington, DC] is now over 50,000, and is increasing rapidly. There seems to be a deficiency of tradespeople, and I have no doubt the profits of retailers are excessive. There is one cotton factory in the District of Columbia, employing one hundred and fifty hands, male and female; a small foundry; a distillery; and two tanneries – all not giving occupation to fifty men; less than two hundred, altogether, out of a resident population of nearly 150,000, being engaged in manufactures. Very few of the remainder are engaged in *productive* occupations. There is water-power near the city, superior to that of Lowell, of which, at present, I understand that no use at all is made ...

Land may be purchased, within twenty miles of Washington, at from ten to twenty dollars an acre. Most of it has been once in cultivation, and, having been exhausted in raising tobacco, has been, for many years, abandoned, and is now covered by a forest growth. Several New Yorkers have lately speculated in the purchase of this sort of land, and, as there is a good market for wood, and the soil, by the decay of leaves upon it, and other natural causes, has been restored to moderate fertility, have made money by clearing and improving it. By deep plowing and limeing, and the judicious use of manures, it is made very productive; and, as equally cheap farms can hardly be found in any free State, in such proximity to so high markets for agricultural produce, as those of Washington and Alexandria, there are good inducements for a considerable Northern immigration hither ...

Not more than a third of the country [between DC and Richmond], visible [from the train] I should say, is cleared; the rest is mainly a pine forest. Of the cleared land, not more than one quarter seems to have been lately in cultivation; the rest is grown over with briars and bushes, and a long, coarse grass of no value ...

A good many substantial old plantation mansions are to be seen; generally standing in a grove of white oaks, upon some hill-top. Most of them are constructed of wood, of two stories, painted white, and have, perhaps, a dozen rude-looking little log-cabins scattered around them, for the slaves ...

The more common sort of habitations of the white people are either of logs or loosely-boarded frames, a brick chimney running up outside, at one end: everything very slovenly and dirty about them. Swine, fox-hounds, and black and white children, are commonly lying very promiscuously together, on the ground about the doors.

I am struck with the close co-habitation and association of black and white – negro women are carrying black and white babies together in their arms; black and white children are playing together (not going to school together); black and white faces are constantly thrust together out of the doors, to see the train go by.

The great mass [of colored persons], as they are seen at work, under overseers, in the fields, appear very dull, idiotic, and brute-like; and it requires an effort to appreciate that they are, very much more than the beasts they drive, our brethren – a part of ourselves. They are very ragged, and the women especially, who work in the field with the men, with no apparent distinction in their labor, disgustingly dirty. They seem to move very awkwardly, slowly, and undecidedly, and almost invariably stop their work while the train is passing.

One tannery and two or three saw-mills afforded the only indications I saw, in seventy-five miles of this old country – settled before any part of Massachusetts – of any industrial occupation other than corn and wheat culture, and fire-wood chopping. At Fredericksburg we passed through the streets of a rather busy, poorly-built town; but, altogether, the country seen from the rail-road, bore less signs of an active and prospering people than any I ever traveled through before, for an equal distance.

...

The hotel at which I am staying [in Richmond], "the American," Milberger Smith, from New York, proprietor, is a very capital one. I have never, this side the Atlantic, had my comforts provided for better, in my private room, with so little annoyance from the servants. The chamber-servants are negroes, and are accomplished in their business; (the dining-room servants are Irish). A man and a woman attend together upon a few assigned rooms, in the hall adjoining which they are constantly in waiting; your bell is answered immediately, your orders are quickly and quietly followed, and your particular personal wants anticipated as much as possible, and provided for, as well as the usual offices performed, when you are out ... I took occasion to speak well of [the male servant] to my neighbor one day, that I might judge whether I was particularly favored.

"Oh yes," he said, "Henry was a very good boy, very – valuable servant – quite so – would be worth two thousand dollars, if he was a little younger – easy."

At dinner, a respectable looking, gray-headed man asked another:

"Niggers are going high now, aint they?"

"Yes, sir."

"What would you consider a fair price for a woman thirty years old, with a young-one two years old?"

"Depends altogether on her physical condition, you know. – Has she any other children?"

"*Yes; four.*"

"– Well – I reckon about seven to eight hundred."

"I bought one yesterday – gave six hundred and fifty."

"Well, sir, if she's tolerable likely, you did well."

...

There were, in the train [heading out from Richmond], two first-class passenger cars, and two freight cars. The latter were occupied by about forty negroes, most of them belonging to traders, who were sending them to the cotton States to be sold. Such kind of evidence of activity in the slave trade of Virginia is to be seen every day; but particulars and statistics of it are not to be obtained by a stranger here. Most gentlemen of character seem to have a special disinclination to converse on the subject; and it is denied, with feeling, that slaves are often reared, as is supposed by the Abolitionists, with the intention of selling them to the traders. It appears to me evident, however, from the manner in which I hear the traffic spoken of incidentally, that the cash value of a slave for sale, above the cost of raising it from infancy to the age at which it commands the highest price, is generally considered among the surest elements of a planter's wealth. Such a nigger is worth such a price, and such another is too old to learn to pick cotton, and such another will bring so much, when it has grown a little more, I have frequently heard people say, in the street, or the public-houses. That a slave woman is commonly esteemed least for her laboring qualities, most for those qualities which give value to a brood-mare is, also, constantly made apparent.*

...

I have been once or twice told that the poor white people [in Virginia], meaning those, I suppose, who bring nothing to market to exchange for money but their labor, although they may own a cabin and a little furniture, and cultivate land enough to supply themselves with (maize) bread, are worse off in almost all respects than the slaves. They are said to be extremely ignorant and immoral, as well as indolent and unambitious. That their condition is not as unfortunate by any means as that of negroes, however, is most obvious, since from among them, men *sometimes* elevate themselves to positions and habits of usefulness, and respectability. They are said to "corrupt" the negroes, and to encourage them to steal, or to work for them at night and on Sundays, and to pay them with liquor ...

...

[A Virginia planter] said that his negroes never worked so hard as to tire themselves – always were lively, and ready to go off on a frolic at night. He did not think they ever did half a fair day's work. They could not be made to work hard: they never would lay out their strength freely, and it was impossible to make them do it.

This is just what I have thought when I have seen slaves at work – they seem to go through the motions of labor without putting strength into them. They keep their powers in reserve for their own use at night, perhaps.

Mr. W. also said that he cultivated only the coarser and lower-priced sorts of tobacco, because the finer sorts required more pains-taking and discretion than it was possible to make a large gang of negroes use. "You can make a nigger work," he said, "*but you cannot make him think.*"

...

Norfolk is a dirty, low, ill-arranged town, nearly divided by a morass. It has a single creditable public building, a number of fine private residences, and the polite society is reputed to be agreeable, refined, and cultivated, receiving a character from the families of the resident naval officers. It has all the immoral and disagreeable characteristics of a large seaport, with very

*A slaveholder writing to me with regard to my cautious statements on this subject, made in the *Daily Times*, says: "In the States of Maryland, Virginia, North Carolina, Kentucky, Tennessee and Missouri, as much attention is paid to the breeding and growth of negroes as to that of horses and mules. Further South, we raise them both for use and for market. Planters command their girls and women (married or unmarried) to have children; and I have known a great many negro girls to be sold off, because they did not have children. A breeding woman is worth from one-sixth to one-fourth more than one that does not breed."

few of the advantages that we should expect to find as relief to them. No lyceum or public libraries, no public gardens, no galleries of art, and though there are two "BETHELS," no "home" for its seamen; no public resorts of healthful and refining amusement, no place better than a filthy, tobacco-impregnated bar-room or a licentious dance-cellar, so far as I have been able to learn, for the stranger of high or low degree to pass the hours unoccupied by business.

[It has been] very well shown what advantages were originally possessed for profitable commerce at this point ... [And as one observer has noted], "Its climate is delightful ... Its harbor is commodious and safe as safe can be. It is never blocked up by ice. It has the double advantage of an inner and an outer harbor. The inner harbor is as smooth as any mill-pond. In it vessels lie with perfect security, where every imaginable facility is offered for loading and unloading ... The *natural* advantages, then, in relation to the sea or the back country, are superior, *beyond comparison,* to those of New York."

There is little, if any exaggeration in this estimate; yet, if a deadly, enervating pestilence had always raged here, this Norfolk could not be a more miserable, sorry little seaport town than it is. It was not possible to prevent the existence of some agency here for the transhipment of goods, and for supplying the needs of vessels, compelled by exterior circumstances to take refuge in the harbor. Beyond this bare supply of a necessitous demand, and what results from the adjoining naval rendezvous of the nation, there is nothing.

Singularly simple, child-like ideas about commercial success, you find among the Virginians – even among the merchants themselves. The agency by which commodities are transferred from the producer to the consumer, they seem to look upon as a kind of swindling operation; they do not see that the merchant acts a useful part in the community, or, that his labor can be other than selfish and malevolent. They speak angrily of New York, as if it fattened on the country without doing the country any good in return. They have no idea that it is *their* business that the New Yorkers are doing, and that whatever tends to facilitate it, and make it simple and secure, is an increase of their wealth by diminishing the costs and lessening the losses upon it.

They gravely demand why the government mail steamers should be sent to New York, when New York has so much business already, and why the nation should build costly custom-houses and post-offices, and mints, and sea defenses, and collect stores and equipments there, and not at Norfolk, and Petersburg, and Richmond, and Danville, and Lynchburg, and Smithtown, and Jones's Cross-Roads? It seems never to have occurred to them that it is because the country needs them there, because the skill, enterprise and energy of New York merchants, the confidence of capitalists in New York merchants, the various facilities for trade offered by New York merchants, enable them to do the business of the country cheaper and better than it can be done anywhere else ...

Then, if it be asked why Norfolk, with its immense natural advantages for commerce, has not been able to do their business for them as well as New York; or why Richmond, with its great natural superiority for manufacturing, has not prospered like Glasgow, or Petersburg like Lowell – why Virginia is not like Pennsylvania, or Kentucky like Ohio? – they will perhaps answer that it is owing to the peculiar tastes they have inherited ...

... Ask any honest stranger who has been brought into intimate intercourse for a short time with the people, why it is that here has been stagnation, and there constant, healthy progress, and he will answer that these people are less enterprising, energetic and sensible in the conduct of their affairs – that they live less in harmony with the laws that govern the accumulation of wealth than those.

Ask him how this difference of character should have arisen, and he will tell you it is not from the blood, but from the education they have received; from the institutions and circumstances they have inherited. It is the old, fettered, barbarian labor-system, in connection with which they have been brought up, against which all their enterprise must struggle, and with the chains of which all their ambition must be bound.

This conviction I find to be universal in the minds of strangers, and it is forced upon one more strongly than it is possible to make you comprehend by a mere statement of isolated facts. You could as well convey an idea of the effect of mist on a landscape, by enumerating the number of particles of vapor that obscure it. Give Virginia blood fair play, remove it from the atmosphere of slavery, and it shows no lack of energy and good sense.

It is strange the Virginians dare not look this in the face. Strange how they bluster in their legislative debates, in their newspapers, and in their barrooms, about the "Yankees," and the "Yorkers," declaring that they are "swindled out of their legitimate trade," when the simple truth is, that the Northern merchants do that for them that they are unable to do for themselves. As well might the Chinese be angry with us for sending our clipper ships for their tea, because it is a business that would be more "legitimately" (however less profitably) carried on in "junks."

Source: Frederick Law Olmsted, *A Journey in the Seaboard Slave States: With Remarks on Their Economy* (London, 1856), pp. 2, 13–14, 16–19, 49–50, 55, 85, 91, 135–141.

3 The *New York Times* Reports on a Millworker Strike in Lynn and Marblehead, 1859

In 1860 the shoe and textile workers of Lynn and Marblehead, Massachusetts, staged what was, at the time, the largest industrial strike in US history. They were responding to the worsening conditions and economic insecurity faced by laborers in the mill towns that were instrumental to American growth in the nineteenth century. Some of these towns had deep roots, such as Lynn and Nashua, New Hampshire, which were settled in the colonial era and only later became centers of shoe and textile production. Others, such as Lowell, Massachusetts, were founded for manufacturing in the early nineteenth century and subsequently developed into complex industrial centers. By harnessing water power, industrialists turned Patterson, New Jersey, into a major center for the production of silk, textiles, firearms, and railroad locomotives.

In these and other industrial cities, hundreds or even thousands of workers would assemble at factory gates each morning to work at jobs that were arduous, insecure, and paid meager wages. Living conditions were also poor. This account of the combined Lynn and Marblehead protests by a New York Times *reporter provides a glimpse into the conversations and concerns of laborers struggling for autonomy and some measure of control over their lives on the eve of the Civil War. The article captures something of workers' moods, their grievances, and their enthusiasm for collective action. Equally evident, meanwhile, is the reporter's impatience with the strike and women's participation, testament to the chasm between the experiences of urban laborers and professionals in the modern industrial metropolis.*

Lynn, Feb. 28, 1860.

In company with some of the Boston correspondents, I yesterday visited the town of Marblehead, where the strikers have obtained an ascendancy equal almost to that of the Lynn malcontents. The immediate cause of our going was a desire to witness the doings of the mass meeting, composed of the combined forces of Lynn and Marblehead ...

About noon, the procession from Lynn, consisting of about 3,500 men, preceded by a brass band, entered the village green, escorted by 500 Marbleheaders. The sight from the hotel steps was a very interesting one. Four thousand men, without work, poor, depending partially upon the charities of their neighbors and partially upon the generosity of the tradesmen of the town, giving up a certainty for an uncertainty, and involving in trouble with themselves many hundreds of women and children, while to a certain extent the wheels of trade are completely blocked, and no immediate prospect of relief appears. Their banners flaunted bravely. Their inscriptions of "Down with tyranny," "We are not slaves," "No sympathy with the rich," "Our bosses grind us," "We work and they ride," "No foreign police," and many others of like import, read very well and look very pretty, but they don't buy dinners or clothing, or keep the men at work or the women at home about their business. By this strike $25,000 *weekly is kept from circulation in Lynn alone*, and who can say what the effect will be on the storekeepers, dealers in articles of home consumption, if such a state of drainage is kept up for any great length of time?

However this may be, they made a grand show. The day was fine, the air balmy, the music good, the crowd great, and all the resolutions for sticking out were passed unanimously; so they passed a few hours on the green, making speeches of encouragement, and then, with three cheers for the Marblehead girls, and three groans for the "*grandizing bosses*," the delegations parted, and the Lynn[ies] returned home, with mud in the road up to their knees, but with enthusiasm waxing stronger at every step.

The most interesting part of the whole movement took place last evening, and will be continued tonight. I refer to the mass meeting of the binders and stitchers held by

THE FEMALE STRIKERS AT LIBERTY HALL

In company with the Boston *Herald and Journal*, the NEW-YORK TIMES mounted the top of a ricketty omnibus, and took fifteen cents' worth of ride over ruts and through mud to Liberty Hall. The streets were thronged with girls of various ages and sizes – some twelve years old, and others forty – some four feet high and ten feet around, and others six feet high and five feet around. The corners were crowded with ["jours"] who cheered each chatty group that passed, saluting them with cries of "Go in, gals," "Remember MOLLY STARK," "Give the bosses fits," &c., &c. Reaching the foot of the stairway, the TIMES happened to be ahead, and with great difficulty pressed his way through the whalebone and rattan to the top of the steps. Here a venerable lady stopped the entrance, and said in a loud voice which attracted the attention of the three hundred occupants (all women), "No, Sir! No sich comes in *here*. You have vilified us and inspersed the purposes of our meetins, and not but one man can come in tonight – but our Chairman, Mr. OLIVER."

... [W]e stood upon a chair, betted the indulgence of the house ... [a] vote was taken, and we were allowed to remain, on condition we would tell the whole truth and nothing but the truth, leaving out what nonsense might be uttered on the spur of the moment ... At our intercession the Herald and Journal were admitted, but not until they purged themselves of all intent to do injustice and had promised to be as good as the TIMES was to be. I hardly think knowledge was ever pursued under more difficult circumstances.

The hall was filled to its utmost capacity. The ladies were such as you can imagine free, self-supporting, fearless, happy women to be. We have seen many assemblages of women, but have never beheld a more intelligent, earnest, "*peart*" set, than were in Liberty Hall last night.

The object of the meeting was the hearing the reports of the Committees who had been deputed to make a list of reasonable prices, and to solicit the girls of Lynn and the surrounding towns to join the strike movement.

There are two classes of workers – those who work in the shops and those [who] work at home – the former use the machines and materials of the bosses, while the latter work on their own machines, or work by hand, furnishing their own materials. It is evident that the latter should receive higher pay than the former, and the report not having considered this fact, was subjected to severe handling. The discussion which followed was rich beyond description – the jealousies, piques and cliques of the various circles being apparent as it proceeded. One opposed the adoption of the report because "the prices set were so high that the bosses wouldn't pay them." Cries of "Put her out," "Shut up," "Scabby," and "Shame!" arose on all sides, but, while the reporters were alarmed, the lady took it all in good part, and made up faces at the crowd. The Chairman stated that, hereafter, pickleeomoonia boots were to be made for three cents a pair less, which announcement was received with expressions of dismay, whereupon he corrected himself, and said they were to be three cents higher; and this announcement drew forth shouts and screams of applause. "There, didn't I *say* so?" said an old lady behind me. "You shut up," was the response of her neighbor, "you think because you've got a couple of machines you're some, but you aint no more than anybody else." ... [T]he Chairman, with the perspiration starting from every pore, said in a loud and authoritative tone of voice: "Ladies! look at me; stop this wranglin." Do you care for your noble cause? Are you descendants of MOLLY STARK or not?" ...

"Here comes the Boston police"; "Pitch 'em in the river"; "Who's afraid?" "We'll put 100 girls at the depot, and *then* see if the police dare arrest anybody." What could the Chairman do? He hammered and yelled "Order," but had to succumb and let the girls talk it out, when they again came to order and resumed business.

A proposition to march in the procession was the next topic which drew forth discussion. Some thought that proper minded women would better stay at home than be gadding about the streets following banners and music.

To this there was some assent, but when a younger girl asked the last speaker what she meant by talking that way, when everybody in Lynn knew that she had been tagging around on the sidewalks after the men's processions the last week, the uproar was tremendous ...

Some of the statements were quite interesting. A MRS. MILLER said that she hired a machine on which she was able to make $6 per week – out of that she paid – for the machine, $1; for the materials, $1.50; for her board, $2; for bastings, $1; – making $5.50 in all, which left her a clear profit of only fifty cents a week ... The leading spirit of the meeting, MISS CLARA BROWN, a very bright, pretty girl, said that she called at a shop that day and found a friend of hers hard at work on a lot of linings. She asked what she was getting for them, and was told *eight cents for sixty*. "Girls of Lynn," said CLARA, "*Girls* of Lynn, do you hear that and will you stand it? Never, *Never*, NEVER. Strike then – strike at once; DEMAND 8 _ cents for your work when the binding isn't closed, and you'll get it. don't let them make niggers of you; [Shame, there are colored persons here] I meant Southern niggers: keep still; don't work your machines; let 'em lie still till we get all we ask, and then go at it, as did our Mothers in the Revolution."

This speech was a good one; it seemed to suit all parties, and they proposed to adjourn to Tuesday night, when they would have speeches and be more orderly. Canvassing Committees were appointed to look up female strikers and to report female "scabs." And with a vote of thanks to the Chairman, the meeting adjourned to meet in Lyceum Hall.

The *Herald and Journal* went into Boston at the close of the meeting, and as the TIMES was a comparative stranger, a committee of five escorted him home. They insisted upon his partaking of a stew and beer, crackers and red sauerkraut, and then with merry laugh and pleasant chat took us to our elegant and really metropolitan quarters at the Sagamore, where we bade them good-night, and retired to the dream of nonpareil, or machines, and eight cents per sixty pair.

Source: "The Bay State Strike. Movement among the Women: Acts and Proceedings of Employers and Workers," *New York Times*, February 29, 1860.

4 Reverend Albert Williams Describes San Francisco's Fires

One Sunday morning in 1851, while preparing his morning service for the First Presbyterian Church in San Francisco, the Reverend Albert Williams looked out of his window and saw smoke billowing from the block where his congregation would soon gather. As he recounts in this excerpt from his

1871 memoir, Williams rushed to the scene and reached the church in time to help its members rescue books, the pulpit, and the organ before the building was consumed by flames.

The size, scale, and density of America's industrial cities created a host of new challenges for residents and local authorities. These places were congested, unsanitary, and largely unregulated, creating numerous safety and public health problems. They were crowded with people unfamiliar to each other and unconnected, creating new opportunities for crime as well as widespread panic about it, regardless of its extent. Urban structures were largely made of wood and filled with flammable materials, so when fires broke out they spread quickly and often destroyed entire neighborhoods. Of course, fire hazards and fires were hardly new to American urban life, and volunteer fire companies had been established in virtually every city by the early nineteenth century. Many of these units were quite large by mid-century and fairly effective, but their members' public drinking and fighting led most cities to disband them in favor of municipal departments with paid staffs. Cincinnati began the trend in 1853. As Williams notes, San Francisco was particularly ill-prepared for the fires that ravaged the city after 1849.

This matter-of-fact account of the city's mid-century fires and the community's response identifies some of the uncertainties that accompanied life in the modern metropolis. Note Williams's inclusion, for example, of a contemporary document (an editorial published in 1851) that reveals popular sentiments about the dangers and challenges posed by urban life.

The destructive fires of San Francisco in the early days were periodical inflictions, which seemed to mark the city as doomed. They had their beginning in '49, and made a part of the crowded incidents of that eventful year. The destroying element was the more sweeping in its effects by reason of the combustible materials of its buildings, high winds, and an insufficient Fire Department, together with a defective supply of water. The most noteworthy fire of 1849 occurred at the close of that year, on the 24th of December. It broke out at four o'clock in the morning, in an "Exchange" on Kearny street, opposite the Plaza, consumed that large and costly building, communicated with the adjoining larger structure, known as the Parker House, and burned it, with other smaller buildings in the vicinity, to ashes. The fabulous incomes from the rents of those principal buildings – from the Parker House $10,000 per month, and from the Exchange in proportion – show the great pecuniary losses sustained.

The next great fires were those of the 4th and 14th of May, 1850. These swept over the central business quarters of the city, and were sufficient to crush the average courage of men. Yet, while the ashes were still glowing with heat, rebuilding was commenced upon the ruins.

The fourth great fire took place on the night of the 17th of September, 1850. Again, to an extraordinary degree, were the endurances of the community tried. Before morning the fire had done its completed work, and destroyed property valued at millions.

So frequent and periodical were these fires, that they came to be regarded in the light of permanent institutions. Fears of a recurrence of the dread evil, in view of the past, were not long in waiting for fulfillment. On the anniversary of the fire of the 4th of May, 1850, came another on the 4th of May, 1851, the fifth general fire. The city was appalled by these repeated calamities. And more, it began to be a confirmed conviction that they were not accidental, but incendiary. On the 22d of June, 1851, the sixth, and, happily the last general fire, and severest of all, occurred. The fact that the point of the beginning of this fire was in a locality quite destitute of water facilities, with other attending circumstances, left hardly a remaining doubt of its incendiary character.

To the congregation of the First Church in general, in the burning of its church edifice, and, in addition, to a large number of its individual members, many of whom lost their all in this fire, the event was deplorably ruinous. The fire began in a small frame house on Pacific street, between Stockton and Powell streets, in the rear of the church, on the same block on which it was situated. When first discovered, a bucket of water might have extinguished the fire, but the preventive was not at command, or timely efforts to apply it were neglected. The time was Sunday morning. At the first bell-ringing for the eleven o'clock service, looking out of my north study window, from my residence on California street, I saw a dark cloud of smoke rising from the region of the church. In anxious haste I left for the threatening scene. On Stockton street I met a friend, who reported the fire as already beyond control, and our church beyond the power of preservation. Very many of the congregation were on the way to the church service at the beginning of the fire. The choir had made special preparation for the music of that day. I reached the church in time to assist members of the congregation in saving the books, organ, and other moveable articles, and last of all, helped to detach the pulpit and bear it to a place of safety. Meanwhile the fire had begun its destructive work upon the west pulpit end of the building, and from the burning masses around had gained such power that in a few minutes the entire structure was enveloped in the consuming flames. The eastern Stockton street front, supporting the belfry, last gave way, and the bell loosened from its lofty height fell into the street and was broken in the fall. In so brief a space of time, the church for which we had waited so long, and in the use of which so much gratification had been derived, was entirely destroyed.

Of course, a conflagration so extensive, with Broadway as its northern limit, southward to the Plaza, and eastward to the line of the Bay, entailed most oppressive losses, and was attended with many striking incidents. Our friends, De Witt and Harrison, saved their large warehouse on Sansome street, with its valuable contents, protecting it with blankets saturated with many thousand gallons of vinegar. Others of our people lost their all. Late in the afternoon, I went outside of the burnt district, seeking such of my congregation as had been extreme sufferers. Not to mention other cases of misfortune, I traced one family, consisting of a father, mother, and two daughters, to their place of retreat, a small room, in the middle of which was the small remnant of articles contained in a blanket, saved from a fully stocked store and a dwelling pleasantly furnished, together with much prized heirlooms from former generations. Only on the previous day, an additional supply of goods had been added to the stock of the store, all of which, according to wont, was fully paid for, but all in a moment was lost.

The lesson of this great fire was not neglected. With the impression of risks from incendiaries, and the fear of repetitions of what was believed to be villainous incendiary work, hundreds of citizens were organized as a *corps* for patrolling the city, especially in May and June, 1852, as a precautionary and preventive measure against incendiarism.

Mechanical labor, building materials, and many other articles of merchandise, rose to greatly enhanced values as a consequence, as had been the case in other preceding fires. Rents were greatly advanced, alike for stores and residences. In the case of the latter, dwellings in the vicinity of, and less commodious than my own residence, readily commanded $300 per month.

Again the congregation was obliged to seek temporary accommodations. Once, on Sunday evening, June 29th, we worshipped, by invitation, in the First Baptist Church. On the first and second Sundays of July, service was held in the Supreme Court Room, Marine Hospital building, on Stockton street. The place was small, and a change was made to the Superior Court Room, St. Francis Hotel, larger but insufficient in capacity.

The spirit of sympathy and the appreciation of religious institutions which prevailed in the community, found utterance in the public prints. Unasked expressions of this interest appeared editorially. One of the class represents so truly the state of the case, including the plans of the congregation looking to rebuilding of the church, that I transfer it to these pages.

> PRESBYTERIAN CHURCH. – We learn that the congregation which were accustomed to assemble at the Presbyterian Church, which was consumed by the conflagration of Sunday last, are taking steps to rebuild, in a more permanent manner, a Temple dedicated to the Most High. We are glad to see

> this. We are well pleased to chronicle to our friends abroad, that while crime stalks through our city, in too many instances unpunished, while good citizens feel constrained to band themselves together for the protection of their lives and property, while it has been deemed necessary in some instances, in different portions of the State, to visit the guilty with the terrible penalty of death, in order to strike terror into the breasts of scores of felons in our midst, there are still so many amongst us who remember the duty they owe their Creator, who are willing to assist with their means in the erection of a Temple to be dedicated to the living God. Such a movement, made at a time when nearly all are oppressed with heavy losses, will inspire a greater confidence in us abroad than any other which could be made. It will be seen and understood that we desire to do our duty, and that we regard the amenities of life more than we prize a few paltry dollars. Let the good work progress, and our word for it, the money thus spent will return fourfold to the generous donors. – *The Pacific Star*, Jan. 25, 1851.

A much longer delay than appears necessary occurred before the rebuilding was accomplished. It was at once decided to rebuild.

Source: Rev. Albert Williams, *Pioneer Pastorate and Times: Embodying Contemporary Local Transactions and Events* (San Francisco: Wallace & Hassett, 1879), pp. 44–49.

Questions for Discussion

1. What forces were shaping urban development by the mid-nineteenth century and what distinguished this period from previous eras of city building? Who and what fueled the settlement of new cities and the expansion of existing ones?
2. Why did immigrants like Mary McCarthy come to the United States, and what sorts of trade-offs did they face by doing so?
3. How did urban change contribute to the nation's geographic, demographic, and economic growth in the mid-nineteenth century?
4. Were the forced removal of indigenous people and the expansion of chattel slavery necessary for urban development?

Part II From Walking City to Industrial Metropolis, 1860–1920

Chapter 3 Commerce and the Metropolis

1 The Pacific Railway Act of 1862 Connects the Nation

Constructing and operating the nation's railroad network required considerable private sector innovation and investment (source 1.1). But the transport revolution depended on public resources, as well, including generous federal aid. Public sector support for infrastructure development predated the Civil War. State governments helped finance canal construction (federal aid was rare) and the first direct federal land grant to a private railroad, for the Illinois Central, came in 1850. Six years later, just after the Army Corps of Engineers completed its transcontinental railroad survey, Congress proposed legislation to promote railway construction, but the bill was blocked by Southern congressmen. Only Southern secession cleared the way for what became the Pacific Railway Act of 1862, which accelerated railroad expansion dramatically through a massive transfer of public lands to private developers. The war gave Northern legislators both the leverage to pass the Act (the opposition had left the government) and a compelling argument for its urgency. Railroad construction was necessary, Republicans insisted, to supply the Union Army and promote economic expansion, both of which were essential for ensuring Union victory.

Some of the Act's far-reaching impacts can be easily enumerated. Within a decade of its passage, the US government had granted over 175 million acres of public land to private rail companies. Between the outbreak of the Civil War and 1880 the miles of track in operation nationwide grew from 30,000 to 166,000 and the first transcontinental link was completed in 1869.

The Modern American Metropolis: A Documentary Reader, First Edition.
Edited by David M. P. Freund.

Railroads and other industrial concerns quickly monopolized the distribution of goods, fueling the antiurban and antitrust sentiments that united farmers and industrial workers behind movements such as the Populist Party. Other legacies of the Act are revealed in its technical, seemingly mundane provisions, which document how public policy helped to literally draw the map for urban and commercial growth in the late nineteenth century. How do the guidelines set out here help explain why certain people and institutions came to monopolize economic power and decision-making in the nation's fast-growing metropolitan regions? How does a statute help us understand the transformation of the landscape, the building of new urbanized places, and Americans' changing relationships to them?

AN ACT to aid in the construction of a railroad and telegraph line from the Missouri river to the Pacific ocean, and to secure to the government the use of the same for postal, military, and other purposes.

Be it enacted by the Senate and House of Representatives of the United States of America in Congress assembled, That Walter S. Burgess, William P. Blodget, Benjamin H. Cheever, Charles Fosdick Fletcher, of Rhode Island; Augustus Brewster, Henry P. Haven, Cornelius S. Bushnell, Henry Hammond, of Connecticut; Isaac Sherman, Dean Richmond, Royal Phelps, William H. Ferry, Henry A. Paddock, Lewis J. Stancliff, Charles A. Secor, Samuel R. Campbell, Alfred E. Tilton, John Anderson, Azariah Boody, John S. Kennedy, H. Carver, Joseph Field, Benjamin F. Camp, Orville W. Childs, Alexander J. Bergen, Ben. Holliday, D. N. Barney, S. De Witt Bloodgood, William H. Grant, Thomas W. Olcott, Samuel B. Ruggles, James B. Wilson, of New York; Ephraim Marsh, Charles M. Harker, of New Jersey ... [*another 124 individuals from 24 states and territories follow*] ... together with commissioners to be appointed by the Secretary of the Interior, and all persons who shall or may be associated with them, and their successors, are hereby created and erected into a corporate and politic in deed and in law, by the name, style, and title of "The Union Pacific Railroad Company"; ... and the said corporation is hereby authorized and empowered to lay out, locate, construct, furnish, maintain, and enjoy a continuous railroad and telegraph, with the appurtenances, from a point on the one-hundredth meridian of longitude west from Greenwich, between the south margin of the valley of the Republican river and the north margin of the valley of the Platte river, in the Territory of Nebraska, to the western boundary of Nevada Territory, upon the route and terms hereinafter provided, and is hereby vested with all the powers, privileges, and immunities necessary to carry into effect the purposes of this act as herein set forth. The capital stock of said company shall consist of one hundred thousand shares of one thousand dollars each, which shall be subscribed for and held in not more than two hundred shares by any one person, and shall be transferable in such manner as the by-laws of said corporation shall provide. The persons hereinbefore named, together with those to be appointed by the Secretary of the Interior, are hereby constituted and appointed commissioners, and such body shall be called the Board of Commissioners of the Union Pacific Railroad and Telegraph Company ...

SEC. 2. *And be it further enacted,* That the right of way through the public lands be, and the same is hereby, granted to said company for the construction of said railroad and telegraph line; and the right, power, and authority is hereby given to said company to take from the public lands adjacent to the line of said road, earth, stone, timber, and other materials for the construction thereof; said right of way is granted to said railroad to the extent of two hundred feet in width on each side of said railroad, where it may pass over the public lands, including all necessary grounds for stations, buildings, workshops and depots, machine shops, switches, side tracks, turn-tables, and water stations. The United States shall extinguish as rapidly as may be, the Indian titles to all lands falling under the operation of this act, and required for the said right of way and grants hereinafter made.

SEC. 3. *And be it further enacted,* That there be, and is hereby, granted to the said company, for the purpose of aiding in the construction of said railroad and telegraph line, and to secure the safe and speedy, transportation of the mails, troops, munitions of war, and public stores thereon, every alternate section of public land, designated by odd numbers, to the amount *of five* alternate sections per mile on each side of said railroad, on the line thereof, and within the limits of ten miles on each side of said road, not sold, reserved, or otherwise disposed of by the United States, and to which a preemption or homestead claim may not have attached, at the time the line of said road is definitely fixed: *Provided,* That all mineral lands shall be excepted from the operation of this act; but where the same shall contain timber, the timber thereon is hereby granted to said company ...

SEC. 4. *And be it further enacted,* That whenever said company shall have completed forty consecutive miles of any portion of said railroad or telegraph line ready for the service contemplated by this act, and supplied with all necessary drains, culverts, viaducts, crossings, sidings, bridges, turnouts, watering places, depots, equipments, furniture, and all other appurtenances of a first-class railroad ... patents shall issue conveying the right and title to said lands to said company, on each side of the road, as far as the same is completed ...

SEC. 5. *And be it further enacted,* … the Secretary of the Treasury shall, upon the certificate in writing of said commissioners of the completion and equipment of forty consecutive miles of said railroad and telegraph, in accordance with the provisions of this act, issue to said company bonds of the United States of one thousand dollars each, payable in thirty years after date, bearing six per centum per annum interest …

SEC. 6. *And be it further enacted,* That the grants aforesaid are made upon condition that said company shall pay said bonds at maturity, and shall keep said railroad and telegraph line in repair and use, and shall at all times transmit dispatches over said telegraph line, and transport mails, troops, and munitions of war, supplies, and public stores upon said railroad for the government whenever required to do so by any department thereof, and that the government shall at all times have the preference in the use of the same for all the purposes aforesaid …

SEC. 9. *And be it further enacted,* That the Leavenworth, Pawnee and Western Railroad Company of Kansas are hereby authorized to construct a railroad and telegraph line from the Missouri river, at the mouth of the Kansas river, on the south side thereof, so as to connect with the Pacific Railroad of Missouri, to the aforesaid point on the one-hundredth meridian of longitude west from Greenwich, as herein provided, upon the same terms and conditions in all respects as are provided in this act for the construction of the railroad and telegraph line first mentioned … The Central Pacific Railroad Company of California, a corporation existing under the laws of the State of California, are hereby authorized to construct a railroad and telegraph line from the Pacific coast, at or near San Francisco, or the navigable waters of the Sacramento river, to the eastern boundary of California, upon the same terms and conditions … and to meet and connect with the first-mentioned railroad and telegraph line on the eastern boundary of California …

SEC. 12. *And be it further enacted,* That whenever the route of said railroad shall cross the boundary of any state or territory or said meridian of longitude, the two companies meeting or uniting there shall agree upon its location at that point, with reference to the most direct and practicable through route, and in case of difference between them as to said location the President of the United States shall determine the said location … The track, upon the entire line of railroad and branches shall be of uniform width, to be determined by the President of the United States, so that, when completed, cars can be run from the Missouri river to the Pacific coast …

SEC. 17. *And be it further enacted,* That in case said company or companies shall fail to comply with the terms and conditions of this act … Congress may pass any act to insure the speedy completion of said road and branches, or to put the same in repair and use, and may direct the income of said railroad and telegraph line to be thereafter devoted to the use of the United States to repay all such expenditures caused by the default or neglect of such company or companies ...

SEC. 18. *And be it further enacted,* That whenever it appears that the net earnings or the entire road and telegraph, including the amount allowed for services rendered for the United States, after deducting all expenditures – including repairs and the furnishing, running, and managing of said road – shall exceed ten per centum upon its cost (exclusive of the five per centum to be paid to the United States), Congress may reduce the rates of fare thereon, if unreasonable in amount, and may fix and establish the same by law ...

Approved July 1, 1862.

Source: Pacific Railway Act, July 1, 1862; 37th Congress, Sess. 2; 12 Statutes at Large 489.

2 William Dean Howells Describes Suburban Boston, 1872

Suburbs were not new to the mid- and late nineteenth century, but they did become far more accessible. The municipal transport revolution, introduced with the omnibus and culminating in the streetcar and interurban rail, put urban hinterlands and their valuable resources – space, access to transport, pastoral settings – within reach of far more Americans. Everyone went. Recent immigrants and working families settled in the periphery near the suburban manufacturing industries that took root in the 1840s and expanded during the Civil War. By mid-century suburban residence also grew increasingly popular among affluent white professionals attracted to the calm, the open spaces and larger homes, and the cachet that came with particular suburban addresses. This mix of populations and land uses led to a persistent contradiction. The "commuting habit" for male professionals and the pastoral image associated with elite residential suburbs existed in tension with real-life suburbs, many of which were multipurpose, multiethnic, and socioeconomically diverse. A privileged suburban ideal was codified while suburban expansion itself remained far more complicated.

Among suburbia's privileged residents was author and magazine editor William Dean Howells, who in 1872 described life in Boston's near northern suburbs – he dubbed his community "Charlesbridge" – in a volume entitled Suburban Sketches. *The excerpts included here illustrate the variety of late nineteenth century suburban development and some of the tensions that resulted. While Howells provides a snapshot of the area's diversity, he also reveals the perspective of self-described "Americans" – white elites who could afford a suburban home and transit fare for the commute – about immigrant newcomers. What does Howells's account suggest about the origins of these multifaceted suburbs? Why did they exist? Meanwhile what forces, both material and cultural, separated their various communities?*

... Charlesbridge appeared to us a kind of Paradise. The wind blew all day from the southwest, and all day in the grove across the way the orioles sang to their nestlings. The butcher's wagon rattled merrily up to our gate every morning; and if we had kept no other reckoning, we should have known it was Thursday by the grocer. We were living in the country with the conveniences and luxuries of the city about us. The house was almost new and in perfect repair ... Breakfast, dinner, and tea came up with illusive regularity, and were all the most perfect of their kind; and we laughed and feasted in our vain security. We had out from the city to banquet with us the friends we loved, and we were inexpressibly proud before them of the Help [a young woman named Jenny], who first wrought miracles of cookery in our honor, and then appeared in a clean white apron, and the glossiest black hair, to wait upon the table ...

... But one day in September she came to her nominal mistress with tears in her beautiful eyes and protestations of unexampled devotion upon her tongue, and said that she was afraid she must leave us. She liked the place, and she never had worked for any one that was more of a lady, but she had made up her mind to go into the city ... Simply, there were no lamps upon our street, and Jenny, after spending Sunday evening with friends in East Charlesbridge, was always alarmed, on her return, in walking from the horse-car to our door ... We had not before this thought it a grave disadvantage that our street was unlighted. Our street was not drained nor graded; no municipal cart ever came to carry away our ashes; there was not a water-butt within half a mile to save us from fire, nor more than the one thousandth part of a policeman to protect us from theft. Yet, as I paid a heavy tax, I somehow felt that we enjoyed the benefits of city government, and never looked upon Charlesbridge as in any way undesirable for residence. But when it became necessary to find help in Jenny's place, the frosty welcome given to application at the intelligence offices renewed a painful doubt awakened by her departure. To be sure, the heads of the offices were polite enough; but when the ... Intelligencer had called out to the invisible expectants in the adjoining room, "Anny wan wants to do giner'l housewark in Charlsbrudge?" there came from the maids invoked so loud, so fierce, so full a "No!" as shook the lady's heart with an indescribable shame and dread ... "You see," said the head of the office, "the gairls doesn't like to live so far away from the city." ...

Doorstep Aquaintance

... In Ferry Street ... so many Italians live that one might think to find it under a softer sky and in a gentler air ... The widow of Giovanni Cascamatto ... was our first Italian acquaintance in Charlesbridge ... I say this woman seemed glad to be greeted in Italian, but not, as far as I could see, surprised; and altogether the most amazing thing about my doorstep acquaintance of her nation is, that they are never surprised to be spoken to in their own tongue, or, if they are, never show it. A chestnut-roaster, who has sold me twice the chestnuts the same money would have bought of him in English, had not otherwise recognized the fact that Tuscan is not the dialect of Charlesbridge ...

There is a little old Genoese lady comes to sell us pins, needles, thread, tape, and the like *roba* ... Her traffic is limited to a certain number of families who speak more or less Italian; and her days ... must be passed in an atmosphere of sympathy and kindliness. The truth is, we Northern and New World folk cannot help but cast a little romance about whoever comes to us from Italy ... [S]he is of a most munificent spirit, and returns every smallest benefit with some present from her basket. She makes me ashamed of things I have written about the sordidness of her race, but I shall vainly seek to atone for them by open-handedness to her.

Pedestrian Tour

Walking for walking's sake I do not like. The diversion appears to me one of the most factitious of modern enjoyments ... Yet it is certain that some sort of recreation is necessary after a day spent within doors; and one is really obliged nowadays to take a little walk instead of medicine; for one's doctor is sure to have a mania on the subject ... For this reason I sometimes go upon a pedestrian tour, which is of no great extent in itself, and which I moreover modify by keeping always within sound of the horse-car bells, or easy reach of some steam-car station.

... As I sally forth upon Benicia Street, the whole suburb of Charlesbridge stretches about me – a vast space upon which I can embroider any fancy I like as I saunter along. I have no associations with it, or memories of it, and, at some seasons, I might wander for days in the most frequented parts of it, and meet hardly any one I know. It is not, however, to these parts that I commonly turn, but northward, up a street upon which a flight of French-roof houses suddenly settled a year or two since, with families in them, and many outward signs of permanence ... [Then] I reach, beyond them, a little bridge which appears to span a small stream. It unites banks lined with a growth of trees and briers nodding their heads above the neighboring levels, and suggesting a quiet water-course; though in fact it is the Fitchburg Railroad that purls between them, with rippling freight and passenger trains and ever-gurgling locomotives … If I descend [the banks] and follow the railroad westward half a mile, I come to vast brick-yards … A little farther on I come to the boarding-house built at the railroad side for the French Canadians who have by this time succeeded the Hebrews in the toil of the brick-yards, and who … loiter in windy-voiced, good-humoured groups about the doors of their lodgings … I take my way up through the brick-yards towards the Irish settlement on the north [called Dublin], passing under the long sheds that shelter the kilns …

Among the houses fronting on the main street of Dublin, every other one … is a grocery, if I may judge by a tin case of cornballs, a jar of candy, and a card of shirt-buttons, with an under layer of primers and ballads, in the windows. You descend from the street by several steps into these haunts, which are contrived to secure the greatest possible dampness and darkness; and if you have made an errand inside, you doubtless find a lady before the counter in the act of putting down a guilty-looking tumbler with one hand, while she neatly wipes her mouth on the back of the other …

In yet earlier spring walks through Dublin, I found a depth of mud appalling even to one who had lived three years in Charlesbridge. The streets were passable only to pedestrians skilled in shifting themselves along the sides of fences and alert to take advantage of every projecting doorstep. There were no dry places, except in front of the groceries, where the ground was beaten hard by the broad feet of loafing geese and the coming and going of admirably small children making purchases there. The number of the little ones was quite as remarkable as their size, and ought to have been even more interesting, if, as sometimes appears probable, such increase shall – together with the well-known ambition of Dubliners to rule the land – one day make an end of us poor Yankees as a dominant plurality.

… It is encouraging, moreover, when any people can flatter themselves upon a superior prosperity and virtue, and we may take heart from the fact that the French Canadians, many of whom have lodgings in Dublin, are not well seen by the higher classes of the citizens there. Mrs. Clannahan, whose house stands over against the main gate of the grave-yard, and who may, therefore, be considered as moving in the best Dublin society, hints, that though good Catholics, the French are not thought perfectly honest … It is amusing to find Dublin fearful of the encroachment of the French, as we, in our turn, dread the advance of the Irish. We must make a jest of our own alarms, and even smile … at the spiritual desolation occasioned by the settlement of an Irish family in one of our suburban neighborhoods.

The householders view with fear and jealousy the erection of any dwelling of less than a stated cost, as portending a possible advent of Irish; and when the calamitous race actually appears, a mortal pang strikes to the bottom of every pocket ... None but the Irish will build near the Irish; and the infection of fear spreads to the elder Yankee homes about, and the owners prepare to abandon them ...

As I leave Dublin, the houses grow larger and handsomer; and as I draw near the Avenue, the Mansard-roofs look down upon me with their dormer-windows, and welcome me back to the American community. There are fences about all the houses, inclosing ampler and ampler dooryards; the children, which had swarmed in the thriftless and unenlightened purlieus of Dublin, diminish in number and finally disappear; the chickens have vanished; and I hear – I hear the pensive music of the horse-car bells ...

...

... The Avenue is our handsomest street ... Commonly, when I emerge upon it ... I behold, looking northward, a monumental horse-car standing ... at the head of Pliny Street; and looking forward I see that other emblem of suburban life, an express-wagon, fading rapidly in the distance. Haply the top of a buggy nods round the bend under the elms near the station; and, if fortune is so lavish, a lady appears from a side street, and, while tarrying for the car, thrusts the point of her sun-umbrella into the sandy sidewalk. This is the mid-afternoon effect of the Avenue; but later in the day, and well into the dusk, it remembers its former gayety as a trotting-course – with here and there a spider-wagon, a twinkling-footed mare, and a guttural driver. On market-days its superb breadth is taken up by flocks of bleating sheep, and a pastoral tone is thus given to its tranquility; anon a herd of beef-cattle appears under the elms; or a drove of pigs, many pausing, inquisitive of the gutters, and quarrelsome as if they were the heirs of prosperity instead of doom, is slowly urged on toward the shambles. In the spring or the autumn, the Avenue is exceptionally enlivened by the progress of a brace or so of students who, in training for one of the University Courses of base-ball or boating, trot slowly and earnestly along the sidewalks, fists up, elbows down, mouths shut, and a sense of immense responsibility visible in their faces.

The summer is waning with the day and I turn from the Avenue into Benicia Street. This is the hour when the fly cedes to the mosquito ... and, as one may add, the frying grasshopper yields to the shrilly cricket in noisiness ... Quick now, the cheerful lamps of kerosene! – without their light, the cry of those crickets ... and the baying of a distant dog, were too much ... This is in fact the hour of supreme trial everywhere, and doubtless no one but a newly-accepted lover can be happy at twilight. In the city, even, it is oppressive; in the country it is desolate; in the suburbs it is a miracle that it is ever lived through. The night-winds have not risen yet to stir the languid foliage of the sidewalk maples; the lamps are not yet lighted, to take away the gloom from the blank, staring windows of the houses near; it is too late for letters, too early for a book. In town your fancy would turn to the theatres; in the country you would occupy yourself with cares of poultry or of stock; in the suburbs you can but sit upon your threshold, and fight the predatory mosquito.

By Horse-Car to Boston

... [O]n the horse-car ... you can, of course, detect certain classes; as, in the morning the business-men going in, to their counters or their desks, and in the afternoon the shoppers coming out, laden with paper parcels. But I think no one can truly claim to know the regular from the occasional passengers by any greater cheerfulness in the faces of the latter. The horse-car will suffer no such inequality as this, but reduces us all to the same level of melancholy. It would be but a very unworthy kind of art which should seek to describe people by such merely external traits as a habit of carrying baskets or large travelling-bags in the car, [or by the] contrasts of splendor and shabbiness, and such intimate association of velvets and patches as you see in the churches of Catholic countries, but nowhere else in the world except in our "coaches of the sovereign people."

Source: William Dean Howells, *Suburban Sketches* (Boston: James R. Osgood, 1872), pp. 12–13, 15–16, 36–37, 45–46, 60–63, 67–68, 70–72, 87–90, 104–105.

3 August Spies Addresses Workers about Their Conditions, 1886

Novels and films depicting life in nineteenth-century cities regularly highlight the harsh conditions endured by American workers, and for good reason. Most unskilled laborers and especially recent immigrants lived in congested, filthy neighborhoods and worked at low-wage, insecure jobs that were arduous and often dangerous. Viewed from today, this squalor and insecurity – immortalized by photographer Lewis Hine and journalist Jacob Riis – can seem like a relic of a distant time, before millions of Americans gained access to better employment and the modern, tidy neighborhoods of the broad middle class. Yet, at the time, laborers had no idea what the future held in store. Most were preoccupied with simply getting by in the face of considerable obstacles, including the indifference and hostility of employers and public officials. Federal and state governments provided working people with minimal, if any, aid or protection. When laborers organized unions to demand higher wages and improved working conditions, employers responded with lockouts and violence, often with aid from public officials who provided police or military units to help crack down on dissent. Conflict between laborers, economic elites, and government authorities was a regular feature of urban life.

One of several turning points in these contests began on May 1, 1886, with a coordinated nationwide protest by tens of thousands of workers calling on state legislatures to mandate an eight-hour workday. Three days into these protests, in Chicago, a group of laborers gathered to hear a speech by August Theodore Spies, a German-born upholsterer, labor leader, and anarchist who published the Arbeiter Zeitung *(Workers' Newspaper). Spies spoke while standing in view of the McCormick Harvesting Machine Company (source 1.2), a firm notorious for responding to workers' grievances with further cost-cutting measures and intimidation. That very spring, McCormick had once again locked out its striking employees.*

Just after Spies completed his remarks, local police fired on strikers who were approaching the McCormick plant, injuring dozens and killing at least two. The next afternoon, Spies returned to address workers for a second time at a rally at Haymarket Square – the speech is excerpted below – and just hours later a bomb exploded, resulting in another wave of police violence, at least 11 deaths, and the eventual prosecution and hanging of eight labor leaders, including Spies. The episode is known as the "Haymarket Affair." Spies's remarks introduce the views of some labor leaders and identify many of the obstacles facing urban immigrant families. We are also left wondering how many of the urban workers involved in the May protests shared the speaker's perspective.

Friends ... I am told that a number of patrol wagons, carrying policemen, were sent to Desplaines street station, and I understand that the militia have been called under arms. There seems to prevail the opinion in certain quarters that this meeting has been called for the purpose of inaugurating a riot, hence these warlike preparations on the part of the so-called "law and order." However, let me tell you at the beginning that this meeting has not been called for any such purpose. The object of this meeting is to explain the general situation of the Eight-Hour Movement, and to throw light upon various incidents in connection with it.

For more than twenty years have the wage workers of this country begged and prayed their masters, the factory lords, to reduce their burdens. It has been in vain. They have pointed out the fact that over a million of willing and strong hands were in a state of enforced idleness and starvation, that to help them to obtain employment it would not only be advisable, nay, it was necessary to reduce the hours of daily toil of those who were fortunate enough in having found a buyer for their muscles, their bones, and their brain. The masters of this earth have treated them with contempt, have condemned them to vagabondage whenever they insisted. The legislatures have been called upon, one petition has succeeded the other, but with no avail.

At last the condition of the disinherited producers has become unbearable. Seeing that neither "boss" nor law would concede anything to them, they have organized for the purpose of helping themselves – a wise and prudent resolution.

All over the land we behold vast armies of producers, no longer begging, but demanding that eight hours shall henceforth constitute a normal working day. And what say the extortionists to this? They demand their pound of flesh, like Shylock. They will not yield one iota. They have grown rich and powerful on *your* labor. They amass stupendous fortunes, while you, who bring them into existence, are suffering from want. In answer to your pleadings they ask for the bodies of your little children, to utilize them in their gold mints, to make dollars out of them! Look at the slaves of McCormick! When they tried to remonstrate with their master he simply called upon "the protectors of these free and glorious institutions" – the police – to silence them. And they did silence them.

You have no doubt heard of the killing and wounding of a number of your brothers at McCormick's, yesterday. Mr. McCormick told a *Times* reporter that Spies was responsible for that massacre committed by the most noble Chicago police. I reply to this that McCormick is an infamous liar. (Cries of "Hang him.") No, make no idle threats. There will be a time, and we are rapidly approaching it, when such men as McCormick will be hanged; there will be a time when monsters who destroy the lives and happiness of the citizens (for their own aggrandizement) will be dealt with like wild beasts. But that time has not yet come. When it has come you will no longer make threats, but you will go and "do it."

The capitalistic press, like the "respectable gentleman" McCormick, howls that the anarchists are responsible for the deeds of violence now committed all over this country. If that were true one would have to conclude that the country was full of anarchists, yet the same press informs us that the anarchists are very few in number. Were the "unlawful" acts in the Southwestern strike committed by anarchists? No, they were committed by Knights of Labor – men who never fail to declare, whenever there is an opportunity, that they are law-and-order-abiding citizens. The attack upon McCormick's yesterday – was it made by anarchists? Let us see. I had been invited by the Central Labor Union to address a meeting of lumber-yard laborers on the Black road. I went out there at the appointed time, about three o'clock in the afternoon. There were at least ten thousand persons assembled. When I was introduced to address them a few Poles or Bohemians in the crowd cried out: "He's a socialist." These cries were followed by a general commotion and derision. "We want no socialist; down with him." These and other exclamations I was treated to. Of course, I spoke anyway. The crowd became quiet and calm, and fifteen minutes later elected me unanimously a delegate to see their bosses. Nevertheless, you can see that these people are not Socialists or Anarchists, but "good, honest, law-abiding, church-going Christians and citizens." Such were the persons who left the meeting, as I afterwards learned, to "make the scabs at McCormick's quit work." In my speech I never mentioned McCormick. Now you may judge for yourselves whether the anarchists were responsible for the bloodshed yesterday or not.

Who is responsible for these many "lawless" acts, you ask me? I have told you that they are generally committed by the most lawful and Christian citizens. In other words, the people are by necessity driven to violence, they can't carry the burden heaped upon them any longer. They try to cast it off, and in so doing break the laws. The law says they must not cast it off, for such an act would alter, yea, revolutionize the existing order of society. These acts of violence are the natural outgrowth of the present industrial system, and every one is responsible for them who supports and upholds that system.

What does it mean when the police of this city, on this evening, rattle along in their patrol wagons?

What does it mean when the militia stands warlike and ready for bloody work at our armories?

What are the gatling guns and cannons for?

Is this military display of barbarism arranged for your entertainment?

All these preparations, my friends, ARE *made in your behalf.*

Your masters have perceived your discontent.

They do not like discontented slaves.

They want to make you contented at all hazards, and if you are stubborn they will force or kill you.

Look at the killing of your brothers at McCormick's yesterday. What did they do? The police tell you that they were a most dangerous crowd, armed to their teeth. The fact is, they, like ignorant children, indulged in the harmless sport of bombarding McCormick's slaughter house with stones. They paid the penalty of this folly with their blood.

The lesson I draw from this occurrence is, that working men must arm themselves for defense, so that they may be able to cope with the government hirelings of their masters.

Source: "The Speech Delivered by August Spies at the Haymarket, May 4, on the Occasion of the Bomb-Throwing," in *A Concise History of the Great Trial of the Chicago Anarchists in 1886*, condensed from the official record by Dyer D. Lum (Chicago, 1886), pp. 35–38.

4 An Engineer Describes the Work Required to Make Seattle Competitive, 1908

Seattle's early twentieth-century development highlights a constant of modern city building: satisfying human needs and preferences can dramatically alter the nonhuman environment, with important consequences for both humans and the environment. Seattle's officials and boosters hoped to make the city an attractive place to do business and thus foster growth by taking advantage of its location and natural assets (compare source 1.1). Part of the solution was to level large sections of the city, a process known as "regrading," and to use the removed earth to transform coastal mudflats into land suitable for development. Equally important was an ambitious project to lower Lake Washington and connect it to the Pacific Ocean by enlarging the Duwamish channel, a task made possible only with considerable technical and financial assistance from the Army Corps of Engineers. This dramatic redesign of Seattle's topography opened up considerable opportunity. Level land is easier to maintain and level roads are easier for transporting goods. Improved access to ports and railroads facilitated a lucrative export of raw materials including lumber and fish, and trade was expected to expand with the opening of the Panama Canal. By creating new salable property – through the landfill process or by reclaiming shoreline – the city accommodated more facilities for the manufacture and processing of goods. Finally, these interventions were designed to control a perennial problem in Seattle: flooding.

Such ambitious engineering projects required technical expertise and considerable investment, as this source details. They also dislocated local residents (usually the poor), further undermined Native people's rights of access to natural resources, and had complicated long-term environmental consequences. For, while these interventions addressed pressing transport, water provision, and drainage problems, they also created new problems by destabilizing nearby tidal regions and triggering other environmental challenges – including, paradoxically, flooding. When a dam constructed 30 miles to the east of Seattle, in the Cascade mountains, failed in 1918, it virtually wiped out the nearby logging town of Edgewick. Water is persistent.

When Louis Zimmerman described Seattle's regradings to his colleagues in this 1908 report published in Engineering News, *he could not anticipate many of its long-term impacts. But as one of the experts involved in authorizing the work, he was well aware of social dislocations and other short-term consequences. What does his discussion suggest about guiding assumptions among the era's planners, engineers, and boosters about the priorities that should guide urban development?*

Seattle, Wash., is confronted with an immense problem that is and must be solved in order that the city may continue to flourish and grow. This problem consists briefly in regrading and leveling the hilly streets and adjacent property on which the city is built.

Commercially, Seattle has every advantage. Here terminate the transcontinental railway systems of the Pacific Northwest; here are the terminal wharves of the steamship lines running to Alaska, the Asiatic ports, the west coast of South America, the Pacific Islands and Canada; and here is found cheap and convenient transportation between many growing towns on the numerous islands and natural harbors of the Puget Sound country.

Seattle fronts on Elliott Bay, a branch of Puget Sound, which forms an extensive deep-water harbor protected from storms, and accessible to the largest vessels afloat, at all times and at all stages of tide ... The surface of the city is hilly, consisting principally of long ridges, which rise to an elevation of about 300 ft. above the level of the sound, with a few higher butters.

These long, hill ridges present a problem to Seattle, the magnitude of which has seldom or never been equaled in any city of the world. To accommodate the great, growing business districts of the city, new ground areas must be produced, with a maximum grade so low that the retail traffic can be moved by teams without exhaustive effort. To get these areas Seattle is carrying out the most extensive regrade of any city in the country. Whole sections are being cut down from 10 to 100 ft., and new blocks are being built up on the hitherto worthless tide flats.

Steam shovels, cars and wagons were so inadequate for this project that, except in special cases, they were not considered. Water, both fresh and salt, is unlimited here in quantity. Hydraulic sluicing was adopted to level Seattle's hills and convert almost worthless buttes into valuable property. Two methods of disposing of the vast amount of earth presented themselves. One, was to waste it into the sound; the other, to sluice it onto the tide flats.

The regrade work in Seattle may be divided into three large and three small areas. The ultimate aim is to level the entire business and abutting sections ...

Considerable difficulty was found in laying the pipe. As laid, it passes under two heavy traffic streets, two street car tracks and several railroad tracks. For a considerable distance over the tide flats it is supported on blocks or suspended from the bridges. Although salt water is obtainable in any quantity and is more effective than fresh water, due to its greater specific gravity, there is the objection of the water foaming and air bubbles being carried in, thus reducing the effective area of the pipe. Four branches lead from this line to four giant cast-iron nozzles, varying in effective diameter from 2.5 to 4 ins. Each giant is mounted on a reducer and a ball and socket joint, so that a sweep of a full circle can be obtained. The nozzles are fitted with handles at the nozzle end, and with a board and box counterweight by means of which adjustment can be made in any direction and at almost any angle.

... The streams are directed only toward the bottom strata and worked to within a foot of the final grade ... This leaves little surfacing to be done by hand ... The yellow clay, loam and sand wash away fairly easily, but the lower strata of hardpan or blue clay requires blasting. In shooting, the clay carries the concussions along the strata and people living on the other side of the hill complain, while those directly above are not affected. Gravel is the hardest to handle. The fine sand washes out and leaves the heavier gravel. This and occasional boulders are disposed of to builders and contractors who haul them away in wagons ...

With the disposal of this immense amount of material and the work on the tide flats, several problems of exceptional engineering interest are encountered. This district is covered with places of business, access to which must be provided by temporary bridges, built on piles and moved as required. New streets are constantly being laid out in the filled tide lands ...

The problem of sanitation and sewage disposal is important because the district is thickly settled. The people living in the district regraded have the choice of tearing down their houses or moving them off ... either of which entails crowded and unnatural conditions. On the adjoining streets and lots houses are crowded together and temporary sewage disposal becomes necessary. This is well effected by means of 1 × 1-ft. box sewers 3 ... feet underground, leading to the tide flats ...

One very striking and beneficial effect has been the cleaning up of the district in which the work is going on. Before, the buildings were all on the low, wet grounds adjoining the tide flats. At high tide they were soaked, and the result was a dirty, filthy region that naturally became the immoral center of Seattle. Since the regrade began, the buildings have been raised from 20 to 40 ft., are now on piles and have plenty of dry air around them. House moving has developed into an important business. The cost is often excessive, in some cases more than the building is worth. A three-story frame building, 60 × 120 ft. in plan, can be raised 40 ft. and blocked for about $2,000 ...

This gigantic work so carefully laid out and so faithfully being carried out by R. H. Thomson, M. Am. Soc. C. E., who has been city engineer for sixteen years, will lay the foundations to make Seattle one of the greatest cities in the United States.

Source: Louis P. Zimmerman, "The Seattle Regrade, with Particular Reference to the Jackson St. Section," *Engineering News*, 60(20) (November 12, 1908), pp. 509–511.

5 New York City Retailers Organize to Protect a Fifth Avenue Shopping District, 1916

In the early twentieth century, American municipalities began adopting laws dictating how property owners could use their land. These "zoning" ordinances – they divided urbanized areas into "zones" for designated use – quickly became powerful development tools in cities and suburbs nationwide. Prior to this, there were few government restrictions on private property, which led to practical problems in the nation's fast-changing, crowded, multiuse metropolitan areas. Many people preferred not to live, for example, next to a slaughterhouse or a factory, hence the appeal of ordinances separating residential from industrial development. Planners and developers calculated, correctly, that dividing cities into zones would make commerce more efficient and residential neighborhoods more pleasant and healthful, in turn improving properties' marketability. Yet, while crafted with these practical concerns in mind, the zoning concept was soon embraced by businesspeople and homeowners for another, complementary, reason: to exclude specific kinds of structures and people from certain residential neighborhoods. As zoning grew in popularity during the 1920s and 1930s, ordinances were regularly used to keep the poor or ethnic and racial minorities (domestic workers excepted) out of affluent residential enclaves. Restriction was defended as a means to protect neighborhood character and property values.

This source demonstrates that the exclusionary impulse was already at work during zoning's experimental phase. In 1916 the nation's first comprehensive zoning ordinance was adopted in New York City. Excerpted here is an influential endorsement of the measure, a paid advertisement in the New York Times. *The ad was run by a private organization called the Fifth Avenue Association, which represented exclusive Manhattan retailers upset by the proliferation of garment plants in the loft spaces above their businesses. Their customers, the New York elite, were uncomfortable that garment workers – people like Sadie Frowne (source 4.1) – were constantly filling the streets of their exclusive shopping, hotel, and residential district. The association had been promoting the zoning idea for years, arguing in an earlier report that restriction was the only means to stop the "vast flood of workers" that every day "literally overwhelms and engulfs shops, shopkeepers, and the shopping public." The 1916 advertisement was an attempt to garner support for the proposed comprehensive ordinance, a law virtually drafted by the association leadership and approved later that year by New York City officials. The ordinance would become an important precedent, cited favorably by the US Supreme Court when it validated municipal zoning in 1926. What does the association's campaign suggest about the forces shaping the era's development politics? What assumptions about urban life, property values, and land uses were guiding that politics?*

Shall We Save New York? A Vital Question to Every One Who Has Pride in This Great City

Shall we save New York from what? Shall we save it from unnatural and unnecessary crowding, from depopulated sections, from being a city unbeautiful, from high rents, from excessive and illy distributed taxation? We can save it from all of these, so far at least as they are caused by one specified industrial evil – the erection of factories in the residential and famous retail section.

The Factory Invasion of the Shopping District

The factories making clothing, cloaks, suits, furs, petticoats, etc., have forced the large stores from one section and followed them to a new one, depleting it of its normal residents and filling it with big loft buildings displacing homes.

The fact of the sections down town now threatens the fine residential and shopping district of Fifth Avenue, Broadway, upper Sixth and Madison Avenues and the cross streets. It requires concentrated co-operative action to stem this invading tide. The evil is constantly increasing; it is growing more serious and more difficult to handle. It needs instant action.

The Trail of Vacant Buildings

Shall the finest retail and residential sections in the world, from Thirty-third Street north, become blighted the way the old parts of New York have been?

The lower wholesale and retail districts are deserted, and there is now enough vacant space to accommodate many times over the manufacturing plants of the city. *If new modern factory buildings are required, why not encourage the erection of such structures in that section instead of erecting factory buildings in the midst of our homes and fine retail sections.*

How it Affects the City and its Citizens

It is impossible to have a city beautiful, comfortable or safe under such conditions. The unnatural congestion sacrifices fine residential blocks for factories, which remain for a time and then move on to devastate or depreciate another section, leaving ugly scars of blocks of empty buildings unused by business and unadapted for residence: thus unsettling real estate values.

How it Affects the Tax-payer

Every man in the city pays taxes either as owner or renter. The wide area of vacant or depreciated property in the lower middle part of town means reduced taxes, leaving a deficit made up by extra assessment on other sections. Taxes have grown to startling figures and this affects all interests.

The Need of Co-operative Action

In order that the impending menace to all interests may be checked and to prevent a destruction similar to that which has occurred below Twenty-third Street:

> *We ask the co-operation of the various garment associations.*
> *We ask the co-operation of the associations of organized labor.*
> *We ask the co-operation of every financial interest.*
> *We ask the co-operation of every man who owns a home or rents an apartment.*
> *We ask the co-operation of every man and woman in New York who has pride in the future development of this great city.*
> ...
> *We ask Citizens, Merchants and Civic bodies to co-operate and send letters endorsing this plan to the committee, care of J. H. Burton, chairman, 267 Fifth Avenue.*

Source: Display Ad 5, *New York Times*, March 5, 1916, p. 5.

Chapter 4 "Natives," Migrants, and Immigrants

1 A Polish Immigrant Describes Life and Work in New York City, 1902

In 1902 the New York Independent *published a series of interviews with Americans from all walks of life to document responses to the nation's fantastic commercial and urban growth. This interview, with a Polish immigrant named Sadie Frowne, provides a rare glimpse into the life and views of a young working-class girl in turn-of-the-century New York City. Frowne's experience was in many ways typical for the "new immigrants" – most hailing from Italy, eastern Europe, Russia, and Greece – who settled in American cities after 1880. Most were escaping poverty, and many were fleeing persecution. Most followed networks of friends and family. And most lived and worked in crowded and impoverished urban areas that posed daily hazards, but that also offered the comfort of familiar faces, language, and culture.*

Frowne's account also highlights a paradox central to immigrants' urban experience. Life in New York City had a lot to offer: work, of course, but also access to new experiences and, for women in particular, new freedoms. Yet the new immigrants like Sadie Frowne were held in contempt by the same "native" Americans (i.e., self-described whites) who relied on their labor. Indeed most whites viewed these new arrivals as unassimilable, as racially suspect, and as a potential threat to the nation's health and democratic institutions (source 3.5). Did Frowne view herself as unassimilable? What do her perspectives on work, sociability, and opportunity tell us about the

The Modern American Metropolis: A Documentary Reader, First Edition.
Edited by David M. P. Freund.

changes underway in America's industrializing cities, and about the contests over citizenship and identity that would loom so large in the early twentieth century (sources 7.2 and 7.4)?

My mother was a tall, handsome, dark complexioned woman with red cheeks, large brown eyes and a great quantity of jet black, wavy hair. She was well educated, being able to talk in Russian, German, Polish and French, and even to read English print, tho, of course, she did not know what it meant. She kept a little grocer's shop in the little village where we lived at first. That was in Poland, somewhere on the frontier, and mother had charge of a gate between the countries, so that everybody who came through the gate had to show her a pass. She was much looked up to by the people, who used to come and ask her for advice. Her word was like law among them.

She had a wagon in which she used to drive about the country, selling her groceries, and sometimes she worked in the fields with my father.

The grocer's shop was only one story high, and had one window, with very small panes of glass. We had two rooms behind it, and were happy while my father lived, altho we had to work very hard. By the time I was six years of age I was able to wash dishes and scrub floors, and by the time I was eight I attended to the shop while my mother was away driving her wagon or working in the fields with my father. She was strong and could work like a man.

When I was a little more than ten years of age my father died. He was a good man and a steady worker, and we never knew what it was to be hungry while he lived. After he died troubles began, for the rent of our shop was about $6 a month and then there were food and clothes to provide. We needed little, it is true, but even soup, black bread and onions we could not always get.

We struggled along till I was nearly thirteen years of age and quite handy at housework and shop keeping, so far as I could learn them there. But we fell behind in the rent and mother kept thinking more and more that we should have to leave Poland and go across the sea to America where we heard it was much easier to make money. Mother wrote to Aunt Fanny, who lived in New York, and told her how hard it was to live in Poland, and Aunt Fanny advised her to come and bring me. I was out at service at this time and mother thought she would leave me as I had a good place and come to this country alone, sending for me afterward. But Aunt Fanny would not hear of this. She said we should both come at once, and she went around among our relatives in New York and took up a subscription for our passage.

We came by steerage on a steamship in a very dark place that smelt dreadfully. There were hundreds of other people packed in with us, men, women and children, and almost all of them were sick. It took us twelve days to cross the sea, and we thought we should die, but at last the voyage was over, and we came up and saw the beautiful bay and the big woman with the spikes on her head and the lamp that is lighted at night in her hand (Goddess of Liberty).

Aunt Fanny and her husband met us at the gate of this country and were very good to us, and soon I had a place to live out (domestic servant), while my mother got work in a factory making white goods … I was only a little over thirteen years of age and a greenhorn, so I received $9 a month and board and lodging, which I thought was doing well. Mother, who, as I have said, was very clever, made $9 a week on white goods, which means all sorts of underclothing, and is high class work.

But mother had a very gay disposition. She liked to go around and see everything, and friends took her about New York at night and she caught a bad cold and coughed and coughed. She really had nasty consumption, but she didn't know it, and I didn't know it, and she tried to keep on working, but it was no use. She had not the strength. Two doctors attended her, but they could do nothing, and at last she died and I was left alone. I had saved money while out at service, but mother's sickness and funeral swept it all away and now I had to begin all over again.

Aunt Fanny had always been anxious for me to get an education, as I did not know how to read or write, and she thought that was wrong. Schools are different in Poland from what they are in this country, and I was always too busy to learn to read and write. So when mother died I thought I would try to learn a trade and then I could go to school at night and learn to speak the English language well.

So I went to work in Allen street (Manhattan) in what they call a sweatshop, making skirts by machine. I was new at the work and the foreman scolded me a great deal.

"Now, then," he would say, "this place is not for you to be looking around in. Attend to your work. That is what you have to do."

I did not know at first that you must not look around and talk, and I made many mistakes with the sewing, so that I was often called a "stupid animal." But I made $4 a week by working six days in the week. For there are two Sabbaths here our own Sabbath, that comes on a Saturday, and the Christian Sabbath that comes on Sunday. It is against our law to work on our own Sabbath, so we work on their Sabbath.

In Poland I and my father and mother used to go to the synagogue on the Sabbath, but here the women don't go to the synagogue much, tho the men do. They are shut up working hard all the week long and when the Sabbath comes they like to sleep long in bed and afterward they must go out where they can breathe the air. The rabbis are strict here, but not so strict as in the old country.

I lived at this time with a girl named Ella, who worked in the same factory and made $5 a week. We had the room all to ourselves, paying $1.50 a week for it, and doing light housekeeping. It was in Allen street, and the window looked out of the back, which was good, because there was an elevated railroad in front, and in summer time a great deal of dust and dirt came in at the front windows. We were on the fourth story and could see all that was going on in the back rooms of the houses behind us, and early in the morning the sun used to come in our window.

We did our cooking on an oil stove, and lived well, as this list of our expenses for one week will show:

ELLA AND SADIE FOR FOOD (ONE WEEK)

Tea $0.06
Cocoa.10
Bread and rolls.40
Canned vegatables.20
Potatoes.10
Milk.21
Fruit.20
Butter.15
Meat.60
Fish.15
Laundry.25
Total $2.42
Add rent 1.50
Grand total $3.92

Of course, we could have lived cheaper, but we are both fond of good things and felt that we could afford them ... Some people who buy at the last of the market, when the men with the carts want to go home, can get things very cheap, but they are likely to be stale, and we did not often do that with fish, fresh vegetables, fruit, milk or meat ... [W]e found a factory where we could buy the finest broken crackers for 3 cents a pound, and another place where we got broken candy for 10 cents a pound. Our cooking was done on an oil stove, and the oil for the stove and the lamp cost us 10 cents a week.

It cost me $2 a week to live, and I had a dollar a week to spend on clothing and pleasure, and saved the other dollar. I went to night school, but it was hard work learning at first as I did not know much English.

Two years ago I came to this place, Brownsville, where so many of my people are, and where I have friends. I got work in a factory making underskirts all sorts of cheap underskirts, like cotton and calico for the summer and woolen for the winter, but never the silk, satin or velvet underskirts. I earned $4.50 a week and lived on $2 a week, the same as before … I got a room in the house of some friends who lived near the factory. I pay $1 a week for the room and am allowed to do light housekeeping that is, cook my meals in it … I am earning $5.50 a week now, and will probably get another increase soon.

It isn't piecework in our factory, but one is paid by the amount of work done just the same. So it is like piecework. All the hands get different amounts, some as low as $3.50 and some of the men as high as $16 a week. The factory is in the third story of a brick building. It is in a room twenty feet long and fourteen broad. There are fourteen machines in it. I and the daughter of the people with whom I live work two of these machines. The other operators are all men, some young and some old.

At first a few of the young men were rude. When they passed me they would touch my hair and talk about my eyes and my red cheeks, and make jokes. I cried and said that if they did not stop I would leave the place. The boss said that that should not be, that no one must annoy me. Some of the other men stood up for me, too, especially Henry, who said two or three times that he wanted to fight. Now the men all treat me very nicely. It was just that some of them did not know better, not being educated.

Henry is tall and dark, and he has a small mustache. His eyes are brown and large. He is pale and much educated, having been to school. He knows a great many things and has some money saved I think nearly $400. He is not going to be in a sweatshop all the time, but will soon be in the real estate business, for a lawyer that knows him well has promised to open an office and pay him to manage it.

Henry has seen me home every night for a long time … He wants me to marry him, but I am not seventeen yet, and I think that is too young. He is only nineteen, so we can wait.

I have been to the fortune teller's three or four times, and she always tells me that tho I have had such a lot of trouble I am to be very rich and happy. I believe her because she has told so many things that have come true. So I will keep on working in the factory for a time. Of course it is hard, but I would have to work hard even if I was married.

I get up at half past five o'clock every morning and make myself a cup of coffee on the oil stove. I eat a bit of bread and perhaps some fruit and then go to work. Often I get there soon after six o'clock so as to be in good time, tho the factory does not open till seven. I have heard that there is a sort of clock that calls you at the very time you want to get up, but I can't believe that because I don't see how the clock would know.

At seven o' clock we all sit down to our machines and the boss brings to each one the pile of work that he or she is to finish during the day, what they call in English their "stint." This pile is put down beside the machine and as soon as a skirt is done it is laid on the other side of the machine. Sometimes the work is not all finished by six o'clock and then the one who is behind must work overtime. Sometimes one is finished ahead of time and gets away at four or five o'clock, but generally we are not done till six o'clock.

The machines go like mad all day, because the faster you work the more money you get. Sometimes in my haste I get my finger caught and the needle goes right through it. It goes so quick tho, that it does not hurt much. I bind the finger up with a piece of cotton and go on working. We all have accidents like that. Where the needle goes through the nail it makes a sore finger, or where it splinters a bone it does much harm. Sometimes a finger has to come off. Generally, tho, one can be cured by a salve.

All the time we are working the boss walks about examining the finished garments and making us do them over again if they are not just right. So we have to be careful as well as swift. But I am getting so good at the work that within a year I will be making $7 a week, and then I can save at least $3.50 a week. I have over $200 saved now.

The machines are all run by foot power, and at the end of the day one feels so weak that there is a great temptation to lie right down and sleep. But you must go out and get air, and have some pleasure. So instead of lying down I go out, generally with Henry. Sometimes we go to Coney Island, where there are good dancing places, and sometimes we go to Ulmer Park to picnics. I am very fond of dancing, and, in fact, all sorts of pleasure. I go to the theater quite often, and like those plays that make you cry a great deal. "The Two Orphans" is good. Last time I saw it I cried all night because of the hard times that the children had in the play. I am going to see it again when it comes here.

For the last two winters I have been going to night school at Public School 84 on Glenmore avenue. I have learned reading, writing and arithmetic. I can read quite well in English now and I look at the newspapers every day. I read English books, too, sometimes. The last one that I read was "A Mad Marriage," by Charlotte Braeme. She's a grand writer and makes things just like real to you. You feel as if you were the poor girl yourself going to get married to a rich duke.

I am going back to night school again this winter. Plenty of my friends go there. Some of the women in my class are more than forty years of age. Like me, they did not have a chance to learn anything in the old country. It is good to have an education; it makes you feel higher. Ignorant people are all low. People say now that I am clever and fine in conversation.

We have just finished a strike in our business. It spread all over and the United Brotherhood of Garment Workers was in it. That takes in the cloak-makers, coatmakers, and all the others. We struck for shorter hours, and after being out four weeks won the fight. We only have to work nine and a half hours a day and we get the same pay as before. So the union does good after all in spite of what some people say against it that it just takes our money and does nothing.

I pay 25 cents a month to the union, but I do not begrudge that because it is for our benefit. The next strike is going to be for a raise of wages, which we all ought to have. But tho I belong to the union I am not a Socialist or an Anarchist I don't know exactly what those things mean. There is a little expense for charity, too. If any worker is injured or sick we all give money to help.

Some of the women blame me very much because I spend so much money on clothes. They say that instead of a dollar a week I ought not to spend more than twenty five cents a week on clothes, and that I should save the rest. But a girl must have clothes if she is to go into high society at Ulmer Park or Coney Island or the theatre. Those who blame me are the old country people who have old fashioned notions, but the people who have been here a long time know better. A girl who does not dress well is stuck in a corner, even if she is pretty, and Aunt Fanny says that I do just right to put on plenty of style.

I have many friends and we often have jolly parties. Many of the young men like to talk to me, but I don't go out with any except Henry.

Lately he has been urging me more and more to get married – but I think I'll wait.

Brooklyn, N.Y.

Source: "The Story of a Sweatshop Girl by Sadie Frowne," *New York Independent*, 54 (September 25, 1902), pp. 2279–2282.

2 Unions Call for Boycott of Chinese and Their Patrons, 1891–1892

Urbanization and industrial development created unprecedented opportunity for millions of Americans and immigrants but also new arenas for conflict. Few cities, company towns, or regions escaped the tensions and violent confrontations that arose between ethnic and racial groups vying for access to jobs and decent living conditions. One contributing factor was the seemingly endless demand for work, which enabled employers to keep wages low, play prospective employees off each other, and undermine strikes by hiring, sometimes literally importing, "scab" laborers. Organized labor also fractured over the question of inclusion; even progressive organizations like the Knights of Labor required its white and black members to form separate union locals.

Further aggravating these tensions was the federal government's concession to rising nativist sentiment, culminating in the passage of race-based immigration restrictions in the late nineteenth and early twentieth centuries. The first, passed under considerable pressure from organized labor, was the Chinese Exclusion Act of 1882, which forbade entry of immigrants from China to work in the mining industry and made entry into the United States increasingly difficult for all Chinese. It also ruled that Chinese immigrants already living in the United States were now ineligible for citizenship. This backdrop helps explain the posters reproduced here, part of a boycott staged by union members in Butte, Montana, and later joined by the city's Chamber of Commerce. Butte was one of the largest cities west of the Mississippi, a mining boomtown flourishing from the demand for gold, silver, and copper. As many as 2,000 Chinese immigrants had settled in Butte since the 1860s to work in placer mines, but most were eventually driven out of the industry, forcibly, by other miners and city officials fearing the competition. Butte's Chinese turned to the service industries, establishing groceries, laundries, and other businesses. Butte's unions rallied support for the boycott and pressured local merchants by posting announcements like those sampled here from 1891 and 1892 (Figure 4.2(a) and 4.2(b)). Chinese merchants eventually won a lawsuit against the Butte unions, but received no compensation, and the city's Chinatown district declined steadily after 1895, as most of its families relocated to other cities.

---

3 *La Crónica* Reports on Challenges Facing the Texan Mexican Community, 1910–1911

Any discussion of the Mexican American experience in the metropolitan Southwest must take into account a complicated history. The region's urban growth depended, as it did throughout the United States in the nineteenth and twentieth centuries, on the work of people who performed exhausting labor, usually in poor conditions and for low wages, and, for many, under conditions of servitude. Meanwhile the region was home to people with a wide range of relationships to the area's colonial and slave pasts. Most of the land that became the states of California, Arizona, New Mexico, Nevada, Colorado, Utah, and Texas had been indigenous, then Spanish, and most recently Mexican territory until it was claimed by the United States and, in the case of the Republic of Texas, by independent Anglo settlers. This history was reflected in the region's remarkably diverse population. Cities from Los Angeles to Phoenix to Houston, and the small towns that dotted the region's hinterlands, were home to indigenous peoples, mestizos, people of Spanish descent, and more recent Anglo arrivals. Texas was also home to a large

(a)

BOYCOTT

A General Boycott has been declared upon all CHINESE and JAPANESE Restaurants, Tailor Shops and Wash Houses. Also all persons employing them in any capacity.

All Friends and Sympathizers of Organized Labor will assist us in this fight against the lowering Asiatic standards of living and of morals.

AMERICA vs. ASIA

Progress vs. Retrogression

Are the considerations involved.

BY ORDER OF

Silver Bow Trades and Labor Assembly and Butte Miners' Union

***Figure* 4.2** Flyers distributed by Silver Bow Trades and Labor Assembly and Butte Miners' Union, 1891–1892.

Source: Exhibits, *Hum Fay v. Frank Baldwin*, Civil and Equity Case Files, U.S. Circuit Court for the District of Montana. Butte Term, Records of the District Courts of the United States, Record Group 21, National Archives at Seattle, 298113.

(b)

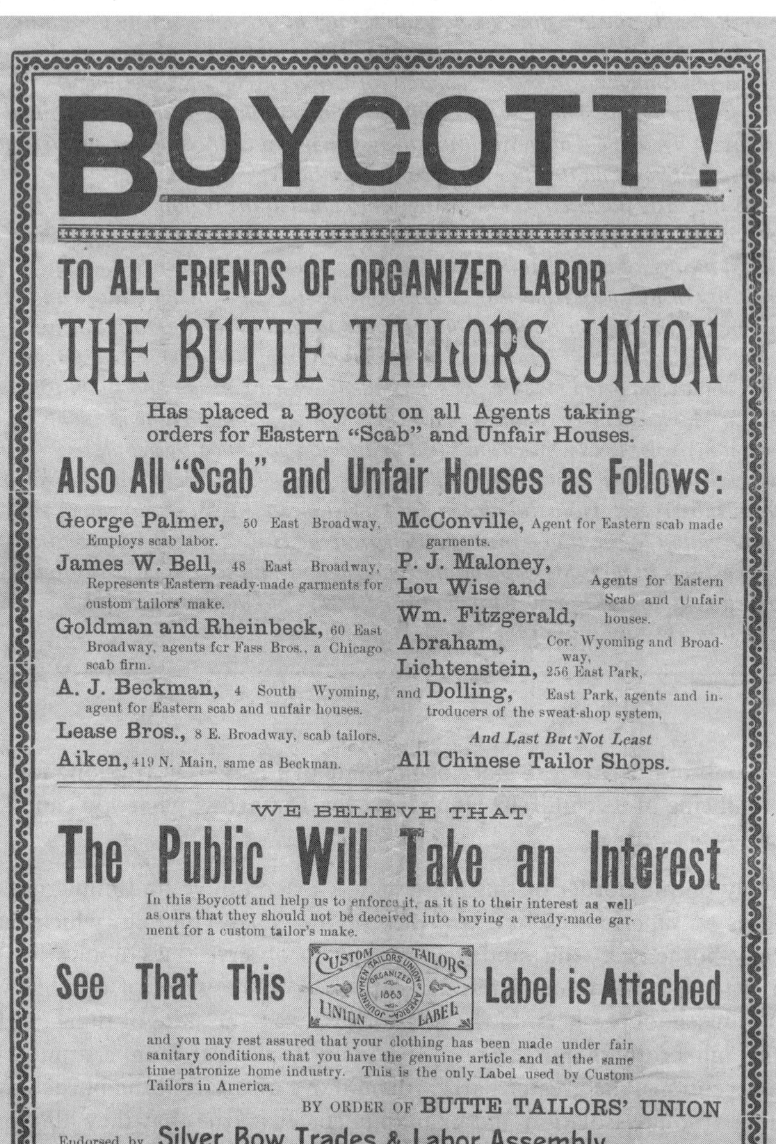

Figure 4.2 (*Continued*)

population of enslaved blacks and, after 1865, former slaves. Throughout the region, finally, the late nineteenth century saw the arrival of a new generation of Mexican immigrants displaced by land reform and political turmoil at home and drawn north by the demand for workers. The US government's restrictions against Japanese and Chinese immigration increased that demand (source 4.2), while a new Mexican rail system and a cadre of labor agents and recruiters facilitated the northward migration.

By the early twentieth century Anglos dominated the region both politically and economically, in part by assuming control, by both legal and illegal means, of land that had belonged to earlier settlers. Hence the vast majority of Mexican Americans were working for wages in agriculture and mining, in the lumber industry, on the railroad, and in service positions in cities. It is in this context that a Laredo-based Spanish-language newspaper, La Crónica, *reported on some of the challenges facing urban and small-town Texan Mexicans in 1910 and 1911. Whether they were longtime residents or recent arrivals, Texan Mexicans lived in a region governed by people dependent on their labor but hostile to their presence and determined to keep them subservient. How did writers for* La Crónica *view Mexican Americans' contribution to the state's metropolitan growth? How did they balance their connections to both Mexico and the Spanish language with their assertion of the citizenship rights assured them by the Treaty of Guadalupe Hidalgo, which marked the end of the US–Mexican war in 1848?*

On Behalf of the Mexican Race of the State of Texas – Do you long for the wellbeing of its children? Don't leave for Tomorrow what you can do today.

... Only on the border of this State with Mexico do we find numerous ... colleges of superior teaching and schools for small children, which have already borne rich fruit, and it is enough to observe the colonies in this region to discover immediately the influence of the work of our beloved Mexican school teachers. In the interior of Texas, the state of things is different: our brothers immigrate to this country in great numbers and with rare exceptions, the greater part of them move away from the border, thus finding absolute isolation and abandonment. It is true that they all work, but in what do they work? In repairing sections of the railroads, in sowing, in the harvest of cotton, in minerals, in the fields as cowboys, in domestic service, etc.; with the exception of a very small number that are dedicated to the various branches of commerce and agriculture, and the majority of those live on the border. As for Mexican professionals in Texas, yes there are some, [but] it is not worth mentioning them, because they are so very scarce.

However, it does not require an extensive analysis of these facts to arrive at the conclusion that increased immigration of Mexican schoolteachers is necessary, so that they come and cultivate the mind[s] of the large colonies of their co-nationals who voluntarily expatriate themselves to a country that denies them the sacred bread of knowledge ... We do not preach the antagonism of races, we are only interested in the conservation and the education of our own [people], so that they cease being seen badly because they do not enlarge their physical and intellectual capacities ...

... We ask that the Mexicans resident in Encinal, Cotullo, Asherton, Carrizo Springs, Millet, Dilley, Lytle, Pearsall, Berclair, Sanderson, Rock Springs, Devine, Big Foot, Floresville, Beeville, Corpus Christi, and all those points of the State where there are numerous colonies of Mexicans permanently located, to write to us WITHOUT DELAY, after discussing with their neighbors the arrangement for the local salary for the school and lodging for the teacher if they want us to help them obtain titled Mexican teachers ... From there, we will give them detailed information on this matter ...

... We need practical work if we want practical results. [November 26, 1910]

To "El Imparcial De Texas"

... In fulfillment of our mission as journalists dedicated to elevating our race we could present ... many letters from Mexicans resident in various parts of this State, in which they ask that we recommend to them Mexican teachers so that they can come to impart the bread of knowledge to their children, who are not admitted into the public schools, or if they are, the American teachers do not make any effort to teach them, it being very common to find children who have attended the schools for four or five years without knowing any English ... [December 10, 1910]

Mexican as well as Mexican-American children excluded from official schools. Consul Miguel E. Diebold renews investigations. Have they already forgotten the Treaty of Guadalupe?

... A complete clarification of the facts will demonstrate, on the one hand, that Mexicans who have been born in this country and despite their American nationality, have not enjoyed in full the extension of the privileges and guarantees that the Federal Constitution offers them; and, on the other hand, that clearly Mexican individuals have also been denied rights and prerogatives that the Treaty of Guadalupe Hidalgo between Mexico and the United States ... conceded to them, with the result that Mexicans and Mexican-Americans are in the same situation ...

Do not think that we are seeking scandal; we are only claiming a right. To the Japanese, to the Irish, to the Scots, to the English, to the Italians and some many other races who have immigrated in great abundance to this country, there has been no obstacle to attendance at public schools in all of the States of the American Republic. Why has one been created for the Mexican-American? In virtue of what law, of what constitutional principle? Perhaps they do not recognize us as of the white race? Have they already forgotten the treaty of Guadalupe Hidalgo? ...

... Mexican-Americans ... pay the personal taxes that the electoral laws of Texas require yearly, in order to exercise the right to vote, and from this tax, part goes to the fund for public education, and the taxes and fees on property and the different branches of business are also put in the coffers of the public treasury, with the consequence that the money of these Mexicans helps to pay for ... Texas teachers and also helps to build public schools in many counties ... [Yet] those who pay the salaries for the teachers of Texas youth and help construct buildings for schools cannot attend them ... [December 24, 1910]

Exclusion in Guadalupe County. Our Investigations Develop and Our Correspondence circulates in the whole state of Texas, Finding out the facts

In what follows we are publishing two letters that speak for themselves, from Seguin, Guadalupe County and Persall, Frio County, Texas, dated 26 and 27 of this month. The first says:

> "Mr. N. Idar,
> Laredo, Texas.
>
> Dear Sir:
>
> I have been very interested in the article that saw public light in your illustrated weekly 'LA CRONICA,' in number 102 of the 17th of this month, headed with these lines: 'The Exclusion of Mexican children in the greater part of the official schools of Texas.' The assertions made in that article are true, because in SEGUIN, GUADALUPE COUNTY, of this same STATE OF TEXAS, they apply exclusion to us equally, since our children are not admitted to the 'WHITE' schools, but that they built us a house of only 20 or 30 feet and without sufficient chairs for the children, while almost the greater part of the children come from outside of the city, they find themselves having to pay 25 cents monthly to rent a chair.
>
> There are also two or three schools outside of the city that we can say are purely Mexican, but in order to build them they have demanded a contribution

from among the whole Mexican Colony, as well as paying certain contribution that they require ...

With the hope that you will continue doing something for the Mexican race ...

RAMON ESCOBEDO"

... The case of Mr. Escobedo, seems to demonstrate that there is indirect and direct exclusion in Seguin: indirect, because if THEY ARE NOT ADMITTED entirely in the official schools for American children, neither do they deny them instruction, but see with what scorn they expel them to a separate neighborhood, in a 20- to 30-foot house, with a lack of seats and seemingly neglected. Direct, because they are not admitted together with the American children, despite the [fact that] the Treaty of Guadalupe Hidalgo specifies that we be recognized as of the white race, and being white, there is no school in the world that can deny us the privilege of its doors ... [December 31, 1910]

The Mexicans of San Angelo Make Demands on the School Board. Protest against the segregation of the Mexican children in the schools.

Reviewing our collection of the last year ... we found the following article, which was sent to us by our correspondent ... It says:

"San Angelo, Texas. June 20.

The board of Directors of the Schools of San Angelo, remain resolved against the demand that Mexican children be admitted in the Schools of the City with the *white* children. Three hundred local Mexicans had a large meeting last Sunday, in which they agreed on resolutions of protest and resolved to employ a lawyer to bring the case before the courts, to obligate the Board of Directors to accede to their demands.

When they received knowledge of this, the members of the Board of Directors stated that they would not change their attitude, and President Samuel Crowther said that if Mexicans were given access to the schools, this would demoralize the system of public schools."

[December 31, 1910]

Unhuman Lynching of a Young Mexican in Thor[n]dale. The Entire World Is Paying Attention to this Savage Crime ...

Antonio Gómez is the name of a boy of 13 or 14 years of age and weighing 40 to 45 pounds who was lynched the night of Monday the 19th of this month in Thorndale, Texas.

The boy was seated on a box in front of an establishment next to the *Garage* of a German, cutting a shingle with a knife when [the German] came out of his establishment and said to his neighbor: if this guy [muchacho] … sits in front of my establishment cutting tile like he is doing there, I'll give him many blows … The German … got close to where he was and he snatched the tile away from him, ordering him to stop cutting there; the boy had the knife in his hand and, on standing up, perhaps in an involuntary movement shielding himself from a blow that the German gave him, he wounded him affecting the artery in the upper part of his heart.

Next the boy threw down the knife and fled. One of the spectators of the event picked up the knife and said to the German – "This knife has blood on it, that boy has wounded you" – "No, you are wrong, he has not wounded me" – said the German.

A half hour later, Charles Zeichung, the German, died as a result of the wound Gómez had inflicted on him. The boy Gómez was arrested immediately by Constable Bob McCoy who took him immediately to the jail.

Dragged with a chain on the neck.

On finding out that Zeichung had died, [McCoy put] a chain around [the boy's] neck [and] took him to a cotton mill, and then he took him to the house of an individual named Penny and there he left him in the charge of Willifred Wilson, whom he deputized to take care of him … A little later several individuals arrived and Penny, according to what he says, tried to escape taking the boy; but he was grabbed by a man mounted on a horse and three other individuals who were with him, and they disappeared in the darkness dragging the boy with the chain that Constable McCoy had put around his neck.

Lynched after death.

An eye witness testified that some minutes later, the boy, already dying, was kicked in the head … More than twenty witnesses testified that still despite the fact that the boy was already dead, they hung him on a ladder that they leaned against a telephone pole.

… We are waiting to see what the Government of Texas will do, but one has to suppose that the lynchers will be charged and freed on bail, and after public opinion has been quieted by a simulacrum of justice, they will discard the case completely; as until now we do not recall any American who has been punished for the lynching of a Mexican, despite the fact that they have committed some.

The death was accidental, he did not commit a crime.

... The Penal Code of Texas says: Art. 710. "Any minor person of sound mind, who illegally kills any rational living person, in this State with MALICIOUS PREMEDIDATION," expressed or implicit, will be considered guilty of murder." ...

As you can see the characteristic that distinguishes a murder, is homicide committed with premeditated malicious intent ...

... Why was he not judged according to the law? Why was he dragged with a chain around his neck through the streets, like a dog?

Race hatred and lynchings in Texas

We do not know to what to attribute such deep-rooted hatred that a great part of the Texan-American population feels for the Mexican element.

... The cultured American, the intelligent American who knows the rights of man, does not treat the Mexican poorly ... The American who is uncultured, who is ignorant, because there are also those ... lets himself be guided by the prejudice that he feels against the Mexican, simply for being Mexican. Because he cannot give any other reason, given that the Mexican does not belong to a degenerate, corrupt, criminal race ...

The barbarous acts of cruelty and savagery committed against Mexicans, burning them alive or lynching them without bringing a charge, excluding them from public schools, robbing them infamously of their work, insulting them in a million ways, awakens compassion for this Mexican people and aversion for the American people; hate that is shared for both the guilty and those who are not, because there is no doubt that there are ... Americans who condemn the acts of cruelty and the injustices that are committed with Mexicans ...

Mexicans in the interior of Texas cannot enter a barbershop, a hotel, or an American restaurant, because they display signs written in such emphatic language as the following: "EXTRICTLY FOR WHITE PEOPLE" [*sic*] ... which is equivalent to saying: Mexicans are not admitted.

Why? Well of course, because they are Mexicans. [June 29, 1911]

Our Duty in this Country: Solidarity and Altruism

... If the wealth and fortunes of the old Mexicans of Texas have slowly been escaping to the possession of other individuals who are not Mexican, this is the moment for Mexicans to interest themselves in regaining them. And why is this wealth necessary for the common good and solidarity of our masses? Because without riches, without interests, without goods, without great wealth in commerce, without displaying great activities in the world of business, we are slowly destroying the reduced grade of liberty, of comfort, and of respectability that we enjoy today …

On the whole border of Texas is found a growing abundance of land agents and buyers, who make their best speculations buying the property of Mexicans at extremely low prices, in order to transfer them to the hands of other individuals who have nothing in common with us, and the logical result of this activity, inevitably will be that in very few years the number of our wealthy men will be greatly reduced, and then, their descendants and their brothers will suffer the consequences of their lack of foresight.

Mexicans need to seek the strong side of every proposal; when we do not get what we want, we expect something more; proceed with the conviction that I CAN; kill our egoisms and banish the excessive love of the SELF; true nobility is not an accumulation of negative virtues but rather a great and positive power that enables a man to make his life greater, richer and more beautiful in all ways and forms than his personal existence … [December 24, 1910]

Editor's Note: *The people charged with lynching Antonio Gómez were acquitted. See "Lo Mismo de Siempre,"* La Crónica, *November 16, 1911.*

Source: "En Pro de la Raza Mexicana del Estado de Texas," *La Crónica*, November 26, 1910, p. 1; "A El Imparcial de Texas," *La Crónica*, December 10, 1910, p. 4; "Tanto los Niños Mexicanos como los Mexico-Americanos son exluidos de las Escuelas Oficiales – ¿ya se Olividaron los Tratados de Guadalupe?" *La Crónica*, December 24, 1910, p. 1; "La Exclusión en el Condado de Guadalupe" and "Los Mexicanos de San Angelo Demandan a Los Síndicos de las Escuelas Públicas," *La Crónica*, December 31, 1910, p. 1; "Cobarde Infame e Inhumano Lynchamiento de un Jovencito Mexicano en Thor[n]dale, Milam Co., Texas," *La Crónica*, June 29, 1911; "Nuestro Deber en Este País: Solidaridad y Altruismo," *La Crónica*, December 24, 1910. Courtesy of the Dolph Briscoe Center for American History, University of Texas, Austin. Translation by Karen D. Caplan.

4 *Good Housekeeping* Counsels "The Commuter's Wife," 1909

The lives of middle-class suburban housewives were dramatically different from those of young women like Sadie Frowne or the prospective migrants who wrote the Chicago Defender *(sources 4.1 and 5). By the late nineteenth century, demand for white-collar professionals had grown significantly while technological innovation was making suburban living more accessible and attractive. The result was the steady expansion of affluent suburban enclaves outside Philadelphia, Boston, New York City,*

Chicago, and other major cities. These communities were unique, by design. Their homeowners were almost exclusively people of northern European descent, Protestant, well educated, with a professional breadwinner who commuted by train to the city. Their homes were sizable and architecturally distinct, sat on large lots with setback requirements, and often had easy access to parks or waterfronts. The most exclusive neighborhoods featured private clubs with golf courses and tennis courts. This was a suburban population with the luxury and means to build, staff, and maintain well-appointed homes and to devote time to discussions of architecture, landscape, and lifestyle.

For counsel on these matters residents regularly turned to the planners, architects, and commentators who shared their assumptions about the superiority of suburban residence, the single family home, and a particular set of domestic and gender ideals. Journalists and advertisers joined the celebration of an exclusive, racially homogeneous, and pastoral suburban ideal, one viewed as the atmosphere most conducive to raising children and marital happiness. The typical reader of Good Housekeeping *was a woman in this small but growing suburban middle class, someone expected to focus on childrearing and keeping the home. Indeed even college-educated women were expected to abandon their professional aspirations for the life of homemaker (source 6.3). A growing market for goods and services gave rise to a variety of periodicals (with titles like* Suburban Life*) that simultaneously celebrated this new ideal and prescribed its terms. In this 1909 article,* Good Housekeeping *advises young housewives who suddenly find themselves isolated from family, friends, and familiar urban resources.*

... [P]roblems and difficulties ... face the many young married people who are leaving the cities for the nearby country, impelled by the spirit of enterprise and a desire for a home that shall be something other than a folding bed and two hooks on a door ... [T]here is more honest return to the lost art of home-making in the suburbs than anywhere else in the country, so far, at least, as young married people are concerned ... The advantages of suburban life have all been set forth by the real estate dealer, by the artistic pamphlet, and by dear human nature's imperishable, if somewhat shame-faced, belief in "love in a cottage." It is a tribute to unspoilable manhood and womanhood that there is today in all these suburban towns so implicit a confidence in this individual home, where the family may sacredly guard its right to live and sleep and eat and develop and love and quarrel and repent – *alone*, albeit there are noted women who, never having known the joy of these things, deny their right to exist.

First among advantages there is a whole house to one's self, with no evil-eyed janitor to say to the humble tenant, "Go, and he goeth"; no unbending neighbor upon whose half of a piazza or a cellar one is forever innocently intruding. Better the dinner of herbs on the peaceful gas stove, a poor thing, but your own, than the contentious kitchen of the combination flat … Again, there is that "lonesome patch of garden ground," where you may experiment at will, raising hollyhocks and cheerfulness, lettuce and humility, nasturtiums, geraniums, good temper and quiet nerves. Also, you may keep chickens if your neighbors' Christian character will bear the strain, and they will provide great funds of interest for little bits of boys and girls …

The young wife in Lonelyville

But you, my dear commuter's wife, refuse to be diverted by these trivial things. It has been hard for you, and you are in no mood to be laughed at. The pretty house is all in order; the husband is away all day; you know nobody; there is nothing to do, nowhere to go; there are no little people to occupy heart and hands, for you are at the beginning of all things, and everything is flat, stale, and unprofitable …

The days are long in these suburban towns. The busy men, an hour or more from the city, leave on early trains, and are at once plunged in the rush of their accustomed life among their usual associates. The little wife, left standing behind the struggling young vines of her brand new piazza, turns back into the house, to face a day devoid of interest and companionship. She may read a little – she who has been brought up on lectures; she may practice a little – she who has been educated on concerts … She may walk [but] all her walking is through endless streets of houses like her own, pretty, with well-kept lawns and drives, and apparently, like her own tenanted by one lonely young woman and perhaps a maid or two … [A]s she walks about, the commuter's wife … wonders a little dismally why she was ever induced to leave New York, or Boston, or Chicago …

The church a social center

… Every suburban town of any pretensions has a church and a schoolhouse and probably a clubhouse … Go, then, to church … Over and over, people have said to me, "Yes, I would like to go to church out there, but it doesn't seem sincere to go now that I want to get something, when I never went before." Yes, it is perfectly sincere, because the church wants just such people as you, and needs you, in a town like yours, quite as much as you need it …

A thorn in the flesh

One serious thorn in the flesh of the suburban woman is her husband's love of a quiet evening. He is tired and wants to rest. She is feeling perfectly fresh, after a dull day, and wants social life ... The commuter and his wife, loving each other dearly, are, through their enforced separation, their different environments, their diverse interests, in great danger of falling after a while into a nagging, fretting, dual existence ... Tom returns late from the city, too tired almost to eat, and his wife meets him, charmingly dressed, with hurry in voice and air: "Make haste, Tom, dear – we're going to dine at the Smiths; your clothes are all laid out. I'm sorry you are so awfully late. They'll just have to wait, but *do* hurry." ... Tom had gone in on the 7.45 that morning; he rushed all day; he ate a cold, hasty, pay-when-it's-over luncheon ... [H]e was jammed and elbowed by the hot and weary crowd of men surging down Barclay street ... [On the returning] train boat ... he stood up all the way home, with a long, uphill walk from the station. It is to his credit that he went to his dressing room without a word, but his wife cried because he neglected to kiss her ... [T]hey spent a strained and uncomfortable evening ...

The servant problem

The servant problem is one of the difficulties of suburban life ... The sources of domestic help are running dry; there are fewer girls and women willing to "live out," as they phrase it, and near a city the difficulty of getting good servants is well-nigh insurmountable ... The city intelligence offices, from which servants are procured for suburban homes, offer only the incapable, unintelligent, or the habitual drunkard. Many low-class women secure entrance to suburban homes, and many a young wife, not well trained before marriage, finds herself on the verge of despair over trying to make a home with such wretched assistance ... The best and most successful way is a hard one ... Let the young mistress go ... to properly credited charitable organizations, to the missionary who meets the immigrant girl, to the matron of the home where friendless girls are sheltered. Let her take a clean, willing, entirely ignorant young girl and train her. It can be done, even if the girl does not speak English. There are many such girls who drift into shops and mills, who might be taught to cook and be trained for domestic service ...

There is no way out of it for the commuter's wife. She *must* herself know how to handle all the affairs of her own home if she expects to be happy or to make her husband contented. In the city it matters less; one can always dine somewhere. In the country one must dine, either well or badly, at home. This stimulates a woman's pride in accomplishment, and that is why one may find more real homes in suburban towns than in some other places ...

When the children come

When the children come into these homes, many of these early trials are things of the past, and all but forgotten, but the commuter's wife is still a woman apart, and even with her children finds that her problems continue to be unique ... The father's hours complicate not only the home life and the child training but they make of Sunday a day which to serve the great purpose of the Sabbath, needs to be recast for suburban [us]age ... A Sunday morning service, held at eleven o'clock, usually receives the attention of everyone ... Granted this, the commuter wants, and will have, and ought to have, the rest of the day for family life ... A certain freedom in family and out-of-door life is natural and right for these men who spend too many weary hours in city offices. Even conscientious women must admit this, and compromise upon a careful observance of the Sunday morning service. Too much church is as bad for a tired-out man as too little, but few men, of the fine type that are making suburban homes, fail to recognize that they owe a certain debt to the little church of the town. It is not wise for women to hold so closely to tradition that they cannot adjust their standards to changed conditions.

Taken at its best, suburban life is sane and wholesome and conducive to the best sort of happiness. It has its trials and difficulties; it has great compensating advantages. It calls for independence, courage, cheerfulness, resource, and it produces by its demands those eminently attractive and capable young women, each one of whom at heart is proud of her home and her children, proud of the little town she lives in, proud of one special man on the 8.17 – proud, in fact, of being a commuter's wife.

Source: Grace Duffield Goodwin, "The Commuter's Wife: A Sisterly Talk by One Who Knows Her Problems," *Good Housekeeping*, 49 (October 1909), pp. 362–366.

5 Black Southerners Write the *Chicago Defender* for Information about Employment, 1916–1918

In the first three decades of the twentieth century, as many as 1.6 million black Americans made their way from homes in the urban and rural south to industrial centers in the Northeast, Midwest, and West. In what was described as the "Great Migration," black communities in cities including

Chicago, Cleveland, New York City, St. Louis, and Detroit grew swiftly and dramatically. Since the Civil War, blacks living in former slave states had mobilized limited material resources to sustain their communities and they had organized constantly to secure basic rights and freedoms. Still, the North had much to offer, including better-paying jobs, comparative freedom of movement and opportunity, and the promise of respite from the systematic restrictions and violence imposed by the sharecropping economy and Jim Crow. Black Southerners learned about these opportunities from friends and family, from churches and social organizations, and in the pages of the Chicago Defender, *a black-owned newspaper that circulated widely in black communities throughout the country. Many readers viewed the* Defender *as an authority on racial issues, because of its candid reporting on life in black America and its celebrations of black community organizations and accomplishments, in Chicago and elsewhere. And, beginning in 1916, when wartime production created an urgent need for laborers in Northern manufacturing centers, the* Defender *actively promoted migration while serving as both a source of practical information and a symbol of the North's promise. Its articles contrasted the racial climates in the North and South, estimated labor demand ("places for 1,500,000 working men in the cities of the North"), and reported on the migration phenomenon itself. Northern employers ran advertisements in the paper claiming to "guarantee you a steady position."*

Southerners anxious to relocate wrote letters to the Defender, *to social organizations including the Chicago Urban League, and directly to firms that advertised jobs. In 1919 the* Journal of Negro History *collected and published dozens of these letters. In the samples excerpted here, prospective migrants discuss their lives in the Jim Crow South, their hopes for resettlement, and the networks of people and institutions that facilitated the dramatic growth of black communities in the urban North and West.*

Dallas, Tex.
April 23, 1917

Dear Sir: Having been informed through the Chicago Defender paper that I can secure information from you. I am a constant reader of the Defender and am contemplating on leaving here for some point north. Having your city in view I thought to inquire of you about conditions for work, housing, wages and everything necessary. I am now employed as a laborer in a structural shop, have worked for the firm five years.

I stored cars for Armour packing co. 3 years, I also claims to know something about candy making, am handy at most anything for an honest living. I am 31 yrs. old have a very industrious wife, no children. If chances are available for work of any kind let me know. Any information you can give me will be highly appreciated.

Selma, Ala.
May 19, 1917.

Dear Sir: I am a reader of the Chicago Defender I think it is one of the Most Wonderful Papers of our race printed. Sirs I am writeing to see if You all will please get me a job. And Sir I can wash dishes, wash iron nursing work in groceries and dry good stores. Just any of these I can do. Sir, who so ever you get the job from please tell them to send me a ticket and I will pay them. When I get their as I have not got enough money to pay my way. I am a girl of 17 years old and in the 8 grade at Knox Academy School. Sir I will thank you with all my heart. May God Bless you all. Please answer in return mail.

Vicksburg, Miss.
May 2, 1917

Sir: I am a reader of the Chicago Defender I am asking you a little information. So many people are leaving south for north it is too big families and we want to come north or middle west for better wages. We all have trade and if you think we all can get position just as we get north if not the middle west. Better please dont publish this is no paper. here is a stamp for reply.

Fayette, Ga.
January 17, 1917.

Dear Sir: I have learned of the splendid work which you are doing in placing colored men in touch with industrial opportunities. I therefore write to ask if you have an opening anywhere for me. I am a college graduate and understand Bookkeeping. But I am not above doing hard labor in a foundry or other industrial establishment. Please let me know if you can place me.

Ellisville, Miss.
May 1, 1917

Kind Sir: I have been takeing the Defender 4 months I injoy reading it very much I dont think that there could be a grander paper printed for the race, then the defender. Dear Editor I am thinking of leaving for Some good places in the North or West one I dont Know just which I learn that Nebraska was a very good climate for the people of the South. I wont you to give me some ideas about it, Or Some good farming country. I have been public working for 10 year. I am tired of that, And want to get out on a good farm. I have a wife and 5 children, and we all wont to get out from town a place an try to buy a good home near good Schools good Churchs. I am going to leave here as soon as I get able to work ... Wages here are so low can scarcely live We can buy enough to eat we only buy enough to Keep up alive I mean the greater part of the Race. Women wages are from $1.25 Some time as high as $2.50. just some time for a whole week.

Hoping Dear Editor that I will get a hearing from you through return mail, giving me Some ideas and Some Sketches on the different Climate suitable for our health.

P.S. You can place my letter in Some of the Defender Columns but done use my name in print, for it might get back down here.

Port Arthur, Texas
May 5, 1917

Dear Sir: Permitt me to inform you that I have had the pleasure of reading the Defender for the first time in my life as I never dreamed that there was such a race paper published and I must say that its some paper ...

... [H]ad I know that there was such a paper in my town or such being handled in my vicinity I would have been a subscriber years ago ...

... In reading the Defender want ad I notice that there is lots of work to be had and if I havent miscomprehended I think I also understand that the transportation is advance to able bodied working men who is out of work and desire work. Am I not right? ...

Jacksonville, Fla.
April 25, 1917

Dear Sir: In reading a copy of the Chicago defender note that if i get in touch with you you would assist me in getting imployment. i am now in Florida East coast R R service road way department and in working line myself and friends would be very glad to get in touch wish as labors ... We are working men with familys. Please answer at once. i am your of esteem. We are not particular about the electric lights and all i want is fairly good wages and steady work.

Moss Point, Miss.
May 5, 1917.

Dear Sirs: Will you please send me in formation a first class cookeing job or washing job I want a job as soom as you can find one for me also I want a job for three your girls ages 13 to 16 years. Pease oblidge.

Jacksonville, Fla.
April 28, 1917

Kind Sir: We have several times read your noted paper and we are delighted with the same because it is a thorough Negro paper. There is a storm of our people toward the North and especially to your city. We have watched your want ad regularly and we are anxious for location with good families (white) where we can be cared for and do domestic work. We want to engage as cook, nurse and maid. We have had some educational advantages, as we have taught in rural schools for a few years but our pay so poor we could not continue ... Will you please assist us in securing places as we are anxious to come but want jobs before we leave. We want to do any kind of honest labor. Our chance here is so poor.

Marcel, Miss.
October 4, 1917

Dear Sir: Although I am a stranger to you but I am a man of the so called colored race and can give you the very best or reference as to my character and ability by prominent citizens of my community by both white and colored people that knows me ... Now I am a reader of your paper the Chicago Defender. After reading your writing ever wek I am compell & persuade to say that I know you are a real man of my color you have I know heard of the south land & I need not tell you any thing about it ... I am a man of a family wide and 1 child I can do just any kind of work in the line of common labor & I have for the present sufficient means to support us till I can obtain a position. Now should I come to your town, would you please to assist me in getting a position I am willing to pay whatever you charge I dont want you to loan me not 1 cent but *help* me to find an occupation there in your town now I has a present position that will keep me employed till the first of Dec. 1917. now please give me your best advice on this subject. I enclose stamp for reply.

Hattiesburg, Miss.
December 4, 1916

HON. JOHN T. CLARK, *Sec. National League on Urban Conditions,* New York City, N.Y. *Sir:* I am writing you on matters pertaining to work and desirable locations for industrious and trust worthy laborers. Me for myself and a good number of Friends especially thousand of our people are moving out from this section of whom all can be largely depended upon for good service, for the past 15 years I have been engaged in insurance work of which I am at the head of one now, And I have a large host of people at my command. I have had a great deal of experience in the lumbering business, Hotel, Agency of most any kind. Any information as to employment and desirable locations especially for good School Conditions Church Etc., will be appreciated.

Natchez, Miss.
Sept. 22, 1917

MR. R.S. ABBOTT, *Editor.*
Dear Sir: I thought that you might help me in Some way either personally or through your influence, is why I am worrying you for which I beg pardon.

I am a married man having wife and mother to support, (I mention this in order to properly convey my plight) conditions here are not altogether good and living expenses growing while wages are small. My greatest desire is to leave for a better place but I am unable to raise the money.

I can write short stories all of which potray negro characters but no burlesque can also write poems, have a gift for cartooning but have never learned the technicalities of comic drawing. these things will never profit me anything here in Natchez. Would like to know if you could use one or two of my short stories in serial form in your great paper they are very interesting and would furnish good reading matter. By this means I could probably leave here in short and thus come in possession of better employment enabling me to take up my drawing which I like best.

Kindly let me hear from you and if you cannot favor me could you refer me to any Negro publication buying fiction from their race.

Lexington, Miss.
May 12, 1917

My dear Mr. H—: I am writing to you for some information and assistance if you can give it.

I am a young man and am disable, in a very great degree, to do hard manual labor. I was educated at Alcorn College and have been teaching a few years: but ah: me the Superintendent under whom we poor colored teachers have to teach cares less for a colored man than he does for the vilest beast. I am compelled to teach 150 children without any assistance and receives only $27.00 a month, the white with 30 get $100.

I am so sick I am so tired of such conditions that I sometime think that life for me is not worth while and most eminently believe with Patrick Henry "Give me liberty or give me death." If I was a strong able bodied man I would have gone from here long ago, but this handicaps me and, I must make inquiries before I leap.

Mr. H—, do you think you can assist me to a position I am good at stenography typewriting and bookkeeping or any kind of work not to rough or heavy. I am 4 feet 6 in high and weigh 105 pounds.

I will gladly give any other information you may desire and will greatly appreciate any assistance you may render me.

Pasca Goula, Miss.
May 8, 1917

Dear Sir & friend: as understand that you ar the man for me to con for to & i want to Com to you & my frend & i has not got the money to Com Will you pleas Sir send me & my frend a ticket to Com an if you will I will glad La Com at onC & will worK et out will Be glad to do so I will not ask you to send the redey Caseh for you dont nae me & if you Will Send me 2 tickets i will gladly take the, & i will Com Jest now hoping to hear from you by re torn male Yors Ever.

New Orleans, LA.
August 27, 1917.

Dear Sir: i am wrighting you for help I haird of you by telling my troble i was told to right you. I wont to come there and work i have been looking for work here for three month and eand find any i once found a place $1 a week for a 15 year old girl and i did not take that. now you may say how can that be but New Orleans is so haird tell some have to work for food and the only help i have is my mother and she have work 2 week now and she have four children young then me and i am 15teen and she have such a hard time tell she is willing for me to go and if you will sin me a pass you will not be sorry i am not no lazy girl i am smart i have got very much learning but i can do any work that come to my hand to do ... i have clothes to bring wenter dress to ware. my grand mama dress me but now she is dead and all i have is my mother now please sire sin me a pass you wont be sorry ... i will work and pay for my pass if you sin it i am so sorry tell i cant talk like i wont to and if you and your famely dont wont to be worry with me I will stay where i work and will come and see you all and do any think i can for you ... excuse bad righting.

Orange City, Fla., May 4, 1917

Dear Sir: Being a reader of the Chicago Defender, I fins a add, stateing laborers wanted. I would like to ask if the add is refering to persons of that state only. Could a person secure a position until he could reach said state?

Now if you would answer this letter of information I would highly appreciate it. During your letter please give information about advanced transportation, etc. This is not as a testimony – don't publish.

Source: "Letters of Negro Migrants of 1916–1918 Collected under the Direction of Emmett J. Scott," *Journal of Negro History*, 4(3) (July 1919), pp. 291, 317, 334, 302, 305–306, 327, 292, 316, 318, 293, 301–302, 304, 316, 334.

Chapter 5 Big City Life

1 Urban Imagery, 1889–1913

As metropolitan regions grew larger, more densely populated, and filled with new technologies, they looked and functioned very differently from their predecessors. To longtime residents and recent arrivals alike, these changes were always novel, often exhilarating, and sometimes overwhelming. Construction was constant and much of the built environment simply new: street cars, electric lights, factories, grand public squares and parks, crowded commercial districts, skyscrapers, tenements, and popular amusements. Work was transformed. Laborers living in isolated "company towns," as well as big-city dwellers employed in loft factories, found themselves in workplaces that were loud, filled with machinery, and filled with dangers (sources 3.3 and 4.1). The growing population of secretaries, clerks, and professionals learned to negotiate the gender and class dynamics of a new office culture. Neighborhoods and living conditions were also transformed. The affluent benefited from new methods of construction and were able to afford new amenities, while the poor generally found themselves in tightly packed neighborhoods and substandard, overcrowded dwellings. No one could ignore perhaps the most striking novelty of the modernizing city: the sheer number of people, be it at work, on the streets, or in places of leisure.

Reproduced here are a few glimpses of those cities and their residents' day-to-day routines (Figures 5.1(a) to (e)). Also captured here is the public nature of urban life. First, it was difficult not to encounter many of the scenes shown in these images. Whether you were a salaried professional,

The Modern American Metropolis: A Documentary Reader, First Edition.
Edited by David M. P. Freund.

a department store employee, or an impoverished factory worker, you were likely to witness sights like those pictured below and to come into contact with people from very different backgrounds. The era's remarkable affluence and its desperate poverty were regularly juxtaposed and on display for anyone to see. Second, some of these images were produced for and consumed by the public. Included is a postcard (from 1913), one of countless artifacts sent to friends and relatives in distant places to spread celebratory images of American city life. Also widely viewed were photographs of factory conditions and slum dwellings, published in exposés by middle-class reformers hoping to draw attention to the plight of the urban poor. Shown here are two examples, a lodging house in New York City from Jacob Riis's How the Other Half Lives, *published in 1890, and Lewis Hine's photo of a young spinner employed by a mill in Georgia.*

(a)

Figure 5.1(a) Traffic jam on Dearborn Street, near Randolph Street, Chicago, 1909.

Source: Chicago History Museum, ICHi-04192. Photo: Frank M. Hallenbeck.

(b)

Figure 5.1(b) MetLife's Industrial Audit and Policy Division, New York City, 1896.

Source: Courtesy of MetLife Archives.

(c)

Figure 5.1(c) Lewis Hine, "A Little Spinner in Globe Cotton Mill," 1909.

Source: Library of Congress, Prints and Photographs Division, LC-DIG-nclc-01583.

(d)

Figure 5.1(d) Boardwalk at Rockaway Beach, NY, postcard, 1913.

Source: Theatre Talks/Cezar Del Valle.

(e)

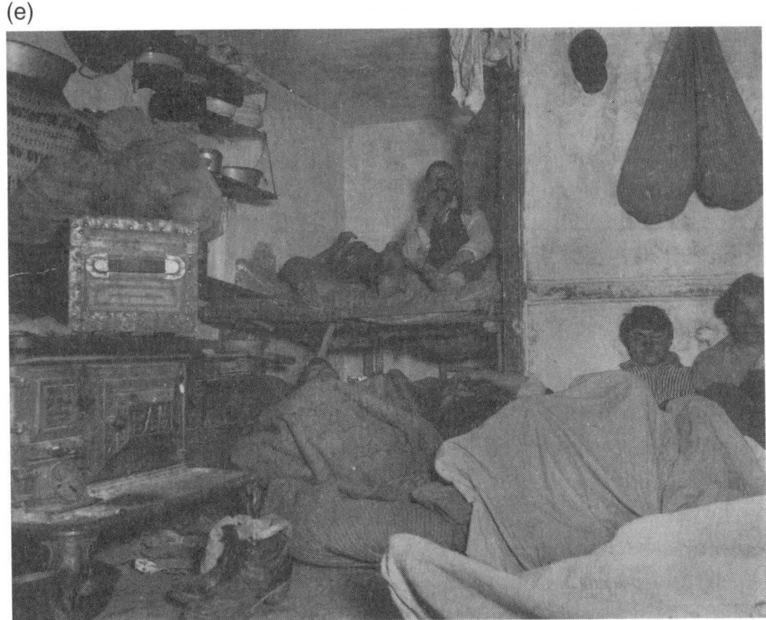

Figure 5.1(e) Jacob August Riis (1849–1914), "Lodgers in Bayard Street Tenement, Five Cents a Spot," 1889, gelatin silver print, printed 1957, $6\frac{3}{16} \times 4\frac{3}{4}$ in. (15.7×12 cm).

Source: New York, Museum of Modern Art, Gift of the Museum of the City of New York. Acc. no. 338.1964. © 2013 Digital image, The Museum of Modern Art, New York/Scala, Florence.

2 A Young Governess Discusses Her New Freedoms, 1903

In her interview with the New York Independent *(see source 4.1) published in 1903, a German immigrant named Agnes M. introduces readers to two very different but intersecting urban worlds: that of the American wage earners able to enjoy some independence and new personal freedoms, and that of the business owners and affluent families that depended on their labor. An important context for Agnes's story was the impact of urban growth on work patterns for white female wage earners, more of whom took jobs not just in manufacturing and domestic service but also in retail positions at department stores and restaurants. Agnes was part of a fast-growing population of single white women who were able to establish a measure of economic and social independence previously unknown to most American women. In Agnes's case the contact between classes was quite intimate: she worked as a governess, caring for the children of affluent New Yorkers. Through her eyes, we learn about the daily life and the aspirations of white female wage laborers, while also viewing a snapshot of the comforts enjoyed by the era's most privileged Americans.*

Consider Agnes M.'s account in light of other people encountered in this volume. She would be quite familiar with much of the public life of industrial cities, and might have rubbed shoulders with James Huneker on one of her visits to Coney Island (sources 5.1, 3–4). How might she have viewed herself in relation to other recent arrivals, such as Sadie Frowne, or the immigrants who turned to Hull House, or to the black Americans who would soon move to New York, Chicago, and other Northern metropolitan areas (sources 4.1, 6.3, and 4.5, respectively)?

The True Life Story of a Nurse Girl

I was born just twenty years ago in the old, old city of Treves, in what was once France, but is now Germany. There were eight children in our family, five girls and three boys, and we were comfortably off until my father died, which happened when I was only three years old.

My father was a truckman, carrying goods from the railway stations to the shops; he had a number of wagons going and had built up a good business, tho he was always ill from some disease that he contracted when a soldier in the war with France. It was consumption, I believe, and it finally carried him off. We were living at the time in a fine new house that he had built near the Moselle, but we were soon obliged to move …

By the time I was five years old my mother had lost everything, except the money she got from the Government, which was enough to keep her, but the family had to break up, and I went away to a school kept by Sisters of Christian Liebe, in another city. The Government paid for me there on account of my being a soldier's orphan …

When I was fifteen years of age I left school and returned to my mother, who was then living in a flat with some of my brothers and sisters. Two of my brothers were in the army and one of my sisters was in America … I went to work for a milliner. The hours were from eight o'clock in the morning till six in the evening, but when there was much business the milliner would keep us till nine o'clock at night. I got no money, and was to serve for two years for nothing as an apprentice …

I heard about how easy it was to make money in America and became very anxious to go there, and very tired of making hats and dresses for nothing for a woman who was selling them at high prices … [We] asked my eldest sister to lend me the money to get to America to my second eldest sister, and a month later I sailed from Antwerp, the fare coming to $55.

My second eldest sister with her husband met me at Ellis Island and they were very glad to see me, and I went to live with them in their flat in West Thirty-Fourth street. A week later I was an apprentice in a Sixth Avenue millinery store earning four dollars a week … [But] I felt that I wanted something different – more time to myself and a different way of living. I wanted more pleasure. Our house was so dull, and tho I went to Coney Island or to a Harlem picnic park with the other girls now and then, I thought I'd like a change.

So I went out to service, getting twenty-two dollars a month as a nursery governess in a family where there were three servants besides the cook.

I had three children to attend to, one four, one six and one seven years of age … I had to look after them, to play with them, to take them about and amuse them, and to teach them German – which was easy to me, because I knew so little English … I got along with these children very well and stayed with them for two years, teaching them what I knew and going out to a picnic or ball or something of that sort about once a week, for I am very fond of dancing …

I enjoyed life with this family and they seemed to like me, for they kept me till the children were ready to go to school. After them I went into another family, where there was a very old man and his son and granddaughter who was married and had two children. They had a house up on Riverside Drive, and the old man was very rich. The house was splendid and they had five carriages and ten horses, and a pair of Shetland ponies for the children. There were twelve servants, and I dined with the housekeeper and butler, of course – because we had to draw the line. I got $25 a month here and two afternoons a week, and if I wanted to go off any place in particular they let me off for it.

These people had a fine place down on Long Island to which we all went in the summer, and there I had to ramble around with the children, boating, bathing, crabbing, fishing and playing all their games. It was good fun, and I grew healthy and strong.

[Later] ... I secured another situation, this time to mind the baby of a very rich young couple. It was the first and only baby of the mistress, and so it had been spoiled till I came to take charge ... I had thought that the place would be an easy one, but I soon found out that this was a great mistake ... When I wasn't on hand they spoiled it by giving it all its own way ... This made discipline impossible, and in the end the baby was too much for me ... [A]t last my health broke down and I actually had to go to a hospital.

When I got out I stayed at my sister's for a month, and then went as a nursery governess in a family where there are three children ... I have recovered my health, but I will never again undertake to manage a strange baby ...

Wherever I have been employed here the food has always been excellent; in fact, precisely the same as that furnished to the employers' families. In Germany it is not so. Servants are all put on an allowance, and their food is very different from that given to their masters.

I like this country. I have a great many friends in New York and I enjoy my outings with them. We go to South Beach or North Beach or Glen Island or Rockaway or Coney Island. If we go on a boat we dance all the way there and all the way back, and we dance nearly all the time we are there.

I like Coney Island best of all. It is a wonderful and beautiful place. I took a German friend, a girl who had just come out, down there last week, and when we had been on the razzle-dazzle, the chute and the loop-the-loop, and down in the coal mine and all over the Bowery, and up in the tower and everywhere else, I asked her how she liked it. She said:

"Ach, it is just like what I see when I dream of heaven."

Yet I have heard some of the high people with whom I have been living say that Coney Island is not tony. The trouble is that these high people don't know how to dance. I have to laugh when I see them at their balls and parties. If only I could get out on the floor and show them how – they would be astonished.

Two years ago, when I was with a friend at Rockaway Beach, I was introduced to a young man who has since asked me to marry him. He is a German from the Rhine country, and has been ten years in this country ... I don't want to get married yet, because when a girl marries she can't have so much fun – or rather, she can't go about with more than one young man ... A good looking girl can have a fine time when she is single, but if she stays single too long she loses her good looks, and then no one will marry her ... I think that I won't wait any longer. Some married women enjoy life almost as much as the young girls.

Herman is the assistant in a large grocery store. He has been there nine years, and knows all the customers. He has money saved, too, and soon will go into business for himself.

And then, again, I like him, because I think he's the best dancer I ever saw.

Source: "The True Life Story of a Nurse Girl by Agnes M.," *New York Independent*, September 24, 1903, pp. 2261–2266.

3 A Columnist Describes the Pleasures and Perils of Coney Island, 1915

Art critic and journalist James Huneker did not like the changes that had come to Coney Island, New York. For decades its beach towns had been a resort destination for affluent tourists seeking to escape Manhattan, nine miles to the east. But the new importance and profitability of commercial amusement venues (thanks in part to the success of the Chicago World's Fair), the growth of New York's immigrant population, and a series of fires that cleared much of West Brighton in 1893 and 1895 opened the way for Coney Island's rapid reinvention. Rebuilt as a series of amusement parks – Sea Lion Park, Steeplechase Park, Luna Park, and Dreamland – it became a bustling meeting place for recreation and consumption, one that challenged Victorian standards of appropriate conduct and leisure. Affluent urbanites and planners in the City Beautiful movement associated leisure time with visits to libraries, public monuments, and public parks. By contrast, Coney Island was the kind of place where Agnes M. and Sadie Frowne went to dance (sources 5.2 and 4.1).

The beach was one appeal of the new Coney Island, but it also offered food vendors, a carnival atmosphere, and attractions including vaudeville, games, circus performers, concerts, and mechanized amusement rides. Along with other popular parks such as the Chutes in San Francisco, Euclid Beach in Cleveland, and Paragon Park in Boston, Coney Island was both symbol and artifact of a mass consumer culture that was revolutionizing leisure in the United States. It attracted a broad range of visitors – working class and middle class, white and black, new immigrant and old. Many came simply to experience this mass of humanity: literally thousands of people congregating to relax and have fun. But the mix of peoples made many New Yorkers uncomfortable. Huneker's critique reveals the preferences of elites who lamented the democratization of public spaces, and with it the decline of "genteel" leisure traditions. Nonetheless, his lively reporting offers a vivid account of what people actually did when they visited Coney Island. Why did people like Huneker, as he writes, not "understand … the lure of the Island for the people who come?"

BY DAY

It was a poster that sent me to Coney Island again, although I had sworn never to tread again that avenue of hideous sights and sounds, had taken a solemn oath to that effect years ago. But that poster! Ah! If these advertising men only knew how their signs and symbols arouse human passions they would be more prudent in giving artists full swing with their suggestion-breeding brushes. This is what I saw on the poster: A tall, energetic band conductor waving his baton over a succulent symphony of crabs, lobsters, fruit, fish, corn, cantaloupes, clams, and water-melons – truly a pretty combination, for the overtones are Afro-American, the undertones Asiatic cholera. Nevertheless, an appealing orchestra to palates jaded by city restaurant fare and hot, humid streets. I was in haste to be off ... I must take the boat at once ...

As I first recall Coney Island, one could walk on a wide, clean, shining space of sand from the Point to the Oriental Hotel ... [But now,] from where the Brighton bathing pavilion stands, down as far as Ravenhall's, is the craziest collection of tumble-down hovels – you can't dignify them with any other term – that ever disgraced a beautiful sea-view ... I do cling to my belief that if the whole horrible aggregation of shanties, low resorts, shacks masquerading as hotels, and the rest were swept off the earth by some beneficent visitation of Providence, the thanksgivings of the community would be in order ...

But the people, the poor people! Must they be deprived of their day's outing, of the innocent, idiotic joys of dear, dear old Coney? ...

I know that you can't make the public enjoy the more refined pleasures of a beach free from vulgarity and rapacious beach-combers, male and female, unless it so wishes. Even mules will not drink unless thirsty ... In a word, it is not a question of restriction but of regulation; decency, good taste, and semibarbarism should not be allowed to go unchecked. Coney Island today, despite the efficiency of the police, is a disgrace to our civilization. It should be abolished and something else substituted.

And now, having abolished the eyesore by a mere waving of my wish-wand, let me tell you of the joys I experienced after I had landed at the Steeplechase Park pier in company with some hundreds of fellow lunatics of all ages and conditions, for when you are at Coney you cast aside your hampering reason and become a plain lunatic ...

The fisherman sits line in hand as we pass; a sign informs that there are twenty-five thousand bathing-suits to hire, and we listlessly gaze at the hulk of the only American vessel captured in the war with Spain. The bakers arouse us. We buy a string of parti-coloured tickets. They are so many keys that unlock to us the magic chambers of this paradise of secular jobs and terrors. You may swim or guzzle; on the hard backs of iron steeds, to the accompaniment of bedlam music, you may caracole or go plunging down perilous declivities, swinging into the gloom of sinister tunnels or, perched aloft, be the envy of small boys.

There is an Italian garden where basket parties are forbidden – the only spot in the establishment – and a vast hall where, as if practicing the attitudes and steps of some strange religious cult, youths and maidens indulge in simian gestures and in native buffoonery. Food, mountains of it, is cooking. The odour ascends to the stars; but you forget as in a monster wheel human beings are swung in a giant circle. Coasting parties clatter by or else are shot down a chute into irritated water. Every device imaginable by which man may be separated from his dimes without adequate return is in operation. You weigh yourself or get it guessed; you go into funny houses – oh, the mockery of the title! – and later are tumbled into the open, insulted, mortified, disgusted, angry, and – laughing. What sights you have seen in that prison-house, what gentlewomen – with shrill voices – desperately holding on to their skirts and their chewing gum.

What I can't understand is the lure of the Island for the people who come. Why, after the hot, narrow, noisy, dirty streets of the city, do these same people crowd in to the narrower, hotter, noisier, dirtier, wooden alleys of Coney? … They leave dirt and disorder to go to greater disorder and dirt. The sky is bluer, but they don't look at the sky; clam chowder is a more agreeable spectacle; and the smacking of a thousand lips as throats gurgle with the suspicious compound is welcome to the ears of them that pocket the cash.

… If I rail at the plague spot, Coney Island, it with the hope that some day it will vanish and be succeeded by pleasant parks, trees, sea-walls, and stone walks. This madland of lunatics, who must go up in the air, down in the earth, who must have clatter and dirt, might be relegated elsewither. Certainly people don't go to Coney for the sea or the air or the view …

But if you want to experience the "emotion of multitude," there is no spot on earth for the purpose like Coney Island.

AT NIGHT

… In Dreamland there is a white tower that might rear itself in Seville and cause no comment. (This was so before fire destroyed the place.) Hemming it about are walls of monstrosities – laughable, shocking, sinister, and desperately depressing. In the center flying boats cleave the air; from the top of a crimson lighthouse flat, sled-like barges plunge down a liquid railroad, while from every cavern issue screams of tortured and delighted humans and the hoarse barking of men with megaphones. They assault your ears with their invitations, protestations, and blasphemies. You are conjured to "go to Hell – gate"; you are singled out by some brawny individual with threatening intonations and bade enter the animal show where a lion or a tiger is warranted to claw a keeper at least once a day. The glare is appalling, the sky a metallic blue, the sun a slayer.

And then the innumerable distractions of the animated walks, the dwarfs and the dogs, the horses and the miniature railway. Inside the various buildings you may see the cosmos in the act of formation, or San Francisco destroyed by fire and quake; the end of life, organic and inorganic, is displayed for a modest pittance; you may sleigh in Switzerland or take a lulling ride in Venetian gondolas. But nothing is real. Doubtless the crowd would be disappointed by a glimpse of the real Venice, the real Switzerland, the real hell, the real heaven. Everything is the reflection of a cracked mirror held in the hand of the clever showman ...

At ten o'clock the crowds had not abated. Noise still reigned over the Bowery, and the cafes, restaurants, dens, and shows were full of gabbling, eating, drinking, cursing, and laughing folk. I had intended to return either to my hotel or to New York, but the heat pinioned my will. In company with thousands, I strolled the beach near the Boulevard. An amiable policeman told me that few people would go back to the city, that, hot as it was at Coney, the East Side was more stifling. The sight of cars coming down crowded at eleven o'clock and returning half-full at midnight determined my plan of action ...

... All the lights of the pleasure palaces were extinguished. Across at Riccadonna's there was still a light, and peering over the Brighton pavilion there was a pillar of luminosity that looked a cross between a corn-cob and a thermometer afire. I sat down on the sand. I would stay out the night. And then I began to look about me. In Hyde Park, London, I had seen hundreds of vagabonds huddled in the grass, their clothes mere rags, their attitudes those of death, but nothing in England or America can match what I saw this particular night. While the poorer classes predominated, there was little suggestion of abject pauperism. Many seemed gay. The white dresses of the women and children relieved the somber masses of black men, who, though coatless for the most part, made black splotches on the sand. In serried array they lay; there was no order in their position, yet a short distance away they gave the impression of an army at rest. The entire beach was thick with humanity. At close range it resolved itself in groups, sweethearts in pairs, families of three or four, six or seven, planted close together. With care, hesitation, and difficulty I navigated around these islets of flesh and blood. Sometimes I stumbled over a foot or an arm. Once I kicked a head, and I was cursed many times and vigorously cursed. But I persisted. Like the "white mice," I was there to see. Policemen plodded through the crowds, and if there was undue hilarity warned the offenders in a low voice. But it was impossible for such a large body of people to be more orderly, more decent. I determined to prowl down the lower beach, between the Boulevard and Sea Gate.

My sporting instinct came to the surface. Here was game. Not in the immemorial mob, joking and snoring, shrieking and buzzing, would I find what I sought. I tried to pass under the bathing-houses, but so densely packed were the paths that I was threatened by a dozen harsh voices. So I pursued a safer way, down Surf Avenue. It was still filled with people – men and women, battered, bleary, drunk or tired, dragged their weary paces, regarding each other as do wolves, ready to spring. We all felt like sticky August salt. Reaching the beach again, I was too fatigued to walk farther. I propped my head against the wooden pillar of an old bath-house and my eyes began to droop. I heard without a quiver of interest the sudden scream of a woman followed by ominous bass laughter. Some one plucked a banjo. Dogs barked. A hymn rose on the hot air. Around me it was like a battle-field of the slain. A curious drone was in the air; it was the monster breathing. A muggy moon shone intermittently over us, its bleached rays painting in one ghastly tone the upturned faces of the sleepers. The stale, sour, rank smell of wretched mankind poisoned the atmosphere, thick with sultry vapors. I wished myself home.

Source: James Huneker, "Coney Island ... By Day" and "Coney Island ... At Night," from *New Cosmopolis: A Book of Images* (New York: Charles Scribner's Sons, 1915), pp. 149, 152–154, 155–157, 158–159, 163–164, 166.

4 A *Harper's Weekly* Columnist Worries about Garbage, 1891

The nation's fast-growing cities were dirty places. Disposing of refuse has always posed challenges in urbanized areas, but the industrial revolution compounded the problem by introducing new kinds of waste while concentrating both production and people geographically. Ash from burnt wood and coal, the latter important by the 1880s for industrial uses and home heating, literally blanketed cities. Local industries added unique problems, such as smoke in iron and steel regions or animal waste near slaughterhouses. Meanwhile, each of the 3.5 million horses in American cities produced 15 to 35 pounds of manure daily, most of which ended up in the streets. Thousands of dead horses were removed from city streets annually, while food waste was constantly scavenged by stray animals. Such conditions were especially hard on the poor, who lived and worked in overcrowded buildings and neighborhoods, with no means of escape from polluted water supplies and landscapes, ubiquitous smoke and fumes, and the ever present garbage. One result was serious health problems and high mortality rates for working-class families, punctuated by occasional outbreaks of infectious disease.

Beginning in the 1870s, municipal authorities began to tackle the problems of water provision and sewage, and efforts to combat smoke and other pollutants followed. But not until the late 1890s did innovation and a municipal commitment to comprehensive waste management strategies begin to address the problem effectively. One key was municipal ownership of utilities and provision of services traditionally handled on a voluntary basis or paid for by private interests. Yet there was no consensus that public authorities ought to shoulder this responsibility. The debate over who was responsible for keeping the industrial metropolis clean was often colored, meanwhile, by elites' discomfort with the immigrant populations that were working in the factories and filling the streets (sources 3.5; 4.1; and 5.3). How does this Harper's Weekly *journalist view the relationship between the practical challenge of keeping cities clean and the other variables that caused urban congestion and made garbage such a problem?*

... [M]unicipal government ... differs from national government in that the objects to which it addresses itself are much more direct and practical. They come home closely to a man's heart and hearth stone, to his daily health and comfort, and they closely affect the surroundings made up of a multiplicity of little things in which, after all, his happiness consists. Yet, strange to say, the average American is more interested in the tariff issue ... than he permits himself to be ... in adequate methods for keeping such cities as New York, Boston, and Chicago in a clean and healthy condition.

... The merchant, intent on reaching his office, cares not a wit if some handcart vendor empties a load of rotten fruit or vegetables into the public thoroughfare, or a house-maid discharges a pailful of slop or garbage under his very nose. Wealthy shopkeepers permit their clerks and porters to sweep a day's accumulation of litter and dirt into the street gutter, which is straightaway blown about the street ... It is owing to the utter limpness of public feeling that municipal action is not more efficient.

... According to testimony of foreigners and Americans alike, the leading cities of this country do not compare favorably in street-cleaning methods and results with the corresponding cities in France, England, and Germany. In Holland, Belgium, and Sweden civic cleanliness is carried to a higher degree than in any other part of Europe, but the cities are very much smaller in extent and population ... Neither are there large foreign colonies, with alien and unsympathetic habits, to complicate the problem of keeping a city clean ...

In this country it is not easy to decide which of the great cities is the most filthy ... New York ... Chicago ... Philadelphia ... St. Louis ... all these rivals for the palm of uncleanliness are vile enough and much worse than they ought to be ... [But] as New York is the biggest in everything ... it is fairly safe to conclude, for the purposes of this article, that she easily surpasses her would-be competition in dirt. She certainly has the largest foreign population among the cities of the land. This fact alone suffices to ensure prominence for filthy streets and tenement houses ... The writer of this article was recently driven through the Italian quarter by a city official on a tour of inspection. The Italian peasant who in the United States blossoms into the organ-grinder, the rag picker, and the railroad [navigator] is probably the dirtiest human animal extant this side the Australian bush ... A city filled with such denizens, and their nearest rivals, Russian or Polish Jews or Bohemians, could only be properly cleansed as Hercules cleansed the Augean stables, or as Carlyle proposed to cure the evils of Ireland by burying it deep under the Atlantic. Who can adequately photograph Mulberry Street, the woes of which, from the street cleaning point of view ... would soon turn gray the hair of any commissioner?

This district is as picturesque as it is foul and unhealthy. The day before it was seen by the writer it had been flushed with water, and thoroughly scrubbed by the sweeping machine. Twenty-four hours had again made it a human pigpen. The pavement was covered with a thick coating of what seemed like grease. A profuse litter of orange and banana peel, withered cabbage leaves, vegetables in different stages of decomposition, and various garbage was scattered all over the street. The intense heat of the day had emptied the tenements, and the population lined the sidewalk ... Nearly all the multitudinous babies were naked, and the mothers, almost nude, suckled their young with the unconcern of the bitch feeding a litter of puppies. A barricade of handcarts on either side made the street a narrow strait, and swarthy men lounged about smoking lazy pipes ... [The] doorways and casements of every house were stained almost to ink with the accretion of smut and pollution coming from foul bodies, foul air, and foul insects ...

... Street-cleaning was not very practicable on a large scale until an adequate system of street paving came into vogue ... [and] it was not until the early days of the present century that systematic and careful paving of streets on a great scale began to be practiced ... In great cities the problem of economical and efficient cleansing must necessarily enter into the *pros* and *cons* of paving methods. Aside from greater durability, ease of traction, and economy of maintenance, granite blocks, asphalt, and wooden blocks have proved to be the most desirable for ends of cleanliness ... When, however, we look at the question of maintenance, ... anyone who uses his eyesight can reach only one conclusion. The pavement after some years becomes filled with ruts and holes, resembling a honey-comb but not full of honey. These, instead of being constantly repaired, are for the most part ignored. The Board of Public Works disdains patchwork ... How any street-cleaning machinery can keep such thoroughfares clean is difficult to see.

... The topographical conditions of Manhattan Island ... are favorable to good drainage ... Other things being equal, New York should be the best sewered and the cleanest of cities. This is precisely what the city is not ... Let us then look at the main causes which conduce to make this city the pigpen that it is, and at those that operate to interfere with the effective work of cleansing the pigpen. The desirable reforms are diminuation of the causes which make dirt, and perfecting the agencies which remove it. Both of these easily lie within the grasp of the people of New York or of that intelligent public opinion which is the force behind administration.

The dirt-producing causes common to all cities exist in excess in New York in three out of four principal classes. These are horse droppings; dirt forced up from the substratum through crevices in the pavement; and the overflow of house and shop refuse in the street ... First, horse droppings. This material, valuable is manure if collected at once, is rapidly ground to powder under the friction of wheel and hoof. It thus adds an offensive element to the body of the street dirt, or, flying in the air, becomes a dangerous fact in the sanitary sense. All commercial use is destroyed by lack of care in gathering it promptly ... There are probably not less than 10,000 horses in the city of New York, and at least half of their excrement is deposited in the public thoroughfares ... Secondly, as to the dirt forced upward through the joints of pavement by various causes ... The tendency of the subsoil to work up ... accounts for a large portion of the street dirt, except in the case of asphalt pavement. Of course the more careless the paving, the greater the uprisal of earth from below it. Again, pavement is rarely patched or mended except in a most desultory way ... Innumerable breaks, ruts, and holes tend to make and hold the dirt. The streetcar system, so universal in American cities, aggravates the problem. The centre and side-bearing rails in general use offer irresistible temptation to the truckman to utilize the car track for his inner wheel. So heavy traffic, instead of being spread over the street with an equal wear, hollows out gutters in the pavement. Another equally potent cause operating under New York methods to destroy the efficiency of pavement comes of the recklessness in granting permits to all manner of companies to tear up the streets for private purposes ... True is it that the companies are presumed to restore the pavement under inspection of city officers. But the latter appears to be the merest farce. So shameless and wretched is the result that it is a standing joke among pedestrians, unless it is viewed in a different light and demonstrated as an audacious swindle ...

The third cause mentioned ... is no less plain to the observer. Even vigilant house-keepers sometimes have difficulty in preventing their servants from depositing illegal matter in the street. But in the tenement house districts ... there seems to be an utter lack of conscience on the subject, an utter ignorance of or indifference to the requirements of municipal statutes ... Not only households of the lower class, but shopkeepers both up and down town, in Broadway as well as on the less important streets, have been in the habit of emptying much of their refuse into the gutters of the streets. Again, the utter lack of proper equipment on the part of the street cleaning bureau causes a percentage of the contents of the ash carts to be deposited prematurely ... [The] vans are mostly uncovered, and they generally leave a wake of ashes and other waste in their track ...

Until 1880 this important work was included within the jurisdiction of the police. A separate department was then organized, in the hope that the time honored inefficiency would be removed by concentrating authority and responsibility. There have been three commissioners since the bureau was established, one of whome was *so* discouraged by the difficulties of his task that he resigned after a few weeks of struggle ... The department owns 94 carts out of 406 in daily use, the remainder being furnished by contractors, and not ten per cent of these are worth much except for firewood and old junk. There are 58 sweeping machines ... [most of them] battered veterans, which do their work in limping fashion.

The appropriation for the expenses of the department is made by the Board of Estimate and Apportionment, each item being rigidly fixed by these pundits, the most of whom probably know but little of the real exigencies of street cleaning ... A deficiency in one category cannot be supplied from the surplus in another ...

... A careful survey of the streets of New York makes it tolerably clear that to keep them measureably clean requires a daily sweeping of every square yard of paved area, involving the use of at least double the number of machines of the most improved type, and more than double the number of hand sweepers. If the street department under its present methods can sweep even the main thoroughfares superficially three times a week it is accomplishing wonders. Even in this case the insufficient supply of carts and carters often causes the redistribution of rubbish before it can be removed, and the worthless carts scatter a portion of their loads before they reach the dumps.

... The contents of the carts are conveyed to the dumping places, of which there are 19, where they are placed in scows, which hold from 400 to 600 loads. There are 19 scows which require shoveling of the material by hand for the final disposition in the deep sea, and 14 self-dumpers, which drop the contents mechanically ... These barges are towed out to sea three miles from

Sandy Hook before the refuse is committed to the deep ... Unutterable abominations are sometimes found on the bathing beaches of Long Island and New Jersey ...

The whole system in New York is radically bad ... Nearly half the work is done by contractors, who have no constraining interest in doing it well. No discipline can be enforced over the men by the department which does not pay them. Contracts are given from year to year to the lowest bidder. The experience of all foreign cities, and some of our own (Boston, for example), is that street cleaning can never be well done except where the city owns its own plant *in toto*, and compels all of the employees under a system of the strictest discipline ... [where] good wages and permanence of employment depend solely on faithful work ...

Source: G. T. Ferris, "The Cleansing of Great Cities," *Harper's Weekly*, 35(1777) (January 10, 1891), pp. 33–36.

Chapter 6 Local Politics in the Gilded Age

1 George Washington Plunkitt Defends Patronage Politics in New York City, 1905

George Washington Plunkitt served as district leader – or "ward boss" – in New York City's Tammany Hall from 1880 to 1905. The urban political "machine," as Tammany and similar organizations were called, represented a local strain of an important nineteenth-century national tradition: the role of patronage, or "spoils," in cementing political coalitions and governing an increasingly complex and fractured polity. Urban patronage politics was one strategy for adapting to a practical problem: the absence of effective tools to govern cities and attend to their multiple constituencies. The machine used existing but inadequate municipal institutions in concert with powerful informal networks to create a hybrid of public and private governance. Managing urban infrastructure and providing services required a sizable public sector, which meant control over municipal jobs (about 12,000 in New York City during the 1880s) and lucrative contracts. Machines like Tammany Hall exerted enough influence at election time to put sympathetic men in positions of legislative power, and these officials, in turn, awarded jobs and contracts to party supporters. Practically speaking, ward bosses and their district or neighborhood-level representatives (called "captains") offered voters material incentives – including, famously, help with community projects or family problems – in return for their support of approved candidates.

The Modern American Metropolis: A Documentary Reader, First Edition.
Edited by David M. P. Freund.

Historians continue to debate the power, effectiveness, and implications of machine governance. In addition, each city's version of patronage operated differently, making it difficult to generalize about the tradition. But there were constants. Local immigrant populations gained political leverage or, at least, a sense of political empowerment. Powerful business interests were able to secure a foothold in the city-building process. Meanwhile the illicit flow of funds regularly enabled machine leaders – men like Plunkitt – to enrich themselves along the way. This account, excerpted from Plunkitt's extended interview with Evening Post *reporter William L. Riordin, poses special challenges. Riordin's vision of machine politics and his desire to spur public debate undoubtedly colored his rendering of the interview. The source is best seen as an amalgam of Plunkitt's experience, as he explained it, and Riordin's vision of Tammany's function in the industrial metropolis. Despite its ambiguities, the memoir raises an important question about urban politics in the Gilded Age: What was the best means of balancing public and private interest in the unwieldy, fractured, and profit-driven industrial city?*

Chapter 1 Honest Graft and Dishonest Graft

EVERYBODY is talkin' these days about Tammany men growin' rich on graft, but nobody thinks of drawin' the distinction between honest graft and dishonest graft. There's all the difference in the world between the two. Yes, many of our men have grown rich in politics. I have myself. I've made a big fortune out of the game, and I'm gettin' richer every day, but I've not gone in for dishonest graft – blackmailin' gamblers, saloonkeepers, disorderly people, etc. – and neither has any of the men who have made big fortunes in politics.

There's an honest graft, and I'm an example of how it works. I might sum up the whole thing by sayin': "I seen my opportunities and I took 'em."

Just let me explain by examples. My party's in power in the city, and it's goin' to undertake a lot of public improvements. Well, I'm tipped off, say, that they're going to lay out a new park at a certain place.

I see my opportunity and I take it. I go to that place and I buy up all the land I can in the neighborhood. Then the board of this or that makes its plan public, and there is a rush to get my land, which nobody cared particular for before.

Ain't it perfectly honest to charge a good price and make a profit on my investment and foresight? Of course, it is. Well, that's honest graft.

Or supposin' it's a new bridge they're goin' to build. I get tipped off and I buy as much property as I can that has to be taken for approaches. I sell at my own price later on and drop some more money in the bank.

Wouldn't you? It's just like lookin' ahead in Wall Street or in the coffee or cotton market. It's honest graft, and I'm lookin' for it every day in the year. I will tell you frankly that I've got a good lot of it, too …

Another kind of honest graft. Tammany has raised a good many salaries. There was an awful howl by the reformers, but don't you know that Tammany gains ten votes for every one it lost by salary raisin'?

The Wall Street banker thinks it shameful to raise a department clerk's salary from $1500 to $1800 a year, but every man who draws a salary himself says: "That's all right. I wish it was me." And he feels very much like votin' the Tammany ticket on election day, just out of sympathy …

Now, in conclusion, I want to say that I don't own a dishonest dollar. If my worst enemy was given the job of writin' my epitaph when I'm gone, he couldn't do more than write:

"George W. Plunkitt. He Seen His Opportunities, and He Took 'Em."

Chapter 2 How to Become a Statesman

THERE'S thousands of young men in this city who will go to the polls for the first time next November. Among them will be many who have watched the careers of successful men in politics, and who are longin' to make names and fortunes for themselves at the same game – It is to these youths that I want to give advice …

… Some young men think they can learn how to be successful in politics from books, and they cram their heads with all sorts of college rot. They couldn't make a bigger mistake. Now, understand me I ain't sayin' nothin' against colleges. I guess they'll have to exist as long as there's book-worms, and I suppose they do some good in a certain way, but they don't count in politics. In fact, a young man who has gone through the college course is handicapped at the outset. He may succeed in politics, but the chances are 100 to 1 against him.

Another mistake: some young men think that the best way to prepare for the political game is to practice speakin' and becomin' orators. That's all wrong. We've got some orators in Tammany Hall, but they're chiefly ornamental. You never heard of Charlie Murphy delivering a speech, did you? Or Richard Croker, or John Kelly, or any other man who has been a real power in the organization? Look at the thirty-six district leaders of Tammany Hall today. How many of them travel on their tongues? Maybe one or two, and they don't count when business is doin' at Tammany Hall …

Now, I've told you what not to do; I guess I can explain best what to do to succeed in politics by tellin' you what I did. After goin' through the apprenticeship of the business while I was a boy by workin' around the district headquarters and hustlin' about the polls on election day, I set out when I cast my first vote to win fame and money in New York City politics. Did I offer my services to the district leader as a stump-speaker? Not much. The woods are always full of speakers. Did I get up a hook on municipal government and show it to the leader? I wasn't such a fool. What I did was to get some marketable goods before goin' to the leaders. What do I mean by marketable goods? Let me tell you: I had a cousin, a young man who didn't take any particular interest in politics. I went to him and said: "Tommy, I'm goin' to be a politician, and I want to get a followin'; can I count on you?" He said: "Sure, George." That's how I started in business. I got a marketable commodity – one vote. Then I went to the district leader and told him I could command two votes on election day, Tommy's and my own. He smiled on me and told me to go ahead ... I soon branched out. Two young men in the flat next to mine were school friends – I went to them, just as I went to Tommy, and they agreed to stand by me. Then I had a followin' of three voters ... And so it went on like a snowball rollin' down a hill. I worked the flat-house that I lived in from the basement to the top floor, and I got about a dozen young men to follow me. Then I tackled the next house and so on down the block and around the corner. Before long I had sixty men back of me, and formed the George Washington Plunkitt Association.

What did the district leader say then when I called at headquarters? I didn't have to call at headquarters. He came after me and said: "George, what do you want? If you don't see what you want, ask for it. Wouldn't you like to have a job or two in the departments for your friends?" ... As time went on, and my association grew, I thought I would like to go to the Assembly. I just had to hint at what I wanted, and three different organizations offered me the nomination. Afterwards, I went to the Board of Aldermen, then to the State Senate, then became leader of the district, and so on up and up till I became a statesman ...

Chapter 3 The Curse of Civil Service Reform

This civil service law is the biggest fraud of the age. It is the curse of the nation. There can't be no real patriotism while it lasts. How are you goin' to interest our young men in their country if you have no offices to give them when they work for their party? Just look at things in this city today. There are ten thousand good offices, but we can't get at more than a few hundred of them. How are we goin' to provide for the thousands of men who worked for the Tammany ticket? It can't be done. These men were full of patriotism a short time ago. They expected to be servin' their city, but when we tell them that we can't place them, do you think their patriotism is goin' to last?

Not much. They say: "What's the use of workin' for your country anyhow? There's nothin' in the game." And what can they do? I don't know, but I'll tell you what I do know. I know more than one young man in past years who worked for the ticket and was just overflowin' with patriotism, but when he was knocked out by the civil service humbug he got to hate his country and became an Anarchist.

... There was once a bright young man in my district who tackled one of these examinations. The next I heard of him he had settled down in Herr Most's saloon smokin' and drinkin' beer and talkin' socialism all day ... And just to think! He might be a patriot but for that cussed civil service.

... What did the people mean when they voted for Tammany? What is representative government, anyhow? Is it all a fake that this is a government of the people, by the people and for the people? If it isn't a fake, then why isn't the people's voice obeyed and Tammany men put in all the offices?

When the people elected Tammany, they knew just what they were doin'. We didn't put up any false pretenses. We didn't go in for humbug civil service and all that rot. We stood as we have always stood, for reward – in the men that won the victory. They call that the spoils system. All right; Tammany is for the spoils system, and when we go in we fire every anti-Tammany man from office that can be fired under the law ...

... This is an awful serious proposition. Free silver and the tariff and imperialism and the Panama Canal are triflin' issues when compared to it.

... First, this great and glorious country was built up by political parties; second, parties can't hold together if their workers don't get the offices when they win; third, if the parties go to pieces, the government they built up must go to pieces ... Now, what is goin' to happen when civil service crushes out patriotism? Only one thing can happen: the republic will go to pieces. Then a czar or a sultan will turn up, which brings me to the fourthly of my argument – that is, there will be h— to pay. And that ain't no lie.

Source: William L. Riordin, *Plunkitt of Tammany Hall: A Series of Very Plain Talks on Very Practical Politics*, edited with an introduction by Terrence J. McDonald (Boston: Bedford Books of St. Martin's Press, 1994), pp. 64–66.

2 Dallas City Commissioner Advocates Running a City Like a Business, 1909

When the voters of Dallas, Texas, adopted the commission form of city government in 1907, they joined a wave of urban political reform aimed at curbing what were viewed as the corruption and inefficiency of urban political machines, the political organizations that helped keep many mayors, most of them Democrats, in office in the late nineteenth and early twentieth centuries (source 6.1). Self-described "reformers," usually middle- or upper-class businesspeople and professionals, mobilized in dozens of cities to replace ward-based electoral systems with at-large elections that used nonpartisan ballots. In most cases this diluted the power of the geographically concentrated working-class and immigrant voters who tended to support local machine government. Many historians criticize reformers for their pro-business, anti-labor, and anti-immigrant stance, but most reformers saw themselves as proponents of professional, nonpartisan, and efficient city management. Founded in 1894, the National Municipal League promoted versions of the reform model nationwide by encouraging municipalities to adopt a commission, strong mayor, or city manager form of government. The stated goal was to remove the "politics" from municipal administration.

Every city's history is different and its politicians face unique challenges. In Dallas, for example, the reform movement was spurred in part by local businessmen's desire to fend off labor activists on the left and a resurgent Ku Klux Klan on the right. Nevertheless, when the city's commissioner of revenue and finance, C. B. Gillespie, spoke before an audience of New York businessmen in 1909, he succinctly captured reformers' belief that efficiency was the most appropriate measure of good urban governance. Consider this excerpt in light of other Texans' experiences of urban and small-town life during these years, such as those documented in source 4.2. More generally, how did reformers' views of urban management differ from those of machine politicians? What trade-offs might result from a turn to citywide, nonpartisan elections? And, given reformers' stated goal of rising above partisan interests, was there nonetheless a politics to their vision?

In the two years' experience of Dallas, under the commission form of government, many miles of streets have been substantially paved; the enforcement of sidewalk construction is general throughout the city; four new parks have been acquired, numerous public buildings have been erected, extensive additions to the waterworks system are under way, and many reforms have been brought about; among which was the reduction of the city's street lighting from $73 per arc light per year to $60. In a financial way the city has shown a decided improvement. Its books are maintained up to date in every respect and the status of any fund or account can be ascertained at any hour as easily as a bank can show a depositor's balance. New methods and systems have been invoked, daily itemized reports of all collections are required, together with a deposit daily with the treasurer of all funds collected, all of which is followed by regularly systematic checking of all departments. The city of Dallas operates thirty-three departments under what is known as its general fund, and which does not include the school, park, library, water and sewerage, street improvement, and interest in sinking funds. Of May 1, 1907, one month before the present board of commissioners assumed control, the general fund of the city was overdrawn $122,575.27, which was the result of two acts of the former council administration ... During the two years ending May 1, 1909, [by contrast,] the board of commissioners maintained those departments at a net saving under the cost of the former administration, and by enforcing the collection of all revenues it was enabled to liquidate the above overdraft and close the fiscal year with a credit balance in its general fund of $10,290.02.

The affairs of the city are treated as a business proposition, and are handled about the same as a bank's directory would manage its affairs, and during the two and a fraction years of the Dallas board of commissioners no disruption of any kind has occurred. Nor has a single speech been made by the mayor or any members of the board at any of its meetings.

Source: C. B. Gillespie, September 30, 1909; quoted in Ford H. McGregor, *City Government by Commission: Bulletin of the University of Wisconsin* (Madison, WI), 423 (1911), pp. 93–94.

3 Jane Addams Describes the Goals of Hull House, 1893

In 1889 Jane Addams and Ellen Gates Starr founded Hull House, a resource center in southwestern Chicago modeled on European "social settlements." Addams grew up in an affluent household in Cedarville, Illinois, and attended college at Rockford Female Seminary, where she befriended Starr, the daughter of a farmer and small businessman. After visiting London's Toynbee Hall in 1887, they opened Hull House to promote the settlement house movement in the United States. The facility provided services for the city's working-class immigrants, ranging from literature classes and concerts to day-care services and assistance with union meetings. Hull House was the most prominent American settlement and an influential symbol of Progressive era reform, for which Addams quickly emerged as a prominent spokesperson. Excerpted here are two of Addams's lectures on Hull House and the settlement house movement, first presented in 1892.

Addams's talks provide insight into many people's experience of the industrial metropolis. While detailing some of the practical resources that Hull House provided for neighborhood residents, she identifies many of the variables that made the lives of urban wage workers and their families so difficult. In discussing her work with and for disadvantaged Americans, Addams articulates the views of privileged, college-educated white women who had professional aspirations but faced considerable obstacles to pursuing their career of choice (source 4.4). In institutions such as Hull House these women carved out a professional niche in which their skills and views would not be dismissed or constantly challenged by middle-class men. Finally, Addams's analysis of urban life and the origins of poverty should be viewed in light of the experiences and analyses of her metropolitan contemporaries. Would the immigrants who benefited from Hull House's resources necessarily agree with all of her conclusions about the obstacles facing the urban poor? (Consider sources 4.1–3; 5.1–4; and 6.1, 4.) How might members of Tammany Hall or municipal government reformers respond to Addams's approach (sources 6.1–2)? Addams would later describe settlement houses as "an experimental effort to aid in the solution of the social and industrial problems which are engendered by the modern conditions of life in a great city." How did Hull House's interventions address these problems and was this strategy sufficient?

The Subjective Necessity of a Social Settlement

Hull House ... was opened by two women, backed by many friends, in the belief that the mere foothold of a house, easily accessible, ample in space, hospitable and tolerant in spirit, situated in the midst of the large foreign colonies which so easily isolate themselves in American cities, would be in itself a serviceable thing for Chicago. Hull House endeavors to make social intercourse express the growing sense of the economic unity of society ... It was opened on the theory that the dependence of classes on each other is reciprocal ...

It is not difficult to see that although America is pledged to the democratic ideal, the view of democracy has been partial ... We conscientiously followed the gift of the ballot hard upon the gift of freedom to the negro, but we are quite unmoved by the fact that he lives among us in a practical social ostracism. We hasten to give the franchise to the immigrant from a sense of justice, from a tradition that he ought to have it, while we dub him with epithets deriding his past life or present occupation, and feel no duty to invite him to our houses ... There are city wards in which many of the votes are sold for drinks and dollars; still there is a remote pretence, at least a fiction current, that a man's vote is his own ...

... The social organism has broken down through large districts of our great cities. Many of the people living there are very poor, the majority of them without leisure or energy for anything but the gain of subsistence. They move often from one wretched lodging to another. They live for the moment side by side, many of them without knowledge of each other, without fellowship, without local tradition or public spirit, without social organization of any kind ... [W]orkingmen are not organized socially; although living in crowded tenement-houses, they are living without a corresponding social contact ... The desire for higher social pleasure is extinct. They have no share in the traditions and social energy which make for progress ...

... [I]f in a democratic country nothing can he permanently achieved save through the masses of the people, it will be impossible to establish a higher political life than the people themselves crave ... [T]he blessings which we associate with a life of refinement and cultivation can be made universal and must be made universal if they are to be permanent ... [T]he good we secure for ourselves is precarious and uncertain ... until it is secured for all of us and incorporated into our common life.

... The public schools in the poorest and most crowded wards of the city are inadequate to the number of children, and many of the teachers are ill-prepared and overworked; but in each ward there is an effort to secure public education. The schoolhouse itself stands as a pledge that the city recognizes and endeavors to fulfil the duty of educating its children. But what becomes of these children when they are no longer in public schools? Many of them never come under the influence of a professional teacher nor a cultivated friend after they are twelve. Society at large does little for their intellectual development ...

... [I]t would, I think, be unfair to Hull House not to emphasize the conviction with which the first residents went there ...; [to] live with opposition to no man, with recognition of the good in every man, even the meanest, I believe that this turning, this renaissance of the early Christian humanitarianism, is going on in America ... Certain it is that spiritual force is found in the Settlement movement, and it is also true that this force must be evoked and must be called into play before the success of any Settlement is assured ...

The Objective Value of a Social Settlement

... Hull House stands on South Halsted Street, next door to the corner of Polk. South Halsted Street is thirty-two miles long and one of the great thoroughfares of Chicago. Polk Street crosses Halsted midway between the stock-yards to the south and the ship-building yards on the north branch of the Chicago River. For the six miles between these two industries the street is lined with shops of butchers and grocers, with dingy and gorgeous saloons, and pretentious establishments for the sale of ready-made clothing. Polk Street, running west from Halsted Street, grows rapidly more respectable; running a mile east to State Street, it grows steadily worse, and crosses a net-work of gilded vice on the corners of Clark Street and Fourth Avenue.

Hull House is an ample old residence, well built and somewhat ornately decorated after the manner of its time, 1856 ... It once stood in the suburbs, but the city has steadily grown up around it and its site now has corners on three or four more or less distinct foreign colonies. Between Halsted Street and the river live about ten thousand Italians: Neopolitans, Sicilians, and Calabrians, with an occasional Lombard or Venetian. To the south on Twelfth Street are many Germans, and side streets are given over almost entirely to Polish and Russian Jews. Still farther south, these Jewish colonies merge into a huge Bohemian colony, so vast that Chicago ranks as the third Bohemian city in the world. To the northwest are many Canadian-French, clannish in spite of their long residence in America, and to the north are many Irish and first-generation Americans. On the streets directly west and farther north are well-to-do English-speaking families, many of whom own their houses and have lived in the neighborhood for years ... This corner of Polk and Halsted Streets is in the fourteenth precinct of the nineteenth ward ... It has had no unusual political scandal connected with it, but its aldermen are generally saloon-keepers and its political manipulations are those to be found in the crowded wards where the activities of the petty politicians are unchecked.

The policy of the public authorities of never taking an initiative, and always waiting to be urged to do their duty, is fatal in a ward where there is no initiative among the citizens. The idea underlying our self-government breaks down in such a ward. The streets are inexpressibly dirty, the number of schools inadequate, factory legislation unenforced, the street-lighting bad, the paving miserable and altogether lacking in the alleys and smaller streets, and the stables defy all laws of sanitation. Hundreds of houses are unconnected with the street sewer. The older and richer inhabitants seem anxious to move away as rapidly as they can afford it. They make room for newly arrived immigrants who are densely ignorant of civic duties. This substitution of the older inhabitants is accomplished industrially also in the south and east quarters of the ward. The Hebrews and Italians do the finishing for the great clothing-manufacturers formerly done by Americans, Irish, and Germans, who refused to submit to the extremely low prices to which the sweating system has reduced their successors. As the design of the sweating system is the elimination of rent from the manufacture of clothing, the "outside work" is begun after the clothing leaves the cutter. An unscrupulous contractor regards no basement as too dark, no stable loft too foul, no rear shanty too provisional, no tenement room too small for his workroom, as these conditions imply low rental. Hence these shops abound in the worst of the foreign districts, where the sweater easily finds his cheap basement and his home finishers. There is a constant tendency to employ school-children, as much of the home and shop work can easily be done by children.

The houses of the ward, for the most part wooden, were originally built for one family and are now occupied by several … There are few huge and foul tenements … Back tenements flourish; many houses have no water supply save the faucet in the back yard; there are no fire escapes; the garbage and ashes are placed in wooden boxes which are fastened to the street pavements. One of the most discouraging features about the present system of tenement houses is that many are owned by sordid and ignorant immigrants. The theory that wealth brings responsibility, that possession entails at length education and refinement, in these cases fails utterly. The children of an Italian immigrant owner do not go to school and are no improvement on their parents. His wife picks rags from the street gutter, and laboriously sorts them in a dingy court. Wealth may do something for her self-complacency and feeling of consequence; it certainly does nothing for her comfort or her children's improvement or for the cleanliness of any one concerned. Another thing that prevents better houses in Chicago is the tentative attitude of the real-estate men. Many unsavory conditions are allowed to continue which would be regarded with horror if they were considered permanent …

Our ward contains two hundred and fifty-five saloons; our own precinct boasts of eight, and the one directly north of us twenty. This allows one saloon to every twenty-eight voters, and there is no doubt that the saloon is the centre of the liveliest political and social life of the ward …

A Settlement which regards social intercourse as the terms of its expression logically brings to its aid all those adjuncts which have been found by experience to free social life … The residents at Hull House find that the better in quality and taste their surroundings are, the more they contribute to the general enjoyment …

… It is an advantage that our cities are diversified by foreign colonies … There are Bohemians, Italians, Poles, Russians, Greeks, and Arabs in Chicago vainly trying to adjust their peasant life to the life of a large city, and coming in contact with only the most ignorant Americans in that city. The more of scholarship, the more of linguistic attainment, the more of beautiful surroundings a Settlement among them can command, the more it can do for them.

… To turn to the educational effort, it will be perhaps better first to describe the people who respond to it. In every neighborhood where poorer people live, because rents are supposed to be cheaper there, is an element … composed of people of former education and opportunity who have cherished ambitions and prospects, but who … come to live in a cheaper neighborhood because they lack the power of making money, because of ill health

... or for various other reasons ... In addition to these there are many young women who teach in the public schools, young men who work at various occupations, but who are bent upon self-improvement and are preparing for professions ... Literature classes until recently have been the most popular. The last winter's Shakespeare class had a regular attendance of forty. The mathematical classes have always been large and flourishing ... During the last term a class in physics, preparatory for a class in electricity, was composed largely of workmen in the Western Electric Works, which are within a few blocks of Hull House. A fee of fifty cents is charged for each course of study ...

... The industrial education of Hull House has always been somewhat limited. From the beginning we have had large and enthusiastic cooking classes ... We have also always had sewing, mending, and embroidery classes. This leads me to speak of the children who meet weekly at Hull House, whose organization is between classes and clubs. There are three hundred of them who come on three days ... A hundred Italian girls come on Monday. They sew and carry home a new garment, which becomes a pattern for the entire family. Tuesday afternoon has always been devoted to school-boys' clubs: they are practically story-telling clubs. The most popular stories are legends and tales of chivalry ... The value of these clubs, I believe, lies almost entirely in their success in arousing the higher imagination ...

... Perhaps the chief value of a Settlement to its neighborhood, certainly to the newly arrived foreigner, is its office as an information and interpretation bureau. It sometimes seems as if the business of the Settlement were that of a commission merchant. Without endowment and without capital itself, it constantly acts between the various institutions of the city and the people for whose benefit these institutions were erected. The hospitals, the county agencies, and State asylums, are often but vague rumors to the people who need them most.

... Passing by our telephone last Sunday morning, I was struck with the list of numbers hung on the wall for easy reference. They were those of the Visiting Nurses' Association; Cook County Hospital; Women's and Children's Hospital; Maxwell Street Police Station for city ambulance; Health Department, City Hall; Cook County Agent, etc. We have been on very good terms with the Hebrew Relief and Aid Society, the Children's Aid, the Humane Society, the Municipal Order League, and with the various church and national relief associations ...

The more definite humanitarian effort of Hull House has taken shape in a day nursery ... A frame cottage of six rooms across our yard has been fitted up as a *creche*. At present we receive from thirty to forty children daily ... Similar in spirit is the Hull House Diet Kitchen, in a little cottage directly back of the nursery ... We have lately opened a boarding club for working girls near Hull House on the co-operative plan. I say advisedly that we have "opened" it; the running of it is quite in the hands of the girls themselves ...

Hull House has had, I hope, a certain value to the women's trades unions of Chicago ... Four women's unions have met regularly at Hull House: the book-binders', the shoemakers', the shirtmakers', and the cloak-makers'. The last two were organized at Hull House ...

... Last May twenty girls from a knitting factory who struck because they were docked for loss of time when they were working by the piece, came directly from the factory to Hull House. They had heard that we "stood by working people." We were able to have the strike arbitrated ... We were helped in this case, as we have been in many others, by the Bureau of Justice. Its office is constantly crowded with working people who hope for redress from the law, but have no money with which to pay for it. There should be an office of this bureau in every ward; "down town" seems far away and inaccessible to the most ignorant. Hull House, in spite of itself, does a good deal of legal work. We have secured support for deserted women, insurance for bewildered widows, damages for injured operators, furniture from the clutches of the instalment store. One function of the Settlement to its neighborhood somewhat resembles that of the big brother whose mere presence on the play-ground protects the little one from bullies ...

Source: Jane Addams, "The Subjective Value of a Social Settlement" and "The Objective Value of a Social Settlement," in *Philanthropy and Social Progress: Seven Essays, Delivered Before the School of Applied Ethics at Plymouth, Massachusetts during the Session of 1892* (New York: Thomas Y. Crowell & Co., 1893), pp. 1–8, 44, 45–46, 47–48, 50–52.

4 An Economist Investigates Employers' Response to Labor Unions

Insight into the metropolitan experience can come from unexpected places. For example, to reconstruct histories of urban labor conflict, scholars have long focused on familiar sites and topics: factories, neighborhoods, contract negotiations, strikes, and violent conflicts (sources 2.3; 3.3; and 4.1–3). But less prominent or visible stories can be equally revealing, such as workers' and employers' routine and often painstaking organizing efforts to gain leverage in contests over wages, conditions, and workplace control. Excerpted here is economist Robert Franklin Hoxie's study of this comparatively mundane topic, Trade Unionism in America, *published in 1917. The book begins by tracing unions' expanding influence and workers' organizing strategies in the decades since the Civil War.*

By pooling resources and sustaining networks of activists, unions such as the Knights of Labor and the American Federation of Labor helped channel workers' discontent into effective, if often short-lived, protest. Later Hoxie turns to the response by business organizations and their frequent collaboration with state and federal authorities. In this excerpt from the chapter on employers' organizing efforts, Hoxie helps explain why business groups consistently maintained the upper hand in the era's battles over work.

Hoxie's "big picture" view of industrial conflict highlights a dynamic central to the metropolitan experience: the ever changing relationship between local, place-specific contests over rights and opportunity – regarding work, housing, access to public resources, or basic constitutional freedoms – and the larger, often national, institutions that shape those local contests. How did the private organizations and government bodies discussed here impact development in local places and the lives of their residents? The study also illustrates the value of different kinds of written accounts. We generally treat scholarly publications as "secondary" sources that capture academics' interpretations of the historical record. Yet they often provide valuable contemporary data and observations, essentially doing work comparable to journalism, as well as insight into the concerns of a scholarly community at the time. What questions and larger issues seem most important to Hoxie?

Chapter VIII Employers' Associations

The social problem of unionism cannot be understood through a study of unions alone. The unions are but one factor in a great struggle going on which involves the fundamental questions of social rights and social welfare. The other factor is the employer, especially employers organized into associations to resist the efforts of unionism. Over against the complex organizations of the workers are the equally complex and perhaps more extensive and more powerful organizations of employers. To grasp the problem fully, therefore, ... we need a knowledge of the employers' organizations created for dealing with, and especially of the militant associations organized for combating, unions – their structure, aims, principles, policies, demands, methods, and attitudes; and the conditions and events which grow out of the existence of these two great organic forces ...

Structurally and functionally the employers' associations offer a striking parallelism to the trade union organizations. In point of structure there is, paralleling the local craft or compound craft and national union of the workers, the local craft or compound craft and national employers' association. The Chicago Team Owners' Association and the National Stove

Founders' Defense Association are illustrations. As a counterpart to similar trade unions, there are local, state and national federations of employers, as, for example, the Chicago Employers' Association, the Illinois Manufacturers' Association, and the National Association of Manufacturers. Where the unions have developed an industrial type of organization, the employers have their local, district or national industrial associations. The local Newspaper Publishers' Association, the Illinois Coal Operators, and the Interstate Coal Operators are in point ... Militant employers' associations, extremely conservative and bitterly opposed to unionism, are the "revolutionary" type among employers. The Metal Trades' Association is one of this group ...

Following upon the great anthracite coal strike of 1902, which suddenly brought out the power of unionism to paralyze social activity, and the fact that unionism had grown stronger than the employers, the latter awoke to the need of better defensive organization and a great growth of radical or militant employers' associations took place. The immediate aims and policies of the employers' associations were accordingly directed to securing mutual aid in the industrial field, rigid enforcement of laws on unions through the courts whenever possible, and new legislation curbing the unions. Injunctions were increasingly sought and suits instituted against union workmen. As a later phase, special employers' associations were formed, such as the Anti-Boycott League. The purpose of this organization was to get the courts to decide that, although unions were voluntary organizations, they could be sued for damages under the Sherman Anti-Trust law as combinations in restraint of trade ... Unionism succeeds in collective bargaining only because it can threaten to strike and it can strike successfully only when there is money laid up to support members on strike. It all goes back to financial resources in the end ...

At the present time the methods of the employers' associations, more especially of the militant, may be summed up as follows:

1. Effective counter organization; employers parallel the union structure, trade against trade (local, district and national), city against city, state against state, national against national, and federation against federation.
2. Uncompromising war on the closed shop by asserting the right to hire and fire, to pay what the individual can be made to work for, and therefore to destroy uniformity and control hours, speed, and the conditions of employment generally; by continuous propaganda, conventions, meetings, literature and personal solicitations, showing the tyranny of the unions under closed shop rule, and the loss and waste in the closed shop from inefficient workers forced by the union upon employers,

from loafing on the job, restrictions on output, and on apprenticeship; showing that the union label is a detriment rather than an advantage to the employer using it; urging employers not to use goods bearing the union label, nor to patronize any concern which does; and opposing the union label on publications of any branch of government.

3. The expulsion of members who sign closed shop agreements, with forfeit of contributions to the reserve fund.
4. Giving financial aid to employers in trouble because of attempts to withstand closed shop demands or to establish the open shop, by inducing banks to refund interest on loans during strikes, and getting owners not to enforce penalties on failure to live up to building contracts. The National Metal Trades Association, for instance, advocates a plan for the cooperation of bankers' associations to extend aid on a wide scale.
5. Mutual aid in time of trial and trouble with unionism; taking orders of a struck shop and returning profit; ... paying members out of the reserve fund for holding out against unions – a kind of strike benefit ...
6. Refusal of aid to any enterprise operating under the closed shop.
7. Advertisements in some newspapers and the withdrawal of advertisements from others friendly to unionism.
8. Detachment of union leaders by promotion or bribery, honorary positions and social advancement, thus constantly depriving unions of the directive force of their strongest men.
9. Discrediting union leaders and unions by exploiting their mistakes in strikes, or mismanagement of funds; appealing to the public by the prosecution of leaders; exposing records of fearful examples as types, e.g., Parks, O'Shea, and Madden, and by inciting to violence.
10. Weeding out agitators and plain union men by blacklists, card catalogs, lists of employees, and by identification systems, for example, the Metal Trades' card catalog, and the Seaman's employment book ...
11. Detaching workers from the union and the union's control by requiring an individual contract with penalties, i.e., the loss of unsettled wages called deposit in case of strike; by welfare plans, insurance and pensions to the workers which depend upon long, continuous service and are forfeited in case of strike ...
12. Conducting trade schools and agitating for continuation schools and vocational training; conducting trade schools themselves or helping to support them ... Advocating trade schools supported at public expense generally, and separate vocational schools; attacking the present system of academic education; donating sums to certain societies for promoting industrial education ...

13. Securing foreknowledge of union plans by the spy system, use of detective agencies, spies in the union, the shadowing of leaders, gaining their confidence or using the dictagraph.
14. Systematic organization and use of strike breakers and counter-sluggers.
15. Organization of counter-unions.
16. Use of the police and militia ... With the law on the side of property, indorsing individual liberty, to gain their ends they resort to force.
17. Systematic appeal to the courts, the use of the injunction, systematic prosecution for violence, the employment of a large corps of legal talent, the bringing into play of law and order leagues, suits for damages in case of strikes, and systematic attacks on the constitutionality of labor laws.
18. Opposition to labor legislation by organizing lobbies to appear before both state and national bodies; by a system of calling upon members of the association to send in letters and telegrams in great numbers; by having employers who will be most affected but who have good labor conditions appear before legislative committees to oppose labor legislation; and by having advertisements in many newspapers denouncing labor bills and calling upon citizens to write to legislators not to support them.
19. Political agitation and action such as ... supporting antilabor statesmen and opposing labor politicians and demagogues, by sending funds, men, and literature into the districts of candidates; ... denouncing the initiative, referendum, and recall, especially the recall of judges and judicial decisions; and defending the courts and the constitution.
20. Appealing to the public by the use of the press, publishing bulletins, and condemning papers which are unfriendly; systematically attacking unions and exploiting their violence; ... giving statements to the press during strikes, pointing out that ... should wages be advanced prices would be higher, and the consumer would have to pay more in the face of the increased cost of living ...; sending out circulars to educators and clergy; ... attacking Socialism and socialists and lauding ministers, educators, judges, and economists who show the fallacies of unionism and set forth the eternal verities.

The underlying assumptions, theories, and attitudes of employers' associations, more particularly those of the militant type, are: that a natural harmony of interests prevails in society and therefore the unions are to be restrained when they use coercive methods; that the employers' interests are always identical with the interests of society and therefore unionism is to be condemned whenever it interferes with their interests; that the interests of the worker and employer are harmonious, and therefore when the unions oppose the employer they are misled by unscrupulous leaders and are to be condemned; that the employer gives work to the laborers and therefore they are ungrateful and immoral and to be condemned when they combine to oppose him; that the employer has an absolute right to manage his own business to suit himself as against his workers, and therefore the unions are to be condemned when they interfere in any way with that …; that the law, the courts, and the police represent absolute and impartial rights and justice, and therefore the unions are to be condemned whenever they violate the law or oppose the police …

The fundamental questions of the source of social rights and the meaning of social welfare lie at the core of a critical consideration of the employers' associations, their theories and viewpoint … Is it right and just to make the workers pay for social progress? … Is there any more basis for the employers' claim of rights and condemnation of attacks of unions upon them, than for the counterclaims of the unions? Is it true that employers give work to laborers any more than that laborers give profits to employers? That the employer has a right to compel men to bargain individually any more than laborers have a right to compel employers to bargain with men collectively? …

Source: Robert Franklin Hoxie, *Trade Unionism in the United States* (New York: D. Appleton & Co., 1917), pp. 188–197.

Questions for Discussion

1. Who lived in the nation's growing cities and suburbs, and why?
2. Why was it so difficult to govern metropolitan America during these decades?
3. Weigh the advantages and disadvantages of urban life for wage workers and their families in the late nineteenth and early twentieth centuries. What generalizations, if any, can we make about their experience of the American metropolis?
4. Why was it impossible for most rural and small-town residents to ignore the urbanization process in the decades following the Civil War?

Part III City and Suburb Ascendant, 1920–1945

Chapter 7 Commerce, Consumption, and the Suburban Trend

1 An Investment Banker Insists that "Everyone Ought to Be Rich," 1929

The American metropolis has always been both a product and promoter of the nation's abundance. Still, the spectacular wealth enjoyed by urbanites during the 1920s was linked to important new developments. For the first time in US history, a plurality of Americans lived in urbanized areas. This concentration was especially potent in light of the steady stream of innovations, corporate consolidation, rising incomes, and the new popularity of installment contracts, an early version of buying on credit. As access to material luxuries grew easier and businesses aggressively marketed the consumer ideal, consumer spending became an important motor of economic growth. And, more than ever before, the purchase of manufactured goods became a defining part of the American experience. Even in rural and small-town America, the new prosperity led to the ascendance of "urban" styles. Harper's Magazine *editor Frederick Lewis Allen described it as "the conquest of the whole country by urban tastes and urban dress and the urban way of living"*[1] *(source 7.2).*

An equally important driver of consumption was speculative investment by the affluent, and even by middle-class Americans, on stocks and real estate.

[1] Frederick Lewis Allen, *Only Yesterday: An Informal History of the 1920's* (New York: Blue Ribbon Books, 1931), p. 176.

The Modern American Metropolis: A Documentary Reader, First Edition.
Edited by David M. P. Freund.

They made these purchases, too, on credit, but this did not dull the widespread confidence that asset prices (for stock shares, homes, undeveloped lots) would rise indefinitely. Americans with disposable income and access to credit looked for financial advice, and found it in periodicals that prescribed investment strategies. This interview with investment banker Jacob Raskob, which appeared in the Ladies' Home Journal *under the headline "Everybody Ought to Be Rich," captures the faith in unlimited growth that helped fuel the conspicuous consumption associated with the Roaring Twenties. The interview was published in August 1929, just two months before the stock market collapse that triggered the Great Depression. Which of the people introduced in other sources were likely to encounter articles like this one and to contemplate similar advice? What were the repercussions in metropolitan America of this enthusiasm for speculative investment?*

Being rich is, of course, a comparative status. A man with a million dollars used to be considered rich, but so many people have at least that much in these days, or are earning incomes in excess of a normal return from a million dollars that a millionaire does not cause any comment.

... Let us ... say that a man is rich when he has an income from invested capital which is sufficient to support him and his family in a decent and comfortable manner ... That amount of prosperity ought to be attainable by anyone. A greater share will come to those who have greater ability.

It seems to me to be a primary duty for people to make it their business to understand how wealth is produced and not to take their ideas from writers and speakers who have the gift of words but not the gift of ordinary common sense ... It is quite true that wealth is not so evenly distributed as it ought to be and as it can be. And part of the reason for the unequal distribution is the lack of systematic investment and also the lack of even moderately sensible investment ... Yet all the while wealth has been here for the asking.

The common stocks of this country have in the past ten years increased enormously in value because the business of the country has increased. Ten thousand dollars invested ten years ago in the common stock of General Motors would now be worth more than a million and a half dollars. And General Motors is only one of many first-class industrial corporations.

It may be said that this is a phenomenal increase and that conditions are going to be different in the next ten years. That prophecy may be true, but it is not founded on experience. In my opinion the wealth of the country is bound to increase at a very rapid rate. The rapidity of the rate will be determined by the increase in consumption, and under [current] investment plans the consumption will steadily increase ...

Suppose a man marries at the age of twenty-three and begins a regular saving of fifteen dollars a month – and almost anyone who is employed can do that if he tries. If he invests in good common stocks and allows the dividends and rights to accumulate, he will at the end of twenty years have at least eighty thousand dollars and an income from investments of around four hundred dollars a month. He will be rich. And because anyone can do that I am firm in my belief that anyone not only can be rich but ought to be rich ...

If [instead of putting their savings in the bank, people] bought ... stock, [they] would be helping some manufacturer to buy a new lathe or a new machine of some kind, which would add to the wealth of the country, and ... by participating in the profits of this machine, [they] would be in a position to buy more goods and cause a demand for more machines ... No one can become rich merely by saving. Putting aside a sum each week or month in a sock at no interest, or in a savings bank at ordinary interest, will not provide enough for old age unless life in the meantime be rigorously skimped down to the level of mere existence. And if everyone skimped in any such fashion then the country would be so poor that living at all would hardly be worth while ...

The personal fortunes of this country have been made not by saving but by producing ... Mere saving is closely akin to the social policy of dividing and likewise runs up against the same objection that there is not enough around to save. The savings that count cannot be static. They must be going into the production of wealth ... The way to wealth is to get into the profit end of wealth production in this country.

Source: Samuel Crowther, "Everybody Ought to Be Rich: An Interview with John J. Raskob," *Ladies' Home Journal*, August, 1929.

2 Commerce and the Good Life

It would be impossible to exaggerate the influence of mass media and advertising on patterns of consumption in the early twentieth century. The market for consumer goods from toothpaste to movie tickets to automobiles assumed a powerful place in the daily life of most Americans, as the modern advertising industry and marketing strategies were born, spending on advertising expanded exponentially, and the distribution of dailies and periodicals soared. The nation's fast-growing metropolitan areas were focal points of these material and cultural changes, continuing their role as centers of commerce, congregation, popular amusement, and cultural production. Thus their residents constantly encountered images, products, and public scenes that forced them to make sense of what consumption meant for them. There was a sensory overload for many recent migrants and immigrants, to be sure, and for anyone encountering more opportunities for leisure and a seemingly endless array of goods and services to buy. Meanwhile everyone had to negotiate the ubiquitous and conflicting messages about the significance of consumer culture in American life. What kind of consumption and what kinds of goods made someone a "true" American? Was enjoying the pleasures of modern metropolitan life – technology, convenience, luxury, free time – a reward for determination and hard work?

Adding to the confusion, different audiences received different messages. Most mainstream publications and advertisements did not depict working-class immigrants, racial minorities, or women of any background as deserving full or equal access to the pleasures of modern urban life. Yet all Americans participated in consumer culture, and marginalized groups advertised and celebrated their experiences in venues rarely viewed by the white middle class. This tiny sample of media representations and candid photographs introduces a few of the messages and contradictions that were daily on display in the American metropolis, and should be considered in light of sources 4.1–5; 5.1–4; 7.3–4; and 8.2–3 in particular. The automobile advertisement was published in Youth's Companion *in 1924. The advertisement for Clara Smith's "Percolatin' Blues" appeared in the* Baltimore Afro-American *on May 7, 1927. The advertisement for Aunt Jemima pancake mix ran in* Ladies' Home Journal *in October 1924, and includes a mail-in coupon for a "jolly family of rag dolls" including "Aunt Jemima" and "Uncle Mose." The* Life *magazine cover ran on July 15, 1926. Two photographs of urban Americans enjoying their leisure time – a group of friends at a Howard University sporting event in the 1920s and another group enjoying a Fourth of July celebration on the beach in Los Angeles in 1931 – further demonstrate how the pleasures and styles of urban life were consumed by more people and in more ways than mainstream media alone would suggest.*

3 Former Employees Describe Finding Work and Building Cars for Ford Motor Company

It was jobs that drew migrants and immigrants to American cities in the 1920s and that afforded many families access to the material benefits and novelties of postwar life. Just as wages dropped and employment disappeared in sectors such as agriculture and coal mining, many urban industries were growing and offered steady work, good pay, and even employer-provided benefits. Still, for most Americans, wage labor continued to be physically demanding, tedious, and often dangerous. Thus, to imagine how most people experienced the Roaring Twenties in American cities, it is important to consider what they did, for most of their waking hours, to earn a living. These interviews (completed in the 1980s) with former Ford Motor Company employees introduce one set of experiences among working people

(a)

for the

YOUNG BUSINESS MAN

The Ford Runabout is a profitable partner and a happy companion for the boy who is making his mark in business and at school.

It reduces distance from a matter of miles to a matter of minutes. By saving time and effort, it makes larger earnings possible. And costing little to buy and keep going, it quickly pays for itself.

When vacation time rolls round the Runabout enables the young business man to reduce by hours the time between work and play.

Let us tell you how easy it is to buy a Ford on the Weekly Purchase Plan.

FORD MOTOR COMPANY, DETROIT, MICHIGAN

THE RUNABOUT

$265

F. O. B. Detroit

Demountable Rims and Starter $85 extra

FORD MOTOR COMPANY
DETROIT, MICH.
Please tell me how I can buy a Ford on small weekly payments.
Name
Address

Ford
THE UNIVERSAL CAR

***Figure** 7.2(a)* "For the Young Business Man," advertisement featuring the 1925 Ford Model T Runabout, 1924. Proposed publication schedule included *Youth's Companion*, May 29, 1924, and *American Boy*, June 1924.

Source: The collections of The Henry Ford, 64.167.19.384.

(b)

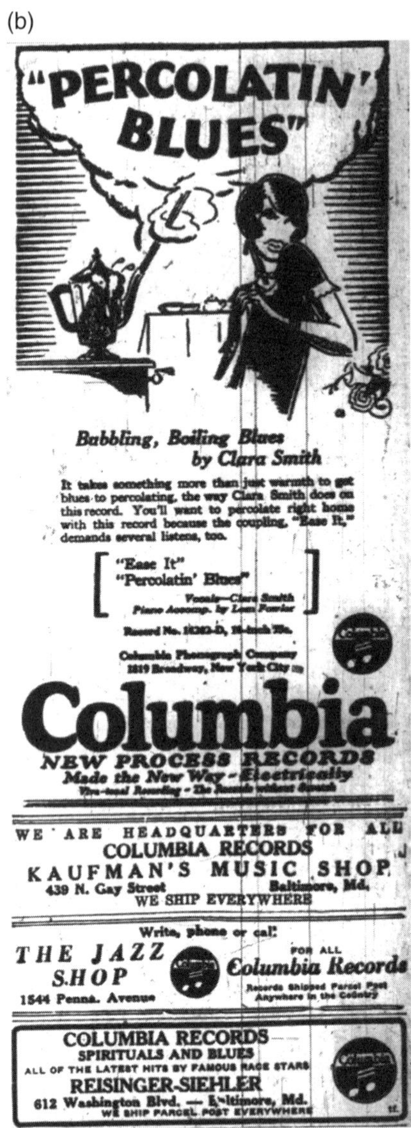

Figure 7.2(b) Advertisement for Clara Smith's "Percolatin' Blues" in the *Baltimore Afro-American*, May 7, 1927.

Source: Courtesy of the *Baltimore Afro-American*.

(c)

Figure 7.2(c) "Tobacco at its best – in a pipe!" Edgeworth advertisement, 1920s.

Source: Virginia Historical Society.

in Detroit, Michigan, a city that showcased many of the advantages of life in the industrialized, consumer-driven metropolis. As noted in these autobiographical accounts, many people sought out work in industrial centers like Detroit when jobs grew scarce in their industry or region. Moreover the men interviewed here secured some of the most coveted and highest-paying jobs in manufacturing: a position at Henry Ford's innovative new production plant, the River Rouge in Dearborn, Michigan, just steps from Detroit. What was it like to produce one of the most prized consumer goods of the era: the automobile?

Paul Boatin

The word got all over the world, and got to New Castle, Pennsylvania, where I was living: $5 for an eight-hour day was better than anybody else was paying ... People came from all over ... during the depression years of 1920, '21, and '22.

There were parking lots for the salaried workers and the office people and the others for the general workers. Those parking lots, for that entire stretch of two miles, were full of people who came there at twelve o'clock and one o'clock at night to wait for the employment office to open at eight o'clock

(d)

Figure 7.2(d) "It cannot be found in cook books," advertisement for Aunt Jemima Pancake Flour, from *Ladies' Home Journal*, October 1924.

Source: Balch Institute Ethnic Images in Advertising Collection, Historical Society of Pennsylvania.

(e)

Figure 7.2(e) "Everything is Hot-tentotsy now," *Life* magazine cover by L. T. Holton, July 15, 1926.

Source: The Granger Collection/TopFoto.

in the morning ... and that went on for five or six weeks, an interminable period of time, and this was July and August.

Kenneth Roche

My parents came from Pennsylvania ... My mother was the daughter of a coal miner, and my father was the son of a coal miner. Their fathers were killed in mining accidents, cave-ins in the mines. They moved to Detroit, and both got jobs working [in the auto industry] at Robert's Brass.

Figure 7.2(f) Addison N. Scurlock, Young women at outdoor sports event, probably football game at Griffith Stadium, black and white photoprint, probably *c.* 1920–1930, print *c.* 1970.

Source: Scurlock Studio Records, Archives Center, National Museum of American History, Smithsonian Institution.

Thomas Yeager

I had a brother and a sister, and had relatives, that worked in what they called Crucible, in Pennsylvania, and there was a big steel outfit and they had their own coal mine. So, I had a half-brother there that took me in the mine with him. And I got my first taste of it, and I was scared to death ...

So after I was there for a while, I met my wife. She was staying with an aunt there in the coal mines ... Her uncle worked in the coal mine there ... And then we stayed there about three years, and I started learning how to cut coal ... But there was no union. And we worked long hours. You go in some nights, and you had a bad night you could be in there all night, come out the next morning, you would meet those guys going [in] ... About three

(g)

Figure 7.2(g) Fourth of July at Venice Beach, photograph, 1931.

Source: Los Angeles Public Library Photo Collection.

years and I got scared. They had a big mine explosion down about maybe seven or eight miles from where I worked in the mine. I worked where they had a big explosion in what they called the "mother mine." It was about 289 miners got killed. I went down there for rescue work, and I saw all that down there, women and children. I came home, and I told my wife, "Hey, I'm going to get out of here." "Where are you going?" I said, "I'm going to Detroit." ... Just before this, ... I went in one afternoon to cut coal, and the place was bad ... [A] cement slate came down ... and caught my toes. They had to haul me out of there with a motor that night ...

I came here to Dearborn [in 1928], and I got a job – imagine, with one shoe on and one bedroom slipper [because of the injury]. They needed men. You can just imagine this big Rouge plant, at one time eighty thousands ... I got a job right away, and I worked in production ... I worked in there off and on ... In those days, there was no union, and you had a job and you didn't have a job ... The old model goes off and the new one follow it.

Sometimes you are off three months, five months out of a job. There was no unemployment compensation. There were no benefits of any kind. You never knew where your next dollar was coming from ...

These [coal] miners, when they were trying to get the unions in, these miners were fired by the company. When they got things straightened out, these people were on the black-list, and never got called back. That's why so many miners were migrating into Michigan. They came here to get jobs, and you got jobs at Ford's.

Archie Acciacca

I went to work at Ford's in 1935 ... at the Rouge plant, on production ... I got in, [but] not by going on a line. There's very few people who are able to go on the line and go to work. I got in. My dad knew a realtor that was pretty well up on the West Side ... and this [man] knew somebody at Ford's ... some wheel in the employment office, I think. He helped my dad get a lot of his friends in. So he gave me a letter ... I brought it to the employment office, and I got into work at what was then known as the "pressed steel," but now they call them "stamping plants."

Dave Moore

A guy living next door to me said, "I got hired at Ford. I slipped in through the line, and I got in the back door. They hired me. One guy dropped his pass, and said, 'I got a pass here if you want to use it.'" On January 17, 1935, I walked all the way from my home. I walked all the way. I left home at 2:30 that morning, and I got out to Ford around 4:00. And that line looked like a million people. At 8:00 the employment office opened up ... One guy said, "All those who got a pass come up to the gate." I had this pass, I went and I got inside ... "You're hired at 62 and ½ cents an hour." Wow! 62 and ½ cents an hour. "You'll work in the foundry on the shake out." Shake out was the worst job you could get. You pour that iron. If you're making a piston, that mold is shaped in a piston. The iron come out of the furnace just like water. Guys would come up, and pour that iron in there, then it would set so long. They would spray water over it, and the steam would come out, and it was hot, and you had to go and shake it out. That's what you call a "shake out." All that fumes coming up ... You would get that mold ... and just take it and shake it, until all that sand come off it ...

I worked in all that fumes there for about three days; and they took me out of there, put me outside on the shipping dock, shipping motors. I was weighing 116, and the motors weighed six hundred pounds. And I had to help a guy put the motors in a box car to be shipped out to different parts of the country ... I worked out there until April ... and, lo and behold, they sent me to a place called the rolling mill. Back in the hell again. That's where they roll all the steel out of. I stayed there ... for a while ...

I was working over on a place, what you call a "pickeling tank," where we'd get the steel, and put it in a big tank to set for awhile 'til it's pickled. And then they would get the fumes cooking up again. I went from hell to double hell.

John Orr

My father worked in the motor building on a crankshaft line. Now, he never weighed more than 135 pounds in his life, and he used to come home at night so darn exhausted that he would just about go wash up come down and eat; and he would lay on the couch and listen to "Amos and Andy" and Kate Smith, who were the tops in radio at that time. Up to bed, to get ready for work. And my mother kept saying [to me and my brother], "You two boys ... are never going to suffer what your father did ... I'm going to take you ... to Henry Ford Trade School," which she did ...

I came here [from Canada], my citizenship papers show, January 25, 1924; and I was nine on January 2. At any rate, my brother and I both went to [Henry Ford] trade school. He went at age fourteen, and I followed a year and half later at age fourteen ... It was very good ... You worked four years. You worked in the shop end of the school two weeks, and then went to school one week. So, we got very little schooling, and I have always been ashamed of my grammar, and what not, on that account, because we had so little of it ...

We had a trolley repair department [at Ford]; and if you ever saw kids work repair, oh, my God! I myself worked on valves, and they were from stead valves, with gates that big, that operated in powerhouses and what not, to little things, very little, on rubber valves, like you change a washer at home. Most of them were metal. Some were so small ... It was quite evident where the leaks were, and you had to sand those out ... Your fingers were like sandpaper. I'd come home with blood oozing out of them. I got bitter in there, although I learned a lot, I'll have to say. I was learning to operate lathes and milling machines ...

When I left the trade school and went in the factory, I was more impressed than ever what my mother meant by saying, "You boys are going to be tradesmen not production workers," because they were like animals, my God. Even today everybody thinks it's easy in a Ford factory, even today if you can get a trip through the Ford assembly plant and see those guys, they are like robots themselves – putting nuts on, putting bolts on, doing this and that. How the hell they stand the pace, it would drive me nuts ... I don't know how they can robotize themselves like that ...

Source: Judith Stepan-Norris and Maurice Zeitlin, *Talking Union* (Urbana: University of Illinois Press, 1996), pp. 27–32, 48–49. Reproduced by permission of the University of Illinois Press.

4 Alfred Kazin Recalls New York City's Ethnic Boundaries Before World War II

In the early twentieth century, New York City was a place of both opportunity and exclusion for recent immigrants and their children. The vast majority of the immigrants who arrived in the United States after 1880 were eastern and southern Europeans – Slavs, Jews, Italians, and others – often escaping poverty or persecution in their homelands (source 4.1). By World War I, these communities were well established in New York, if still vulnerable in a political and economic climate that held little certainty for immigrant laborers and merchants. And during the 1920s they were enjoying the benefits of the nation's economic growth, including access to more leisure time and to the novelties, conveniences, and freedoms of an expanding consumer culture (sources 7.1–2). Still, these immigrant groups were repeatedly reminded of their marginal status. Constantly exhorted by politicians and educators to embrace an American cultural ideal, they were simultaneously labeled as foreign, unassimilable, even as racially inferior. Testament to nativist resentment was Congress's passage in 1922 and 1924 of restrictive legislation that cut off most immigration of Asian and European peoples deemed nonwhite or not "fully" white.

Included in this category were people like Alfred Kazin, son of Jewish immigrants living in Brooklyn, New York, who later established himself as a nationally prominent author and literary critic. In these excerpts from his 1946 memoir, he describes how the metropolis helped reinforce social and ethnic differences in the 1920s and beyond. In what ways did the built environment – the city's geography, buildings, and institutions – repeatedly remind Kazin of his community's status? Why, historically, did the boroughs of New York City look and feel this way to people like Kazin? And why might a young immigrant nonetheless feel drawn to urban places and to an urban culture that seemed to constantly reject him? (Consider sources 3.5; 4.2–3; and 5.1–3.)

When I was a child I thought we lived at the end of the world. It was the eternity of the subway ride into the city that first gave me this idea. I took a long time getting to "New York"; it seemed longer getting back. Even the I.R.T. got tired by the time it came to us, and ran up into the open for a breath of air before it got locked into its terminus at New Lots. As the train left the tunnel to rattle along the elevated tracks, I felt that I was being jostled on a camel past the last way stations in the desert. Oh that ride from New York! Light came only at Sutter Avenue. First across the many stations of the Gentiles to the East River. Then clear across Brooklyn, almost to the brink of the ocean all our fathers crossed. All those first stations in Brooklyn – Clark, Borough Hall, Hoyt, Nevins, the junction of the East and West Side express lines – told me only that I was on the last leg home, though there was always a stirring of my heart at Hoyt, where the grimy subway platform was suddenly enlivened by Abraham and Straus's windows of ladies' wear. Atlantic Avenue was vaguely exciting, a crossroads, the Long Island railroad; I never saw a soul get in or out at Bergen Street; the Grand Army Plaza, with its great empty caverns smoky with dust and chewing-gum wrappers, meant Prospect Park and that stone path beside a meadow where as a child I ran off from my father one summer twilight just in time to see the lamplighter go up the path lighting from the end of his pole each gas mantle suddenly flaring within its corolla of pleated paper – then, that summer I first strayed off the block for myself, the steps leading up from the boathouse, the long stalks of grass wound between the steps thick with the dust and smell of summer – then, that great summer at sixteen, my discovery in the Brooklyn Museum of Albert Pinkham Ryder's cracked oily fishing boats drifting under the moon. Franklin Avenue was where the Jews began – but all middle-class Jews, *alrightniks*, making out "all right" in the New World, they were still Gentiles to me as they went out into the wide and tree-lined Eastern Parkway. For us the journey went on and on – past Nostrand, past Kingston, past Utica, and only then out into the open at Sutter, overlooking Lincoln Terrace Park, "Tickle-Her" Park, the zoo of our adolescence, through which no girl could pass on a summer evening without its being understood forever after that she was "in"; past the rickety "two-family" private houses built in the fever of Brownsville's last real-estate boom; and then into Brownsville itself – Saratoga, Rockaway, and home. For those who lived still beyond, in East New York, there was Junius, there was Pennsylvania, there was Van Siclen, and so at last into New Lots, where the city goes back to the marsh, and even the subway ends.

Yet it was not just the long pent-up subway ride that led me to think of Brownsville as the margin of the city, the last place, the car barns where they locked up the subway and the trolley cars at night. There were always raw patches of unused city land all around us filled with "monument works" where they cut and stored tombstones, as there were still on our street farmhouses and the remains of old cobbled driveways down which chickens came squealing into our punchball games – but most of it dead land, neither country nor city, with that look of prairies waste I have so often seen on my walks along the fringes of American cities near the freight yards. We were nearer the ocean than the city, but our front on the ocean was Canarsie – in those days the great refuse dump through which I made my first and grimmest walks into the city – a place so celebrated in New York vaudeville houses for its squalor that the very sound of the word was always good for a laugh. CAN-NARR-SIE! They fell into the aisles. But that was the way to the ocean we always took summer evenings – through silent streets of old broken houses whose smoky red Victorian fronts looked as if the paint had clotted like blood and had then been mixed with soot – past infinite weedy lots, the smell of freshly cut boards in the lumber yards, the junk yards, the marshland eating the pavement, the truck farms, the bungalows that had lost a window or a door as they tottered on their poles against the damp and the ocean winds. The place as I have it in my mind still reeks of the fires burning in the refuse dumps. Farms that had once been the outposts of settlers in Revolutionary days had crumbled and sunk like wet sand. Canarsie was where they opened the sluice gates to let the city's muck out into the ocean. But at the end was the roar of the Atlantic and the summer house where we stood outside watching through lattices the sports being served with great pitchers of beer foaming into the red-checked tablecloths. Summer, my summer! Summer!

We were of the city, but somehow not in it. Whenever I went off on my favorite walk to Highland Park in the "American" district to the north, on the border of Queens, and climbed the hill to the old reservoir from which I could look straight across to the skyscrapers of Manhattan, I saw New York as a foreign city. There, brilliant and neutral, the city had its life, as Brownsville was ours. That the two were joined in me I never knew then – not even on those glorious summer nights of my last weeks in high school when, with what an ache, I would come back into Brownsville along Liberty Avenue, and, as soon as I could see blocks ahead of me the Labor Lyceum, the malted milk and Fatima signs over the candy stores, the old women in their housedresses sitting in front of the tenements like priestesses of an ancient cult, knew I was home.

We were at the end of the line. We were the children of the immigrants who had camped at the city's back door, in New York's rawest, remotest, cheapest ghetto, enclosed on one side by the Canarsie flats and on the other by the hallowed middle-class districts that showed the way to New York. "New York" was what we put last on our address, but first in thinking of the others around us. *They* were New York, the Gentiles, America; we were Brownsville – *Brunzvil*, as the old folks said – the dust of the earth to all

Jews with money, and notoriously a place that measured all success by our skill in getting away from it. So that when poor Jews left, *even* Negroes, as we said, found it easy to settle on the margins of Brownsville, and with the coming of spring, bands of Gypsies, who would rent empty stores, hand their rugs around them like a desert ten, and bring a dusty and faintly sinister air of carnival into our neighborhood …

…

It was never learning I associated with … school: only the necessity to succeed, to get ahead of the others in the daily struggle to "make a good impression" on our teachers, who grimly, wearily, and often with ill-concealed distaste watched against our relapsing into the natural savagery they expected of Brownsville boys …

All teachers were to be respected like gods … They were the delegates of all visible and invisible power on earth – of the mothers who waited on the stoops every day after three for us to bring home tales of our daily triumphs; of the glacially remote Anglo-Saxon principal, whose very name was King; of the incalculably important Superintendent of Schools who would someday rubberstamp his name to the bottom of our diplomas in grim acknowledgment that we had, at last, given satisfaction to him, to the Board of Superintendents, and to our benefactor the City of New York … The road to a professional future would be shown us only as we pleased [our teachers]. *Make a good impression the first day of the term, and they'll help you out. Make a bad impression, and you might as well cut your throat.* This was the first article of school folklore, whispered around the classroom the opening day of each term. You made the "good impression" by sitting firmly at your wooden desk, … by silence for the greatest part of the live-long day; … by "speaking nicely," which meant reproducing their painfully exact enunciation; … by bringing little gifts at Christmas, on their birthdays, and at the end of the term …

It was not just our quickness and memory that were always being tested. Above all, in that word I could never hear without automatically seeing it raised before me in gold-plated letters, it was our *character* … Character was never something you had; it had to be trained in you, like a technique. I was never clear about it. On our side *character* meant demonstrative obedience; but teachers already had it – how else could they have become teachers? They had it; the aloof Anglo-Saxon principal whom we remotely saw only on ceremonial occasions in the assembly was positively encased in it; it glittered off his bald head in spokes of triumphant light; the President of the United States had the greatest conceivable amount of it. Character belonged to great adults …

I was awed by this system, I believed in it, I respected its force. The alternative was "going bad." … Anything less than absolute perfection in school always suggested to my mind that I might fall out of the daily race, be kept back in the working class forever, or – dared I think of it? – fall into the criminal class itself …

…

Chester Street at last … On my right hand the "Stadium" movie house – the sanctuary every Saturday afternoon of my childhood, the great dark place of all my dream life. On my left the little wooden synagogue where I learned my duties as a Jew and at thirteen, having reached the moral estate of a man, stood up at the high desk before the Ark … and was confirmed in the faith of my fathers.

Right hand and left hand: two doorways to the East. But the first led to music I heard in the dark, to inwardness; the other to ambiguity. That poor worn synagogue could never in my affections compete with that movie house, whose very lounge looked and smelled to me like an Oriental temple. It had Persian rugs, and was marvelously half-lit at all hours of the day; there were great semi-arcs of colored glass above the entrance to the toilets, and out of the gents' came a vaguely foreign, deliciously stinging deodorant that prepared me, on the very threshold of the movie auditorium itself, for the magic within. There was never anything with such expectancy to it as that twilit lounge. I would even delay in it a little, to increase my pleasure in what lay ahead; and often shut my eyes just as I entered the auditorium, knowing that as soon as I opened them again a better world would take me in.

In the wonderful darkness of the movies there was nothing to remind me of Brownsville – nothing but the sudden alarm of a boy who, reminding himself at six o'clock that it was really time to get home, would in haste let himself out by the great metal fire door in front. Then the gritty light on Bristol Street would break up the images on the screen with a meanness that made me shudder.

I always feared that light for the same reason: it seemed to mock imagination … There was something in the everyday look of the streets that reproached me; they seemed to know I had come back to them unwillingly …

…

… [T]he Catholic church on East New York Avenue … marked the boundary, as I used to think of it, between us and the Italians stretching down Rockaway and Saratoga to Fulton … I remember the hymns that rolled out of the church on Sunday mornings, and how we sniffed as we went by. All those earnest, faded-looking people in their carefully brushed and strangely old-fashioned clothes must have come down there from a long way off. I never saw any of them except on Sunday mornings – the women often surprisingly quite fat, if not so fat as ours, and looking rather timid in their severe dresses and great straw hats with clusters of artificial flowers and wax berries along the brim ... [T]he men very stiff in their long four-buttoned jackets. They did not belong with us at all; I could never entirely believe that they were really there. One afternoon on my way back from school my curiosity got the better of me despite all my fear of Gentiles, and I stealthily crept in, never having entered a church in my life before, to examine what I was sure would be an exotic and idolatrous horror. It was the plainest thing I had ever seen ... so varnished-clean and empty and austere, like our school auditorium ... that the chief impression it made on me, who expected all Christians to be as fantastic as albinos, was that these people were not, apparently, so completely different from us as I had imagined. I was bewildered. What really held me there was the number of things written in English. I had associated God only with a foreign language ...

Source: Alfred Kazin, *A Walker in the City* (New York: Harcourt, Brace, 1951), pp. 8–12, 17–20, 39–41, 15–17.

5 A Social Scientist Explains the "Suburban Trend," 1925

This famous sociological account of suburban life in the 1920s is revealing both for the information that it provides and for its insights into conventional assumptions. Before Harlan Paul Douglas published The Suburban Trend *in 1925, no study had offered such a comprehensive view of American metropolitan growth. His exhaustive research debunks common myths by documenting the variety of suburban forms and the range of people – rich and poor, minority and white, native and immigrant – who called them home, while also demonstrating suburbs' complex interdependence with their anchor cities. His analysis also reveals a tension visible in academic and popular treatments of metropolitan change. Despite the variety of suburban types in the early twentieth century, most commentators insisted that the affluent residential suburb represented the typical or normative model of growth and that its popularity reflected larger, universal trends in American society (compare source 3.2).*

This focus on affluent suburbs was in part a product of their new economic and cultural prominence after World War I. As rising incomes and the automobile helped make these communities far more accessible to white salaried professionals, suburban residence and styles assumed a prominent place in advertising, political discourse, and the imagination of countless Americans. For many, suburban life was associated with middle-class comforts, "pastoral" or "small-town" atmospheres, and a particular domestic ideal, centered around nuclear families with a breadwinning father and stay-at-home mother (source 4.4). It often mattered little to observers that a great many suburban communities looked quite different, and that modest working-class suburbs filled with self-built homes were flourishing not far from their celebrated, affluent neighbors. Note the contradictions between Douglas's descriptions of suburban types, on the one hand, and his analysis of "decentralization" and the separation between "work" and "home," on the other. Who works and lives in these places, by the author's own account? How does this variety at times undermine his generalizations about work, consumption, gender roles, family, and class in the American suburb?

Out toward the fringes and margins of cities comes a region where they begin to be less themselves than they are at the center, a place where the city looks countryward. No sharp boundary line defines it; there is rather a gradual tapering off from the urban type of civilization toward the rural type. It is the city thinned out ... [Thus] even though it is a town in form, the brand of the city is stamped upon it. It straddles the arbitrary line which statistics draw between the urban and rural spheres; but in reality it is the push of the city outward ...

The Major Suburban Types

Suburbs so manifestly differ from one another that even the most generalized account of their character ... could not ignore the fact. At one extreme, for example, we [find] the resort and amusement suburbs given over exclusively to the pleasure of people of the near-by city ... At the other extreme is such a manufacturing suburb as Harrison, New Jersey, with a total population of some 15,000, but with 13,000 wage-earners, most of whom come in from the outside to their daily toll ... It is almost exclusively a place for work in contrast with play or even with rest ...

Turning to the underlying philosophy of the matter, we are to distinguish one set of suburbs in which it is primarily the home which has separated itself from the city and which has settled down in specialized areas in which business and industry have little part. In another set of suburbs, industry has separated itself from the city and taken over suburban communities for its more or less exclusive and dominating use. Why should such differences exist? ...

The Decentralization of Consumption

... The residential suburb represents the decentralization of consumption. Man creates wealth in the central city and spends it in the suburbs. He makes his living in town but lives at home in an intentionally contrasting environment. He leaves his work in the city but takes wife and children and moves out to the country, going back and forth daily in order to keep both aspects of life going.

Part of the pay which he receives for his work in the city he immediately pays out there in return for services or goods, but the goods which he buys are chiefly consumed at home, and in the suburb are his major expenditures – for rent and taxes, for most of his food, for doctor and dentist, for automobile, church and club, for charity, self-improvement and self-indulgence. There could hardly be a greater error than to think of the residential suburbs as mere dormitories. They are rather the realms of consumption as over against production, of play in contrast with work, of leisure in exchange for business. Only incidentally are they places to sleep.

Of course some work is done in the residential suburbs, but it is primarily in the service of rest, recreation, and refreshment for others. The gainfully employed breadwinner goes to the city, but the work of the homemaker ... is decentralized along with the home; and round it gather the types of business immediately related to consumption.

Indeed, more domestic work takes place in the residential suburb than in the city. It moves the woman from the apartment-house with its centralized heating-plant, its elevator, laundry, incinerator, and janitor service, and with no premises outside of the house, to the single or double house with its independent equipment for each family and its grounds to look after. More work is necessary to make the process of consumption efficient and agreeable and to maintain esthetic standards under these circumstances. Nevertheless in the largest sense it is the mark of the residential suburb to have left productive work in the city and to have solved the problem of the worker by daily movement from home in the morning to the shop, factory, or office and back again at night.

The Decentralization of Production

... Urban congestion as experienced by populations is largely due to the reception, transportation, handling and processing, storage and reshipment of material things. The sidewalks are blocked by barrels of produce and bales of goods, and the streets are crowded with trucks.

In the industrial suburb these things are decentralized, together with the manufacturing plants and facilities which go with them. The factory becomes suburban as well as the home. Production moves out as consumption has already done. Both halves of the city reestablish themselves in the country in a roomier environment. The industrial suburb is more independent of the parent city than is the residential one because the workers work near home as well as live there. Nevertheless, marked relations to the city continue ... The city constitutes the major center where brains, credit facilities, the docks and railroad terminals which are the ultimate factors of transportation, and the primary labor markets all remain.

Industrial suburbs and residential suburbs thus constitute the major suburban types. For both the city continues [to be] the economic center as well as the focus of ideals and imagination.

Demographic and Economic Variations: Rich Suburbs and Poor Suburbs

Within the boundaries of the city the social complexion of its more prosperous districts is in most glaring contrast with that of its poverty-stricken ones. The same contrasts occur along the margins of the city and out into the suburbs. Rich and poor suburbs constitute for practical purposes different kinds.

It follows from the ordinary distribution of human fortunes that the residential suburbs are richer than the industrial ones ... Housing costs in the better residential suburbs catering to the upper middle class are so high as to exclude all but about ten per cent. of the population of the urban area ...

Most suburbs, either residential or industrial, are inhabited by people of the middle class on the economic scale. This is because there are relatively few rich people and because ... the suburb is not generally available for the very poor. There are, however, many residential suburbs of the better-paid industrial classes, but they are usually closer to cities, especially to minor cities within the suburban zone. The industrial worker cannot ordinarily commute so far as the salaried man ...

Besides the very poor industrial suburbs where foreign immigrants in industry live on a characteristically low level in the shadow of the factory, many purely residential suburbs exist on exceedingly unsatisfactory economic planes. Thus the projection of the Delaware River Bridge between Philadelphia and Camden started hordes of poorly paid workers to building mushroom suburbs in the country beyond. Many of them were cheap, planless, vulgar, and inconvenient to the last degree. Some indeed started in temporary summer bungalow communities and adapted their style of architecture and standards to year-round living. Without civic coherence or community consciousness, suburbs of this sort present many of the aspects of the frontier mining-camp. Scores of them exist along the edges of the Los Angeles oil-fields ... [and] nearly every great city since the war shows similar phenomena ... There are also numerous examples of downright suburban slums ...

A second very profound series of differences between suburbs reflects the varying population elements which compose them ...

Foreign and Negro Suburbs

… The heaviest concentrations of foreign-born populations in the United States are not urban but suburban. Also … no Northern city has massed so large a proportion of negro population as some of the Northern suburbs.

The relation between industry and the presence of these alien groups of population is well understood. It is in the industrial suburb, therefore, that we must look for these extreme concentrations of alien population … No great city … has so high a number of foreigners as East Chicago, Indiana, or Passaic, Garfield, and Perth Amboy, New Jersey. No Northern city has relatively so many negroes as the residential suburbs of Englewood, East Orange, and Montclair, New Jersey, and Evanston, Illinois, where the negro colonies represent primarily domestic service groups.

On the other hand, there are distinctly industrial suburbs actually with fewer foreigners than the average residential suburbs of the cities have. Examples are Hammond, Indiana, and Plainfield, New Jersey. These strikingly American suburbs may, as already noted, stand on a high economic level.

Source: Harlan Paul Douglas, *The Suburban Trend* (New York: Arno, 1925), pp. 3–4, 74–75, 84–87, 94–98.

6 Suburban Speculation Creates Empty Subdivisions, 1925

Real estate booms and busts have been recurring and formative phenomena in American metropolitan development, even if popular memory of these cycles is often short-lived. Many of the nation's founding fathers were land speculators, and both urban and industrial expansion depended on waves of investment in undeveloped property (sources 1.1–4, 2.1, and 3.1, 4). By the early twentieth century speculation in residential real estate had become an especially powerful motor of growth, symbolized famously by the 1920s real estate bubble in South Florida. Developers inundated prospective investors nationwide with advertisements and enticements to visit the state for tours; thousands flocked to Florida to buy properties, while others purchased developments unseen that were, too often, nonexistent. Miami's population grew from 30,000 in 1920 to 75,000 (a conservative estimate) just three years later. Henry S. Villard, writing in The Nation *in 1928, after boom turned to bust and a hurricane added to the devastation, describes the drive into Miami: "Dead subdivisions line the highway, their pompous names half-obliterated on crumbling stucco gates." By decade's end, numerous Florida boomtowns were defaulting on the bonds issued to pay for infrastructural development.*

Figure 7.6 Aerial view of Dearborn, Michigan, August 28, 1925.

Source: Aerial Surveys, Inc., Cleveland, Ohio. Courtesy of Dearborn Historical Museum, Dearborn, Michigan.

If the Florida case was dramatic and the focus of considerable publicity in the 1920s, a comparable process played out on a smaller scale in metropolitan regions nationwide (source 7.1). Within existing municipal boundaries (both urban and suburban) and in unincorporated areas, speculators bought property, usually on credit, in anticipation of rising prices and presumably endless demand. Real estate sales were a key component of the speculative activity that triggered the Great Depression. And after the Wall Street and housing bubbles collapsed, these platted areas – sometimes partially developed – sat dormant for years. When this aerial photo of Detroit's near western suburbs was taken in 1925, new streets had been marked out but few of the planned homes had been built. At the time these unfilled subdivisions signified promise and progress to local residents and investors. But, four years later and throughout the 1930s, this scene remained largely unchanged, and thus served as an inescapable symbol of economic stagnation. Indeed most of the neighborhood's lots remained empty until the late 1940s and 1950s, when prosperity and a new housing market built the missing pieces of a neighborhood designed decades earlier. When you get to the sources in Part IV, return to this image and consider how postwar developments transformed undeveloped suburban areas like this one, both materially and culturally.

Chapter 8 Economic Collapse and Metropolitan Crisis

1 The New Deal Rebuilds the Metropolis during the Great Depression

Throughout the nineteenth and early twentieth centuries the American economy, and with it the nation's cities, experienced frequent episodes of stalling growth and financial instability. But the downturn that followed the crash of 1929 endured longer and impacted a far broader range of Americans than did any previous crisis. So severe was this Great Depression that federal authorities were compelled to assume an unprecedented new role in American economic life. Beginning in 1933, the federal state devoted considerable spending to the task of putting people to work and building infrastructure, both urban and rural. It secured laborers' right to organize and regulated workplace conditions. It regulated the financial industry, subsidized markets such as housing and agriculture, and created the first federal safety net for many American workers, including unemployment insurance and retirement benefits. Much of the pressure for federal involvement came from America's cities, specifically their working populations and the mayors who turned to Washington, DC, for help. The Roosevelt administration's support for these programs, in turn, helped solidify a powerful Democratic electoral coalition well into the postwar era.

Depression era programs also had a very public presence. In the depths of the crisis, Americans regularly encountered Works Progress Administration (WPA) crews engaged in construction, as pictured here, and ubiquitous

The Modern American Metropolis: A Documentary Reader, First Edition.
Edited by David M. P. Freund.

promotional materials distributed and displayed by New Deal agencies. In addition, Americans were surrounded by physical products of federal intervention such as bridges, schools, roads, and other infrastructure. Notably, it is these visible manifestations of federal spending that are most often associated with the New Deal's legacy. The activist federal state has been a fixture of American life since the 1930s and has been especially influential in shaping patterns of metropolitan and regional economic development (sources 9.1–4; 10.1; 11.1–3; 12.2–4; 13.1–4; and 14.2, 5). Yet people generally associate the New Deal's impact on the American metropolis with a narrow range of interventions, especially employment programs and public works projects. Why have these artifacts of the federal role, and not other equally powerful interventions, dominated discussions of the New Deal's legacy?

(a)

Figure 8.1(a) The New Deal rebuilds the metropolis, Tuskegee, Alabama. Photographer unknown, 1936.

Source: Courtesy National Archives, 69 MP-56-1, box 5.

(b)

Figure 8.1(b) WPA road grading project, Pennsylvania.

Source: Pittsburgh City Photographer Collection, 1901–2002, AIS.1971.05, Archives Service Center, University of Pittsburgh.

(c)

Figure 8.1(c) WPA sewer project, San Diego. Photo by Russell Lee, 1941.

Source: Library of Congress, Prints and Photographs Division, LC-USF34-039412.

2 Jane Yoder Describes Living through the Depression in a Central Illinois Mining Town

When considering the Great Depression's significance in US history, it is useful to think on a metropolitan scale. The economic crisis had differential impacts by region, by industry, and by social class; thus it manifested itself very differently in distinct American places. For Jane Yoder, daughter of a blacksmith living in a small Illinois mining town, the Depression meant desperate poverty for her family when closure of the local mines forced her father to travel elsewhere in search of work. In this oral account, related to author Studs Terkel in the 1960s, she describes her family's experience, their reliance on federal aid, and a moment when she was reminded that people with backgrounds unlike hers could be insulated from the worst of the crisis.

Of equal importance, the Depression began a fundamental change in the federal government's relationship to the American metropolis. The US government had long influenced development patterns, as illustrated in many of the sources collected above. But the Depression began an era – one that continues to this day – of active federal involvement in virtually every arena of American life, from protecting the public welfare, to investing directly in infrastructure, to regulating and promoting a range of industries and markets (source 8.1). As a result, Americans of all backgrounds have come to count on government action to protect their well-being and their interests. During the 1930s, working-class Americans like the Yoders were among the first beneficiaries of the expanded federal role. New Deal policies provided jobs (for Jane Yoder's father, for example), guaranteed many workers the right to organize, and created a social safety net unimaginable for the laborers introduced in previous sources. A host of public policies eased some of the Depression's hardships for working people and thus linked them to the federal state in new ways, both practically and politically. As Yoder's account reveals, the implications of government intervention were open to multiple interpretations at the time. When you reach the sources in Part IV, consider how families that endured the Depression would look back, decades later, and view the significance of the New Deal. When Yoder gave this account in the 1960s, she was married to a junior executive and living a comfortable middle-class life in Evanston, Illinois. Her eldest son was a lieutenant in the Air Force.

During the Depression ... [w]e were struggling, just desperate to be warm. No blankets, no coats. At this time I was in fourth grade. [My sister] went to Chicago and bought an Indian blanket coat. I remember this incident of that Indian blanket coat. (Gasps.) Oh, because Katie came home with it and had it in her clothes closet for quite a while. And I didn't have a coat. I can remember putting on that coat in Sue Pond's house. I thought, oh, this is marvelous, gee. I took that coat home, and I waited till Sunday and wore it to church. And then everybody laughed. I looked horrid. Here was this black-haired kid, with a tendency to be overweight. My God, when I think of that ... But I wore that coat, laugh or not. And I can remember thinking: the hell with it. I don't care what ... it doesn't mean a thing. Laugh hard, you'll get it out of your system. I was warm.

Before that I had one coat. It must have been a terrible lightweight coat or what, but I can remember being cold, just shivering. And came home, and nothing to do but go to bed, because if you went to bed, then you put the coat on the bed and you got warm.

The cold that I've known. I never had boots. I think when I got married [in 1940], I had my first set of boots. In rainy weather, you just ran for it, you ran between the raindrops or whatever. This was luxuriating to have boots. You simply wore your old shoes if it was raining. Save the others ...

If we had a cold or we threw up, nobody ever took your temperature. We had no thermometer. But if you threw up and you were hot, my mother felt your head. She somehow felt that by bringing you oranges and bananas and these things you never had – there's nothing wrong with you, this is what she'd always say in Croatian; you'll be all right. Then she gave you all these good things. Oh, gee, you almost looked forward to the day you could throw up. I could remember dreaming about oranges and bananas, dreaming about them.

My oldest brother, terribly bright, wanted to go on to school to help pay those grocery bills that were back there ... Did it cost much? No matter what you brought in: bread and eggs and Karo syrup. Oh, Karo syrup was such a treat. I don't remember so much *my* going to the store and buying food. I must have been terribly proud and felt: I can't do it. How early we all stayed away from going to the store, because we sensed my father didn't have the money. So we stayed hungry. And we talked about it.

I can think of the WPA ... my father immediately got employed in this WPA. This was a godsend. This was the greatest thing. It meant food, you know. Survival, just survival.

How stark it was for me to come into nurses' training and have the girls – one of them, Susan Stewart, lived across the hall from me, her father was a doctor – their impressions of the WPA. How it struck me. Before I could ever say that my father was employed in the WPA, discussions in the bull sessions in our rooms immediately was: these lazy people, the shovel leaners. I'd just sit there and listen to them. I'd look around and realize: sure, Susan Stewart was talking this way, but her father was a doctor, and her mother was a nurse. Well, how nice. They had respectable employment. In my family, there was no respectable employment. I thought, you don't know what it's like.

How can I defend him? I was never a person who could control this. I just had to come out or I think I'd just blow up. So I would say, "I wonder how much we know until we go through it. Just like the patients we take care of. None of them are in that hospital by choice." I would relate it in abstractions. I think it saved me from just blowing up.

I would come back after that and I'd just say: Gee, these are just two separate, separate worlds.

Source: Interview with Jane Yoder, in Studs Terkel, *Hard Times: An Oral History of the Great Depression* (New York: Washington Square Press, 1970), pp. 106–109.

3 Langston Hughes Remembers Rent Parties in Harlem

While historians commonly organize the past into tidy chronological periods – captured by terms like "The Roaring Twenties," "The Great Depression," or "The Civil Rights Era" – primary source materials regularly demonstrate the limits of this strategy. Sources highlight continuities, and remind us that the people we study are generally unaware, at the time, that they have transitioned between "eras" that we now treat as discrete. Consider, for example, the recollections of essayist and poet Langston Hughes about the African American urban experience in the 1920s and 1930s. Recalling his years living in New York City, Hughes reflects on two challenges commonly faced by working- and middle-class blacks: dealing with de facto segregation, and avoiding poverty. Urban blacks certainly benefited from the opportunities created by World War I and postwar economic growth (sources 4.5 and 7.2). But those opportunities were still limited, most often to poorly paid domestic or unskilled labor, and whites continued to police residential boundaries and exclude racial minorities from places of business and many public spaces. Thus both the attention lavished by white New Yorkers on black artists in the 1920s, during the so-called Harlem Renaissance, and the economic collapse that followed had complicated repercussions for Harlem's residents. Interest in black culture brought attention and white consumers to black neighborhoods, but it simultaneously reinforced the "color line." And while the Great Depression hit the black community especially hard, the challenge of scraping by on low wages and insecure employment was not new to most black Harlemites. To get by in the 1930s they turned to long-standing community traditions.

In discussing black New Yorkers' responses to discrimination and poverty, Hughes reveals that countless black Harlemites did not make sharp distinctions between – or even think in terms of – neatly defined eras like the Harlem Renaissance or the Great Depression. Consider, also, that throughout American history black communities relied on social networks and various family and neighborhood safety nets to sustain themselves in the face of systemic discrimination. These strategies were not new, nor was this, as Hughes reveals in the closing discussion, the last time that sociability helped provide African Americans with economic security. The first account excerpted here, from 1940, was published in Hughes's autobiography, The Big Sea. *Then in 1957 he recalled Depression era Harlem in an article for the* Chicago Defender.

1940

[In the 1920s] white people began to come to Harlem in droves. For several years they packed the expensive Cotton Club on Lenox Avenue. But I was never there, because the Cotton Club was a Jim Crow club for gangsters and monied whites. They were not cordial to Negro patronage, unless you were a celebrity like Bojangles. So Harlem Negroes did not like the Cotton Club and never appreciated its Jim Crow policy in the very heart of their dark community. Nor did ordinary Negroes like the growing influx of whites toward Harlem after sundown, flooding the little cabarets and bars where formerly only colored people laughed and sang, and where now the strangers were given the best ringside tables to sit and stare at the Negro customers – like amusing animals in a zoo ...

The ordinary Negroes hadn't heard of the Negro Renaissance. And if they had, it hadn't raised their wages any. As for all those white folks in the speakeasies and night clubs of Harlem – well, maybe a colored man could find *some* place to have a drink that the tourists hadn't yet discovered.

Then it was that house-rent parties began to flourish – and not always to raise the rent either. But, as often as not, to have a get-together of one's own, where you could do the black-bottom with no stranger behind you trying to do it, too. Non-theatrical, non-intellectual Harlem was an unwilling victim of its own vogue. It didn't like to be stared at by white folks. But perhaps the downtowners never knew this – for the cabaret owners, the entertainers, and the speakeasy proprietors treated them fine – as long as they paid.

The Saturday night rent parties that I attended were often more amusing than any night club, in small apartments where God knows who lived – because the guests seldom did – but where the piano would often be augmented by guitar, or an odd cornet, or somebody with a pair of drums walking in off the street. And where awful bootleg whiskey and good fried fish or steaming chitterling were sold at very low prices. And the dancing and singing and impromptu entertaining went on until dawn came in at the windows.

These parties, often termed whist parties or dances, were usually announced by brightly colored cards stuck in the grille of apartment house elevators ... Almost every Saturday night when I was in Harlem I went to a house-rent party ... I met ladies' maids and truck drivers, laundry workers and shoe shine boys, seamstresses and porters. I can still hear their laughter in my ears, hear the soft slow music, and feel the floor shaking as the dancers danced.

1957

After the Stock Market Crash of 1929, followed by the closing of many factories, shops, and banks, numbers of people in Harlem had no work. But they still wanted to have a little fun once in a while even during the Depression, so the custom of giving pay parties in some homes came into being, with a small charge made at the door, and also for refreshments inside. Such parties became very popular.

Sometimes, at the end of the month, people would give pay parties to help them get the rent together. So these parties came to be known as House Rent Parties, whether the purpose was always to help raise the rent or not. These parties were often announced by small printed cards given out to friends, put into neighborhood mail boxes, or stuck in the elevator grills of apartment houses ...

To come into the party might be a dime or a quarter at that time. For fifteen or twenty cents a hot fish sandwich or a golden-brown chicken leg could be enjoyed. There was dancing, often to very good music. Some of the best piano players in Harlem played at House Rent Parties in the late Twenties and early Thirties – maybe J. P. Johnson, Willie "The Lion" Smith, Dan Burley, or Fats Waller, all of whom eventually became famous. At these parties young pianists developed their styles, had fun themselves, and worked out ways of playing that influenced other jazz pianists.

When I first came to Harlem, as a poet I was intrigued by the little rhymes at the top of most House Rent Party cards, so I saved them. Now I have quite a collection ...

A card announcing a September, 1929 party was headed:

Some wear pajamas
Some wear pants.
What does it matter,
Just so you can dance?

And Lucille and Minnie's card, dated Nov. 2 of that year said:

Fall in line and watch
your step –
There'll be lots of browns
With plenty of pep.

... Usually a good time was had by all, with the piano playing well into the wee hours of the morning.

But with the passing of the depression, such pay parties disappeared from the Harlem scene. Lately, they seem to be coming back into favor again. Maybe it is inflation today and the high cost of living that is causing the return of the pay-at-the-door and buy-your-refreshments parties. Only, unfortunately, instead of live music and all-night-long piano players, now, the juke box, the phonograph, or radios usually furnish the music ...

Source: Langston Hughes, *The Big Sea* (1940; New York: Hill & Wang, 1963), pp. 224–225, 228–229, 233; "House Rent Parties Are Again Returning to Harlem," *Chicago Defender*, March 9, 1957. Reproduced by permission of Real Times Media.

4 Jose Yglesias Describes the 1930s in Tampa and New York City

Compare the accounts above by Jane Yoder (source 8.2) and Langston Hughes (source 8.3) to that of Jose Yglesias, who experienced the Great Depression in Tampa's Ybor City neighborhood – an enclave of Spanish, Cuban, and Italian immigrants – and later in New York City. First, Yglesias's description of cigar workers' protest highlights the impact of New Deal policies on labor protest in urban America. In 1935 Congress passed the Wagner Act, which secured workers' right to form unions, strike, and engage in collective bargaining. Yglesias's family and neighbors took considerable risk by organizing protests in the early 1930s, whereas just years later the federal government was formally committed to protecting similar actions. One result of federal protection and labor's new legitimacy was the formation of a national organization, the Congress of Industrial Organizations, in 1935. The CIO embraced industry-wide organizing and competed fiercely, as discussed here, with "craft" unionists in the American Federation of Labor (AFL). New Deal legislation simultaneously protected the rights of Tampa's immigrant workers and helped set the stage for new contests over political strategies and local control. As Yglesias notes – and the comparison with Yoder and Hughes is revealing – there was widespread disagreement among working-class Americans about the meaning of the government's new interventions.

Consider also how the residents of Ybor City related to the city of Tampa and to other locales, both in the United States and abroad. The son of Cuban and Spanish immigrants, Yglesias did not learn English until he entered public school. Here he recounts the kind of journeys between metropolitan regions and the connections to other nations that were commonplace among American immigrants and their children. By the 1920s, this population outnumbered that of "native" whites in most urban areas.

In the sunlit town, the Depression came imperceptibly. The realization came to me when Aunt Lila said there's no food in the house. My aunt, who owned the house we lived in, would no longer charge rent. It would be shameful to charge rent with $9 a week coming in.

The grocery man would come by and take a little order, which he would bring the next day. When my mother would not order anything because she owed, he'd insist: Why are you cutting down on the beans?

There was a certain difference between the Depression in my home town than elsewhere. They weren't dark, satanic mills. The streets were not like a city ghetto. There were poor homes, that hadn't been painted in years. But it was out in the open. You played in the sunlight. I don't remember real deprivation.

Ybor City was an island in the South. When an American got mad at any Latin, he called him a Cuban nigger. This was one of the first feelings I remember: I want to be an American. You become ashamed of the community. I was an ardent supporter of Henry Ford at the age of twelve.

The strike of 1931 revolved around readers in the factory. The workers themselves used to pay twenty-five to fifty cents a week and would hire a man to read to them during work. A cigar factory is one enormous open area, with tables at which people work. A platform would be erected, so that he'd look down at the cigar makers as he read to them some four hours a day. He would read from newspapers and magazines and a book would be read as a serial. The choice of the book was democratically decided. Some of the readers were marvelous natural actors. They wouldn't just read a book. They'd act out the scenes. Consequently, many cigar makers, who were illiterate, knew the novels of Zola and Dickens and Cervantes and Tolstoy. And the works of the anarchist, Kropotkin. Among the newspapers read were *The Daily Worker* and the *Socialist Call.*

The factory owners decided to put an end to this, though it didn't cost them a penny. Everyone went on strike when they arrived one morning and found the lecture platform torn down. The strike was lost. Every strike in my home town was always lost. The readers never came back.

The Depression began in 1930, with seasonal unemployment. Factories would close down before Christmas, after having worked very hard to fill orders throughout the summer and fall ...

My uncle was a foreman. He was ill-equipped for the job because he couldn't bear to fire anybody. He would discuss it with his wife: We have to cut off so many people. What am I going to do? My aunt would say: You can't fire him. They have twelve children. You'd hear a great deal of talk. You knew things were getting worse. No more apprentices were taken in. My sister was in the last batch.

The strike left a psychological scar on me. I was in junior high school and a member of the student patrol. I wore an arm band. During the strike, workers marched into the schools to close them down, bring the children out. The principal closed the gates, and had the student patrols guard them. If they come, what do I do? My mother was in the strike.

One member of the top strike committee was a woman. That day I stood patrol, she was taken off to jail. Her daughter was kept in the principal's office. I remember walking home from school, about a block behind her, trying to decide whether to tell her of my sympathies, to ask about her mother. I never got to say it. I used to feel bad about that. Years later, in New York, at a meeting for Loyalist Spain, I met her and told her.

Everybody gave ten percent of their pay for the Republic. It was wild. The total community was with Loyalist Spain. They used to send enormous amounts of things. It was totally organized. The song "No pasarán" that was taken to be Spanish was really by a Tampa cigar maker ... It was an extraordinarily radical strike. The cigar makers tried to march to City Hall with red flags, singing the old Italian anarchist song, "Avanti popolo," "Scarlet Banner." ...

It was a Latin town. Men didn't sit at home. They went to cafes, on street corners, at the Labor Temple, which they built themselves. It was very radical talk. The factory owners acted out of fright. The 1931 strike was openly radical. By then, there was a Communist Party in Ybor City. Leaflets would be distributed by people whom you knew. (Laughs.)

During the strike, the KKK would come into the Labor Temple with guns, and break up meetings. Very frequently, they were police in hoods. Though they were called the Citizens' Committee, everyone would call them Los Cuckoo Klan. (Laughs.) The picket lines would hold hands, and the KKK would beat them and cart them off ...

When the strike was lost, the Tampa paper published a full page, in large type: the names of all the members of the strike committee. They were indicted for conspiracy and spent a year in jail. None of them got their jobs back ... There were, of course, many little wildcat strikes. Cigar makers were just incredible ...

There were attempts to organize the CIO. I remember one of my older cousins going around in a very secretive manner. You'd think he was planning the assassination of the czar. He was trying to sign people up for the CIO. The AF of L International was very conservative and always considered as an enemy. They never gave the strike any support. It was considered the work of agitators.

People began to go off to New York to look for jobs. Almost all my family were in New York by 1937. You'd take that bus far to New York. There, we all stayed together. The only place people didn't sleep in was the kitchen. A bed was even in the foyer. People would show up from Tampa, and you'd put them up. We were the Puerto Rican immigrants of that time. In any cafeteria, in the kitchen, the busboys, the dishwashers, you were bound to find at least two from Ybor City.

Some would drift back as jobs would open up again in Tampa. Some went on the WPA. People would put off governmental aid as long as possible. Aunt Lila and her husband were the first in our family, and the last, to go on WPA. This was considered a terrible tragedy, because it was charity. You did not mention it to them.

That didn't mean you didn't accept another thing. There was no payday in any cigar factory that there wasn't a collection for anyone in trouble. If a father died, there was a collection for the funeral. When my father went to Havana for an operation, there was a collection. That was all right. You yourself didn't ask. Someone said: "Listen, so and so's in trouble." When Havana cigar makers would go on strike, it was a matter of honor; you sent money to them. It has to do with the Spanish-Cuban tradition ...

My family thought very highly of Roosevelt, except my grandfather. As a young man, he had known José Martí the Cuban liberator ... He'd say, "Hoover was just a mean old skinflint and Roosevelt is just another Mussolini." But the New Deal did become the basis of a new union drive. And people did find work ...

Source: Interview with Jose Yglesias, in Studs Terkel, *Hard Times: An Oral History of the Great Depression* (New York: Washington Square Press, 1970), pp. 133–137.

Chapter 9 The Metropolis at War

1 The LA Chamber of Commerce Coordinates the Region's War Production Efforts, 1942–1943

World War II created spectacular opportunities for the nation's metropolitan regions. Each year the federal government spent millions of dollars on war materials and services, quickly reviving the fortunes of local and regional economies still staggering from the Great Depression and drawing a wave of migrants to major cities from Los Angeles to Philadelphia. Meanwhile the Department of Defense financed and built manufacturing plants for large private firms, in exchange for their commitment to devote the facilities, temporarily, to war production. Military spending would steadily increase throughout the Cold War and remain a decisive force in metropolitan and regional development (source 11.2).

Cities' mobilization for war was facilitated by the long-standing development tradition of boosterism, as local civic and business leaders coordinated efforts to secure the benefits of federal spending (sources 1.1, 3 and 3.4). Boosters in select locales worked to attract military installations in the 1920s and 1930s, but the mobilization for World War II quickly drew numerous municipalities, especially in Pacific Coast and Southwestern states, into competition for lucrative federal contracts. The cities that prevailed, in states from Oregon to Texas to Virginia, were transformed by the resultant economic expansion and population growth. This sample of articles from Southern California Business, *a publication of the Los Angeles Chamber of Commerce, reveals the depth of public–private cooperation necessary*

The Modern American Metropolis: A Documentary Reader, First Edition.
Edited by David M. P. Freund.

to coordinate production and meet wartime demand, itself a remarkable technical and managerial accomplishment. Also documented here is Southern California's heavy reliance on federal spending, the lobbying efforts required to secure military contracts, and widespread concern about the future of the region's economy once those contracts dried up. How did the Chamber view the US government's role in Los Angeles's wartime expansion? How did it understand the balance between federal spending and private initiative?

Millions in Blocked L.A. Trade Opened up by Chamber of Commerce

A $2,000,000 annual trade between Los Angeles and Peru, blocked by wartime red tape and confusion, has been reopened for a single local company through the Washington service of the Los Angeles Chamber of Commerce.

... Harry C. Reed, of the firm of Reed & Romano ... wrote [to us] as follows:

"We have a project in South America for the canning of fish, and as far back as last October we made application with our Government for export licenses and priorities to ship empty cans and cases to Peru, which are vitally necessary for the operation of our plant. Our application had been rejected and was delayed for various reasons."

... Mr. Reed ... turned to the Chamber of Commerce ... [which] put him in touch with the Washington office of the Chamber ... Mr. Reed [continues]:

"I just want to state that assistance was immediately forthcoming, and within a very short time the Government issued the necessary licenses."

"What we were unable to do in several months' negotiation by correspondence your office was able to accomplish in a few weeks' time."

"Securing these licenses will permit us to do an annual business of $2,000,000 with Peru – all of which will be handled through the Port of Los Angeles ... All of our cans, cases and labels will be purchased from Los Angeles manufacturers, so in assisting us your organization is helping to create business for others in Los Angeles County, too."

Look! Nation getting View of Something We Always Saw

Always it has been known in this region, and now the nation is being told about it.

The national magazine, *Look*, in its August 25 issue, is featuring "California – Arsenal of Our Air Power" in the lead article. Five full pages of story and pictures are presented, telling how eight manufacturing plants in Los Angeles and San Diego Counties have performed a miracle that the people did not believe could happen.

J. C. Herric, *Look's* West Coast editor ... says, in fact, that miracles just "don't happen – somebody makes them happen." He pays high tribute to Southern California's eight "young men" (average age 45) who made California the arsenal of U.S. airpower. They are Richard Millar, formerly of Vultee Aircraft ..., Donald Douglas of Douglas Aircraft, Harry Woodhead of Consolidated Aircraft, J. H. Kindelberger of North American, Robert Gross of Lockheed Aircraft, Courtlandt Gross of Vega Airplane, and T. Claude Ryan of Ryan Aeronautical.

Source: *Southern California Business*, 4(27), August 17, 1942. University of Southern California Libraries, Special Collections.

Industrial Expansion Here in 9 Months Creates 100,000 jobs

Creation of jobs for 100,000 workers in Los Angeles County in the first nine months this year, through investment of $77,600,000 for new industrial plants and expansion of existing ones, is announced by the Los Angeles Chamber of Commerce Industrial Department.

... Among the new industries, those for the manufacture of synthetic rubber are notable in interest and size ... but there are many others of importance to this area. For example, a plant will soon be in operation for the production of welding rods suitable for shipyard use, a new venture in this region. Another factory will be devoted to the manufacture of almost microscopic jeweled bearings for Army and Navy instruments, which likewise is a "first" in the West.

A new plant already is producing tungsten carbide cutting tools ... Many new airplane parts manufacturing establishments have been started.

Among the 286 plants spending $30,300,000 for increased facilities, airplane factories and their industrial satellites making airplane parts take first place.

Other important expansions include plants engaged in the manufacture of aluminum tubing, screw machine products, tools, uniform caps, salesbooks, gears, food products, high-octane gasoline, open hearth steel, and steel, brass and magnesium castings.

Source: *Southern California Business*, 4(36), October 19, 1942. University of Southern California Libraries, Special Collections.

50 New War Construction Contracts Awarded

The Chamber's Construction Industries Department reports that the latest release from the War Department lists award of 50 contracts for war construction in Southern California.

One contract was for $1,000,000 to $5,000,000. One was for $500,000 to $1,000,000. Ten were for $100,000 to $500,000. Nine were for $50,000 to $100,000. Twenty-nine were for contracts under $50,000.

ODT Certificates of War Necessity Slated Soon

Applications for certificates of war necessity in connection with the Office of Defense Transportation's new program of transport conservation should not be sent to Washington, the ODT says.

Application blanks, together with complete instructions on how to fill them out, will be mailed soon to every person registered … as the owner of a truck, bus, taxicab, ambulance, hearse, jitney or other type of motor vehicle …

WPB Wants 2,470 Miles of Pipe for War Project

… Urgent need for this enormous quantity of vari-sized pipe lengths is announced by the San Francisco Regional War Production Board to fill an order for emergency war project …

All pipe offered must be No. 1 pipe plain end or threaded and coupled and in carload lots.

Congratulations to:

Louis Breer, president of Lohman Brothers Co., Los Angeles, who has been appointed a member of the Heating Contractors Industry Advisory Committee to the War Production Board.

J. Hauerwass, of the Boyle Manufacturing Co., Los Angeles, who has been appointed a member of the Galvanized Ware Manufacturers Industry Advisory Committee to the War Production Board.

Domestic Trade Department Reports War Services

War services performed by the Domestic Trade Department of the Chamber in August are reported as follows:

A total of 2,902 calls for bid were analyzed and referred to Los Angeles manufacturers and wholesalers.

A total of 1,506 opportunities for war business were referred to Los Angeles firms.

Personal calls were made by staff members on 14 shipbuilding companies and 37 chemical and electrical firms to give assistance in problems of war conversion, contracts, and purchasing.

Assistance was given to purchasing offices of the Pan-American Highway Commission, the Marine Corps Base at San Diego, Camp Young at Indio, the Engineers Corps at Douglas, Ariz., and the San Bernardino Quartermaster Depot.

Source: *Southern California Business*, 4(32), September 21, 1942. University of Southern California Libraries, Special Collections.

Manpower Drive on in 2 Weeks

Machinery for the vast job of conducting a house-to-house canvass in every residential section of the city and county, to recruit workers for critical war industries and smaller plants in the area, is making rapid progress.

LeRoy M. Edwards, general chairman of the city and county sponsored Citizens' Manpower Committee [explained]:

"We hope to recruit sufficient workers not only to man the essential aircraft, shipbuilding and high-octane gasoline plants, but also our painstakingly nurtured small industries ... and our thousands of civilian services upon which home front workers depend as much in war as in peacetime." ...

... A subcommittee, headed by Sam Leask Jr., former OPA head and now vice-president of J.W. Robinson Co., has been prepared after consultation with the United States Employment Service and personnel managers of the aircraft, shipbuilding and the high-octane gasoline industry ...

Source: *Southern California Business*, 5(40), November 1, 1943. University of Southern California Libraries, Special Collections.

Kenneth T. Norris on Industry Advisory Committee

Kenneth T. Norris, president of the Norris Stamping and Manufacturing Co. of Los Angeles, has just won national distinction in being the only businessman in the western part of the United States chosen to sit on President Roosevelt's new industrial advisory committee.

The committee was named by Mr. Roosevelt to meet with him at frequent intervals and keep the Chief Executive advised as to policies needed to make industry's role in the war effort most effective ...

Source: *Southern California Business*, 5(41), November 8, 1943. University of Southern California Libraries, Special Collections.

Chamber Acts to End Labor Crisis

With Los Angeles facing immediate threat of cancellation of many war contracts unless sufficient manpower can be developed to keep wheels turning in industry, the Chamber of Commerce Board of Directors has approved a plan for action recommended by the Emergency Manpower Committee ... A committee of directors ... has been instructed to call on city and county officials and invite their sponsorship of the manpower campaign as a civil enterprise ...

[F]ear has been expressed that the closing of many factories and the concentration of employment in aircraft and shipbuilding industries may result ... That such a concentration would have serious adverse effects upon the community's economic stability and on postwar conversion is openly acknowledged ...

Tip-off on Contract Cancellation Formula

... Industrialists were warned that manufacturing plants with the lowest man-hour efficiency and the highest scrap piles would be the first to lose their government business.

Revelation came during a program put on by officials of the Smaller War Plants Corporation ...

"Every holder of a war contract," [the audience was informed,] *"should immediately draft plans for future activities based upon the possibility of contract cancellation any time within the next three to 18 months."*

Source: *Southern California Business*, 5(36), October 4, 1943. University of Southern California Libraries, Special Collections.

2 Henry Cervantes Describes His Journey from Migrant Farm Worker to World War II Hero

This 2004 interview with Henry Cervantes might not, at first glance, seem like a source in metropolitan history. Yet, in describing his path from immigrant laborer to Air Force pilot in World War II, Cervantes connects many of the variables – industrialization and innovation, migration and immigration, expanding state power, the growth of mass media, new kinds of opportunity and exclusion – that together forged the mid-twentieth-century city. His story also shows how these variables helped sustain a deeply patriotic public, one largely unified behind the war effort despite the tensions and divisions that characterized everyday life. American cities, their industrial production, and their residents' tireless efforts were essential ingredients in turning the tide in World War II. Catching a glimpse of those residents' lives and their travels through the American metropolis helps us see how the nation mobilized human and material resources to effectively prosecute the war.

This account also helps us think about how marginalized groups viewed patriotism in light of their limited access to rights and opportunity, and how the urbanization process continued to shape people's views about and struggles for inclusion. The domestic front during World War II saw considerable debate and protest over the meaning of American citizenship. When wartime production drew women into professions previously reserved for men, it generated increasing conflict over their proper "role" both in the workplace and at home, while exacerbating tensions between women of different ethnic and racial backgrounds. Meanwhile, despite the endurance of Jim Crow and widespread discrimination and violence against racial minorities, black Americans expressed considerable support for the war. Indeed they viewed that support as part of an ongoing struggle to secure political equality and economic opportunity. Hispanic and Asian Americans, whether longtime residents or recent immigrants, were also supportive of the war but nonetheless faced constant discrimination and hostility. The internment of Japanese Americans, the Zoot Suit Riots, and numerous shopfloor "hate strikes" were among the most widely publicized attacks on minorities' status and rights (sources 9.3–4).

Cervantes also juxtaposes two facets of urban war production that are too often treated separately: what it was like to work in the industries that produced for the war, and how the aircraft and supplies built in in those places were eventually used (source 9.1). Cervantes was employed in a production center just northeast of San Francisco Bay.

RODRIGUEZ: We're sitting at ... the National Archives building in Washington, D.C. ... and Colonel Hank Cervantes has been nice enough to let us interview him for the U.S. Latino and Latina World War Two Oral History Project ... Mr. Cervantes ... it's the middle of the ... 60th anniversary of ... D-day. And there's lots of events going on for this Memorial Day ... And so I really appreciate you taking the time.

CERVANTES: Good morning ...

ASHCROFT: Thank you ... [a]nd it's my sincere pleasure to have the chance to meet you and talk with you. And one of the things that I'm always curious about is what inspired you to become an Air Force pilot?

CERVANTES: My aspiration ... began at, very early in, in my, in age. It was a very unusual circumstance ... I was ... a child of ... very, very poor parents ... [W]e moved about in central California picking crops. But ... regardless of how often we moved about, my mother always ... insisted that my brother and I ... not ... miss school. And ... when I was in third grade ... [t]he teacher held me over late one afternoon. And she said ... "Henry, because you speak Spanish at home, there's no reason for you not to learn to speak English here." ... [Later, on my eighth birthday], she gave me a ... card, wrote a little poem on it, and gave it to me as a present ... "Dream your dreams upon a star. Dream them high, and dream them far. For the dreams that we dream in you make us what we are." ... I thought that it had to do with aviation, with flying, high ... [a]nd I began thinking about being a pilot at that age. I'm sure that you and everyone else will agree that some little guy looking like a discarded rag pile out in the middle of a vegetable field and thinking about being a pilot isn't thinking. He's dreaming ... We're talking now about the early 1930s ... I wanted to go up there so badly because I felt so ashamed of being Mexican, brown, and poor.

ASHCROFT: And some of the pilots that I have talked to from the World War Two [era] mentioned the movies from the 1930s and 1940s ...

CERVANTES: Yeah ... [w]hat did inspire me ... was ... "A Guy Named Joe." ... [I]t was all about B-38s and the uh, the flying situation. And ... I wanted obviously to be one of those guys, that leather jacket was my big inspiration ... [A]lthough I was a very good high school athlete, I, we could not afford for me to have a letterman sweater with a big chenille letter on it. And so that was my next desire, if you will ...

...

RODRIGUEZ: ... I know that you were working in the fields with your family when you were a kid. How old were you when you started working in the fields? ...

CERVANTES: I'm sure, I would guess that around seven or eight, eight years old ... by 10 or 11, there's no question I was out there ... The whole family did, the whole family went out. We uh, we lived in a tent. We dug a hole in the ground, and my mother put a grate over it, and that's where my mother cooked. Uh at night we hung a kerosene lantern for illumination. We fashioned mattresses from uh gunny ... sacks filled with corn husks. And we burned horse manure to get rid of the mosquitoes. And we, the entire family got up at uh four o'clock in the morning. We had a simple breakfast. Then my mother wrapped our heads with towels and rags to ward off the sun ... The entire family went out and began working as soon as daylight came. And uh, uh if a woman had to go, other women formed a circle around her. If a man had to go, he went behind a tree. Water came in a ten gallon milk can with a ladle tied to it. Uh by ten o'clock when the sun was starting to beat down on us, our backs were wet like wet cellophane, uh clouds of mosquitoes and gnats just rose and fell on us, landed on us like little vultures as we moved about. Uh the kids were crying. Uh our knees were bleeding. Our cuticles were bleeding. The back of our legs hurt. Uh noon time came, and we uh, we'd sit under a, if we were picking grapes, we'd try to sit in the shade of a grape vine. If we were out in the fields, we'd sit on the clods under the dirt, under the tree and eat our cold tacos. The gnats and bugs had ate the tacos along with us. We ate them as condiments ...

And at night we'd have to, we lived in a, one place I can recall, we lived in a, in a little motel, and the room was so small that we had to move the kitchen table outside so that we could put the mattress down on the floor so we could sleep on it. But we didn't have it as bad as other people. Other people were living in little huddles fashioned from, from cardboard, uh old mattress springs and, and tree branches, next to creeks ... We lived from day to day. Whatever we uh earned today was what we spent the next day.

...

ASHCROFT: [I]n your squadron ... or combat wing, were there other Hispanic pilots ... or ground crew?

CERVANTES: I was in ... flight school in Phoenix ... They gave us three days off. And so I went into Phoenix to look around, walked into a hotel and saw a Mexican family sitting on a, on a van, mother, father, three, four kids. And their eldest son, who was a brand new ... Second Lietentant in the infantry. I had never seen Mexican officer before. Uh I'd seen many number of privates ... [Y]ou could see the pride the mother had in him, and his father, and his little brothers and sisters were just looking at him like he was a god ... And ... so I said to myself, "Mud, flood, or blood you're going to stay in this program, even if it kills you." And it wasn't easy because I took all my flying training in Arizona from ... Phoenix to Tuscan [*sic*] to Douglas. And Douglas was right on the border. And it doesn't take much imagination to, to picture all of the slurs and, and insults, and the bad jokes I had to endure in those days.

...

RODRIGUEZ: ... You mentioned that, that there, that you had not met uh another Hispanic officer when you were in the military. Why was that? Why were there not more Hank Cervanteses? ...

CERVANTES: ... I can't answer your question truthfully because I don't know why. Uh I'm sure that uh many of the Mexican soldiers didn't think that they could make it anymore than I did ... [When] I was inducted into the Army ... I was taken in with a very good friend of mine named Phil Samora ... One day we were walking down the Army camp ... and he said, "Hey Hank, mira they're looking for pilots." And I said, "Where, guy?" And he said, "Over there, you see the sign?" And he says, "It says, 'take a test and become a pilot in the United States Army Corps.'" And he said, "Let's go take the test." ... "Even if we fail it, maybe they'll let us work around the airplanes. It's better than dragging this rifle around." I said, "Okay, let's go take it." So, so that's how, that's how, how it happened with me ... I'm sure there were many other Mexican kids who felt exactly the way I did at the moment, that they couldn't make it, and I'm sure that there were many people in, in the positions of authority that made sure they couldn't make it if they did try. But some of us were able to slip through uh those people. Uh what I think was more difficult for me was that I'm darker than some of the lighter-skinned guys, you know, would expect, would've gotten through easier. But because I was darker, I think I was the exception. I never did a, anyone as dark as I in an officer's uniform, other than black officers. So I was always some-, someone different, you know, people would always approach me with a, a little feeling of, "Who in the hell is this?" And when I'd walk up, you know, after I retired, and I'd walk into a group of people like I have in the last two, three days. And I say, "Well, I was a pilot too." And uh they look at me like out of the corner eye like, "Where'd this guy come from. You know, this guy's trying to come on with something." Something happened uh yesterday. This guy was, he knew he was putting me down. And I knew he was putting down, me down. But nobody else did. And he caught up in emphasizing "Mister." And so when he was through with his little exercise, I went up close ... to his ear, and I said, "I'm a Colonel." And he immediately started saying, "Yes, sir. No, sir." So I have experience that, experienced that all my life. And I love playing with him, I loved it, bring him on in and then teach him a little lesson of how to be respectful to people … I let them play their little game … until I think I've got 'em pretty well roped in. And then I'll lay it upon 'em one way or the other … For example they'll say, "What'd you fly? Well, did you fly transports?" "Yeah, I flew transports. I also flew bombers, and I flew fighters. And I was a test pilot …"

…

RODRIGUEZ: [W]here were you born?

CERVANTES: Fresno, California … [in 1923] …

RODRIGUEZ: [A]nd where did you go to school …?

CERVANTES: … Easterby … Grammar School in the east side of Fresno … [also] in Pittsburgh, California … Then I graduated from grammar school in Oakley, California … I attended high school in Brentwood, California … [and] my … Vice Principal … [encouraged me to take] college preparatory courses … And I said, "What's this? I don't need this. I, I can't go to college. My, my parents can't send me to college. We work in the fields." … The very next day, we were out picking apricots. I knew what I was going to be. I was going to be a farm worker …

RODRIGUEZ: Now you graduated in, in '41, and so what did you do right after graduation until you ended up in the military?

CERVANTES: I worked in the fields uh for a considerable period at the time. And within about less than a year before I went into the service, I got a job on a labor gang in the steel mill … [i]n Pittsburgh, out in California, Columbia Steel Company. And … I did the … dirtiest, hardest, most, most difficult jobs I could ever imagined. They were just horrible jobs … [W]e were working around open-hearth furnaces … [W]e would wear clogs over our shoes and while we were working, a fellow would be standing outside with a water hose, throwing water at us so our shoes wouldn't catch on fire …

…

RODRIGUEZ: … What does it mean to be a test pilot? How does that set someone apart …?

CERVANTES: … There are a number of different types of test pilots. There are experimental test pilots such as Chuck Yeager. And there are acceptance test pilots, pilots who accept new airplanes coming into the, into the inventory … I was … an engineering test pilot. And I tested airplanes that had … major maintenance for example, changes … of engines and wings or the modification of equipment. And … what made it uh a very dicey situation in my day was that it was right after we had began … getting … jet airplanes in the, in the Air Force. And so not only were we learning high speed, high altitude ... flight, but our mechanics were learning how to maintain a jet airplane. And so uh they often, often made mistakes ...

... I was certified to fly ... a C-47, a C-45, a B-25, a B-26, a B-47, a B-58, ... an F-80, a T-33, a F-84, F-84F, uh F-102. That's all that comes to mind ...

...

CERVANTES: ... When I took my first trip down to Mexico, I went to Mexico City ... after I'd retired ... I checked in the Ritz hotel in downtown Mexico City. And I immediately went out for a walk ... to experience Mexico City. And I hadn't gone two blocks when I felt this sense of relief. It was like somebody had lifted a 50 pound sack off my back. And it was ... so palpable that I went to a uh bus stop, and I sat down on a bench and tried to figure out what it was. And I finally realized that, that it was ... because I was among Mexicans, I didn't have to be on my guard ... I was there among people who, who weren't judging me. And I, and I ... clearly remember I wanted to climb on top of one of those huge monuments and stand up there and face north and say, "God damn you! [pause] You gave me all those medals. Why is it I have to come down here to feel like a man?" That's how I felt. They give you the medals and yet they discriminate you. And that's the way it is folks. We're not over it yet.

...

ASHCROFT: [Y]ou were part of a very famous or infamous group during the war [known as] the Bloody 110th ... [and you] had an encounter with an ME262, I believe ...

CERVANTES: We ... had several encounters with the 262s. They were the first jet fighters in the world ... They were deadly. The first time I ever saw one, we were flying over Brunswick ... [A]ll of the sudden we, without a warning, we saw these two ... airplanes come flashing into the forma[tion] ... and we'd never seen an airplane like that ... Uh now these things are flying fast, 100 miles an hour faster than anything I'd ever seen. It didn't have propellers. Uh this black smoke was streaming out of the back of it ... And we were totally mystified ... [It] fired at the leader, the first of [our] two airplanes ... [which] immediately caught on fire ... [T]he pilot held the airplane, his name was Jack Thrasher, very good friend of mine. He continued to hold the airplane steady ... while his crew bailed out. And immediately after that, it blew up with him at the controls. Uh great loss, a fine, fine young man ...

Source: Henry "Hank" Cervantes, interviewed by Maggie Rivas-Rodriguez and Bruce Ashcroft, Washington, DC, May 30, 2004, videotape recording, U.S. Latino and Latina World War II Oral History Project. Reproduced with permission from VOCES Oral History Project, The University of Texas at Austin.

3 White Transit Workers Walk Off the Job in Philadelphia, 1944

In August of 1944, while Philadelphia's manufacturers were struggling to fulfill the demands of war production, the federal government required that the city's streetcar line, the Philadelphia Transportation Company (PTC), permit its black employees to work in the skilled and better-paying positions of motorman and conductor. The PTC's white employees insisted that blacks be restricted to menial positions, and responded to the federal order by walking off the job for five days. By August 6, a day after this report appeared in the local press, the government had settled the dispute and secured more positions for black PTC employees by assuming control of the transit system and threatening strikers with punishment.

The event marked one of many flashpoints, nationwide, in the struggle over access to the opportunities afforded by modern metropolitan life. Another wartime wave of migration from the South, again spurred by the demand for industrial labor, continued to expand the African American populations of Northern cities like Philadelphia (source 4.5). And the demand for black workers, coupled with the rhetoric of a war to "defend democracy," helped to energize blacks' long-standing efforts to assert their constitutional rights and their right to economic opportunity, articulated in the national "Double V" campaign – fighting for victory both in the war and in the domestic struggle for rights – sponsored by a black-owned newspaper, the Pittsburgh Courier. *World War II became an important turning point in the civil rights struggle. The US government, engaged in a war against an openly racist state, was especially vulnerable to challenges by civil rights activists. Two years before the PTC strike, A. Philip Randolph used the threat of a mass demonstration to pressure Franklin Delano Roosevelt to require that businesses receiving federal war contracts commit to fair hiring practices. This was the first executive or legislative action on behalf of black Americans' rights since the end of Reconstruction. In light of this national victory, the success of local efforts in places like Philadelphia helped to create momentum and to train future activists for the protests that would revolutionize the politics of race and rights in the following decades (sources 12.1–2, 4). What does this account of the strike by a* Philadelphia Tribune *reporter reveal about the wartime politics of race and opportunity and their impacts on urban life? Why did white and black PTC employees interpret their obligations and privileges so differently?*

The Jap sneak attack at Pearl Harbor had nothing on the one launched on citizens here by the employees of the Philadelphia Transportation Company, Tuesday.

Led by Frank P. Carney, president of the deposed PRT Employees Union, 6000 trolley, bus and subway-elevated line operators and conductors went on strike, paralyzing the city's transit system, and tying up war plants and private industry. Twenty-five hundred trolleys and buses stand idle in the yards while Philadelphia's million and a half car riders trudge wearily to their jobs, or, if they are fortunate share a ride with kindly neighbors.

Many war plants whose production was cut twenty-five percent, including the Navy Yard and the Philadelphia Signal Corps, have made arrangements to pick up their workers at strategic points throughout the city.

Federal officials, members of the War Labor Board, the War Production Board, the Fair Employment Practice Committee and the War Manpower Commission, have given up all attempts to negotiate with the strikers and have referred the situation to Washington for settlement, where it was formally certified to the War Labor Board early Wednesday morning.

It is expected that a report will be sent to President Roosevelt, who will have the final say on whether or not the Army shall take over the system.

Violence flared in various sections of the city Tuesday night but there were no serious injuries reported and no fatalities.

Monday night, at the Frankford car house Carney and an associate, William Fogg, addressed employees of the company urging that their "D Day" had arrived and that the company's move to place Negroes on the trolleys was threatening the very existence of those operators who were already employed and jeopardizing the jobs of the men who were in the armed forces.

"We must keep them (Negroes) in their places. They are allright as porters or maintenance workers, but we can't have them running trolleys," he said.

From the Frankford house Carney and Fogg went to the Richmond barn, at Richmond and Allegheny avenues, and made a similar statement. The well-planned walk-out was underway.

In less than an hour the word had spread throughout the city and PTO and City officials were warned that there would be a tie-up of transportation facilities in the morning.

Crew men, completing the night shift, were apprised of the situation. Day shift men were told and if they insisted on taking their runs were advised. "You're sick, if you take that car out you are apt to have an accident." They heeded the striker's admonition.

By noon on Tuesday there wasn't a single unit of the PTC in operation ..., leaving thousands of Philadelphians stranded in the downtown section ...

Hurried consultations with Mayor Bernard Samuel and the PTC officials joining with Governmental representatives failed to produce any agreement.

At one of the meetings ... [PTC officials] proposed that the following notice ... be posted in car barn bulletin boards:

NOTICE:

Stoppage of PTC service has crippled every war industry in the Philadelphia area. Service must be restored immediately to prevent critical interference with vital war production.

The first duty of this company is to provide service to the war effort and the public.

Therefore, provisions of the notice dated July 7, 1944, regarding changes in employment practices to comply with the directive of the War Manpower Commission, are suspended.

Philadelphia Transportation Company

[Federal officials responded] that acceptance of the PTC proposal would be tantamount to surrendering the Federal Government's authority in the manpower situation in the United States.

Source: George Lyle, Jr., "Army Intervention Looms as Deadlock Continues," *Philadelphia Tribune*, August 5, 1944, pp. 1, 3.

4 Jeanne Wakatsuki Houston Recounts Her Family's Forced Relocation from Santa Monica, California

In February of 1942, President Franklin D. Roosevelt issued Executive Order 9066, authorizing US officials to remove Japanese American civilians from designated areas of the country and confine them in government-run internment camps. As many as 120,000 Japanese Americans from California, Washington, Oregon, and Arizona were ordered to abandon their communities and relocated to ten hastily built camps in locations from northern California to southeastern Arkansas, where most remained until the war's end. Two-thirds of the detainees were US citizens. The episode was a stark reminder of the power of racial ideology and state authority in shaping American places. Neither German nor Italian Americans were targeted solely because of their national origin. Well-established Japanese American enclaves were cleared of their populations, families lost personal property including homes and businesses, and all were denied their constitutional rights.

Jeanne Wakatsuki Houston's narrative of her family's relocation to the camp at Manzanar, in California's Central Valley, begins with Japan's attack on Pearl Harbor and ends with her family's return to the site of the abandoned camp in 1972. The facility stood on land that was originally Paiute territory before the US Army removed them in the 1860s to Fort Tejon (see sources 1.3 and 14.5), clearing the way for Anglo settlers to farm the region. Then, between the 1910s and 1930s, the city of Los Angeles purchased most of the valley's property and with it rights to the water, which it channeled southward to satisfy its growing population. This left the valley comparatively desolate by the time that the US War Relocation Authority opened the Manzanar camp in 1942, on land leased from the city of Los Angeles. Within months the facility held over 10,000 people and was in effect the largest city between Los Angeles, California, and Reno, Nevada. Its detainees shared rooms in poorly built barracks without plumbing and withstood the Central Valley's climatic extremes. Still, they managed to sustain families and communities until their release in 1945, when they were given little more than transit fare and instructions to return home. Those who refused to leave – because they had nowhere to go – were forcibly removed. In this excerpt Houston describes the first months of her family's ordeal following the Japanese attack on Pearl Harbor, providing a glimpse of the Japanese American urban communities that were relocated by war throughout the American West.

On that first weekend in December there must have been twenty or twenty-five boats getting ready to leave. I had just turned seven. I remember it was Sunday because I was out of school, which meant I could go down to the wharf and watch. In those days – 1941 – there was no smog around Long Beach. The water was clean, the sky a sharp Sunday blue, with all the engines of that white sardine fleet puttering up into it, and a lot of yelling, especially around Papa's boat. Papa loved to give orders. He had attended military school in Japan until the age of seventeen, and part of him never got over that. My oldest brothers, Bill and Woody, were his crew. They would have to check the nets again, and check the fuel tanks again, and run back to the grocery store for some more cigarettes, and then somehow everything had been done, and they were easing away from the wharf, joining the line of boats heading out past the lighthouse, into the harbor.

Papa's boat was called the *Nereid* ... He had another smaller boat, called *The Waka* (a short version of our name), which he kept in Santa Monica, where we lived. But *The Nereid* was his pride. It was worth about $25,000 before the war ...

Through one of the big canneries he had made a deal to pay for *The Nereid* with percentages of each catch, and he was anxious to get it paid off.

He didn't much like working for someone else if he could help it. A lot of fishermen around San Pedro Harbor had similar contracts with the canneries. In typical Japanese fashion, they all wanted to be independent commercial fishermen, yet they almost always fished together. They would take off from Terminal Island, help each other find the schools of sardine, share nets and radio equipment – competing and cooperating at the same time.

You never knew how long they'd be gone, a couple of days, sometimes a week, sometimes a month, depending on the fish. From the wharf we waved good-bye – my mother, Bill's wife, Woody's wife, Chizu, and me. We yelled at them to have a good trip, and after they were out of earshot and the sea had swallowed their engine noises, we kept waving. Then we just stood there with the other women, watching … We watched until the boats became a row of tiny white gulls on the horizon. Our vigil would end when they slipped over the edge and disappeared …

But this time they didn't disappear. They kept floating out there, suspended, as if the horizon had finally become what it always seemed to be from shore: the sea's limit, beyond which no man could sail. They floated awhile, then they began to grow, tiny gulls becoming boats again, a white armada cruising toward us.

"They're coming back," my mother said.

"Why would they be coming back?" Chizu said.

"Something with the engine."

"Maybe somebody got hurt."

"But they wouldn't *all* come back," Mama said, bewildered.

Another woman said, "Maybe there's a storm coming."

They all glanced at the sky, scanning the unmarred horizon. Mama shook her head. There was no explanation. No one had ever seen anything like this before. We watched and waited, and when the boats were still about half a mile off the lighthouse, a fellow from the cannery came running down to the wharf shouting that the Japanese had just bombed Pearl Harbor.

Chizu said to Mama, "What does that mean? What is Pearl Harbor?"

Mama yelled at him, "What is Pearl Harbor?"

But he was running along the docks, like Paul Revere, bringing the news, and didn't have time to explain.

That night Papa burned the flag he had brought with him from Hiroshima thirty-five years earlier … He burned a lot of papers too, documents, anything that might suggest he still had some connection with Japan. These precautions didn't do him much good. He was not only an alien; he held a commercial fishing license, and in the early days of the war the FBI was picking up all such men, for fear they were somehow making contact with enemy ships off the coast. Papa himself knew it would only be a matter of time.

They got him two weeks later, when we were staying overnight at Woody's place, on Terminal Island. Five hundred Japanese families lived there then, and FBI deputies had been questioning everyone, ransacking houses for anything that could conceivably be used for signaling planes or ships or that indicated loyalty to the Emperor. Most of the houses had radios with a short-wave band and a high aerial on the roof so that wives could make contact with the fishing boats during these long cruises. To the FBI every radio owner was a potential saboteur. The confiscators were often deputies sworn in hastily during the turbulent days right after Pearl Harbor, and these men seemed to be acting out the general panic, seeing sinister possibilities in the most ordinary household items: flashlights, kitchen knives, cameras, lanterns, toy swords.

If Papa were trying to avoid arrest, he wouldn't have gone near that island. But I think he knew it was futile to hide out or resist. The next morning two FBI men in fedora hats and trench coats – like out of a thirties movie – knocked on Woody's door, and when they left, Papa was between them. He didn't struggle. There was no point to it. He had become a man without a country. The land of his birth was at war with America; yet after thirty-five years here he was still prevented by law from becoming an American citizen. He was suddenly a man with no rights who looked exactly like the enemy ...

About all he had left at this point was his tremendous dignity ... He was over fifty. Ten children and a lot of hard luck had worn him down ... But he still had dignity, and he would not let those deputies push him out the door. He led them.

Mama knew they were taking all the alien men first to an interrogation center right there on the island. Some were simply being questioned and released ... But it grew dark and he wasn't back. Another day went by and we still had heard nothing. Then word came that he had been taken into custody and shipped out. Where to, or for how long? No one knew ...

What had they charged him with? We didn't know that either, until an article appeared the next day in the Santa Monica paper, saying he had been arrested for delivering oil to Japanese submarines offshore.

My mother began to weep ... This was the beginning of a terrible, frantic time for all my family ...

In December of 1941 Papa's disappearance didn't bother me nearly so much as the world I soon found myself in.

He had been a jack-of-all-trades. When I was born he was farming near Inglewood. Later, when he started fishing, we moved to Ocean Park, near

Santa Monica, and until they picked him up, that's where we lived, in a big frame house with a brick fireplace, a block back from the beach. We were the only Japanese family in the neighborhood ... But with him gone and no way of knowing what to expect, my mother moved all of us down to Terminal Island. Woody already lived there, and one of my older sisters had married a Terminal Island boy. Mama's first concern now was to keep the family together, and once the war began, she felt safer there than isolated racially in Ocean Park. But for me, at age seven, the island was a country as foreign as India or Arabia would have been. It was the first time I had lived among other Japanese, or gone to school with them ...

In those days it was a company town, a ghetto owned and controlled by the canneries. The men went after fish, and whenever the boats came back – day or night – the women would be called to process the catch while it was fresh ... My mother had to go to work right after we moved there. I can still hear the whistle – two toots for French's, three for Van Camp's – and she and Chizu would be out of bed in the middle of the night, heading for the cannery.

The house we lived in was nothing more than a shack, a barracks with single plank walls and rough wooden floors, like the cheapest kind of migrant workers' housing. The people around us were hardworking, boisterous, a little proud of their nick-name, *yo-go-re*, which meant literally *uncouth one*, or roughneck, or dead-end kid. They not only spoke Japanese exclusively, they spoke a dialect peculiar to Kyushu, where their families had come from in Japan ... They would swagger and pick on outsiders and persecute anyone who didn't speak as they did ... I had never spoken anything but English, and the other kids in the second grade despised me for it ... Each day after school I dreaded their ambush. My brother Kiyo, three years older, would wait for me at the door, where we would decide whether to run straight home together, or split up, or try a new and unexpected route ...

None of these kids ever actually attacked. It was the threat that frightened us, their fearful looks ...

... [W]e lived there about two months [when] the navy decided to clear Terminal Island completely. Even though most of us were American-born, it was dangerous having that many Orientals so close to the Long Beach Naval State, on the opposite end of the island ... There were four of us kids still young enough to be living with Mama, plus Granny, her mother, sixty-five then, speaking no English, and nearly blind. Mama didn't know where else she could get work, and we had nowhere else to move *to*. On February 25 the choice was made for us. We were given forty-eight hours to clear out.

The secondhand dealers had been prowling around for weeks, like wolves, offering humiliating prices for goods and furniture they knew many of us would have to sell sooner or later ...

The American Friends Service helped us find a small house in Boyle Heights, another minority ghetto, in downtown Los Angeles, now inhabited briefly by a few hundred Terminal Island refugees. Executive Order 9066 had been signed by President Roosevelt ... There was a lot of talk about internment, or moving inland, or something like that in store for all Japanese Americans ... Just before leaving Terminal Island Mama had received her first letter [from Papa] from Bismarck, North Dakota. He had been imprisoned at Fort Lincoln, in an all-male camp for enemy aliens ...

Mama and Woody went to work packing celery for a Japanese produce dealer. Kiyo and my sister May and I enrolled in the local school, and what sticks in my memory from those few weeks is the teacher – not her looks, her remoteness ... [S]he would never help me out. She would have nothing to do with me.

This was the first time I had felt outright hostility from a Caucasian. Looking back, it is easy enough to explain. Public attitudes toward the Japanese in California were shifting rapidly ... Tolerance had turned to distrust and irrational fear. The hundred-year-old tradition of anti-Orientalism on the west coast soon resurfaced, more vicious than ever. Its result became clear about a month later, when we were told to make our third and final move.

The name Manzanar meant nothing to us when we left Boyle Heights. We didn't know where it was or what it was. We went because the government ordered us to. And in the case of my older brothers and sisters, we went with a certain amount of relief. They had all heard stories of Japanese homes being attacked, of beatings in the streets of California towns. They were as frightened of the Caucasians as Caucasians were of us ...

Our pickup point was a Buddhist church in Los Angeles ... I remember sitting on a duffel bag trying to be friendly with the Greyhound driver. I smiled at him. He didn't smile back. He was befriending no one. Someone tied a numbered tag to my collar and to the duffel bag (each family was given a number, and that became our official designation until the camps were closed), someone else passed out box lunches for the trip, and we climbed aboard ...

Source: Jeanne Wakatsuki Houston and James D. Houston, *Farewell to Manzanar* (New York: Bantam, 1973), pp. 3–18.

Questions for Discussion

1. The development and uses of urbanized places in the United States in the twentieth century have been shaped by private decision-making (by businesses and consumers) and by government policy. How would you weigh the relative influence of the private and public roles?
2. Use the experiences of average Americans, as documented in this part, to explore some of the reasons that the urbanization process had such radically different impacts on different people during this era.
3. How would you characterize the urban "home front" in the United States during World War II?

Part IV Creating a Suburban Nation, 1945–1970s

Chapter 10 "The Affluent Society"

1 Veterans Line Up for Homes in Long Island, 1949

Variations on the scene reported here by the New York Times *– crowds of prospective homebuyers descending on new suburban subdivisions – were commonplace in the 1940s and 1950s. Housing was in short supply nationwide. The Depression and wartime materials rationing had limited construction for years, and then returning soldiers and young families compounded the problem, forcing people in every region to move in temporarily with friends and relatives. Developers were anxious to fill the demand and rose to the challenge. By streamlining the construction process, large-scale builders such as William Levitt brought costs down considerably and raised new dwellings quickly. And now ownership was within reach of millions of Americans, thanks to the federal mortgage programs that created a robust market for the sale of single family homes, especially in restricted, all-white suburbs like the Levittowns (see sources 11.1 and 12.2). Returning soldiers were in an especially enviable position, as the "GI Bill" gave most applicants access to homeownership without a down payment. They needed only to qualify for the loan and then commit to a modest mortgage payment, comparable to the cost of monthly rent. Desperate for space, anxious to get settled after the grueling experience of combat, and aspiring to a comfortable and much celebrated suburban lifestyle, veterans nationwide jumped at the opportunity. Millions took advantage of these and other GI benefits in the years to follow.*

The Modern American Metropolis: A Documentary Reader, First Edition.
Edited by David M. P. Freund.

Episodes like this one at Levittown in Long Island, New York, highlight two important facets of the suburban housing boom. It was a shared experience. If you were eligible for a mortgage, the incentives were hard to turn down and the pressures to participate considerable, be it from advertising, word of mouth, or constant political celebrations of American affluence and its suburban trappings (source 10.2). Meanwhile it was a very visible phenomenon. Even if you were not joining the migration to the suburbs or jockeying to purchase a more spacious home in yet another new development, you were still likely to witness it: in local real estate advertising and promotions, in the ubiquitous construction sites that were transforming forest and farmland into new subdivisions, or driving by one of the mob scenes like the one described here by the Times.

Line Forms Early in Sale of Houses

Veterans Arrive 3 Days Ahead of Time to Purchase 350 Homes on Long Island

Roslyn, L.I., March 6 – If William J. Levitt, Long Island mass building contractor, had any illusions about the end of the housing shortage, they were rudely dispelled this morning when he found nearly 300 home-hungry veterans camping on the doorstep of his model home here.

In the last two months, since the model home went on display at 275 Willis Avenue, 5,000 prospective buyers had indicated their interest and been put on a waiting list. Last week those on the list were notified by letter that 350 of these houses would go on sale at 9 A.M. tomorrow.

About 11 o'clock Friday night Roger Williams of Bayside, Queens, appeared at the model home and announced that he was in line for Monday's sale. Within the next two hours a dozen other veterans had followed suit and ensconced themselves in deck chairs and sleeping bags on the lawn.

By Saturday morning the number had grown to nearly fifty, and Mr. Levitt decided that the police guard, which had watched over the house since its opening, would have to be augmented. Six patrolmen were assigned to guide new arrivals and maintain order in the line.

Meanwhile, the veterans had set up an organization of their own and had assigned a number to each new home-hunter as he fell into line. In this way husbands were able to take a few hours off for sleeping, eating and seeing their wives, and still retain their priority.

As the line grew Saturday and looped around into the back yard, word arrived that the wife of one of the [w]aiting veterans had presented him with twins in a local hospital. Unperturbed, he received the congratulations of his companions and kept right on standing in line.

This morning, after two nights and a day had produced nearly 300 persistent customers, with others to follow later, Mr. Levitt decided that enough was enough. He gave each a number, guaranteed that it would entitle the holder to buy a house, and sent all home to bed.

The first half of the 350 number-holders will report to the model house to sign their contracts at 9 A.M. tomorrow, when the sale was to have taken place. The others will have the same opportunity Tuesday morning.

This arrangement broke up the encampment, but it left 4,500 buyers who had been advised of the sale with nothing to purchase when they report tomorrow. Mr. Levitt said he expected the police guard would be necessary for several days more.

The veterans who buy the $7,990 homes tomorrow and Tuesday will pay $90 down and the remainder in $58 monthly installments. This price will include a four-room house equipped with radiant heating, automatic laundry, refrigerator and stove, and will cover taxes, water and fire insurance.

The 350 homes, which will be ready for occupancy in mid-July, will bring to 1,100 the number that Mr. Levitt has sold in the last two months. They are part of 4,000 houses of a new model to be erected in Levittown, which will raise the population to 10,000 families.

Source: "Line Forms Early in Sale of Houses," *New York Times*, March 7, 1949, p. 21. Reproduced by permission of The New York Times Company.

2 *Sunset* Magazine Markets a Suburban Way of Living, 1946 and 1958

Several measures of the postwar suburban boom are quantifiable: millions of new single family homes; thousands of new suburban municipalities that expanded metropolitan borders and fragmented regional politics; the dramatic increase in homeownership rates. Less easily measured is the influence of cultural and political narratives that generated enthusiasm for the suburban revolution. By the 1950s, pundits and politicians were constantly declaring homeownership and a suburban lifestyle to be defining traits of the American experience and a reward for citizens' commitment to the capitalist system and democratic institutions. At the 1959 American National Exhibition in Moscow, for example, a model of an American suburban kitchen provided the backdrop when Vice President Richard Nixon famously lectured Soviet premier Nikita Khrushchev about the personal and material advantages that US housewives enjoyed over women in the Soviet Union. (Observers would dub their exchange the "Kitchen Debate.") Throughout the postwar era, advertisers aggressively marketed the suburban ideal and its amenities, along with its widely accepted class, gender, and racial norms (sources 10.3–4 and 11.1). Builders, architects, and realtors circulated publications promoting the advantages of suburban homeownership and recent design trends, including the increasingly popular "ranch house," a detached dwelling recognizable by its low rooflines, open floorplans, and sliding glass doors.

Among the most prominent of these promotional efforts was a book published by Sunset *magazine called* Western Ranch Houses, *first appearing in 1946 and revised in 1958 as* Western Ranch Houses by Cliff May. Sunset *was a major proponent of ranch-style living, and collaborated on these volumes with its most prominent architect (May) to celebrate the new style and its possibilities. These are lengthy publications (160 and 176 pages, respectively) dominated by architectural renderings, floor plans, photographs, and practical design advice. Meanwhile, running throughout each edition – and excerpted here – is commentary about a suburban lifestyle that could be realized, the authors argue, by respecting certain planning principles. These volumes sample the era's celebratory rhetoric about suburban homeownership and its presumed advantages. Also notable is the effort to root this brand of postwar living in supposedly timeless, "Western" traditions and even the Spanish colonial past, a striking claim in light of the contested history of Western metropolitan settlement (see sources 1.1–4; 2.4; 3.1, 4; and 4.2–3).*

From *Sunset: Western Ranch Houses* (1946)

What is a ranch house?

In your mind, you may have a clear picture of the ranch house you would like to build.

Architecturally, however, no such clarity exists.

Today, almost any house that provides for an informal type of living and is not definitely marked by unmistakable style symbols is called a *ranch house*.

The fact that there is no definite form labeled *ranch house* should not disturb the prospective builder. He can go ahead and build according to the way he wants to live, without fear of violating any rules.

... The purpose of this book is to explore the many ways in which the ranch-house type of living has prevailed in Western homes in the past, and how it may be built into them now.

... The real crime against the ranch house lies not in the failure to reproduce its historic appearance or characteristics, but in the failure to take advantage of what it has to offer as a way of living. A house can look like a ranch house and not serve as a ranch house.

The close-to-the-ground look of a ranch house is of secondary importance to its being actually on ground level. The ability to move in and out of your house freely, without the hindrance of steps, is one of the things that makes living in it pleasant and informal.

The eye appeal of the house that rambles around the site means little if the protected, out-door areas created by the ramblings are not accessible from the house.

Wide, protected porches immediately suggest outdoor living – lazy summer afternoons, informal entertaining – but if those porches face the street and are, therefore, without privacy, you merely have a house that *looks* like a ranch house but does not function as one.

The form called the ranch house has many roots. They go deep into the Western soil. Some feed directly on the Spanish period. Some draw upon the pioneer years. But the ranch-house growth has never been limited to its roots. It has never known a set style. It was shaped by needs for a special way of living – informal, yet gracious.

History of the ranch house

The history of the Western ranch house is the personal history of many [Spanish, Mexican, British, and American] families ... Each brought to the West his own mental blueprint of a home; each had his influence on the development of the Western architectural pattern.

Those blueprints were not followed to the letter. The Western sun and the Western terrain stimulated some changes in them. The availability of a few building materials and the lack of others with which to build undoubtedly simplified many former complex designs. But the greatest and most lasting influence on the blueprints brought into California was the way of living developed by the Spanish colonists. A few hundred people found themselves separated from the rest of the world in a new and gentle place. Almost immediately they established a pattern of living to fit that place ...

What does ranch-house history mean to today's home builder?

Looking back at the old ranch houses should help you look ahead and see the real values in tomorrow's house ... There is no single fixed form to be copied. But the virtues of the ranch houses of the past have been built into the ranch houses of today as illustrated in plan, sketch, and photograph on the following pages ...

Houses of today must meet certain living requirements. They must give a feeling of spaciousness, privacy, indoor-outdoor living, etc. To assist you in your appraisal, the houses shown here have been grouped under the requirement they illustrate particularly well ...

Planning livable space

You expect the house you build to do many things for you.

Not only should it give you greater comfort with less work, but it must also give you a more satisfying way of living. In short, you expect an emotional as well as a functional reward.

If, emotionally, you rebel at restraint, abhor fussiness, and in your heart are listening for the jingle of silver spurs to drown out the clank, clank of modern machines, you should call the house you build a *ranch house*. A ranch house, because of its name alone, borrows friendliness, simplicity, informality, and gaiety from the men and women who, in the past, found those pleasures in ranch-house living.

If you call it a ranch house, you'll probably live that way. But be careful that you don't use symbols – spurs and boots and saddles – as substitutes for the real living needs that make for ranch house living ...

[And] when you analyze the living of the past you realize that the house itself was but a small part of the story. The out-of-doors invariably played the major role ... It is impossible to consider a ranch house without thinking of the outdoor living areas connected with it ...

...

Living space should be defined as space that can be used comfortably, at least part of the time, for play, resting, eating, entertaining, etc. You cannot call just any area within the boundaries of your lot *living space*. If there is no connection between it and the house, the space will be used infrequently. If the space is in full view of the neighbors, its use will be limited. If it is unprotected from rain, wind, or hot sun, it could not honestly be counted as livable space.

Source: Editorial Staff of *Sunset* magazine, in collaboration with Cliff May, *Sunset: Western Ranch Houses* (San Francisco: Lane Publishing Co., 1946; republished 1976; reprinted Santa Monica, CA: Hennessey & Ingalls, 1999), pp. ix, 11, 24–26, 39.

From *Western Ranch Houses by Cliff May* (1958)

Beginnings of the ranch house

The story of the ranch houses in this book stretches back a century and a half to the homes built by a handful of Spanish colonizers in what is now Southern California ...

In the sense that architecture mirrors the life of a people at any point in time, we can perhaps reach a better understanding of the ranch house as a structure if we see what the people were like who originally designed, built, and lived in it.

In 1882, the novelist Helen Hunt Jackson visited Rancho Camulos to gather material for her famous romance, *Ramona*. She lived in the rambling adobe house for several days as the guest of the del Valle family who had built it 30 years before and had been operating the rancho ever since. The house and the family made such an impression on her that she worked them both into her novel. In perceptive words that might be applied to early California ranch houses in general and to the people who created them, she wrote: "the house was one of the best specimens to be found in California of the representative house of the half barbaric, half elegant, wholly generous and free-handed life led there by Mexican men and women of degree in the early part of this century, under the rule of the Spanish and Mexican viceroys ... It was a picturesque life, with more of sentiment and gayety in it, more also that was truly dramatic, more romance, than will ever be seen again on these sunny shores. The aroma of it all lingers there still; industries and inventions have not yet slain it; it will last out its century."

Source: Editorial Staff of Sunset Magazine and Books, *Western Ranch Houses by Cliff May* (San Francisco: Lane Publishing Co., 1958; reprinted Santa Monica, CA: Hennessey & Ingalls, 1997), pp. 8–10.

3 *Ebony* Discusses Homeownership and Domestic Life for a Steelworker's Family in Gary, Indiana, 1957

Most journalism, advertising, film, and television in the post-World War II period depicted the ideal domestic life in very narrow terms: it took place in neighborhoods of suburban homes populated by whites. The reality of metropolitan life was far more complex. To be sure, people of European descent were the primary beneficiaries of higher salaries, white-collar or union-scale jobs, and loans for homes, businesses, and college education. But economic growth also helped more racial minorities gain access to some of the stability, comforts, and trappings of middle-class domestic life. As this profile of a family in Gary, Indiana, demonstrates, people of color did not equate homeownership and domesticity with all-white suburbs.

Through a combination of necessity and preference, black Americans in all parts of the country had sustained separate residential neighborhoods, often for generations. Most whites resisted neighborhood integration and used a combination of tools to maintain the color line, including race restrictive covenants, zoning law, informal real estate practices, and violence. All-black suburban communities often developed just outside cities with industries open to black laborers, and sometimes in the vicinity of affluent white enclaves dependent on black domestics. In the early twentieth century, homes in modest and largely unplanned black suburbs were often "self-built" or financed with the help of family and friends, while in parts of the Jim Crow South white officials avoided conflicts over integration by negotiating with black leaders to create "Negro expansion zones." Regardless of region, economic growth after World War II expanded black urban and suburban communities alike, most of which included a mix of single-family housing and multiple-unit dwellings, owner-occupied homes and rental properties. In this 1957 feature in Ebony *magazine, readers saw a snapshot of Denver and Willa Lee's experience of life in the expanding middle class. Other photographs show the family grocery shopping, visiting the doctor, and socializing with neighbors.*

During the first seven years of their married life, Denver Lee and his wife, Willa, lived with in-laws. "We learned a lot about handling money in those years," Denver recalls. "Before we got married, both of us sort of let it run through our fingers. After a while, though, we acquired the habit of saving."

Mrs. Lee did social work in Gary for eight years after graduating from Fisk University but decided to quit when her first child, Denise, was born in January, 1952. She is a full-time housewife now, has worked for only a few months in the past five years. Yet the saving program continues. Each month, Denver puts $40 into bonds, another $30 into life insurance and endowment policies for the future.

Good management of their finances enabled the couple to buy their own home in 1952. It is a neat, two-story brick house containing six rooms. "It cost us nearly $15,000," says Mrs. Lee, "and when we moved into it, it seemed plenty big. It doesn't seem large at all now, mainly because of the children. We hadn't counted on *three*."

The arrival of the children changed the Lees' life in many ways. "We settled down then," Denver recalls. "We used to take long vacations together, just driving around the country in our car. There was hardly a week passed when we didn't take in a show or drive to Chicago to a party or a club or to visit. We've gotten out of the habit of doing things like that now. Our life is more centered around the home."

Mrs. Lee's activities, like those of most wives with children, are much more restricted than her husband's. She probably puts in a 110-hour week on her homework: cooking, cleaning, washing clothes and diapers, preparing

Figure 10.3 Photo of Denver Lee and family from *Ebony* magazine, September 1, 1957, p. 46.

Source: Courtesy Johnson Publishing Company, LLC.

bottles. Denver's social and civic activities revolve around the Eureka Club, of which he is an active member. He is also active in the Elks, in the labor unit of the NAACP and in Local 1014 of the United Steel Workers union whose meetings he regularly attends. "I'd probably do more," he says, "if I just had the time and the energy, but when you work in a mill you don't seem to have much of either." He works one week from 8 a.m. until 4 p.m.; the second from 4 p.m. until midnight; the third from midnight until 8 a.m. Breakfast time may be at 7 a.m. in the Lee household for one week and 2 a.m. the next. The alarm clock and the mill whistle decide everything.

The family budget runs to $533 a month. Mrs. Lee actually keeps a mental budget rather than a formal one. "One thing is sure, though," she confesses, "the money goes. There was a time when Denver and I believed that $6,400 a year was a small fortune. Now we know it's no fortune at all, just a livable wage. But we still think we are well off. We are happy and healthy and we lead a full life."

Source: "Careful Management Has Enabled Couple to Buy Home," *Ebony*, September 1, 1957, pp. 46–49.

4 Catherine Marshall Defends a Woman's Right to Work, 1954

In 1954 Life *magazine devoted a special issue to "The Modern Woman." Here was a celebration, the editors wrote, of women who were "successful on many fronts: keeping themselves healthy and good-looking, ... producing more and healthier babies than any women in the nation's history, ... well organized as wives, influential in politics, a power in economics." A sample of the issue's articles and photo essays suggests the range of coverage: "Changing Roles in Modern Marriage"; "Price Puzzle Illustrates why U.S. Women are the Best Dressed"; "Women Work for the Church All Year – And Especially at Christmas"; "Women Have Earned a Place in Politics"; "The First Baby is a Rich Experience."*

The introductory essay, written by Catherine Marshall (called "Mrs. Peter Marshall" in the byline), previews the collection and speaks to contemporary debates concerning women's appropriate role in postwar America. This was a matter for "debate" for many readers because the era's affluence allowed far more middle-class women the option of staying out of the wage labor force. Meanwhile these women were widely viewed as vital decision-makers in the growing market for domestic goods and services. Yet, to many observers' surprise, a greater percentage of married middle-class women were entering the workforce. Why, asked critics, should they abandon the comfortable life of a suburban housewife for the life of a wage earner? Just months before this issue of Life *appeared, an article in* Esquire *magazine described working women as a "menace."*

Of course, most American women did not have this option. They had always worked, either by command or necessity. Who was Marshall's audience, and who might she have claimed to speak for? How might women with very different backgrounds and experiences have responded to her prescriptions and warnings (sources 10.3; 11.3 and 12.1)?

To be an American woman today is to be cast in an exciting, challenging and difficult role – exciting because the sky seems to be the limit, in education, work and freedom; challenging because the whole concept of "woman's rights" is still relatively new – scarcely more than 50 years old; and difficult because the new freedom has produced a backwash of unforeseen emotional and psychological problems for the emancipated woman. Caught as she is in conflicting currents, the American woman of today finds herself being analyzed and admired, envied and criticized as never before.

The Editors of *Life* have devoted this special issue to the achievements and troubles of this fascinating, puzzling, eminently noticeable figure, the American woman. It is an appropriate time for such an issue because woman today is in a time of transition. As the [articles] show, she is still torn between using her freedom wisely and using it wastefully.

The case of the woman and the automobile may be a sort of parable for our day. Men invented the horseless carriage. Women, wearing coquettish dusters, were at first only eager passengers. To them the actual mechanics of the car were an enigma. Not for the world would a woman have tried to crank the thing or change a tire.

Then the car grew more attractive. Self-starters replaced cranks, and tires did not have to be changed so often. Women found that they, too, could handle a car. Right away they wanted to drive. Soon many of them had permits, and for a while driving was heady wine. They did not have to be beholden to any male for transportation. It was sweet release to go where they wanted whenever they wanted. But even in the transportation field rights inevitably have duties and responsibilities attached. In our day many a suburban housewife finds that the wonderful "freedom to drive" means that she is chained to the family car, beholden indeed, serving continually every member of her family ...

This same pattern applies to any area in which women have won their rights – the right to bring home a pay check, to enter business, industry or politics. In each of these fields all the steps have seemed exciting and enjoyable – until the last one. Freedom always seems like fun; duties and responsibilities not always so. In addition to her new responsibilities this present-day woman finds that she has certain strong urges and instinctive needs. If she is to be a truly happy person, these needs must be met. Ask any thoughtful, honest woman what the most satisfying moments of her life have been, and she will never mention the day she got her first job or the day she outwitted her boss on his ground. But she will always speak of the night when, as a teen-ager, she wore her first formal ... and twirled in the arms of a not-so-bad date to tingly music. Or the night the man she loved took her in his arms, bringing a special look to her face ... Then there was the moment when she held her first baby in her arms. It was not just releasing, it was completely fulfilling ...

When women do *not* have the deep satisfaction of these experiences, their troubles begin ... Can it be that many of woman's current troubles began with the period of her preoccupation with her "rights"? Perhaps so, for there are only two basic approaches to any aspect of human life: one approach sees life as a "right," the other as a "privilege."

We women have always had certain privileges that no man could take from us: our differentness; our unique femininity; the prerogative of bearing children; our devotion to beauty in ourselves and our environment. But privileges no longer cherished have a way of disappearing. It is possible that the difficulties in which we women now find ourselves are but another manifestation of that ancient but inexorable law: "Whosoever will save his life shall lose it." Historians of the future may speak of the 20th Century as "the era of the feminist revolution." As in all revolutions, there have been many worthwhile gains, some agonizing losses, and no possibility of returning to the status quo. To be sure, the modern woman has no desire to surrender a single gain she has made. Today she is healthier, loses fewer babies in infancy, is more attractive than ever before ... Indeed, she is something of a phenomenon ...

[W]oman has shown through the ages that though she has limitations, she also has resilience. She has lived out revolutions before. With the kind of information implicit in this kind of thoughtful journalism, plus a new kind of dedication to the task before her, the modern American woman will yet be grateful to be herself, proud to be a woman.

Source: "The American Woman: An Introduction by Mrs. Peter Marshall," *Life*, 41(26) (December 24, 1954), pp. 49–50.

Chapter 11 Public Policy and "Best Use" in American Neighborhoods

1 The Federal Housing Administration Defines Value in Single-Family Suburban Housing

It was after World War II that suburban residence and homeownership became norms for most Americans, and both trends were made possible by federal programs established years earlier. Between 1933 and 1944, Congress created agencies including the Federal Housing Administration (FHA), the Federal National Mortgage Association (FNMA), and the Veterans Administration (VA), which together restructured and subsidized the market for mortgage debt. After the war, legislators repeatedly expanded these agencies' powers and their budgets, with the result that patterns of tenancy and metropolitan development were revolutionized in a generation's time.

Federal mortgage programs did not lend money. Rather, by insuring private lenders, standardizing construction and appraisal practices, and buying unmarketable loans, these programs enabled banks to expand lending on very generous terms for home repairs and purchases. It was an arrangement that few eligible bankers or borrowers could refuse. For lenders the federal insurance system created virtually risk-free opportunities to make profits in the mortgage business. Meanwhile borrowers saw average down payments shrink from about 50 to 10 percent and waived for most veterans, while repayment periods were extended from about three years to as many as 30. To remain competitive, noninsured lenders offered mortgages with comparable terms. Coupled with aggressive marketing and innovations in homebuilding, the result was an unprecedented wave of suburban

The Modern American Metropolis: A Documentary Reader, First Edition.
Edited by David M. P. Freund.

development. Beginning in 1946 and until the mid-1960s, between one and two million housing units were built every year in the United States, the vast majority of them single-family, detached, suburban homes, and ownership rates skyrocketed nationwide (sources 10.1–2).

Essential to these programs' effectiveness was the creation of uniform standards in the housing market. If a property was to qualify for government insurance, it needed to comply with strict federal guidelines concerning construction, design, and occupancy. Those guidelines were spelled out in the FHA's Underwriting Manual, *a lengthy technical volume that instructed appraisers, realtors, builders, and lenders about topics such as materials standards, subdivision design, and the superior marketability of suburban housing. This excerpt, regarding "Rating of Location" from the 1936 edition, captures the manual's tone and coverage, and also introduces the agency's rules about race. The FHA deemed minority-occupied properties a financial risk and described their presence as a threat to the value of white-owned homes. Concerted protest by civil rights activists forced the FHA to renounce explicit racial restrictions by 1950, but the agency nonetheless followed its original guidelines and refused mortgage insurance to most minority applicants until passage of the Civil Rights Act of 1968. Noninsured lenders followed their lead. As a result, most nonwhites were excluded from the new postwar market for affordable housing credit, not because they were unable to afford the loans but because most realtors and government officials insisted that minorities brought down property values. The* Manual *illustrates how public policy helped give physical shape to the postwar metropolis and determine access to some of its most valuable resources.*

Rating of Location: Protection from Adverse Influences

226. This feature [is] one of the most important features in the Rating of Location ... Where little or no protection is provided against adverse influences the Valuator must not hesitate to make a reject rating of this feature.

227. Protection in the form of zoning restrictions is becoming almost universal. The best artificial means of providing protection from adverse influences is through the medium of appropriate and well drawn zoning ordinances. If the framers of the zoning ordinance have used excellent judgment in establishing areas, and if the provisions of the ordinance have been well worded and drawn from a thorough knowledge of conditions existing in the city and those which will most probably exist in the future, and if the zoning ordinance receives the backing of public approval, an excellent basis for protection against adverse influences exists ...

228. Deed restrictions are apt to prove more effective than a zoning ordinance in providing protection from adverse influences. Where the same deed restrictions apply over a broad area and where these restrictions relate to types of structures, use to which improvements may be put, and racial occupancy, a favorable condition is apt to exist. Where adjacent lots or blocks possess altogether different restrictions, especially for type and use of structures and racial occupancy, the effect of such restrictions is minimized and adequate protection cannot be considered to be present ... It must be realized that deed restrictions, to be effective, must be enforced ...

229. The geographical position of a location may afford in certain instances reliable protection against adverse influences. If the location lies in the middle of an area well developed with a uniform type of residential properties, and if the location is away from main arteries which would logically be used for business purposes, probability of a change in type, use, or occupancy of properties at this location is remote. The Valuator should consider carefully the immunity or lack of immunity offered to the location because of its geographical position within the city. Natural or artificially established barriers will prove effective in protecting a neighborhood and the locations within it from adverse influences. Usually the protection against adverse influences afforded by these means include prevention of the infiltration of business and industrial uses, lower class occupancy, and inharmonious racial groups. A location close to a public park or area of similar nature is usually well protected from infiltration of business and lower social occupancy coming from that direction. Hills and ravines and other peculiarities of topography many times make encroachment of inharmonious uses so difficult that protection is afforded ...

230. ... It is difficult to overemphasize the importance of the presence or absence of well-executed neighborhood planning in rating locations. Narrow streets, excessive lot coverage, inadequate light and air, and poor circulation within the neighborhood area, as well as the intermixture of types, price levels, and a general absence of architectural attractiveness in dwellings represent adverse influences in themselves ...

232. When nuisances are present in a neighborhood little protection is offered to locations close to such undesirable elements ... A few nuisances may be listed: Presence of billboards, undesirable domestic animals, stables, chicken coops and runs, liquor dispensing establishments, rooming houses, ... schools, churches, mercantile and industrial establishments, ... offensive noises and odors, and poorly-kept, unsightly properties.

233. The Valuator should investigate areas surrounding the location to determine whether or not incompatible racial and social groups are present,

to the end that an intelligent prediction may be made regarding the possibility or probability of the location being invaded by such groups. If a neighborhood is to retain stability it is necessary that properties shall continue to be occupied by the same social and racial classes. A change in social or racial occupancy generally leads to instability and a reduction in values ...

Source: US Federal Housing Administration, *Underwriting Manual: Underwriting and Valuation Procedure under Title II of the National Housing Act* (Washington, DC: US Government Printing Office), 1936, part 2, sections 226–230, 232–233.

2 A US Senator Argues That Military Spending Is Producing Inequality, 1962

In this excerpt from a 1962 Congressional hearing on defense policy, a US senator and an administration official discuss the impact of federal spending on patterns of postwar metropolitan growth. The hearing concerned a short-lived program, the Area Redevelopment Administration (ARA), created in 1961 to channel federal defense dollars to impoverished regions in Appalachia and the South. Like a range of federal initiatives – including the programs of the Public Housing Administration and Aid for Families with Dependent Children – the ARA was designed to direct resources to populations that had benefited minimally from the nation's remarkable postwar growth. And, like these programs, the ARA faced considerable Congressional and popular opposition and thus struggled for funds and legitimacy. It ceased operations in 1965.

In this exchange with ARA director Harry W. Williams, Senator Hubert H. Humphrey argues for expanding the program's reach by reminding legislators of an incontrovertible fact: key national industries and entire metropolitan regions depended heavily on federal defense spending. US military expenditures provided an enormous boost to postwar economic activity, in effect subsidizing the fantastic growth of targeted industries and the urbanized areas that depended on them. Large sections of the American South and Southwest were among the biggest beneficiaries. By 1962, for example, over 42 percent of all manufacturing employment in Los Angeles was in private sector production paid for with public monies via defense contracts. Meanwhile military installations from coast to coast provided employment and created local demand for everything from fuel and housing to groceries and movie tickets (see source 9.1).

As Humphrey notes, he and other critics of the disparities in federal allocations were dismissed by opponents as "big spenders." Also targeted were the grassroots organizations and advocacy groups that mobilized throughout the postwar decades to increase funding for public housing, urban development programs, and welfare recipients. By the late 1960s, these activists and supportive Democratic officials such as Humphrey were labeled as "big government liberals," and political attacks on their agenda helped the Republican Party garner considerable support in congressional and presidential elections. How does this testimony, seen in light of other sources (for example 8.1; 9.1; 11.1, 3; and 12.3–4), help explain why some types of federal spending were successfully defended as legitimate and necessary while others were characterized as "redistribution" or "government handouts"? In what ways were both metropolitan prosperity and poverty shaped by federal policy after World War II?

Statement of Senator Humphrey:

According to most recent Department of Labor figures, there were 517 areas of substantial and persistent unemployment existing in May of this year. The 20 million people of these areas work and do business under extremely adverse conditions. Over 9 percent of their 8.9 million man-laboring force is unemployed, with little prospect of finding work in the extremely tight job markets. The economic growth and progress of these areas is hampered by lack of capital, and thus is considerably slower than that of the rest of the Nation. Businesses are discouraged from entering these areas because the tax base has been jeopardized – by that I mean the outflow is there, those that remain take on the burden of the tax – and they consequently feel that they may have to bear an inordinate share of the cost of public facilities and services.

Such distressed areas work hardship on the entire Nation. Their manpower and resources are idle – not serving the Nation's consumers ... [T]he Nation lost $175 billion in the last 10 years by not fully using our productive capacity.

If we had as many people worried about that figure as they are about the unbalanced budget, we would have had this thing whipped a long time ago. We have people worrying about the apples that are stolen rather than making bigger orchards ...

... The only way to redeem these pockets of unemployment is through long-term rebuilding, as is now attempted by the Area Redevelopment Administration. We must apply every tool at our command to accelerate ARA's present work ... I might say that it has a toothpick to do the work of a crowbar. Frankly, the capital resources of the ARA in terms of the enormous nature of the task are totally inadequate ...

I am one of the Senators who feels this way and I do not mind having people call me a spender or whatever else they want to, because the worst spender of all is the person who does not spend enough. If you are going to need penicillin, do not take less than required or you are wasting your money – take enough. It is going to cost you a little more ... What I worry about is that we approach these tasks with inadequate enthusiasm and resources ... We just do not make a real impact.

What is the ARA's response so far? It is 30,000 jobs?

MR. WILLIAMS: Right.

SEN. HUMPHREY: That is inadequate ... [I]t is not your fault, it is just that we did not tool you up to do the job. It is perfectly obvious that an organization that is supposed to provide for redevelopment should do better than 30,000 jobs.

I realize the importance of a defense budget, but nearly a tenth of our gross national product is accounted for by our defense program.

Whether we wish to or not, we cannot ignore the fact that the allocation of defense funds has an inevitable and tremendous economic impact upon the pattern of the national economy. The changing distribution of defense spending can actually be detrimental to certain areas of the country. For example, during World War II, our military needs required the concentration of resources for the production of tanks, trucks, and similar equipment in the Midwest. As this sort of material gave way to missiles and other weapons and materials, less money was spent in these Midwest plants. The impact of this spending shift is now being felt by numerous communities throughout the Midwest. The detrimental effects of defense-spending changes may be modified by intelligent planning to insure that the defense dollar is spent not only to produce military material that is both of high quality and low cost, but also to relieve economic conditions in areas which have the skills and resources to do the production job as well as more economically fortunate areas of the country ... After all, the greatest redevelopment program in the country is a defense program. What is your total capital?

MR. WILLIAMS: We have $375 million total authorized for loans and grants.

SEN. HUMPHREY: Great. What is the appropriation for the Department of Defense?

MR. WILLIAMS: Sir, I am not an expert on that. It is about $60 billion or $50 billion.

SEN. HUMPHREY: That is just defense. That does not include NASA; that does not include Atomic Energy. So when you really start to compare, you have to admit you are not exactly one of the big agencies in Government, are you?

MR. WILLIAMS: No, sir.

SEN. HUMPHREY: ... The very nature of distressed areas, we are told, makes it inherently difficult to allocate money to such areas without paying undesirable premiums on the cost of procurement ... I realize it is difficult to get prime contracts in a distressed area if you have a policy that says: "Well, there is nobody there to take care of it." There was nobody out in California to take of it at first, either. They put them there. They did not have anybody in Florida to take care of those rockets. They put them there. They did not have any people at Offutt Air Base; they put them there. Any time the Defense Department wants to make a going community, they will do it. I am going to get them all irritated here so they will answer me when they get up here [to testify] ... If you can build a base down at the South Pole, you can implement a distressed-area set-aside. You are not kidding Humphrey. If they want to do anything, they can do it, including getting to the moon.

... How much influence do you think you have with the Defense Department, Mr. Williams, you and that big agency you have over there?

MR. WILLIAMS: We try to influence them.

SEN. HUMPHREY: I did not ask you that. I said how much do you think you have.

MR. WILLIAMS: I think the figures will indicate that we do not have very much influence at all ...

SEN. HUMPHREY: You understand ... in the building of ships, that we have ... a 6-percent differential? We permit certain west coast shipyards to have a 6-percent differential [from government agencies]; is that right?

MR. WILLIAMS: I believe so.

SEN. HUMPHREY: I believe that is a fact; it is the law. If you can give one area of America 6-percent differential on building ships, which the government of the United States subsidizes for private concerns, why can't you have some kind of little old 1- or 2-percent differential to get started in distressed areas? The principle has been established that we do pay a differential in order to give some degree of equity, alleged equity, and equality in the price structure and to bring a certain amount of building and construction into certain areas ...

Source: "Impact of Defense Spending on Labor-Surplus Areas – 1962," Hearing Before the Select Committee on Small Business, US Senate, Eighty-Seventh Congress, Second Session, on Effect of Defense Spending on Small Business in Labor-Surplus Areas, August 29, 1962, testimony of Hon. Hubert H. Humphrey, US Senator, Minnesota, pp. 8–12.

3 Herbert Gans Critiques Federal Urban Renewal Programs, 1959

The Housing Act of 1949 initiated an era of federally sponsored redevelopment – or "urban renewal" – that eventually transformed American downtowns. Under Title I of the program, municipalities used their power of "eminent domain" to confiscate private property deemed "substandard," and then qualified for federal funds to defray the cost of demolishing structures on that land. Once cleared, these properties were redeveloped by private builders. The areas targeted for renewal were either commercial districts or, commonly, residential and mixed-used neighborhoods inhabited by renters and owners with modest and often very low incomes. Most areas were cleared to make room for high-end residential and commercial projects. Developers benefited from drastic reductions in costs (public monies cleared the land), while municipal officials attracted new businesses, consumers, and revenue-producing properties. Yet the process of urban renewal displaced tens of thousands of households and countless small businesses nationwide, with neighborhoods occupied by racial and ethnic minorities hit especially hard. Reforms to the nation's renewal programs in the late 1960s helped redirect some federal resources more equitably, but neighborhood clearings for commercial and interstate development continued to devastate communities that lacked the clout to stop these federally funded efforts.

Many contemporaries criticized the Act for permitting an ostensible "renewal" program to channel its greatest benefits to private developers and affluent consumers. Housing, civil rights, and labor activists challenged the program for discriminating against the poor, minorities, and single women, a critique echoed by many professional planners and public officials. Among the most prominent was Herbert Gans, a planner (and later professor of planning) who spent years researching the impact of urban renewal on Boston's West End neighborhood. In 1959 he published some of his findings – excerpted here – in an academic planning journal, explaining how competing priorities and the politics of municipal development compromised the Housing Act's more progressive aims. Why, according to Gans, were the needs and concerns of residents in these targeted neighborhoods ignored by the federal agencies that financed urban renewal?

A number of large cities are currently initiating or carrying out renewal projects which involve the clearance of a neighborhood and the relocation of a large number of families. [Here I attempt] to analyze and evaluate some of the social and planning problems in this process, as they were observed in the redevelopment of Boston's West End ... [M]any of the conditions described exist in other American cities.

The forty-eight acre West End project area is part of a seventy-two-acre working-class residential district in downtown Boston. The project area is covered almost solidly with five-story apartment buildings, which replaced older three-story single- and multifamily structures around the turn of the century ... In the last twenty-five years, the West End has been mainly an area of first and second settlement for Italian and Polish families. In 1950, the area was estimated to have 12,000 residents. At the time of the city's "taking" the land under eminent domain in May, 1958, about 2,800 households and 7,500 residents remained.

The redevelopment plan proposes total clearance, except for a half dozen community-wide institutions and buildings of architectural interest. The area is to be redeveloped with up to 2,400 apartments, most of them in elevator buildings, at rents currently estimated to be $45 per room, and with parks, shops, and parking areas for the new tenants. Massachusetts General Hospital is also expanding its plant and parking areas on an adjacent site.

The Redevelopment Plan

A planning analysis of this redevelopment project must begin with the question of whether or not the area is a slum. The term slum is an evaluative not an empirical one ... Popular definitions of the slum include two criteria, the social image of the area and its physical condition. Federal standards for determining eligibility for renewal funds focus almost exclusively on the latter. However, it is the local agency which selects the area to be proposed for clearance; and, in most communities, the area's physical condition is a necessary but not sufficient criterion. What seems to happen is that neighborhoods come to be described as slums if they are inhabited by residents who, for a variety of economic, cultural, and psychological reasons, indulge in overt and visible behavior considered undesirable by the majority of the community ... Usually, the physical condition of the area is such that it is eligible for redevelopment; however, there are areas, such as Boston's North End, which meet physical criteria, but which are socially and politically strong enough to discourage any official or politician from suggesting them for clearance.

The federal and local housing standards which are applied to slum areas reflect the value pattern of middle-class professionals. These professionals, like the rest of the middle class ... place greater emphasis on the status functions of housing than does the working class. Their evaluation of the behavior of slum residents is also based on class-defined standards, and these often confuse behavior which is only culturally different with pathological or antisocial acts.

Generally speaking, these standards are desirable bases for public policy, despite their class bias: and many of them should be applied to the poorer areas of the city, *if they were followed by a program which provided the residents of these areas with better housing*. Presently, however, these standards are used to tear down poor neighborhoods; but the better housing for the residents is not provided ...

Slum and Low-Rent Districts: A Redefinition

... Existing physical standards fail to make a distinction between *low-rent* and *slum* districts, or low-rent and slum housing, community facilities, street patterns, etc. This distinction is an important one. *Slum dwellings, etc., may be defined as those which are proven to be physically, socially, or emotionally harmful to their residents or to the community at large. On the other hand, low-rent dwellings, etc., provide housing and the necessary facilities which are not harmful, to people who want, or for economic reasons* must *maintain, low rental payments and are willing to accept lack of modernity, high density, lack of privacy, stair climbing, and other inconveniences as alternative costs* ...

The West End as a Low-Rent District

In my opinion, and given existing renewal policies, most of the West End cannot be described as a slum. I would estimate that at the time of the land taking [through eminent domain], probably from 25 to 35 per cent of the buildings in the project area were structurally unsound, uninhabitable because they had been vacant for some time, or located on alleys too narrow for proper sanitation and fire prevention. Some of the deterioration was due to the fact that in 1950, when the plans for redevelopment were first announced, landlords were advised not to make extensive repairs on their properties. Many residents claim – with some justification – that parts of the area deteriorated rapidly as a result, especially where apartment or entire buildings became and remained vacant in the years that followed. However, reduction of maintenance ... especially by absentee landlords with big holdings, also contributed to the decay.

Nevertheless, the majority of the structures provide low-rent rather than slum dwellings. Rents are extremely low ... and during the postwar prosperity, most West Enders were able to modernize the interiors of their apartments. The low rents enable the many people in the area who have never escaped the threat of work layoffs to keep their fixed housing costs low enough to survive such a layoff, and the location of the area is within walking distance of the central business district where most of the residents are employed. Also, the minimal rents and the familiar neighbors enable the many old people in the area who retired on social security and some income ... to maintain independent households.

The exteriors of the buildings have not been well maintained. This is in part because West Enders pay little attention to the status symbols connected with housing. The proximity of family and ethnic group and the availability of local institutions catering to their needs are valued by residents more highly than the status image of the neighborhood ...

Nor does the West End satisfy the social criteria which would make it a slum. There are "problem residents" in the area ... But ... problems are not created by the neighborhood. In fact ... the highly developed system of informal social control in the West End makes it possible for people with different standards of living and ethnic backgrounds to live together peaceably, tolerant of those with problems.

... Because of its central location adjacent to Beacon Hill and near the downtown retail area, real estate men had long felt the West End was "ripe for higher uses." The Charles River frontage was considered desirable for high-rent apartments. Moreover, the desire of the hospital and other powerful Boston institutions that the low-income population be moved out of the area, the city's desperate need for a higher tax base and its equally urgent search for some signs of economic revival, and the belief that the shrinkage of the central retail area could and should be halted by settling "quality shoppers" nearby, all contributed to justify clearance of the area. The fact that a developer was available made the plan a potential reality. Meanwhile, other Boston neighborhoods in which the housing is more deteriorated and even dangerous receive a much lower priority for renewal, because they are not suitable for high-income housing or because there is less interest among the community's major decision-makers.

Costs and Benefits of Redevelopment

... The project has been planned on the assumption that high- and middle-income residents are of benefit to the city, whereas low-income residents are only a burden and a source of public expense. The assumption ignores the vital economic and social functions played in the city by low-income people – and by the availability of low-rent housing. The reduction of the city's low-rent housing supply by close to 3000 units makes it more difficult for the present and future industrial [labor] force of a low-wage city to find centrally located, economic housing ...

The Hidden Costs

... West Enders must bear the financial burdens that result from having to pay higher rentals for new apartments that are unlikely to be better in quality than the old ones ... Landlords who were able to live modestly from the rentals of one or more West End buildings will lose their incomes ... Many small businessmen in the area will lose their incomes and livelihood. Although federal relocation regulations allot them $2,500 for moving expenses if they re-establish their business, many will be unable to find a new location, since Boston is already oversupplied with small stores. Many of these businessmen are too old to be hired by employers, so both economically and psychologically their future is grim ... [Finally], [c]learance destroys not only housing, but also a functioning social system ... The scattering of family units and friends is likely to be especially harmful to the many older people ...

The variety of costs which West Enders will pay as a result of clearance and relocation ... represent hidden subsidies to the redevelopment program. In effect, the present low-income population will subsidize the clearance of their neighborhood and the apartments of their high-income successors, both by their own losses and by their share of the federal and local tax monies used to clear the site. To balance these costs, the only benefit to be received by most residents is the moving allowance ...

...

[Moreover,] beliefs about the virtues of relocation and the unilateral desirability of redevelopment are written into existing local and federal renewal policy. *As a result, when redevelopment officials take action affecting project area residents, they are not required to take into account the attitudes and the situation of the residents.* There is no opportunity for the correction of such actions by feedback from the residents.

Source: Herbert J. Gans, "The Human Implications of Current Redevelopment and Relocation Planning," *Journal of the American Institute of Planners*, 25(1), February 1959, pp. 15–19, 22. Reproduced by permission from Taylor & Francis and H. J. Gans.

4 *U.S. News and World Report* Warns of Contaminated Suburban Water Supplies, 1963

The pace and scale of metropolitan development after World War II aggravated existing environmental problems and created many new ones. It was not only that population growth and migration added more people to metropolitan areas, but also that these areas were growing much larger (this was the age of suburban "sprawl"), decentered, and resource intensive.

The proliferation of single family homes increased the demands for water, in part to maintain private landscapes, and for energy to power larger homes, more cars, and longer commutes. Demand for electricity by residential customers alone increased almost four times between 1950 and 1970. Meanwhile Americans were consuming more – the increase in materials consumption outpaced population growth – and producing more waste, much of it made of plastics, other synthetic products, and toxic chemicals. In 1966 packaging materials alone produced 52 million tons of waste products, and over the course of the decade the amount of industrial waste dumped into waterways and the ocean in the Northeast doubled. Complicating matters further were standard methods of waste disposal. Because of increasing dependence on landfills, toxins were leaching into surrounding groundwater. When suburban developers cut costs by installing septic tanks instead of sewer lines, leakage from these tanks further polluted water supplies.

The result, as this 1963 U.S. News and World Report *article documents, was a growing chorus of concern over the environmental consequences of unplanned growth, and water was usually front and center. Water had come a long way in American urban development. With the late nineteenth-century expansion of municipally owned or managed water systems, more and more urban residents, and certainly the affluent, had come to expect easy access to clean running water. Well-managed municipal systems helped encourage sanitation and healthier living conditions. Yet easy access also encouraged a dramatic increase in consumption. Fast-growing metropolitan centers, particularly in Western states, came to depend on water transported across state lines and often managed and distributed by federally funded dam projects. In the eyes of the expanding middle class, at the very least, water appeared to be manageable and its supply under control. Thus the news that the water supply might be filled with toxic hazards came as a wake-up call to countless Americans.*

Here's something new to start worrying about. This time it is the quality and safety of your drinking water.

To most Americans, the thought that tap water in their homes has been used in other homes and discharged as sewage is repugnant. Yet, for millions of people in the U.S., that has become a fact of life. Their tap water smells and tastes of chemicals used to kill bacteria. Or it foams from the residue of modern detergents.

Today, an estimated 40 per cent of the U.S. population is using water that has been used at least once before for domestic or industrial purposes. In some cities, water flowing from taps has been used as many as five times by other human beings …

Congress is considering a number of bills that would crack down hard on practices that pollute water ... [including] bills to ban detergents that do not decompose when treated.

Two congressional committees are holding extensive hearings on water pollution. They have been told that the reuse of water in the U.S. today is nothing compared to what it will be in the future as an exploding population crowds increasingly into urban areas.

... One expert has warned ... "You can't escape from the fact that the water we have will need to be used, reused, and used again. That is going to require sewage treatment methods that we do not presently have in most places."

At the moment pollution by modern detergents is drawing the most attention. Cause of the trouble is a chemical known as ABS – alkyl benzine sulfonate. It comes from petroleum and is basic in most of these detergents ... ABS doesn't decompose, as soap does, through the action of bacteria in sewage treatment facilities. In a river, ABS can travel downstream more than 100 miles and still be less than one-third decomposed. When the water is reused by a downstream city, another batch of ABS is added and the double dose passes downriver to still another city.

In areas where homes discharge sewage into septic tanks, the chemical seeps down into the underground water and then is pumped up from wells ... Tests have shown that ABS persists in underground water for years, and the concentration is building up rapidly.

Effect on Health. Says the Secretary of Health, Education, and Welfare, Anthony J. Celebrezze ... "The potential health hazard presented by these detergents is still under investigation. Chemical tests have indicated that these waters are acutely toxic to fish and wildlife when present in water in large accumulations. We do not yet know the adverse effects, if any, of these wastes on human health when ingested over a long period in the minute quantities in which they may be present in the public water supply."

The foaming of detergent residue in drinking water has been reported thus far only in supplies drawn from wells in areas where septic tanks are used.

This warning, however, comes from Representative Henry S. Reuss (Dem.), of Wisconsin, who is sponsoring a bill to prohibit the manufacture and importation of present detergents: "We may look forward to foam in municipal water unless we take timely preventative action."

Action abroad ... In the cities of Germany, where modern detergents have been in use since World War I, ... some waterways are so saturated with detergent residue that billowing suds interfere with navigation. Foam frequently is picked up by the wind and splattered on windshields of nearby autos.

What irks people. Tests in Wisconsin have shown that some of the underground water in 64 of 71 of the state's counties is polluted by ABS … At Oregon, Ill., last winter, a pile of suds 40 feet high accumulated in front of ice that had jammed up in the Rock River just below a dam … The Indians of Isleta Pueblo, below Albuquerque, avoid irrigating on Wednesday because by then the heavy discharge of laundry detergents used by housewives of Albuquerque on Monday reaches their irrigation inlets … Operators of sand and gravel pits at Phoenix, Ariz., complain that detergent has found its way into pits, and as a result, the aggregate they sell makes "lousy concrete." … Sewage treatment plants are fighting a losing battle against detergent suds. The foam covers machinery, makes catwalks slimy, cuts off the oxygen and light necessary for the treatment process.

What States are doing. Legislatures [in many states] are considering bills to ban detergents, [while] U.S. manufacturers are racing to get a "soft" detergent on the market …

[Meanwhile] experts on water pollution are looking beyond the detergent dilemma at other problems that will have to be resolved as the nation turns increasingly to reusing water. Research on these problems by the U.S. Public Health Service … [demonstrates] that detergent pollution is only one of many problems that must be solved … [He reports that] the Government is spending around $750,000 a year on "advanced waste treatment research" … to find improved ways of treating sewage so that it will be possible to reuse water again and again with safety.

Source: "Just How Safe Is Your Drinking Water?" *U.S. News and World Report*, 55(3), July 15, 1963. Reproduced by permission of U.S. News and World Report LLC.

Chapter 12 Metropolitan Contests over Citizenship, Rights, and Access

1 Local Activists Organize a Boycott in Montgomery, Alabama, 1954

The successful boycott of the municipal bus system in Montgomery, Alabama, was a major victory for activists who challenged state-sanctioned discrimination against African Americans and a pivotal moment in a long history of black civil rights protest. Media coverage of the events in Montgomery provided national exposure to activists and organizations, including the newly formed Southern Christian Leadership Council (SCLC), which would help spur a new generation of protest.

The boycott's success was also a metropolitan story. While black protest traditions were generations old and efforts to desegregate trolleys and trains had begun in the nineteenth century, the post-World War II city afforded African American communities new opportunities and leverage. Far more blacks were living in urban areas, North and South, which helped build affluence in their communities and facilitated political organizing. Meanwhile metropolitan whites depended on black workers, be they domestics, janitors, or employees in other select industries, as well as revenues from black consumers (sources 9.3 and 10.3). Postwar civil rights activism owed its success to many variables, including the experience of black veterans, the reality of Jim Crow violence against African Americans, and the sharp contrast between televised instances of such violence and Cold War era celebrations of American democracy and opportunity. But the remarkable florescence of organization building and protest activity owes a great deal to

The Modern American Metropolis: A Documentary Reader, First Edition.
Edited by David M. P. Freund.

transformations in metropolitan America that reconfigured black communities and their relationships to whites. New housing and commercial development, an expanding infrastructure, and continued population growth ensured that access to metropolitan spaces and opportunities – buses and streetcars, restaurants and workplaces, schools and universities – would remain symbolic of American freedom. These sites remained fertile ground for struggles over equality and opportunity.

What do these accounts of the boycott reveal about the dynamics of Southern black urban communities and the work that made the civil rights revolution possible? The interviews with Montgomery's residents were conducted in the 1970s and 1980s for the documentary film Eyes on the Prize. *Ralph Abernathy was the pastor of the city's First Baptist Church. Rosa Parks was a longtime activist and tailor's assistant. E. D. Nixon was a Pullman car porter, labor leader, and activist who had long worked with Parks on political issues. Jo Ann Robinson, founder of the Women's Political Council, taught English at Alabama State College. Coretta Scott King was a civil rights activist; her husband was the Rev. Martin Luther King, Jr. Rufus Lewis was a funeral director. Virginia Durr was a white civil rights activist; her husband was attorney Clifford Durr. Georgia Gilmore lived, worked, and commuted in Montgomery.*

Ralph Abernathy

In the mid-1950s, life was most difficult for all poor people, but it was much better for poor white people than for black people in the South. Blacks were permitted to hold only the menial jobs, domestic workers and common and ordinary laborers. The only professional jobs that were open to blacks were the field of pastoring a black church and the schoolteaching profession, which was open because of segregated schools. In the whole state of Alabama we had probably less than five black doctors. And we didn't do anything but dig ditches and work with some white supervisor that told us everything to do. We were the last to be hired and first to be fired.

All of the restaurants were segregated, the hotels and motels were segregated ... Even in the public courthouse, blacks could not drink water except from the fountain labeled "Colored." ... And the janitor never would clean up the restroom for the colored people.

Rosa Parks

Having to take a certain section [on the bus] because of your race was humiliating, but having to stand up because a particular driver wanted to keep a white person from having to stand was, to my mind, most inhumane.

More than seventy-five, between eighty-five and I think ninety, percent of the patronage on the buses were black people, because more white people could own and drive their own cars than blacks.

I happened to be the secretary of the Montgomery branch of the NAACP as well as the NAACP Youth Council adviser. Many cases did come to my attention that nothing came out of 'cause the person that was abused would be too intimidated to sign an affidavit, or to make a statement. Over the years, I had had my own problems with the bus drivers. In fact, some did tell me not to ride their buses if I felt that I was too important to go to the back door to get on. One had evicted me from the bus in 1943, which did not cause anything more than just a passing glance.

On December 1, 1955, I had finished my day's work as a tailor's assistant in the Montgomery Fair department store and I was on my way home. There was one vacant seat on the Cleveland Avenue bus, which I took, alongside a man and two women across the aisle. There were still a few vacant seats in the white section in the front, of course. We went to the next stop without being disturbed. On the third, the front seats were occupied and this one man, a white man, was standing. The driver asked us to stand up and let him have those seats, and when none of us moved at his first words, he said, "You all make it light on yourselves and let me have those seats." And the man who was sitting next to the window stood up, and I made room for him to pass by me. The two women across the aisle stood up and moved out.

When the driver saw me still sitting, he asked if I was going to stand up and I said, "No, I'm not."

And he said, "Well, if you don't stand up, I'm going to call the police and have you arrested."

I said, "You may do that."

He did get off the bus, and I still stayed where I was. Two policemen came on the bus. One of the policemen asked me if the bus driver had asked me to stand and I said yes.

He said, "Why don't you stand up?"

And I asked him, "Why do you push us around?"

He said, "I do not know, but the law is the law and you're under arrest."

E. D. Nixon

I made bond for Mrs. Parks and got her out ... Fred Gray, our local lawyer, who had just come out of law school about a year, was out of the city at the time. So I turned to a white lawyer that I had known for some years, Clifford Durr. I went by, and his wife come runnin' down the stairs with him, so the three of us went down there. Mrs. Parks's husband came up, and we followed them to our house. I talked to her for a couple of hours and I ended up saying to her point-blank, "Mrs. Parks, with your permissions we can break down segregation on the bus with your case. If I wasn't convinced that we can do it, I wouldn't bother you by it."

She asked her mother what she thought about it. She said, "I'll go along with Mr. Nixon."

And her husband, he said, "I'll support it."

Then I went home and I said to my wife, "Baby, we're going to boycott the Montgomery buses."

The next morning at five o'clock I went to calling people. Number one, I called Ralph D. Abernathy. And he said he'd go along with it. Second, I called the late Reverend H. H. Hubbard. And I called Reverend King, number three ... I went on and called eighteen other people ... [and] told them to meet at [King's] church at three o'clock ...

Jo Ann Robinson

Fred Gray told me Rosa Parks was arrested. Her case would be on Monday. He said to me, "Jo Ann, if you have ever planned to do anything with the [Women's Political] [C]ouncil, now is your time." I called the officers of the three chapters, I called as many of the men who had supported us as I could reach, and told them that Rosa Parks had been arrested and she would be tried. They said, "You have the plans, put them into organization." We had worked for at least three years getting that thing organized.

The Women's Political Council had begun in 1946, after just dozens of black people had been arrested on the buses for segregation purposes. By 1955, we had members in every elementary, junior high, and senior high school, and in federal, state, and local jobs. Wherever there were more than ten blacks employed, we had a member there. We were prepared to the point that we knew that in a matter of hours, we could corral the whole city.

I didn't go to bed that night. I cut stencils and took them to the college. The fellow who let me in during the night, John Cannon ... was in the business department. We ran off thirty-five thousand copies. After I talked with every WPC member in the elementary, junior high, and senior high schools to have somebody on campus during my day so I could deliver them, I took them to school with me in my car. I taught my classes from eight o'clock to ten o'clock. When my ten o'clock class was over, I took two senior students with me and I had the flyers in my car, bundled and ready to be given out. I would drive to the place of dissemination, and a kid would be there to grab them. I was on the campus and off before anybody knew that I was there.

... [O]ne lone black woman ... went back to work and took one of the circulars to [her white employer] so she would know what the blacks had planned ... [S]he immediately called the media. After that, the television, the radio, the evening newspapers told those persons whom we had not reached that there would be the boycott. So the die was cast.

Monday morning, December the fifth, 1955, I shall never forget because many of us had not gone to bed that night. It was the day of the boycott. We had been up waiting for the first buses to pass to see if any riders were on them. It was a cold morning, cloudy, there was a threat of rain, and we were afraid that if it rained the people would get on the bus. But as the buses began to roll, and there were one or two on some of them, none on some of them, then we began to realize that the people were cooperating and that they were going to stay off the bus that first day.

Coretta Scott King

The Monday night, December the fifth, there was to be a mass meeting at the Holt Street Baptist Church. In the afternoon of the fifth, there was another meeting of the leadership. And that was the time when they decided to form the Montgomery Improvement Association and to select a spokesperson. When E. D. Nixon proposed Martin's name, Martin said, "Well, I'm not sure I'm the best person for this position, since I'm new in the community, but if no one else is going to serve, I'd be glad to try."

He came home very excited that he had to give the keynote speech that night at the mass meeting. He only had twenty minutes to prepare his speech.

When he got there, he told me, there were so many people, they couldn't get near the church. They almost had to be carried over the shoulders of people, he and Reverend Abernathy, in order to get to the pulpit ...

Rufus Lewis

I think I was made chairman of the transportation committee because I had access to cars at the funeral home. When we needed cars, I could get a car right then, and go and do what was necessary. But to organize the transportation was a much bigger job. Therefore, we asked for persons who had cars and would voluntarily put them in the transportation pool to let us know.

The people who worked in the various outlying areas of the city would register their place of working and the time they'll get off and where they would be for cars to pick them up. And those folks who had cars would register them in the pool, and register the time that they would be usable, and from that we could serve the people.

We had a transportation center downtown, a parking lot. The cars that came from the various sections of the city, they would bring all the people in that area, and they would make the transfer. People would call in, say, "I'm out here on Cloverdale Road in such-and-such a block, and I'll be ready at such-and-such a time." This was being done all through the day. And we would know what time they was to go to be picked up, and where they were. When we bring them to the center, then all of those people who lived in North Montgomery would get into a car and be carried to their place in North Montgomery.

Virginia Durr

The strange thing that happened was a kind of play between white women and black women, in that none of the white women wanted to lose their help. The mayor of the town issued an order that all black maids had to be dismissed to break the boycott. Well, their reply was, "Tell the mayor to come and do my work for me, then." So the white women went and got the black women in the car. They said that they did it because the bus had broken down, or any excuse you could possibly think of. And the black women, if you picked one of them up who was walking, they'll tell you that they were walking because the lady that brought them to work, her child was sick. So here was this absurd sort of dance going on. I saw a woman that worked for my mother-in-law, and they were asking her, "Do any of your family take part in the boycott?" She said, "No ma'am, they don't have anything to do with the boycott at all." … And so when we got out of the room, I said to Mary, "You know, you had been really the biggest storyteller in the world. You know everybody in your family's involved in the boycott." And she says, "Well, you know, when you have your hand in the lion's mouth, the best thing to do is pat it on the head." I always thought that was a wonderful phrase …

Georgia Gilmore

Sometime I walked by myself and sometime I walked with different people, and I began to enjoy walking … I walked a mile, maybe two miles, some days. Going to and from. A lot of times some of the young whites would come along and they would say, "Nigger, don't you know it's better to ride the bus than it is to walk?" And we would say, "No, cracker, no. We rather walk." ...

The maids, the cooks, they were the ones that really and truly kept the bus running. And after the maids and the cooks stopped riding the bus, well, the bus didn't have any need to run ...

Source: Henry Hampton and Steve Fayer (eds.), *Voices of Freedom: An Oral History of the Civil Rights Movement from the 1950s through the 1980s* (New York: Bantam Books, 1990), pp. 17–24, 26–27, 29–31.

2 Suburban Homeowners Mobilize to Exclude "Incompatible" Development, 1950–1951

As suburban houses became more easily attainable and a powerful symbol of middle-class status following World War II, homeowners worked hard to protect this residential ideal (sources 10.1–2 and 11.1). By chartering home rule governments and adopting municipal zoning ordinances, suburban property owners gained considerable power to control local development and land use. They regularly forbade construction of multiple-unit dwellings and sharply segregated commercial uses deemed "incompatible" with suburban residence. (On zoning's origins, see source 3.5.) Local realtors and their national organizations generally supported these efforts, in part by coordinating with the federal programs that privileged suburban growth and denied access to many Americans (source 11.1). Still, there were constant challenges to the suburban status quo. An entrepreneur who wanted to open a nightclub or light manufacturing plant in a neighborhood zoned residential could petition to alter the ordinance. Likewise the high demand for affordable rental housing encouraged developers to propose apartment construction in otherwise restricted areas. Finally, people excluded from these neighborhoods, including racial minorities, attempted to rent or buy homes there, both to assert their constitutional rights and to access the new housing and well-funded public services concentrated in the nation's all-white suburban enclaves.

In response to these challenges and to press for area improvements, homeowners throughout the country formed community organizations, usually called "neighborhood," "civic," or "homeowners' associations." Their members filled city council and zoning board meetings to influence local debates over development and ordinance revision. They rallied, often successfully, to block construction of low-rent or government-subsidized housing units. And they regularly supported racial exclusion, further enforcing the array of policies and practices that secured the residential color line. Reproduced here are excerpts from the monthly newsletter of the Southwest Dearborn Civic Association (SDCA), which represented hundreds of residents in a suburb just west of Detroit. The SDCA formed when the postwar housing boom filled Dearborn's undeveloped subdivisions with detached, single-family structures. The plats pictured in source 7.6, left empty for decades, later gave rise to the homes now represented by the SDCA. These excerpts from the October 1950 newsletter, and from a membership appeal run in April 1951, document the association's efforts to control land use and occupancy. How did members characterize the advantages, privileges, and responsibilities of suburban residence? And why did they describe racial exclusion as a property owner's right? Note that in 1948 the US Supreme Court ruled in Shelley v. Kraemer *that race restrictive covenants – prohibitions against minority occupancy that were regularly included in property deeds – were not legally enforceable.*

In Unity ... There is strength

The civic organization is a necessary part of any healthy neighborhood or area setup. Without such organizations, the elected politicians ... are handed a blank check as they enter office and can write in what they like so long as there is no united opposition.

Those who give freely of their time and energy to build a strong area group must sometime think of the money which could be theirs if the same effort were put in a gainful occupation.

Perhaps the tangible gains from active community effort [are] worth a great deal to the individual for he finds as time goes on that his whole outlook on life has broadened and that he has gained dignity and self-assurance in his daily contact with other people.

The civic organization is the neighborhood watchdog, to see that undesirable projects are kept out and to fight for projects which are good for the community.

The Bulletin ... is our method of keeping the area informed of various problems, and provides a method for alerting the home owners to any development which is against their best interests ...

Your home is your gem and as such, requires the bulk of your attention, but like any other gem it requires a beautiful neighborhood for a setting and that setting can only be maintained through united effort of the people.

Next Tuesday a new group of officers will be elected for this association and many of those elected will be chosen from those who volunteered as area leaders last year. They will need a lot of assistance and we hope that the people of this area will volunteer to give it.

Did you know ...

We have an ordinance regulating the size of signs which may be erected on residential lots. Residence A and B (single and double homes), four square feet. Residence C and D (four-family and multiple), six square feet.

If you see a sign that is objectionable, you can notify the complaint department at the City Hall.

Warning

The Civic Association has received information that certain unscrupulous real estate dealers are attempting to buy up Dearborn property to resell to people of other than the Caucasian race. Exorbitant price offers are one of the indications of this deal.

Anyone contemplating selling his home is asked to get in touch with one of the officers of this Association to check the background of the firm with which he is dealing.

Listing your property with members of the DEARBORN real estate board is one safeguard you can offer your neighbor. Dearborn realtors have been most co-operative in upholding the restrictions here in this city. Patronize your local business men and be sure.

A New Year

Now is the time to let the Association know if your neighborhood is in need of more street lights or other facilities which the city provides.

Let's hear from you on what you think could be done to make ours a better city.

Source: *Southwest Dearborn Civic Association* (newsletter), October 1950. Dearborn Historical Museum, Dearborn, Michigan. Reproduced by permission of the Dearborn Historical Museum.

What is the object of this association?
A united effort toward neighborliness and to obtain through united effort of all association members the proper improvements and maintenance in the area this association covers ...

Who can be a member?
All residents and business proprietors of the area who contribute the yearly dues of one dollar.

What happens to the membership fees?
Printing and postage to keep members informed of association activities.

Is this a political organization?
No, it is not. This is an organization to promote a better community.

What is the Association doing?
Cooperates with the Dearborn Federation of Civic Associations to secure worthwhile city improvements. Works for better housing inspection and better homes, maintaining better zoning of our area.

What are the future plans?
Improve our zoning restrictions.
Secure more parks and playgrounds and improve those already established.
To be continually on guard to maintain our present occupancy standards and housing restrictions.
To assist in all ways to prevent juvenile delinquency by working with other agencies.
To become the largest and most respected Civic Association in the City of Dearborn.

Source: *Southwest Dearborn Civic Association* (newsletter), April 1951. Dearborn Historical Museum, Dearborn, Michigan. Reproduced by permission of the Dearborn Historical Museum.

3 Residents of a Memphis Neighborhood Block Construction of the Interstate, 1967

Since the 1930s, activists who mobilize over local development issues have usually been negotiating, in some way, with the federal government. The New Deal initiated a new level of federal involvement in urban issues, and postwar policies gave the federal state or local authorities funded by congressional action even more power to shape the built environment. The GI Bill expanded the federal presence in the housing market while helping send a generation of veterans to college, in turn assisting the rise of our modern university system and, with it, new patterns of regional development. Federal urban renewal and public housing policies remade American neighborhoods, often displacing communities that lacked the influence to shape local decision-making. The Federal Interstate and Defense Act of 1956 committed the federal government to paying for 90 percent of a new Interstate System, which connected metropolitan regions and provided easier automobile links between cities and suburbs. If you drive on highways in your region, you are likely to spend part, and in some cases all, of your time on a federally subsidized road (sources 8.1; 9.1, 3; 10.1; 11.1–3; 12.6; and 13.4).

In all of these arenas, local populations engaged the authorities responsible for publicly funded efforts. When public housing was introduced to urban and suburban neighborhoods, opponents mobilized to block its construction and, if they failed, public housing residents mobilized to maintain its standards. Urban renewal efforts – which often dovetailed with highway construction – brought out considerable opposition from the local communities most at risk of displacement. Meanwhile communities and activists have battled for years with public and private interests to contain metropolitan sprawl and prevent environmental damage (sources 11.3–4, 12.1–2, and 14.5). The letter excerpted below introduces the work of Memphis residents who successfully organized to prevent construction of Interstate I-40 through the neighborhood of Overton Park. They faced tremendous obstacles and battled numerous opponents, from road-building agencies and highway engineers to the municipal and private sector boosters who viewed an interstate link to downtown Memphis as a panacea for urban decline. This letter from the Citizens to Preserve Overton Park to President Lyndon B. Johnson illustrates organizers' immersion in the details of metropolitan development and their savvy use of the law and public pressure to protect their local environments. Groups that failed in similar efforts nationwide generally demonstrated the same attention to detail, but often lacked the strategic leverage to protect their communities from what critics called the "Federal Bulldozer."

Citizens to Preserve Overton Park
192 Williford Street
Memphis, Tennessee, 38112

January 5, 1967

The President of the United States
The White House
Washington, D.C.

Mr. President:

Because of the accelerated plans for building Interstate 40 in Overton Park, we again come to you with this controversy.

In light of the recent legislation and future proposals to save natural park land, and in light of the organization of a new Department of Transportation, we feel that you may appreciate a report of the current status of the expressway plans and our recent experience with the Bureau of Public Roads. Some facts follow:

1. Right of Way acquisitions on Sections 1 and 2 of I-40 in the city with emphasis on western portion of Section 2 which is within about two miles of Overton Park. Plans are reported to be ready for the State Highway Department's approval now for Section 3 ... The plans for Section 4 – from Collins to McLean Avenue through Overton Park are expected to be ready for the Tennessee Highway Department's approval on or before January 16th.

   Mid-town Interchange: a contract recently was let for its construction ... We contend that the interchange does not necessarily have to serve the eastern portion of I-40 planned to go through Overton Park ... [T]he western portion of I-40 can function, for [it] will carry traffic to the vicinity of the downtown area and across the new Mississippi river bridge ...
2. Misleading statements:

   One of the greatest problems of the preservationists is to give the public the truth. Many people cannot believe that the park will be violated – the Woods has always been there (made into a city park in 1901 and named in 1902).

   Statements such as the following lead the public to believe only a little disturbance will occur in the Park:

   a. Acreage
      The "Cost of Progress" TV program November 27, 1966:
      Memphis City Commissioner of Public Works stated "the bus lane will be a major portion of the expressway."

      The present bus lane is approximately thirty (30) feet wide; right of way is (50) feet ... Since the 1957 public hearing on I-40 the public was given the impression that the road construction would be just a widening of the present bus lane which is now used by the Memphis Transit Authority which runs one gasoline bus through the park with a stop at the zoo entrance. No other traffic uses the bus lane. It is well screened and planted. Running cross-country interstate traffic through the park is very different from one city bus.

From the beginning of planning the public has been led to believe that the highway would be depressed and therefore less obnoxious in the park ... There will be an elevated cross-road over the highway which will take considerable land and which has received little publicity ... [And] there is an access ramp road in the park in addition to the main highway. The public knows little of this. The Design Engineering firm presently completing the plans still tells us that the total acreage is "undetermined." ...

b. "Mayor Edmund Orgill reminded that that when city and county officials met early this year with state and Federal representatives and expressway engineers, assurance was given that the utility of the park would not be diminished." – The Commercial Appeal

   The "utility" of Overton Park as a natural recreation park and spot of beauty will be greatly impaired and irreparably changed with a highway in it, in the opinion of many citizens.

c. Senator Albert Gore wrote to a Memphian October 26, 1966: "Officials in the Tennessee Highway Department express the views that damage to Overton Park will be minimal. Under the law, these highways will be constructed to standards adequate to meet traffic needs for a period of at least 20 years."

   (Shall Memphis sacrifice a park forever to meet so-called "traffic needs" for only 20 years?) ...

...

4. Power and autonomy in the Bureau of Public Roads:

   ... The chairman of the Advisory Committee on Urban Highway Location and Design advises us that the committee is to write a report on principles of highway design and possibly a book ...

   We call attention to the fact that the [Federal Highway] Administrator has written directives since 1963 setting forth "desirable principles" and asking for "respect for the amenities of the cities."

   July 28, 1965, he wrote, "it is admittedly undesirable to cross the (Overton) park." ...

   When will the Bureau's directives and public statements ... be put into ACTION? By the time they are translated into action, if ever, many natural areas will have been destroyed ...

We are not knowledgeable in ways of political implementation; we are people who exercise our rights as good citizens and are interested in the whole good of our country and in preserving our natural heritage ...

Sincerely,
CITIZENS to PRESERVE OVERTON PARK
Arlo I. Smith, Chairman

(Mrs.) Anona Stoner
Secretary

Source: (Mrs.) Anona Stoner, Secretary, Citizens to Preserve Overton Park to President Lyndon B. Johnson, January 5, 1967. Tennessee Department of Highways and Public Works, Record Group 84, Box 26, Folder 3, Tennessee State Library and Archives, Nashville. Courtesy of the Tennessee State Library and Archives.

4 Activists Define Black Power, 1967

The history of black radicalism during the 1960s and 1970s cannot be reduced to a story about urban militancy, or captured solely with images of urban riots and armed Black Panther activists. There were important organizing and intellectual traditions, as well as changes in metropolitan America, which shaped civil rights protest and black activism across the political spectrum. Prominent organizations that advocated Black Power, such as the Black Panther Party, the Congress of Racial Equality (CORE), and the Student Nonviolent Coordinating Committee (SNCC), came to their positions from different trajectories, but all were building on generations of opposition to institutional racism, discriminatory public policy, and police brutality. Meanwhile many proponents of nonviolent direct action saw eye to eye with their so-called militant counterparts about the origins of racial inequality and appropriate political solutions. (Compare the source excerpted below with Martin Luther King, Jr.'s 1963 essay "The Days to Come.") Regardless of the labels we may use today, anyone who engaged in civil rights protest in this era – be it joining a sit-in, supporting the Black Panthers' breakfast programs for kids, or resisting police harassment – asserted blacks' right to power and equal treatment in the American system. And white Americans regularly viewed such assertions as "radical." Many self-identified white liberals who supported the principle of racial equality nonetheless opposed fair housing campaigns or school desegregation rulings that directly impacted their communities. Most middle-class whites could not sympathize with proposed expansions to the country's social safety net, including the National Welfare Rights Organization's claim that impoverished black mothers had a right to higher benefits.

These excerpts from Stokely Carmichael and Charles V. Hamilton's Black Power: The Politics of Liberation, *published in 1967, introduce some of the analytical traditions that informed civil rights and urban radicalism throughout the era. A participant in CORE and SNCC protests since college, the Trinidad-born Carmichael (later Kwame Ture) suffered repeated arrest and violent attacks from whites because of his activism, including work on a successful voter registration drive in majority-black Lowndes County, Alabama. In 1966, while serving as director of SNCC, he famously invoked the slogan of "Black Power" during a protest in Greenwood, Mississippi. In* Black Power, *he and coauthor Charles Hamilton, a professor of political science, draw on the work of community activists and public intellectuals and use America's impoverished ghettos as a key site of analysis both to explore the history of institutional racism and to propose political strategies for undoing its legacy. What is their analysis, and how do they distinguish Black Power from other approaches to securing civil rights? Why did many Americans view this kind of analysis as a threat?*

This country is known by its cities: those amazing aggregations of people and housing, offices and factories, which constitute the heart of our civilization, the nerve center of our collective being. America is increasingly dominated by her cities, as they draw into them the brawn and brains and wealth of the hinterland. Seventy percent of the American people now reside in urban areas – all of which are in a state of crisis ... For a number of reasons, the city has become the major domestic problem facing this nation in the second half of the twentieth century ...

The problems of the city and of institutional racism are clearly intertwined. Nowhere are people so expendable in the forward march of corporate power as in the ghetto. At the same time, nowhere is the potential political power of black people greater. If the crisis we face in the city is to be dealt with, the problem of the ghetto must be solved first ...

What problems did black people face [in the 20th century] as they moved into [Northern and Western] urban areas? Most ... were crowded into the slums of the cities. In the face of bombs and riots, they fought for a place to live and room for relatives and friends who followed them. They also faced a daily fight for jobs [and] education ... History clearly indicates that the disturbances in our cities are not just isolated reactions to the cry of "Black Power," but part of a pattern. The problems of Harlem in the 1960s are not much different from those of Harlem in 1920 ...

The core problem within the ghetto is the vicious circle created by the lack of decent housing, decent jobs and adequate education. The failure of these three fundamental institutions to work has led to alienation of the ghetto from the rest of the urban area as well as to deep political rifts between the two communities …

The black man lives in incredibly inadequate housing, shabby shelters that are dangerous to mental and physical health and to life itself … The shelter shortage for the black person is not only acute and perennial, but getting increasingly tighter … Urban renewal and highway clearance programs have forced black people more and more into congested pockets of the inner city. Since suburban zoning laws have kept out low-income housing, and the Federal Government has failed to pass open-occupancy laws, black people are forced to stay in the deteriorating ghettos. Thus crowding increases, and slum conditions worsen … The struggle for employment … perpetuates the breakdown of the black family structure … Children growing up in a welfare situation often leave school because of a lack of incentive or because they often do not have enough food to eat or clothes to wear … [Some] turn to petty crime, pushing dope, prostitution … and the cycle continues …

These are the conditions which create dynamite in the ghettos … This country, with its pervasive institutional racism, has itself created socially undesirable conditions; it merely perpetuates those conditions when it lays the blame on people who, through whatever means at their disposal, seek to strike out at the conditions. What has to be understood is that thus far there have been virtually no *legitimate* programs to deal with the alienation and the oppressive conditions in the ghettos …

When the dynamite does go off, pious pronouncements of patience should not go forth. Blame should not be placed on "outside agitators" or on "Communist influence" or on advocates of Black Power. That dynamite was placed there by white racism and it was ignited by white racist indifference and unwillingness to act justly.

…

The black community perceives the "white power structure" in very concrete terms. The man in the ghetto sees his white landlord come only to collect exorbitant rents and fail to make necessary repairs, while both know that the white-dominated city building inspection department will wink at violations or impose only slight fines. The man in the ghetto sees the white policeman on the corner brutally manhandle a black drunkard in a doorway, and at the same time accept a pay-off from one of the agents of the white-controlled rackets. He sees the streets in the city lined with uncollected garbage, and he knows that the powers which could send trucks in to collect that garbage are white. When they don't, he knows the reason: the low political esteem in which the black community is held. He looks at the absence of a meaningful curriculum in the ghetto schools – for example, the history books that woefully overlook the historical achievements of black people – and he knows that the school board is controlled by whites. He is not about to listen to intellectual discourses on the pluralistic and fragmented nature of political power. He is faced with a "white power structure" as monolithic as Europe's colonial offices have been to African and Asian colonies.

It is a stark reality that the black communities are becoming more and more economically depressed. In June, 1966, the Bureau of Labor Statistics reported on the deteriorating condition of black people in this country. In 1948, the jobless rate of non-white males between the ages of fourteen and nineteen was 7.6 percent. In 1965, the percentage of unemployment in this age group was 22.6 percent. The corresponding figures for unemployed white male teen-agers were 8.3 percent in 1948, and 11.8 percent in 1965. ... *Unemployment rates in 1965 were higher for non-white high school graduates than for white high school drop-outs* ...

The black community has been the creation of, and dominated by, a combination of oppressive forces and special interests in the white community. The groups which have access to the necessary resources and the ability to effect change benefit politically and economically from the continued subordinate status of the black community. This is not to say that every single white American consciously oppresses black people. He does not need to. Institutional racism has been maintained deliberately by the power structure and through indifference, inertia and lack [of] courage on the part of white masses as well as petty officials ... In the face of such realities, it becomes ludicrous to condemn black people for "not showing more initiative." Black people are not in a depressed condition because of some defect in their character ...

"To carve out a place for itself in the politico-social order," V. O. Key, Jr. wrote in *Politics, Parties and Pressure Groups*, "a new group may have to fight for reorientation of many of the values of the old order" (p. 57). This is especially true when that group is composed of black people in the American society – a society that has for centuries deliberately and systematically excluded them from political participation ...

The next step is what we shall call the process of political modernization – a process which must take place if the society is to be rid of racism. "Political modernization" includes many things, but we mean by it three major concepts: (1) questioning old values and institutions of the society; (2) searching for new and different forms of political structure to solve political and economic problems; and (3) broadening the base of political participation to include more people in the decision-making process ...

The values of this society support a racist system; we find it incongruous to ask black people to adopt and support most of these values. We reject the assumption that the basic institutions of this society must be preserved ... The values of [middle-class America] are based on material aggrandizement, not the expansion of humanity. The values of that class ultimately support cloistered little closed societies tucked away neatly in tree-lined suburbia ... That class *mouths* its preference for a free, competitive society, while at the same time forcefully and even viciously denying to black people as a group the opportunity to compete ... The adoption of the concept of Black Power is ... a call to reject the racist institutions and values of this society ...

Black Power means, for example, that in Lowndes County, Alabama, a black sheriff can end police brutality. A black tax assessor and tax collector and county board of revenue can lay, collect, and channel tax monies for the building of better roads, and schools serving black people. In such areas as Lowndes, where black people have a majority, they will attempt to use power to exercise control. That is what they seek: control. When black people lack a majority, Black Power means proper representation and sharing of control. It means the creation of power bases, of strength, from which black people can press to change local or nation-wide patterns of oppression – instead of from weakness ... It does not mean *merely* putting black faces into office. Black visibility is not Black Power ... The power must be that of a community, and emanate from there ...

... Some observers have labeled those who advocate Black Power as racists; they have said that the call for self-identification and self-determination is "racism in reverse" or "black supremacy." This is a deliberate and absurd lie. There is no analogy ... between the advocates of Black Power and white racists. Racism is not merely exclusion on the basis of race but exclusion for the purpose of subjugating or maintaining subjugation. The goal of the racists is to keep black people on the bottom, arbitrarily and dictatorially, as they have done in this country for over three hundred years. The goal of black self-determination and black self-identity – Black Power – is full participation in the decision-making processes affecting the lives of black people. The black people of this country have not lynched whites, bombed their churches, murdered their children and manipulated laws and institutions to maintain oppression. White racists have. Congressional laws, one after the other, have not been necessary to stop black people from oppressing others and denying others the full enjoyment of their rights. White racists have made such laws necessary. The goal of Black Power is positive and functional to a free and viable society. No white racist can make this claim.

A great deal of public attention and press space was devoted to the hysterical accusation of "black racism" when the call for Black Power was first sounded.

A national committee of influential black churchmen affiliated with the National Council of Churches, despite their obvious respectability and responsibility, had to resort to a paid advertisement to articulate their position, while anyone yapping "black racism" made front-page news. In their statement, published in the *New York Times* of July 31, 1966, the churchmen said:

> We ... are deeply disturbed ... by historic distortions of important human realities in the controversy over "black power." What we see shining through the variety of rhetoric is not anything new but the same old problem of power and race which has faced our beloved country since 1619.
>
> ... We deplore the overt violence of riots, but we feel it is more important to focus on the real sources of these eruptions. These sources may be abetted inside the Ghetto, but their basic cause lies in the silent and covert violence which white middle class America inflicts upon the victims of the inner city.
>
> ... Without the capacity to participate in power, i.e., to have some organized political and economic strength to really influence people with whom one interacts, integration is not meaningful.
>
> ... America has asked its Negro citizens to fight for opportunity as *individuals*, whereas at certain points in our history what we have needed most has been opportunity for *the whole group* ... We must not apologize for the existence of this form of group power, for we have been oppressed as a group and not as individuals. We will not find our way out of that oppression until both we and America accept the need for Negro Americans, as well as for Jews, Italians, Poles, and white Anglo-Saxon Protestants, among others, to have and to wield group power ...

When the concept of Black Power is set forth, many people immediately conjure up notions of violence. The country's reaction to the Deacons for Defense and Justice, which originated in Louisiana, is instructive. Here is a group which realized that the "law" and law enforcement agencies would not protect people, so they had to do it themselves. If a nation fails to protect its citizens, then that nation cannot condemn those who take up the task themselves. The Deacons and all other blacks who resort to self-defense represent a simple answer to a simple question: what man would not defend his family and home from attack?

But this frightened some white people, because they knew that black people would now fight back. They knew that this was precisely what *they* would have long since done if *they* were subjected to the injustices and oppression heaped on blacks. Those of us who advocate Black Power are quite clear in our own minds that a "non-violent" approach to civil rights is an approach that black people cannot afford and a luxury white people do not deserve. It is crystal clear to us ... *that there can be no social order without social justice*. White people must be made to understand that they must stop messing with black people, or the blacks *will* fight back!

The goals of integrationists are middle-class goals, articulated primarily by a small group of Negroes with middle-class aspirations or status ... Such people will state that they would prefer to be treated "only as individuals, not as Negroes"; that they "are not and should not be preoccupied with race." This is a totally unrealistic position ... Black people have not suffered as individuals but as members of a group; therefore, their liberation lies in group action. This is why SNCC – and the concept of Black Power – affirms that helping *individual* black people to solve their problems on an *individual* basis does little to alleviate the mass of black people.

Source: Kwame Ture and Charles V. Hamilton, *Black Power: The Politics of Liberation in America* (1967; New York: Vintage, 1992), pp. 147–149, 152, 155–156, 160–162, 9–10, 18–19, 22–23, 34, 39–40, 44, 46–49, 52–54.

5 Gays and Lesbians in New York City Organize to Combat Discrimination, 1969

American cities have long afforded socially and politically marginalized groups new opportunities to live, work, congregate, and organize. The decades following World War II marked a notable opportunity, as many central city neighborhoods lost higher-income residents (which brought down rents and property values for some) and seemed like havens for people estranged by the new suburban ideal: socially homogeneous, status-conscious, and peopled by heterosexual two-parent families with "stay at home" moms (sources 10.1–2 and 11.1). In central cities, artists and activists could find affordable housing and some distance from what they viewed as a shallow "bourgeois" culture. Gays, lesbians, and transgender people could find supportive communities and places to socialize, away from the scrutiny of men and women uncomfortable with homosexuality. But even in these enclaves, gays faced constant harassment from employers, anonymous strangers, and public officials. Municipal police officers regularly raided gay bars and beat their patrons. On June 28, 1969, the patrons of the Stonewall Inn, a bar on Christopher Street in New York City's Greenwich Village, resisted one of those police raids. Their response sparked a riot and days of protest against the police, as well as politicians and business people who failed to accept or respect members of the gay community.

The gay rights movement was not new to the United States. Formal groups had been organizing for decades, most prominently the Mattachine Society and Daughters of Bilitis. But the successes of the modern Civil Rights Movement and the new visibility of other rights campaigns for women,

Chicanos, and Native Americans helped spark a new willingness in the gay community to publicly assert the right to equal treatment. In the months following the Stonewall riots, several activist organizations and newspapers were formed in New York City to promote gay and lesbian rights, and this level of organization soon spread to cities nationwide and worldwide. This flyer was distributed in Greenwich Village to organize the community following the riots. What does it document about the challenges and new opportunities for gays and lesbians in the United States? What does it suggest about activists' political strategies and the obstacles to organizing?

6 A Photograph Captures Divisions in Boston over Court-Ordered Busing, 1976

Contests over access to metropolitan resources entered a new phase in the wake of the civil rights revolution. Pictured here is a scene from an April 5, 1976 protest against court-ordered school busing in Boston. Opponents had marched to City Hall that day to challenge an order by District Court Judge W. Arthur Garrity, Jr., requiring compulsory racial integration of specific Boston schools. Garrity was acting in accordance with federal and state laws passed to address the problem of racial imbalance. Busing advocates applauded the plan for addressing the legacy of private and public sector discrimination against minorities. Opponents in the affected white neighborhoods – enclaves dominated by working-class Irish and Italian Americans – lashed out at the disruption of neighborhood school districts and accused suburban whites, largely unaffected by the ruling, of hypocrisy. Violent confrontations became commonplace: white students hurled rocks and insults at black students; blacks and whites alike assaulted students and innocent bystanders; riot police attempted to maintain order. A photographer for the Boston Herald American *captured this April 5 scene when a group of white student activists, just leaving a meeting with a prominent antibusing leader on Boston's city council, confronted architect and lawyer Theodore Landsmark, who was on his way to conduct unrelated business at City Hall. During the attack on Landsmark, one protester swung an American flag (he was not, as it appears, trying to spear the man) while another attempted to get the lawyer out of harm's way. Landsmark suffered a broken nose and severe bruising, and the nation's media broadcast an image that came to symbolize urban conflicts over race and rights nearly a decade after passage of the Civil Rights Act.*

Resistance to school desegregation was an important ingredient of the white backlash against the Civil Rights Movement and the Democratic Party, some members of which supported policies aimed at securing rights and opportunity for racial minorities. And while "white flight" from American cities to its suburbs had been underway since the 1940s, the new politics of

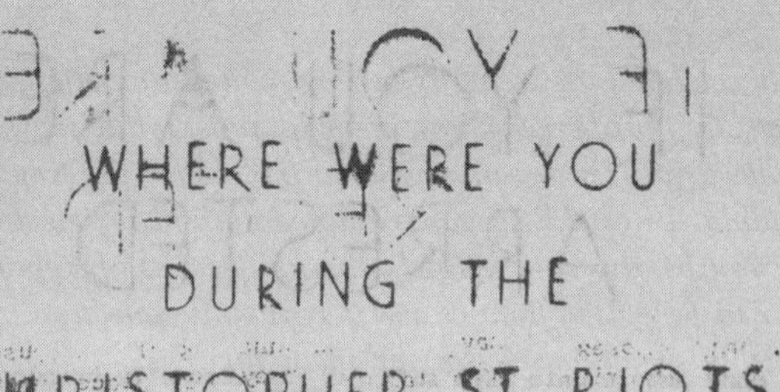

WHERE WERE YOU DURING THE CHRISTOPHER ST. RIOTS?

On the evenings of June 27th and 28th, hundreds of homosexuals violently protested the attempted closing of another gay bar in Greenwich Village. The police raided the well-known bar near Sheridan Square on the charge that liquor was being served without a license. This is a legitimate reason but WHY WAS THIS BAR ALLOWED TO OPERATE FOR YEARS WITH HARDLY ANY POLICE INTERFERENCE? WHY DID THE POLICE PICK THIS TIME TO CRACKDOWN ON ILLEGAL OPERATIONS? These and many other questions deserve answering.

IF YOU ARE TIRED OF -

* Police officials who have decided to harass homosexuals again
* Syndicate leaders who exploit homosexuals
* A State Liquor Authority which will not grant licenses for legitimate gay bars
* Mayoral candidates who use "Law and Order" issues to persecute minorities, including the homosexual minority
* Private citizens who form vigilante groups to rout homosexuals from their community, as has happened in Queens County
* A Governor who has failed to legalize consensual homosexual acts between adults in private due to to his political cowardice

JOIN AND ACTIVELY PARTICIPATE IN MATTACHINE . . . NOW IS THE TIME FOR ALL HOMOSEXUALS TO UNITE IN COMMON ACTION!

MATTACHINE

243 West End Avenue 799-0916

Figure 12.5 Mattachine Society of New York, "Where Were You during the Christopher St. Riots?", typescript flyer, 1969. Mattachine Society, Inc. of New York Records, 1951–1976.

Source: Manuscripts and Archives Division, The New York Public Library, Astor, Lenox and Tilden Foundations.

race and rights accelerated the trend by fueling whites' anxieties about integration, safety, and property values. In 1980, most white working-class voters, for decades loyal Democrats, cast their ballots for the Republican presidential candidate, Ronald Reagan. Coupled with heavy electoral support from all-white suburbs, this shift helped usher in decades of Republican Party dominance in American politics and a systematic rejection of efforts to rectify the history of structural racism and inequality.

Read this photograph in the context of twentieth-century metropolitan change. Why would a white working-class teenager view school desegregation and a well-dressed black man as a threat to his rights and well-being? How did the history of the built environment and Americans' relationship to it shape the electorate? What is the best means to ensure access to metropolitan resources, and who decides?

Figure 12.6 Stanley Forman, *The Soiling of Old Glory, Boston, April 5, 1976.*

Source: Stanley Forman Photos (www.stanleyformanphotos.com).

Questions for Discussion

1. Why did the rate of homeownership in the United States increase so dramatically between 1930 and 1970? Why were the vast majority of new housing units built during these years in the suburbs rather than in cities?
2. The nation's residential neighborhoods were segregated by race before World War II. Why did segregation continue and what new patterns emerged in the decades immediately after the war? What distinguished segregation in states that practiced Jim Crow?
3. Weigh the relative importance of the following forces in shaping life in the postwar metropolis: innovation; expansion of the middle class; federal policy; municipal policy; local activism; mass media and advertising.
4. Looking back from 1970, had the American metropolis grown more inclusive since the turn of the century?

Part V What Makes a City? The "Postindustrial" Metropolis

Chapter 13 Redefining "Urban" and "Suburban"

1 U.S. Steel Demolishes Its Plant in Youngstown, Ohio, 1983

This 1983 photograph of a demolition in Youngstown, Ohio, tells a story about urban decline that had been decades in the making. Many of the industries that anchored metropolitan growth in the nineteenth and twentieth centuries were literally taken apart in the decades after World War II. Of course, it was not new for manufacturers to relocate when deemed profitable or necessary; for example, Henry Ford shifted much of his company's production to Detroit's near suburbs in the 1920s (source 7.3). But the movement and dismantling of plants accelerated significantly in the 1950s and 1960s, as firms sought out more space, easier access to transport, and lower labor costs. Many relocated to "right to work" states in the American South and Southwest, where restrictions on union organizing enabled employers to reduce wages and avoid paying benefits. Foreign production was equally lucrative: by 1980, Ford Motor Company was investing about 40 percent of its capital budget overseas and earning over 90 percent of its profits from those markets. Accelerating the decline of US industrial centers were foreign competition, mismanagement, and a wave of corporate takeovers that saw companies secure profits by shifting from manufacturing to other fields. By the mid-1980s, American Can Company no longer made cans, then soon merged with a financial services company and renamed itself Primerica.

A key turning point in this long history came with the collapse of manufacturing profits in the 1970s, which turned a steady stream of plant

The Modern American Metropolis: A Documentary Reader, First Edition.
Edited by David M. P. Freund.

relocation and abandonment into a flood, devastating communities in cities from Pittsburgh and Cleveland to Oakland and Los Angeles. In places dependent on single industries – like Youngstown, Ohio; Flint, Michigan; and Kenosha, Wisconsin – workers had few alternatives when jobs disappeared. Home foreclosures and even community abandonment soon followed. When three plant closures in Youngstown between 1977 and 1979 eliminated 8,000 high-wage jobs, 60 percent of the newly unemployed relocated, were forced into early retirement, or remained jobless.

Here many of Youngstown's residents watched the Ohio Works of U.S. Steel demolished after a nearly decade-long battle to save the plant from a merger with Ling Temco Vought, a US corporation which viewed disinvestment in steel production as key to maintaining profitability in its other ventures. The image provides a vivid reminder of the modern metropolis's dependence on costly, sophisticated infrastructure and raises a pressing question as the US economy is steadily reinvented: Who shoulders responsibility for sustaining or remaking communities devastated by structural change and its impacts on the built environment?

Figure 13.1 The demolition of Ohio Works, Youngstown, 1983.

Source: Photo courtesy of the Ohio Historical Society, AL04499.

2 Hoboken Residents Debate the "Yuppie" Invasion, 1984–1987

The rapid disappearance of well-paying manufacturing jobs in the 1970s devastated working- and middle-class families in metropolitan centers nationwide (source 13.1). Places with diversified economies provided wage earners with more options, but the economic downturn coupled with rising inflation left millions of Americans vulnerable. Complicating matters in many working-class neighborhoods was a new challenge: affluent urbanites were moving in, and transforming the communities.

The newcomers were beneficiaries of deindustrialization's "upside": the growth of service, technology, and financial sectors that produced lucrative employment for college-educated professionals. The result was a spike in demand for housing in older neighborhoods of urban centers such as San Francisco, Chicago, Boston, and New York City. Jobs and, for many, the lure of city living fueled a wave of investment in modest-income and poor neighborhoods. Individuals bought older properties, often well-built but rundown row houses, which they renovated for personal use or resale. Recognizing the potential for profits, real estate developers followed, converting existing apartment buildings into condominiums and eventually building new multiunit structures designed and marketed as distinctly "urban." New construction units featured high ceilings, exposed brickwork, and exposed ductwork, intended to mimic the industrial loft spaces in Lower Manhattan that artists had converted into apartment studios. (For these lofts' original uses, see sources 3.5 and 4.1.)

By the 1980s, this process of neighborhood turnover had been dubbed "gentrification" and was reshaping many "ethnic" European, Hispanic, and black working-class neighborhoods in Manhattan and its near neighbors: Brooklyn to the east and the cities of Hoboken and Jersey City, New Jersey, to the west. (For similar trends in Los Angeles, see source 13.4.) There were no condominiums in Hoboken in 1970, only 41 in 1980, and 3,062 by 1990. Given the economic struggles facing places like Hoboken, many residents welcomed the revival of business and the demand for real estate. But many were uncomfortable with the trade-offs, as hundreds of letters to the Hoboken Reporter *in the 1980s revealed. Excerpted here is a small sample, including responses by defenders of the gentrification process.*

Dear Editor:

I'm a Hoboken resident for 35 years, losing my home to Yuppies. Seeing these weird people with sneakers and dresses every morning dashing for a crosstown bus just turns my stomach. But please have some compassion for my privacy. Realtors coming to show my apartment at suppertime without notice is unpleasant. Again I have to see sneakers and dresses and men with shoulder bags and cameras only in my house at my special time. Give me a break – or a little advanced notice.

Thank you.

Once lived on a tree-lined street
July 9, 1986

Dear Editor:

... I once lived in Hoboken.

My building was sold, my rent tripled, and after 18 years in my apartment, I was forced out. My family helped to build Hoboken. I have roots in Hoboken from the very early beginning. Too bad I can't enjoy living there any more.

I am not welcome into the restaurants or old haunts that I used to visit with my friends. (We are all professional people, not bums!) We no longer "fit in."

Hoboken is now a cold city. What happened to my neighborhood? My rights were ignored and so were so many others. Being displaced is a terrible thing to do to people.

There is and always will be resentment towards those who "took over our neighborhoods." Yes, Yuppies didn't move in, they took over.

Hoboken people were the hard working laborers. Now they, we, us, and I can't afford to live in my town, our town.

Where do I and these others like me go when you take over my new home? Out in the streets like so many other displaced people are, or will I be "burned out" one night like so many other people whose homes were gone as a result of "suspicious fires." It's scary facing those odds. So understand that we were scared for our lives as well as our homes ...

A. D. Emahs
Aug. 6, 1986

Dear Editor:

... I too once lived in Hoboken, that was before I was forced out by a suspicious fire. I lost everything I owned. If you yuppies wouldn't pay such high rents, knowing that people before you were paying low rents, we never would have lost our homes. It's too late to do anything about it now, but one day a new generation will want to move in and I hope you people suffer as much as we did.

Sonia Rodriguez
Aug. 24, 1986

Dear Editor:

In response to "Once lived in Hoboken," we so-called "Yuppies" are sorry for taking over your town, but what do you want from us? We didn't know that the landlords in Hoboken were so desperate for money that they would do anything to get you people out of the city. We just want a place to live just like you. How do you think we feel being treated like we are millionaires, having to pay such high rents for a cheap run-down apartment in "Hoboken."

Palmer Monroe
A "Yuppie" Citizen
Aug. 31, 1986

Dear Editor:

[Nothing has] stopped the invasion of hordes of harried househunters from across the Hudson and the hinterlands who have descended on our tiny urban hamlet of Hoboken like a plague of biblical locusts. As regards the [new] homeowner[s] and the high interest rates and the vulnerable rent-paying tenant, many of the so-called "hip" avant-garde genre, supposedly wise to the ways of the our wicked, wicked world, they simply lend credence to the cretin philosophy of P.T. Barnum who once remarked that there is a sucker born every minute.

Yours truly,
Ralph Ruggiere
July 4, 1984

Dear Editor:

May I reply to a recent letter by Ralph Ruggiere by saying – Come out of the dark ages, Mr. R.

My husband and I bought a condominium apartment here in Hoboken a month ago ... [W]e do not qualify as part of the "so-called hip, avant garde generation" ...

Dumb as it may seem to Mr. R., we left a home in suburbia because we were tired of the toll (mental, physical and financial) of four hours commuting every day, were tired of a big house we never had time to care for or enjoy, and were tired of our lifestyle in general.

Here in Hoboken, we think we have found again the urban atmosphere we were seeking when we left Wisconsin 25 years ago. Our apartment suits our new lifestyle and we don't feel we were "suckers" for buying it. Especially considering the cost of housing in the suburbs. We like the multi-ethnic nature of the town and hope that its deteriorating housing stock will continue to be restored by funds both public and private.

We are productive people, work hard, pay taxes and don't want to be relegated to the suburbs!

Thanks for your "welcome" Mr. R.

Janet Civalor
Aug. 1984

Dear Editor:

The Renaissance continues and the city is literally being ripped up block by block ... Dumpsters occupy two or three parking locations all over town, not for days or weeks, but now for months ... You can hardly walk a few blocks on our city streets before you are forced out into the street as sidewalks are blocked by construction companies.

Hoboken has become a mile of duplexes, condos, and camocondos – a camouflaged condo is an old wooden tinder box house cosmetically done up with a stone-faced front.

These are the same apartments that my grandparents paid $23 per month, six railroad rooms (which I used to rollerskate through 'til I'd get caught).

These same rooms have now been razed and split into two three room exclusive apartments, $700 for you and $695 for me.

Some of the remodeling leaves only the front of the building, held together with wooden beams for support ...

Displacement runs rampant – there was a time when if rent on First Street went up to $85 per month, you'd look for an apartment on Second Street. For $60 ...

Jack O'Brien
Nov. 13, 1985

Dear Editor:

As a New Yorker, I would like to put in a good word for gentrification. It has made an amazing improvement in a stagnant and dying Hoboken. When I first came here, in 1963, Hoboken was a slum, choked by welfare recipients the way algae kills a lake ...

... Hoboken's renaissance, begun in the seventies, was the work of ... successful "Noo Yawkuhs" who bought and renovated the unwanted houses and made the rebirth possible ...

Sincerely,
D. M. Weed
Nov. 20, 1985

Dear Editor:

Renaissance in Hoboken?

A revival of Arts and Letters?

Hardly!

Yuppie hordes trail each morning to the Big City trough for their parasitic feed.

To monotonous clerkdoms at the stock market [or] advertising agencies ...

At day's end they trail back to Hoboken to their co-signed cubicles to await the next exciting morning.

However, on weekends they break out and "brunch it up." Whee!!!!!

This entire yuppie population crowded into a giant Italian style grape squeezer wouldn't yield one drop of talent.

Joseph Trincellita
Dec. 21, 1986

Dear Editor:

In response to Joseph Trincellita's December 21 letter ... His claim that the entire Hoboken Yuppie population would not yield one drop of talent makes him blind to the fact that there are many people in this town who have well respected jobs and have talents far beyond his capabilities. It would not surprise me one bit if Mr. Trincellita's occupation was that of urinal cleaner ... Mr. Trincellita can gripe all he wants. It's his own fault if he never made it big in life ...

The Lurker Group, Inc.
Jan. 11, 1987

Dear Editor:

I am a janitor for a large firm on Wall Street. I was very insulted when I read your letter insulting Mr. Trincellita by calling him a urinal cleaner ... For your information, I am a urinal cleaner and damn proud of it ... You folks work in nice clean offices and use the nice clean restrooms. Who do you think cleans those toilets and makes sure the bathroom is sanitized ...

So next time you use a toilet, think about the people who have to clean up your crap!

Lawrence Donnelly
A Janitor and Damn Proud of it!!!!!
Jan. 25, 1987

Dear Editor:

... I'm tired of being scorned because I am young, ambitious and making it in the New York metro area. If people are being displaced by a new wave of people, perhaps the fault lies with "natives" who didn't take the necessary steps to insure the stability of their lifestyles ...

Edward Dolinger
Aug. 1, 1984

Source: Joseph Barry and John Derevlany (eds.), *Yuppies Invade My House at Dinnertime: A Tale of Brunch, Bombs, and Gentrification in an American City* (Hoboken, NJ: Big River Publishing, 1987), pp. ix–xiii, 9–11, 26, 77–80, 125–126. Reproduced with permission from J. Derevlany and the *Hudson Reporter.*

3 Jersey City Markets Itself to a New Demographic, 2003 and 2006

As Hoboken's rental and real estate prices soared and the population of affluent professionals continued to expand in the 1990s (source 13.2), the "gentrification" process accelerated in neighboring Jersey City. For much of the nineteenth and twentieth centuries, Jersey City attracted German, Irish, Italian, and black American migrants who found work at its docks, railroads, and manufacturing plants. But by the 1970s a stalling national economy had devastated large portions of the city and impoverished many of its residents. Meanwhile students and artists priced out of Manhattan and Hoboken moved to Jersey City to find cheap rent and, often, to live in what they viewed as more "diverse" neighborhoods. This helped fuel the gentrification process, which saw investors redevelop Jersey City's waterfront, formerly the site of rail yards, manufacturing plants, and warehouses. By the 1990s, the redevelopment process had moved inland, as individuals and corporate investors purchased brownstones, apartments, and retail properties in the city's old downtown, just minutes by train from Lower Manhattan.

Two documents highlight some of the design and marketing strategies commonly employed to attract affluent renters and homebuyers to places like Jersey City. A 2003 brochure for "The Majestic Theater Condominiums" pictures residential units marketed as part of an historic restoration project; in fact they were new construction, attached to the facade of a restored landmark movie house (similar to the theater pictured in Figure 5.1(d)). Individual condominiums ranged in size from 700 to 1,500 square feet, with starting prices from $175,000 to $500,000. How might prospective owners see the Majestic as – to borrow the advertisement's language – a "synthesis of suburban and urban living"? This is followed by an excerpt from a 2006 article in Jersey City Magazine *entitled "Sugar House Lofts: A Bit of History*

A New View In Urban Living!

The circa 1907 Majestic Theatre and the surrounding landmarks have been transformed into a brand new cosmopolitan residence along with dynamic new retail shops.

A synthesis of suburban and urban living!

The Majestic Theatre Condominiums are unsurpassed in efficiency and affordability. It provides residents the best of both worlds: a charming community and graceful living just minutes from Manhattan. Within each home are all the amenities you could hope for:marble bathrooms with radiant heated flooring, sleek stainless steel kitchens and high ceilings highlighted with oversized windows offering the maximum in light and space.

Figure 13.3 The Majestic Theatre Condominiums sales brochure.

Source: Silverman – Building Neighborhoods.

Restored for Fine Living." The reporter describes this luxury waterfront development as a "collection of homes that mix a strong sense of history with the best of modern living." What history is being preserved or celebrated in these residential developments?

"Sugar House Lofts: A bit of history restored for fine living"

Residents of the Sugar House Lofts, located on the cusp of Jersey City's historic Paulus Hook neighborhood, say they frequently get letters from realtors asking them if they want to sell. Considering the elegance, history, accessibility, and stunning view offered by these units, it's no surprise.

One pair of owners agreed to let *Jersey City Magazine* take a peek inside their spacious abode to see how they have made Jersey City their home.

Their two-bedroom, two-bath unit ... features numerous brickface walls and vaulted ceilings that evoke the building's days as a warehouse for refined sugar.

"In that loft-like building, you have higher ceiling spaces. You don't get that in new construction," says Paul Somerville of Hoboken's Somerville Design, who designed many of the rooms in this and other units in the Sugar House. "It's a higher standard of quality [of construction] than most of [the county]."

The value of this particular space is a secret, but comparable lofts in the building have sold for over $1 million.

Amenities at the Sugar House include a 24-hour concierge, a health club, and underground parking. Not that residents necessarily need a car to hit the town: there's a Light Rail station literally around the corner ...

The building overlooks the Hudson River inlet of the former Morris Canal ... Many of the building's units ... feature unrivaled views of the Statue of Liberty, the historic CRRNJ train terminal, New York City, and Liberty State Park ...

But today's residents of the Sugar House very nearly didn't get the chance to enjoy those views. The building has lived through two fires and a complete overhaul, from factory floors into family units.

The Sugar House was created in 1863 by Danish architect Detleft Lineau, a founder of the American Institute of Architects. It served as a sugar warehouse for F.O. Matthiessen and Wiechers and, later, the American Sugar Refining Company.

The building was nearly destroyed in one of the worst fires in Jersey City history on Nov. 14, 1924, but survived. It then survived a second fire in 1955.

From 2000 to 2002, Diversified Management Systems converted the former warehouse into the 64-unit condominium it is today. The result is a collection of homes that mix a strong sense of history with the best of modern city living.

Source: Christopher Zinzli, "Sugar House Lofts: A Bit of History Restored for Fine Living," *Jersey City Magazine*, Spring/Summer 2006, pp. 32–33. Reproduced by permission of Hudson Reporter Association, L.P.

4 A Professor Explains How Urban Redevelopment Has Impacted Los Angeles's Minority Communities, 1987/1988

To what degree does our knowledge of metropolitan history inform contemporary debates about pressing urban issues? Excerpted here is a trenchant analysis of development politics and racial inequality in twentieth-century Los Angeles that helps us think about this question. In 1987 Professor Cynthia Hamilton intervened in a prominent national conversation about inner-city poverty and crime by publishing "Apartheid in an American City," which was reprinted the following year in the LA Weekly, *an independent newspaper. Drawing on existing scholarship and knowledge from her work in the community, Hamilton traces the complex origins of racial segregation and minority poverty in South Central Los Angeles. She documents a history familiar to students of the subject: private practices and public interventions had for decades maintained strict racial boundaries in Los Angeles, denying blacks and Hispanics in South Central access to resources and opportunities that had enabled other local communities to thrive (sources 9.2–3; 10.1, 3; 11.1–3; and 12.1–2, 4, 6). Notably, Hamilton's work echoed the findings of several studies commissioned by the government in the 1960s and 1970s to examine the endurance of urban poverty and the waves of riots that broke out in American cities. These authors agreed that it was impossible to understand inner-city poverty and episodes of urban unrest without examining the legacies of systemic discrimination, including development policies, hiring practices, racial profiling, and police violence.*

Hamilton's essay and similar studies were largely ignored during the 1980s and 1990s in mainstream discussions of the "urban crisis." When pundits and policy-makers addressed minority poverty or drug-related violence or urban decay, they pointed instead to a "culture of poverty" that had supposedly sapped inner-city residents' will to aspire and dedicate themselves to productive work. Critics also placed considerable blame on the expansion of the "welfare state," accusing government programs such as public housing,

Aid to Families with Dependent Children (AFDC), food stamps, and Head Start of creating a "culture of dependency" among the minority poor (source 11.2). Four years after Hamilton's article appeared, South Central Los Angeles became the center of massive rioting when an all-white jury acquitted police officers caught on tape beating a black motorist named Rodney King. The public debate that ensued focused not on the history of structural inequality, sentencing guidelines, and incarceration rates, nor on police violence against minorities, but rather on the "character" of minority neighborhoods and the life choices of their residents. Why did most media outlets and public officials fail to discuss the well-documented history explored in studies by Hamilton and others? To what extent has this history informed recent discussions of race, poverty, incarceration, and violence in your city or region, or in high-profile incidents such as the 2012 shooting death of Trayvon Martin and the ensuing acquittal of the shooter, George Zimmerman, in Sanford, Florida?

Southward, beyond the highrise towers of downtown Los Angeles a symmetrical grid pattern of streets is barely discernible through the usual dim haze. These streets, stretching south to the horizon (Crenshaw, Western, Normandie, Vermont, Hoover, Figueroa, Broadway, San Pedro, Main, Avalon, Central, Hooper, Compton, Alameda) and east to west (Washington, Adams, Jefferson, Vernon, Slauson, Florence, Manchester, Century, Imperial, El Segundo, Rosecrans) are unknown to most white Angelenos. These are the arteries of South Central Los Angeles. Hundreds of thousands of blacks move along these pathways daily. The fortunate go to places of employment in the metropolitan area, but for most the movement is circular, cyclical and to nowhere. These streets have become the skeletal structure of another "Bantustan" in an American city – another defoliated community, manipulated and robbed of its vitality by the ever present growth pressures of the local economy.

Los Angeles has never been an integrated community. The restrictive racial covenants of the prewar years saw to that; the Ku Klux Klan based in Compton and Long Beach saw to that. Old-timers will tell you about the days when they couldn't live south of Slauson, or they reminisce about their teenage years when it was an adventure to transverse [*sic*] the taunting white neighborhoods that separated the Central/Jefferson part of the black community from the black out-post in Watts. Those native to South Central have always known that blacks live south of downtown, Latinos to the east and whites on the Westside or in the Valley. In more than 40 years this fundamental pattern has not changed.

... [T]here is a [unique] sort of emptiness and starkness [in South Central], one caused by what appears to be a systematic pattern of displacement and removal of all the things that contribute to a liveable environment and viable community. If one were to take the very long view, one would have to say that the larger society has denuded the community for the society's own long-term profitable ends. Much like the bulldozing of black encampments on the fringe of Johannesburg or Durban, it can be argued, South Central is inevitably slated by the historical process to be replaced without a trace: cleared land ready for development for a more prosperous – and probably whiter – class of people. For the larger, unspoken malady affecting South Central stems from the idea that the land is valuable and the present tenants are not. This "bantustan," like its counterparts in South Africa, serves now only as a holding space for blacks and browns no longer of use to the larger economy.

On the street you get a different view. First, nobody knows he or she lives in South Central. Nobody calls the area Watts or "Greater Watts." ... Nor do people call South Central the "curfew zone" ... as did the McCone Commission ... after the 1965 "Watts" uprising. The area is simply home and neighborhood: many neighborhoods centering around churches and schools. These supportive environments, however, have become a shadow of what they once were, as recently as 30 years ago ...

South Central ... is 73.9 percent black, 22.9 percent Latino, with a growing number of undocumented ... It is a vast wasteland with few jobs, no industry, few functioning services. The largest percentage of L.A.'s homeless population can be found in South Central ... Only 3.6% of the total land mass in South Central is zoned for industry ... More industry has moved out of the South Central area since 1971 than has moved in ... The major health facilities ... are underfinanced, overused county institutions. The housing stock in the area is older than most in the city. Forty percent of the housing ... was built prior to 1940; only 2 percent of the housing was built after 1970; only 46% of the property is owneroccupied. The vast bulk of those who are employed must commute outside the community to work each day. For the 20 percent who are unemployed, survival is a function of subsistence inside the area. With no jobs, the underground economy takes over – that is, crime: theft, drugs, prostitution ... A cursory view of health conditions is equally shocking ... [with] a higher [infant mortality rate and higher] death rate due to cancer [and] heart and liver diseases ... Yet the county Board of Supervisors has slashed health-care budgets and closed trauma centers throughout the area.

These social and economic conditions of deterioration, coupled with the growing volume of abandoned space, make South Central vulnerable to new development because its real estate costs have been reduced ... As rents peak across the city developers will seek new opportunities in areas presently under-capitalized. Community residents know this and fear their own displacement – many perhaps to the streets – as a consequence of gentrification ... and new zoning that could change residential patterns and add new development projects.

The fears of the community are well founded in light of recent experience. Since construction began in 1967, the Century Freeway displaced more than 27,150 people, 7,150 dwellings, 294 businesses, 1,140 community jobs and 38 cultural institutions. One-third of the cultural institutions lost along [the] entire freeway route were in the black community, as were one-third of the small businesses, 40 percent of the dwellings and one-third of the jobs. To the northeast, USC expansion transformed the Hoover and Jefferson area (with the assistance of the Community Redevelopment Agency [CRA] and through the use of police power, eminent domain and condemnation). Additionally, USC has incorporated a multimillion-dollar real estate company to build student and faculty housing, research and development facilities and commercial projects in the surrounding neighborhood ...

Public Dollars for Private Growth

... L.A. primarily is still a service economy, and its job structure reflects this. The scarcity of industry and product manufacturing has been a serious handicap for the working class, although the explosion in the undocumented immigrant population has resulted in a temporary expansion in non-aerospace manufacturing (light industry, garment trades) that will continue as long as employers can pay salaries below the minimum wage.

But this kind of economy has little to sustain the black population, whose initial immigration to the West was accelerated by assembly-line war production at the shipyards and aircraft plants ... [And since the war, meanwhile, as larger companies began marketing their goods to the black community], most blackowned businesses collapsed under the pressure of competition from white-owned giants – and with them, the jobs they had created ... [T]hus we see ... the decline of black newspapers and black-owned centers of entertainment, banks and insurance companies. The irony is that deterioration and loss of black ownership occurred after "Jim Crow" conditions began to break down here ...

... The location of industrial corporations outside the inner city, which was also facilitated by government subsidies, has been another major factor in the underdevelopment of the black community. As firms found new homes after the war, the relocation of the white population outside of L.A.

began ... Growth of the peripheral areas of Los Angeles County, including the San Fernando Valley and Orange County, boomed during the 1950s. Many Valley residents worked for Lockheed in Burbank or for one of the many subcontractors in the area. In Orange County the number of aircraft workers skyrocketed from 5,100 in 1956 to 73,500 by 1968 ...

"Slum Clearance" for Profit

... Odd as it now seems, blacks had to fight to move into what is now a large portion of South Central. From the '20s to the early '50s downtown business interests were allied with real estate blockbusters in maintaining restrictive racial housing covenants in most of the areas surrounding downtown ... [Yet] a peculiar development pattern for South Central has emerged in recent years as a result of such housing manipulation.

In the early-1970s post-"War on Poverty" era, after the Nixon administration eliminated most of the low-income housing programs, government subsidies became more plentiful for commercial rehabilitation and development. New construction of badly needed low-cost residential units has therefore been minimal ... Most of the housing units in South Central therefore remain single-family units built before 1940. The depreciation of values that results from redlining, from lack of services and from the area's general deterioration compounds the problem: neither private financial institutions nor the Federal Housing Authority consider the "curfew zone" an attractive market ... [R]esidents today still face redlining and home ownership is even further beyond the reach of most black families ...

More needful of social services than other communities because of lack of jobs, South Central in fact gets less ... Basic needs are not being met by the state, county, or city agencies. Some sections ... have never been visited by the Bureau of Sanitation's regular weekly trash trucks and street sweepers. This is a neighborhood where individuals and families try desperately to solve their problems alone because there is little or no help ...

The explanation given – and accepted – is that conditions of severe poverty routinely plague the "underclass," a group separate from the general population whose problems are largely a consequence of their own cultural past and habits ... "Underclass," of course, is simply the latest rationalization for the racism and neglect of the larger society. It conditions both residents of South Central and the public at large to accept government passivity, corporate hostility and citizen apathy to conditions of homelessness and unemployment. Furthermore, it prepares the population to accept repressive legislation – everything from L.A.'s police sweeps to the mayor and police chief's order to sweep the homeless away from downtown business fronts.

The Big Plan

Los Angeles is becoming the model American city. It exemplifies the corporate growth that all urban areas have sought to achieve since World War II in an effort to overcome the industrial flight to the suburbs. Cities have relied on the growth process to facilitate consolidation of their central business districts; they have relied on urban-renewal strategies to transform and transplant old residential communities that in another era encircled downtown areas. Growth has become the primary concern of government. …

However, this strategy has also created a contradictory role for local government … Public money that should have been available to build and maintain that community, rather than let it slip into blight, has been absorbed by the more profitable downtown building binge. Meanwhile, largely working-class black neighborhoods adjacent to downtown are being gentrified, with a huge push from the city and developers …

Source: Cynthia Hamilton, *Apartheid in an American City: The Case of the Black Community in Los Angeles* (Los Angeles: Labor/Community Strategy Center, January 1, 1987), pp. 1–8. Reprinted as "The Making of an American Bantustan," *LA Weekly*, December 30, 1988.

5 Planners Assess an Experiment in "New Urbanism" (Before the Great Recession), 1999

This thoughtful analysis of a New Urbanism project in the Detroit suburb of Novi, Michigan, raises important questions about redevelopment politics in the twenty-first century. Advocates of New Urbanism promote community development along what are deemed "urban" principles: mixing land uses, reducing the footprint of residential and commercial construction, promoting socioeconomic diversity, and encouraging walking and reliance on public transportation. The project discussed here highlights key differences between older, "traditional" central cities and recent efforts to recreate urban efficiencies, diversity, and "feel." What structural, political, and cultural variables make Novi's new Main Street distinct from the urban environments encountered in Parts V through VII? What does it mean for a neighborhood unit to be "self-sufficient" in the early twenty-first century? Why do the authors question the new project's economic viability?

The timing of this report – it was published in 1999 – illustrates one of the obstacles faced by proponents of New Urbanism. The Detroit region's economy stalled over the following decade and was devastated by the crisis and recession that began in 2007. How do public and private interests effectively plan for metropolitan redevelopment and growth, as these parties in Novi attempted to do, when long-term economic trends are not predictable? The jobs and growth anticipated here did not fulfill expectations. Who, then, absorbs the costs of such failed, or at best delayed, investments in city building?

Novi's Main Street: Neotraditional Neighborhood Planning and Design

Introduction

Recently, there has been interest in many suburban communities around the United States to revive traditional styles of commercial and residential land development. These neotraditional developments are characterized by a land-use intensive style of zoning in which densely spaced residential neighborhoods are integrated with commercial areas. One of the primary objectives of these districts is to form self-sufficient neighborhood communities. Although such land use is common in many large urban areas and rural cities, this type of combined land use is rarely seen in suburban communities. One effort to revive this traditional urban style of land development within a suburban community is the Main Street project in the city of Novi, Mich.

Traditionally styled land-use developments are desirable from a number of standpoints. Among the anticipated benefits is a decrease in traffic demand resulting from the pedestrian-oriented nature of the development. Neo-traditional developments are also pleasing from the standpoint of convenience. The integration of residential and commercial land use into a single community allow[s] residents to live in close proximity to places of employment, shopping, and entertainment. Some recent projects, like Novi's Main Street, also incorporate decorative enhancement features such as ornate street lighting fixtures, brick paver sidewalks, and other land/streetscape amenities. These features allow the neotraditional community to revive an ambience absent from most suburban communities.

Although a project such as Main Street can have many positive aspects, these types of developments can also be difficult to initiate and implement due to their unique requirements ... [including] unique design and zoning issues [and] ... the lack of published guidelines and standards to direct the design of the project. Present planning and engineering practices provide relatively little guidance for the development of neotraditional neighborhood development ... Another significant impediment to the project was its cost. The type of community desired by the city carried a substantially higher development cost than more conventional developments. As such, it became difficult to find a private developer willing to take the risks of initiating such a plan.

The Main Street project has overcome these obstacles to create a downtown area where none had existed before ... Through a series of public/private funding initiatives, open community forums, and careful planning and engineering the 22.3-ha (55-acre) project is nearing completion. Whether the Main Street project can grow into a commercially viable and "community-friendly" neighborhood, remains to be seen.

Project History

The city of Novi is a suburban community of approximately 50,000 residents located 50km (30 mi) northwest of downtown Detroit. Novi originated in the 1920s as a stop on the Detroit-to-Grand Rapids railroad line. The city was officially chartered in 1969. During the past 15 years the city has ridden the crest of an economic development wave to become the fastest growing city in the state of Michigan. In response to this anticipated growth, the city adopted a master plan for land use [which included] a framework for a commercial business district in the center of the city ... The Town Center District, as it is known, now occupies an area of 2.5 km (1 mi) and serves as the commercial hub for the city and one of the largest retail centers in the state.

Two decades of rapid growth has given Novi the image of a city on the move. The Town Center served as its commercial heart; however, the city's Office of Community Development felt it lacked a true central business district and meeting place for residents, workers, and visitors to the city. In addition, ... city administrators felt the city lacked a unique identity among the many suburban communities of metropolitan Detroit ... A recent *Newsweek* magazine article has criticized what in their view is a lack of effective planning in most modern suburban communities, stating: "The 'civic center' of many suburbs, designed for the convenience of the car, is a strip mall along a six-lane highway" (Adler 1993). The Main Street concept was initiated by the city's Community Development Department in 1988 to address these deficiencies.

Project Planning

In any land development project there are a great number of factors that influence the final design of the project. In the case of Main Street ... [it involved] individuals from engineering, planning, and landscape architecture ... closely allied with professionals specializing in construction, architecture, real estate development, banking, and public administration to work out the details of land exchange and project financing. The public nature of the project also required contributions from citizen advisory groups and community steering committees ...

Zoning

The first step to initiate the Main Street project was to develop a zoning ordinance that would promote the city's Community Development Department's vision of a traditional neighborhood community ... The new zoning ordinance, called TC-1, was written to "promote the development of a pedestrian accessible, commercial service district" [as well as] combined parking facilities for all businesses [while discouraging] vehicular-oriented commercial land uses such as car washes, gas stations, [or] drive-through restaurants that would "have a disruptive effect on the pedestrian orientation of the districts." The TC-1 ordinance promoted service-oriented tenants such as banks, cleaners, law and medical offices, and tailors. This was to establish a codependent connection between the residential and commercial sections of the district ...

Partner Planning

An important element of the planning process was establishment of numerous public and private partnerships. A close partnership between the city and the Main Street developer was crucial to the life of the project. The land parcel for the Main Street district was spread over both privately and publicly owned land. As such, both the city and real estate developer were required to make considerable funding commitments to one another. Agreements for the purchase and trade of property, road and utility rights-of-way, parking areas, park land, and infrastructure utility service had to be worked out prior to any final design or construction. These agreements also had to include contingency clauses to protect the city's interests in the event of any financial failure from the project's private interests.

The joint nature of the project has resulted in both costs and benefits to the city and the developer ... The monetary outlays by the city totaled over a million dollars for sewer and water main construction as well as the accompanying engineering and environmental studies. Repayment to the city for these costs will come in the form of increased real estate taxes and utility tap charges. The benefits to the city, aside from the realization of a new city center, were the enhanced commercial tax base, income from municipal parking fees, and the enhancement of the city's transportation infrastructure. The costs to the developer were associated with the construction of the roadway, accompanying streetscape amenities, parking lots, and land donations. These costs totaled over $4,100,000. For his investment, the developer is expected to reap rewards from the enhanced property values resulting from newly gained road frontage, utility extensions through the subject property, and the acquisition of additional property for the construction of parking areas ...

Another element in the planning process was to evaluate the impact of the project on the community in terms of future economic development and community involvement. It has been estimated that the project will ultimately result in the addition of some 1,200 permanent jobs and 300 new businesses. Another 500 jobs were expected to result from the construction of the project. In addition to the employment opportunities, the project is also regarded as the catalyst to drive future expansion of existing visitor and entertainment businesses in the area. When complete the Main Street community is expected to feature a dinner theater and microbrewery to complement the existing Novi Exposition Center, Motor Sports Hall of Fame, ice arena, and regional shopping mall ...

Current status and future plans

At the time of writing, the construction of the Main Street project was about half complete. All underground infrastructure including water main storm and sanitary sewer, roadway, and streetscape features have been constructed. The fruit market has been in successful operation since 1995. Three of the nine Main Street building phases ... are under construction. The Main Street Village residential district is complete and is fully occupied. The microbrewery and shop plaza at the east end of the site have also recently begun operation and have generated a great deal of interest and anticipation for the remainder of the commercial buildings. The next phases of approved development will include the construction of phases four through nine, with future plans to include a five-story hotel building and a dinner theater ...

Near term growth within the Main Street vicinity also looks promising. A conceptual design study is underway to evaluate options for the 8.09-ha (20 acre) parcel west of Novi Road. It is anticipated that this property will become "Main Street West" and will house 65,032 m (700,000 ft) of commercial building and parking space. While considerable obstacles remain, such as the relocation of existing businesses, several real estate developers are interested in the project. Discussions are also underway to expand the existing Main Street District further to the south and east to incorporate more commercial and residential areas.

Some of these expansion plans have also met with considerable resistance from owners of existing businesses immediately adjacent to the proposed TC1 district expansion. Most of the land surrounding or adjoining the proposed TC-1 vicinity is currently zoned for light industrial uses. Current property owners feel that an expansion of the existing Main Street area will one day lead to a call for rezoning of their properties and ultimately the need to relocate their buildings.

The long-term economic viability of Main Street is unknown ... [N]o one can accurately predict if the combination of the residential and commercial land uses in a suburban area will be a passing fad or a growing trend. The interest to reduce suburban sprawl and create more livable communities exists ... Main Street represents a real effort to improve the community of Novi, Mich. The question of whether it can accomplish all of its goals will be answered in the next 5–10 years.

Source: Brian Wolshon and James Wahl, "Novi's Main Street: Neotraditional Neighborhood Planning and Design," *Journal of Urban Planning and Development*, 125(1) (March 1999), pp. 2–7, 13, 16. Reproduced by permission of the American Society of Civil Engineers.

Editor's note: *As of August 2013, an aerial view of central Novi (just south of the intersection of Grand River and Main Street) illustrates the recession's impact on this project and highlights other practical challenges facing New Urbanist development. Much of the plan described in the 1999 report was never realized. "Main Street" itself was completed, but only a portion of its planned pedestrian-friendly commercial development has been built. The remainder of the new roadway is surrounded by undeveloped green space.*

In addition, while people living in the development's new townhouses can walk to Main Street via Potomac or Pennsylvania Avenues, most Novi residents have to drive there and park in one of the large lots that accommodate the commercial strip (or at the mall, across 11 Mile Road). Even neighborhood residents living in older subdivisions adjacent to the redevelopment region (for example, on Fountain Park Drive or Cherry Hill Road) have limited pedestrian access to Main Street. To patronize its retail establishments, it might be easier and safer for them to drive, around the corner, and then park on site.

Chapter 14 Growth and Its Challenges

1 The Global Economy and Global Politics Create New Challenges in the Twin Cities Region, 2012

Read, view, or listen to contemporary accounts of American places and you will encounter topics and themes that have long been central to metropolitan history. Reprinted here is a story about electoral politics that speaks to the long history of immigration and global economic change.

On February 14, 2012, the Minneapolis Star Tribune *reported on local efforts to redraw municipal ward boundaries, so that the city's growing immigrant populations would be adequately represented in council elections. The ethnic makeup of the Minneapolis–St. Paul region changed dramatically in the late twentieth century, as white outmigration was matched with the arrival of Latinos, Africans (especially Somalis), and Asians (especially people of Hmong, Asian Indian, and Chinese descent). Migrants and immigrants came seeking work – in the high-tech industry, for example – or, in some cases, political refuge. According to US Bureau of Census figures, between 1970 and 2010 the non-Hispanic white population of Minneapolis shrank from about 90 percent to just over 60 percent, and the change in St. Paul was comparable. New arrivals to the region came with a wide range of educational and work experience, as well as incomes; two of the fastest-growing immigrant concentrations have been in working-class, trailer-park communities, on the one hand, and Falcon Heights, a suburb in which over 70 percent of residents have college degrees and nearly 40 percent have professional degrees, on the other. The demographic shift has not always*

The Modern American Metropolis: A Documentary Reader, First Edition.
Edited by David M. P. Freund.

been smooth, with numerous conflicts arising over cultural practices and the provision of public services for immigrants who are impoverished, less educated, or have limited English skills.

The debate discussed here is specific to Minneapolis politics. But it is part of a process that all metropolitan regions continue to negotiate: adapting to demographic, economic, technological, political, and cultural changes through some kind of political process. In this case, local activists are attempting to give minority populations equal access to power in the Minneapolis City Council. What has changed to differentiate this debate from a similar one, a century earlier, concerning strategies for municipal governance in the "immigrant city"? (See sources in Chapters 4 and 6.)

"Immigrants draw lines for change in Minneapolis"

Activists and redistricting officials are drafting revised political wards in Minneapolis to consolidate and increase influence.

The increasing influence of immigrants in Minneapolis shows up in the bustle of Latino plazas and Somali malls, from East Lake Street to Cedar-Riverside – but not on the dais of the City Council, where two of 13 representatives are members of racial minorities.

Ward boundaries divide two fast-growing groups, Latinos and East African immigrants, in ways that some redistricting officials and immigrant activists say dilute their voting power and lessen the likelihood that they will win election.

Some see an opportunity to broaden political participation through the once-a-decade redistricting process underway in Minneapolis, where a 24-member group is studying how to revise ward lines to reflect demographic changes following the U.S. census.

The panel's latest draft map – to be presented at a meeting Wednesday – would shift more blacks and Latinos into the Sixth Ward, which now spans Ventura Village, Phillips West, Whittier and Stevens Square-Loring Heights. The proposal increases the combined Latino and black population from 48 to 63 percent by expanding the ward to take in part of Cedar-Riverside, including Riverside Plaza, home to many of the city's Somali-Americans. It also adds Midtown Phillips and parts of East Phillips to boost the Hispanic population, while shifting a chunk of Whittier into another ward.

The Redistricting Group wants "to increase opportunities for minority voters," member Andrea Rubinstein said at a meeting last week. "There have been enormous demographic changes in Minneapolis ... and this is a great opportunity for us to recognize those things."

Minneapolis' population of 382,578 barely budged in the last decade. Yet as blacks increasingly left north and south Minneapolis, Latino and East African immigrants continued their influx into the city from the 1990s. Minneapolis is now 36 percent non-white, up about 1 percentage point in the past decade, and 15 percent of the population is foreign-born.

Political representation has not kept pace. The City Council's only racial minorities are Robert Lilligren, an American Indian, and Don Samuels, who is black.

"What would it do for our kids to have a council member from our community?" asked Abdulkadir Warsame, a Somali-American who lives in Cedar-Riverside. "It would encourage them; it would get more people to participate in the process."

After Somali-American Mohamud Noor lost the DFL primary in last year's special election in Senate District 59, Warsame and others who campaigned for him brainstormed about their next step. They consulted a former state demographer and formed a committee called Citizens for Fair Redistricting, then submitted a map proposing three wards with higher concentrations of minorities and immigrants.

Most of Minnesota's 32,000 Somalis live in Minneapolis. And the number of the city's East African-born residents jumped 53 percent to 14,497 in the last decade.

Terra Cole, a member of the redistricting panel, said that the group's proposal had influenced their approach.

"We didn't see what they saw, and it got us to think differently," she said.

The North Side's Fifth Ward is more than half black, but few of those residents are of East African descent. Redistricting Group Chairman Barry Clegg said it will be impossible to create an additional ward in which one minority group makes up more than 50 percent of the population; other parts of Minneapolis lack a similarly high concentration of one non-white community.

All of these ideas are fluid, as the Redistricting Group meets over the next few weeks to continue refining a new map and hear from the public. The deadline is April 3.

Hispanics have been less visible in redistricting hearings this year, even though their population in Minneapolis jumped 37 percent to about 40,000 since 2000.

Efforts are underway to boost political participation in the community, which is mostly Mexican. Mariano Espinoza, a trainer for political leadership at Minnesota Immigrant Freedom Network who lives in Powderhorn, said he is meeting with Latinos in south Minneapolis about redistricting and other public issues.

Source: Maya Rao, "Immigrants Draw Lines for Change in Minneapolis," *Star Tribune*, February 14, 2012.

2 College Students in Merced Rent Empty McMansions, 2011

Beginning in the 1990s, the US housing market underwent a new and unprecedented wave of expansion. Thanks to effective marketing of innovative – some thought risky – new mortgage loans with unusually liberal terms, homeownership came within reach of far more Americans. The abundant flow of credit also enabled borrowers to finance much larger and more expensive residences, commonly referred to as "McMansions." In a wave of construction and sales that transformed existing suburban areas and undeveloped rural areas nationwide, sizable large-lot homes became a new symbol and for many a new standard of middle-class success. Four-bedroom houses with 4,000 or more square feet of floor space quickly rose up nationwide.

The collapse of the housing market after 2007 – echoing comparable episodes of real estate speculation in US history (source 7.6) – left millions of investors and homeowners in debt and countless housing units empty. Individual structures and often entire subdivisions were left unfinished. More often, neighborhoods of newly built homes could not find buyers. One hard-hit region was the San Joaquin Valley in Central California, where cash-strapped homeowners resorted to renting out new properties to defray the expense of ownership. Late in 2011, Patricia Leigh Brown reported for the New York Times *on a rental strategy that had grown in popularity because of the city's proximity to a captive rental market: college students. How do the people interviewed for this piece view the value of homeownership and the meaning of living in an expansive, luxurious dwelling? How do they view the implications of the market's collapse?*

MERCED, Calif. – Heather Alarab, a junior at the University of California, Merced, and Jill Foster, a freshman, know that their sudden popularity has little to do with their sparkling personalities, intelligence or athletic prowess.

"Hey, what are you doing?" throngs of friends perpetually text. "Hot tub today?"

While students at other colleges cram into shoebox-size dorm rooms, Ms. Alarab, a management major, and Ms. Foster, who is studying applied math, come home from midterms to chill out under the stars in a curvaceous swimming pool and an adjoining Jacuzzi behind the rapidly depreciating McMansion that they have rented for a song.

Here in Merced, a city in the heart of the San Joaquin Valley and one of the country's hardest hit by home foreclosures, the downturn in the real estate market has presented an unusual housing opportunity for thousands of college students. Facing a shortage of dorm space, they are moving into hundreds of luxurious homes in overbuilt planned communities.

Forget the off-to-college checklist of yesteryear (bedside lamp, laundry bag, under-the-bed storage trays). This is "Animal House" 2011.

Double-height Great Room? Check.

Five bedrooms? Check.

Chandeliers? Check.

Then there are the three-car garages, wall-to-wall carpeting, whirlpool baths, granite kitchen countertops, walk-in closets and inviting gas fireplaces.

"I mean, I have it all!" said Patricia Dugan, a senior majoring in management, who was reading Dario Fo's "Accidental Death of an Anarchist" in her light-filled living room while soaking a silk caftan in one of two master bathroom sinks.

The finances of subdivision life are compelling: the university estimates yearly on-campus room and board at $13,720 a year, compared with roughly $7,000 off-campus. Sprawl rats sharing a McMansion – with each getting a bedroom and often a private bath – pay $200 to $350 a month each, depending on the amenities.

Gurbir Dhillon, a senior majoring in molecular cell biology, pays $70 more than his four housemates each month for the privilege of having what they enviously call "the penthouse suite" – a princely boudoir with a whirlpool tub worthy of Caesars Palace and a huge walk-in closet, which Mr. Dhillon has filled with baseball caps and T-shirts.

The pool table in the young men's Great Room is the site of raucous games and taco dinners. "You definitely appreciate it when you visit your friends at other schools and they say, 'O.K., sleep on the floor,'" Mr. Dhillon said.

A confluence of factors led to the unlikely presence of students in subdivisions, where the collegiate promise of sleeping in on a Saturday morning may be rudely interrupted by neighborhood children selling Girl Scout cookies door to door.

This city of 79,000 is ranked third nationally in metropolitan-area home foreclosures, behind Las Vegas and Vallejo, Calif., said Daren Blomquist, a spokesman for RealtyTrac, a company based in Irvine, Calif., that tracks housing sales. The speculative fever that gripped the region and drew waves of outside investors to this predominantly agricultural area was fueled in part by the promise of the university itself, which opened in 2005 as the first new University of California campus in 40 years.

The crash crashed harder here. "Builders were coming into the area by the bulkload," said Loren M. Gonella, who owns a real estate company here. "It was, 'Holy moly, let's get on this gravy train.'"

But visions of an instant Berkeley materializing in the cow pastures were premature. The stylishly designed university planned for a gradual expansion, adding 600 new students a year. That has meant phased dorm construction, which is financed with tax-exempt bonds repaid by student revenue. There is room for only 1,600 students in the campus dorms, but 5,200 are enrolled.

With hundreds of homes standing empty, many of them likely foreclosures, students willing to share houses have been "a blessing," said Ellie Wooten, a former mayor of Merced and a real estate broker. Five students paying $200 a month each trump families who cannot afford more than $800 a month.

The university's free transit system, Cat Tracks, stops at student-heavy subdivisions. There are also limitless creative possibilities, with decor ranging from a Kappa Kappa Gamma sorority bedroom motif to an archetypal male nightstand overflowing with empty bags of Flamin' Hot Cheetos.

Not all neighbors are amused.

"Everybody on this street is underwater and can't see any relief," said John Angus, an out-of-work English teacher who paid $532,000 for a house that is now worth $221,000. "This was supposed to be an edge-of-town, Desperate Housewifey community," he said. "These students are the reverse."

Mr. Angus pays $3,000 a month, while student neighbors pay one-tenth of that. "I think they're the luckiest students I've ever come across," he said somewhat bitterly.

Nevertheless, students quickly learn that the cul-de-sac life is not risk-free. Lance Eber, the crime analyst for the Merced Police Department, said vacant houses were frequent targets of theft, most recently of copper wiring. They also attract squatters, who sometimes encamp beneath covered patios, he said.

Ms. Wooten ... added, "There are some odd scenarios going on around here."

They include the case of absentee landlord parents like Rhonda Castillo and her husband, who bought a house for their son, Jason, when times were flush in 2005. Jason was in the first class at the Merced campus.

The untimely investment was ultimately less important than "an investment in our son," Mrs. Castillo said. "It gave him a preview of real life: buying groceries, preparing food, doing the laundry and taking care of the yard." (He is now in medical school, and four female students rent the house.)

Indeed, managing a four- or five-bedroom house – not to mention all the cars – can be tricky business for young people.

Sitting in her kitchen, a planet of granite, Katilyn McIntire, a human biology major, explained how she and her four roommates rotated cars – one parks on the street, two park in the garage and two in the driveway. Whoever is getting up for an 8 a.m. class parks last. After an unsuccessful attempt at tending the yard with a hand mower, they now pay $50 a month to a gardener.

The student equivalent of "keeping up with the Joneses" has emerged, too.

Jaron Brandon, a sophomore and a senator in the student government, does his homework in the Jacuzzi in his six-bedroom house, on a waterproof countertop that he rigged over the tub.

Seeking housemates, he posted a beguiling ad on Craigslist: "For a small amount more than a nameless house in the suburbs," it read, "you could be living in a mansion right by school."

Source: Patricia Leigh Brown, "Animal McMansion: Students Trade Dorm for Suburban Luxury," *New York Times*, November 13, 2011, p. A1. Reproduced by permission of The New York Times Company.

3 The *Great Wall of Los Angeles* Pictures the Region's Development History, 1974 to the Present

You might regularly encounter examples of a well-established urban tradition: public art. Some pieces are sanctioned, notably the sculptures that adorn parks, squares, and the grounds of office buildings. Others are often not welcomed and sometimes illicit, including graffiti, street performances, and murals. For insight into the culture and politics of any American place, consider how various forms of public expression are received by different populations. In New York City during the 1970s, for example, graffiti artists redecorated a lot of real estate and hundreds of the city's subway trains. Many people viewed this as street art, a form of self-expression by marginalized New Yorkers who claimed public spaces and offered a running commentary on urban decline, poverty, and the policing of minorities. Others saw graffiti as vandalism, produced by New Yorkers unwilling to engage in constructive pursuits and contemptuous of people and the property of those who did. By the 1980s, however, some of these same critics were celebrating graffiti – when found in certain venues – as fine art. Works by Brooklyn-born painter Jean-Michel Basquiat were fetching top dollar at SoHo art auctions, and soon the iconography introduced by Keith Haring would be ubiquitous in popular culture, even adorning tee shirts sold at Urban Outfitters.

One prominent sample of the public art tradition, the Great Wall of Los Angeles, *is a sanctioned work with roots in the contested history of street mural painting. The project began in 1974 when the Army Corps of Engineers invited a local mural artist, Judith Francisca Baca, to contribute to the renovation of the Tujunga Wash, a concrete flood-control channel built in the 1930s to facilitate development in the San Fernando Valley. Baca recruited hundreds of youths, mostly low-income and many referred by the city's Criminal Justice department, to contribute to a painting that recounted California's history from the perspective of its marginalized communities. The mural's topics include colonial occupation, Dust Bowl refugees, Japanese internment, and the Zoot Suit Riots. By 1983 it measured more than 2,000 feet in length, easily visible to pedestrians and drivers. Renovations, extensions, and public celebrations of the project continue to this day. But paintings like this have not always been accepted as art, especially by the region's Anglo population, and the city's murals – there are thousands – are still viewed by many as unnecessarily "political" or as eyesores. Pictured here are three segments from the* Great Wall *depicting California in the 1950s: the first shows the "return" of American women to their domestic roles following World War II, the second depicts the destruction of the Chicano community in Chavez Ravine for the construction of Dodger Stadium, and the third depicts a celebration of Asian Americans' success in gaining the right to become naturalized US citizens and own property. (Color reproductions viewable at www.sparcmurals.org.)*

(a)

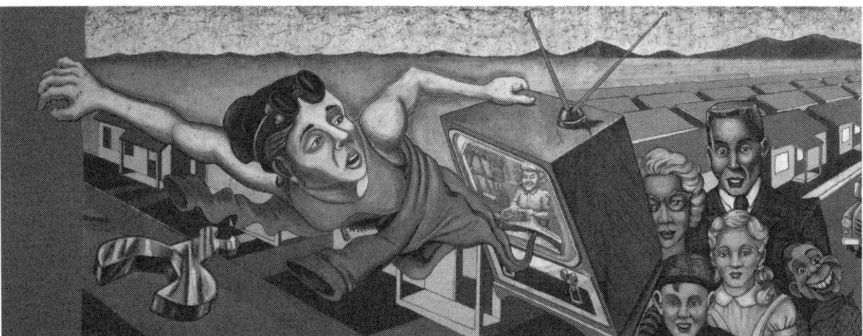

Figure 14.3(a) Judith F. Baca, "Farewell to Rosie the Riveter," detail from 1950s section of the *Great Wall of Los Angeles*, 1983.

Source: Courtesy of SPARC (www.sparcmurals.org).

(b)

Figure 14.3(b) Judith F. Baca, “Division of the Barrios,” detail from 1950s section of the *Great Wall of Los Angeles*, 1983.

Source: Courtesy of SPARC (www.sparcmurals.org).

(c)

Figure 14.3(c) Judith F. Baca, “Asians Gain Citizenship and Property,” detail from 1950s section of the *Great Wall of Los Angeles*, 1983.

Source: Courtesy of SPARC (www.sparcmurals.org).

4 City Building in Kansas: An Immigrant’s Perspective, 2007

The modern American metropolis continues to dramatically shape the countryside. For one, the mechanization of agriculture and ranching that began in the nineteenth century continues to dictate how food is produced and processed, who performs the labor to bring it to market, and how different people benefit from these markets' growth and scale. American consumers have long reaped an important reward in the form of lower food prices. But corporate control of farming, ranching, and processing – each industry grew even more concentrated during the twentieth century – continues to make it very difficult for family farms and other independently owned businesses to remain profitable. Instead, these industries operate largely on factory principles, with most labor performed by an unskilled, low-wage, and predominantly immigrant workforce.

The big business of food production has also given rise to new kinds of urban development in the agricultural "heartland," by transforming places like Garden City and Dodge City, Kansas. Both were settled in the nineteenth century: the former by speculators and aspiring farm families, the latter to aid and protect westward migrants (sources 1.1–2). Dodge City was later, briefly, a booming cattle town. But their modern forms, characterized by large populations, diversified economies, and median incomes ranging from $40,000 to $50,000 per household, depend heavily on the meat packing and other food production industries. Immigrants fill most of the low-wage jobs and are among the cities' most impoverished residents. Overall, Latinos – predominantly of Mexican origin – make up 50 percent of the population in Garden City and 60 percent in Dodge City.

In 2007 a 29-year-old meatpacker and dairy worker agreed to be interviewed, anonymously, about his immigration to the United States (he had arrived in 1999) and his life in urban Kansas. He chose the pseudonym "El Mojado" as a comment on his marginal status. This is a single story among countless others, and his perspective is not necessarily shared by all of his peers. But his experience is quite common, and highlights dynamics of the urbanization process that sustain the modern metropolis but remain invisible to many Americans.

I was born in the Sierra de Porvenir, Guerrero, Mexico. It's on the coast. You can camp, fish, hunt. It's a small city, mostly fields. It's like Dodge City if there was no Home Depot, Dillon's, Burger King, Wal-Mart, or Sears. The only thing is, there's no beach here in Kansas. And there's no feedlots in Porvenir. Here in Kansas, at seven in the evening, every day, you're smelling the pestilence of the feedlot.

I wasn't like a normal boy who finished primary school. I felt really separate from the other kids. When I was six in primary school, we sometimes went the day without lunch. We had to sell things like tender corn on the cob, turkeys, chickens, eggs, and bread rolls. We had to sell things to make one peso, two pesos. We also had to walk almost for an hour to wash in the river ... My brother and I both didn't finish secondary school.

It was better for us to start working. My sister stayed in school and studied English and French. My mother's working to try and support herself and my sister because right now I can't even afford to send her money. My mother cleans. She cleans office buildings ...

... My wife and I have four children. My wife is twenty-eight years old. She is very nice, a hard worker and a good cook – she makes really good tamales, which we sometimes sell. I like the way she takes care of the house. She's also taking classes to learn English. And I tell her not to leave school. For her it will be a big help. It will help me, too. She'll be able to translate. At least she gets ahead, since I can't study. We get by with what I earn. It's the only thing we count on ...

... You come here with a dream. I came here for one reason: I was told I'd earn double what I was making in Mexico. But the bad thing is that your dream never comes true. You just want to see the greens. A lot of people have died wanting to see those greens. Here everything moves with money. My wife also wanted to come here. She thought it would be a better place for children, that there are more opportunities here for kids.

We spent about eight months living on the border in Juarez before crossing over. To support my family I worked in a kitchen as a cook. I crossed first, alone, with a coyote and some other guys. I left my family in Juarez. You hear stories about the border, of women who are raped. People who are assaulted. Money stolen ... The big problem we had was climbing a fence, which was about twelve feet high. It had this sharp wire at the top of it. I had to help a guy, a friend, who got caught on that wire. He was bleeding. He'd cut his foot. The coyote left us. He was running ahead with the others. But the truth is I couldn't leave a friend like that, hooked on this piece of wire. If Immigration had taken him down who knows what would have happened to him. I helped him off the fence and cleaned his foot with a shirt. We had to throw that shirt away.

Later, we ran across a four-lane highway. Honestly, I felt like a thief. Then we ran towards the town of El Paso to look for a hotel to spend the night ... Then a half day later, they put me on a bus that came straight to Garden City in November of 1999. I came to Kansas because my wife had family here. I was twenty-two years old.

My family crossed over in March 2000. My wife came over as an American citizen. She walked across the bridge with a fake ID she bought at the border ... My oldest son was three years old at the time. He also had the papers of a citizen. He passed alone, without my wife, with the son of a coyote, a twelve-year-old kid. My wife was already waiting on the other side ...

At first we stayed with my wife's family. Nine of us lived in one small trailer. The first job I had here in Garden City was at the Montfort beefpacking plant. My brother-in-law worked there and helped me get the job. I used my fake papers. When I first saw the cow at the slaughterhouse I was surprised. I had never seen animals like that, all cut up, with blood everywhere. There is always work with the slaughterhouse. They don't stop work because of snow or rain. So on the one hand, it's good to have work, but on the other hand, it's not good because they discriminate. They make certain people work more than other people. They do give you training, but too little training. Someone just tells you, "Move your wrist, warm up the fingers." But you never warm up your back and you're standing up the whole time. It depends on the job they give you, but I was standing the whole time for the job they gave me. My fingers would lock up. They're still locked up …

At the plant, I would work sometimes ten, twelve hours a day. It depended on the hours that they gave me. The salary was very little – I made about $8.00, $8.50 an hour. They told me how to use the equipment, but charged us for it. They charged for the boots, the gloves, helmet, goggles – all the equipment. The most expensive piece of equipment was the steel glove. The glove cost about $30, I think. I don't know for sure. They don't give a list of how much things are. The checks I received were supposedly for about $300. I ended up with something around $150 after they charged me for the equipment.

I was on the line. There were three of us on the line. One did the flat cut, and I would take the bone. Then when I worked on the flat, another one did the bone … And we would take turns like that. And we had to do it quickly – in less than two minutes – or else it would all end up together, the work would stack up on you …

There's two kinds of climates in the slaughterhouse: very hot and very cold. I was in processing, so the place where I ended up was very cold. It keeps the bacteria out of the meat. I wore a vest, sleeves, an apron, and four gloves. I was wet all the time. Inside I trembled. When I took off my clothes I would catch a fever. Sometimes the body acclimates to the environment. Other times, as time passes, you end up with respiratory problems. Or you get heart problems. I got a lot of colds, too many. I also got sinusitis.

They only gave us two breaks – one fifteen-minute and another one for half an hour … Sometimes I had to do work for somebody else if they were absent. And since I was new, I sometimes had to do the jobs nobody wanted to do. But I had to do them. I needed a stable job. I was afraid that they would fire me. And where I am going to go without papers? …

I had an accident … A guy who would give us rides to work locked his keys in his car [and the window broke as we tried to reach in to get them] … I cut my hand. I had to go to the hospital. I didn't have insurance. I paid all $495 in cash. They sewed me up, but left glass inside. I could hardly work, even though I wanted to … My hand was looking really bad – green.

I thought I would end up without a hand. It was all swollen. I couldn't put gloves on or anything ...

... I had to ... support my family in whatever way I could. I sold chickens. I'd go to the city park and look for people and tell them, "Look, I'm selling chicken." ... If I sold fourteen chickens in a day I could pay my bills ... I found other jobs. I got into touching up car dents, preparing them for paint jobs and a body shop ... [But the boss] accused me of stealing. He fired me ... after eight months ... I had another job working with large farming sprinklers, the kind that irrigate corn ... They paid me about $6.50 an hour; we worked over twelve hours a day. They never gave us a raise ... In 2003, I worked in roofing and made three hundred dollars a week ... With my fake papers I was able to work at lots of jobs. I never did my taxes, so I never got money back from the government. I was paying in, but not getting money back.

In June 2006, I applied for a job on the cleanup crew at the IBP meatpacking plant ... An American girl at the office there took applications. She took my picture and checked the picture and my papers on the computer. She saw the photos weren't the same. She said, "If you don't leave, I'm either going to call the police or call Immigration." She got a person – some big American guy from the office, and he was in agreement that they should take the papers from me, and they took them. From then on I haven't had any papers.

After they took my papers, I went to work at the dairy farm. The hours were long, twelve hours. It's a job you have to be careful with, because a cow could hurt you or a fence could hurt you. I cleaned the pens, took the poop off the cows. I was in charge of the corrals, maybe fifteen corrals, more, with half an hour to clean each corral. I rushed to finish it all in one day ... I had to take care of everything – the cows, the machinery ...

It was a lot of pressure. The pay was little. It turned out to be about $6.50 or $7.50 an hour for twelve hours a day. There was no insurance. When we started there, we had to sign a sheet that said that we could be let go at any time. At any instant. But if we chose to quit, we had to give them two weeks' notice.

I had headaches, I felt very tense, I had nosebleeds. My ears hurt. I had to go to the doctor. They drew blood. They gave me pills. They gave me a letter for the boss. The foreman told me he didn't care. "You still have to work. Many people come in sick." He said, "I knew a person who drove a tractor. He was sick. He kept driving that tractor, and he just died in that tractor. You don't have to worry about it. God is good." My foreman said I could come back. I told him I wasn't going to come back. I had to keep my health.

Right now, I work in carpeting. Again, I work about twelve hours a day. It's very hard on the knees, on the back. The knees get swollen ...

Truly I don't see a difference since when I got here. I don't have more money. I don't have any land. I was supposed to earn double what I was making in my country. For the eight years that I've been here – nothing.

The trailer we live in is okay enough, but it's missing lots of details. There are three holes in the roof that leak. The insulation underneath is all broken. If I had seen how the trailer was, I wouldn't have paid $2,000. I pay $180 for the lot rent and cable; $82 for water and trash; $140 for electricity and gas … I'm also not done paying my coyote. He lives in the area. I paid about $12,000 for the whole family to come over. Right now I still owe $2,500 … And I can't tell on him for anything. He would call the police on me or Immigration on me. My coyote's legal here.

That's the world. That's the life of the immigrant … People from El Salvador, Honduras, Guatemala – they pay even more … Guatemalans pay five thousand dollars to come here …

Immigrants need documents. They need at least an ID or license. But here's no way to get a license. Here in Kansas, you must drive to get to the store, to the hospital, everywhere. And everything we do is a crime. You don't have papers, it's a crime. You buy fake papers, it's a crime. You live a crime.

The Americans want us to do the job harder, faster, but for less money. If we at least had insurance or a raise … We come here to find a different life …

Americans with papers can go to Mexico and drive. They are able to work there, too. Why can't we work here? A lot of Americans in Mexico have hotels, restaurants. They live well there. Nobody bothers them. And here, nobody wants us here … We do things an American wouldn't do … Who works the oranges? Who works the construction? Dairies? Fields? Hog farms? Cleaning homes? Who does that? Immigrants. I don't think anyone who has papers is going to be doing that. An American, when is he gonna be picking oranges? Who is going to milk cows for ten hours straight, then get a five-minute lunch?

Source: "El Mojado," in Peter Orner (ed.), *Underground America: Narratives of Undocumented Lives* (San Francisco: McSweeney's, 2008), pp. 205–216. Reproduced by permission.

5 Developers in Los Angeles County Spark a Twenty-First-Century Debate over City Building and Environmental Protection, 2009

The technical and environmental challenges encountered by nineteenth-century city builders, some of them documented in Chapters 1–3, continue today in a very different political and institutional context. A great deal has changed. Developers have the expertise, the resources, and considerable public sector support to expand metropolitan regions with ever more ambitious projects. Meanwhile scientists, planners, activists, and housing reformers have publicized the risks of unchecked and unregulated development, risks for both natural environments and residents. Together with the modern environmental movement, these critics have raised public awareness and often forced public authorities to protect less powerful stakeholders and to curb dangerous practices. Building American places still requires compromises, but now we have considerable knowledge about the advantages and disadvantages posed by alternative approaches to development.

This is a good thing, because development is necessary: to maintain and replace existing structures, to accommodate population growth, to sustain markets for a variety of goods and services, and to raise revenues for municipal, county, and state governments. How, then, should the interested parties reconcile the practical need to build and maintain human communities, on the one hand, with the need to pursue sustainable models of development, on the other? Edward Humes's coverage of the ongoing debate over the Tejon Ranch development just north of Los Angeles does not attempt to answer these questions. But it introduces key players in contemporary development contests, their competing priorities and visions, and the political processes that ultimately decide what gets built and on what terms (see also source 9.4). Humes's reporting aptly closes this volume by exploring the complexity of the contemporary built environment and the constant negotiations and trade-offs that it demands. His brief history of Tejon Ranch reminds us, in the meantime, that every parcel of land in the United States, whether we call it urban, suburban, or rural, has been continually and steadily transformed by the processes that gave rise to the modern metropolis.

Between the asphalt sprawl of the Los Angeles basin and the fertile flatlands of the Great Central Valley, where the Okies flocked during the Dust Bowl days and *The Grapes of Wrath* was set (and banned), a vast and surprising wilderness still thrives. Broad pastures, granite-studded hillsides, and icy blue mountain lakes all lie within an hour's drive of L.A. smog and concrete, hidden in plain sight as traffic snakes by on the one major freeway through the Tehachapi Mountains. Ancient oak groves offer cool shade; thick stands of piñon pines beckon in the breeze; forests of twisted Joshua trees grope toward the clouds.

The landscape has barely changed for thousands of years, which is why more than 80 rare or endangered species continue to prey, roam, roost, flower, and rear their young here. The nearly extinct California condor comes to forage in small numbers where long ago colonies nested in this last Southern California wilderness, this blank spot on the map 18 times the size of Manhattan. There is no other place like it in California and few to rival it on earth. To stand on a windswept hill at Tejon Ranch is to be at once humbled, enthralled, and saddened by vistas that in years past defined California and the West by their plenty rather than their dearth. The United Nations has recognized the region encompassing much of the ranch as one of 25 irreplaceable hot spots of biodiversity in the world – a designation reserved for just 2.4 percent of the earth's surface.

The ranch's owners want to build a city there. Called Centennial, it would have 23,000 homes and at least 64,000 residents. They also plan to create a resort and shopping malls, along with industrial parks, cargo terminals, and a system for delivering water no one in this drought-ridden state can spare. Where cattle grazing and hunting have been the main activities for the last 150 years, the Tejon Ranch Company and its investors want to construct the largest master-planned community California has ever seen. This is the rough equivalent of dropping a Boulder, Colorado, into the Arctic National Wildlife Refuge or a couple iterations of Harrisburg, Pennsylvania, down into Yosemite.

After years of preliminaries, an initial environmental impact statement and a habitat conservation plan – federally mandated studies that must be hashed out before a patch of grass can be disturbed – were released for public comment in January. The documents were pushed out the door three days after Barack Obama took office and before new administration appointments had been made, despite the new president's memorandum to delay all environmental reports so they could be reevaluated.

Normally this would have created an uproar among California environmental organizations. Instead there has been silence. That's because a number of the biggest environmental players in the state – Audubon California, the Sierra Club, and the Natural Resources Defense Council among them – that once opposed the project as an ecological disaster are now working with the Tejon Ranch Company. Facing the likelihood of years of litigation, the owners of the Tejon Ranch last year agreed to something so extraordinary that it fractured the environmental opposition. They offered to dedicate up to 90 percent of the ranch land to conservation, giving environmental groups equal control of the property. In one stroke, the single largest development in state history would also become the single largest wilderness preservation project in the state.

"This is one of the great conservation achievements in California history," said Joel Reynolds, senior attorney and director of the NRDC's urban program, when the deal was announced. "This agreement is the Mount Everest of conservation."

There was a catch, however. Those same environmental groups would have to drop public opposition to the resort, the city, the industrial parks, and all other development on the remaining 10 percent of the ranch, no matter what form it took. The greens would have to remain on the sidelines instead of digging into those recently released reports. Five of six environmental organizations that had been allied to fight the ranch development have removed themselves from contention by signing the conservation agreement.

It was a brilliant move by the Tejon Ranch Company, a publicly traded corporation with Wall Street money behind it – Third Avenue Management being the biggest investor, with nearly 30 percent of the company's shares and a seat on the board. Sums as monumental as the landscape are at stake. The raw land alone was reportedly valued at $1.5 billion in 1999, and if developed as envisioned, the ranch would be worth up to 30 times that amount, perhaps much more when all is said and done. More than 37,000 jobs could be added to a struggling local economy. Completing the project would demand, on average, the construction of a new house every eight hours, 365 days a year, for 20 years.

To those who see progress in a bulldozer's blade and beauty in the taming of nature, Tejon Ranch is an irresistible plum: 270,000 contiguous acres lying 60 miles from downtown Los Angeles, a straight shot up Interstate 5 – the Golden State Freeway transformed into the ultimate driveway to the ultimate bedroom community. The *New York Times* admiringly described the plan as "Playing SimCity for Real." The investors know the economic downturn won't last forever, and they want their plans and permits ready to roll as soon as the market picks up. Sacrificing up to 90 percent of the ranch – more than half of which was too rugged or remote to ever be developed – just may be the quickest way to make that city a reality.

Standing in the path of this future Tejon Ranch is a relatively little-known environmental group with a small budget and outsize ambitions, the Center for Biological Diversity, whose representatives have called the agreement "a classic greenwash." This is the sixth group, the one that opted out of the negotiations with Tejon. "If we can't save a pristine piece of wilderness that the United Nations considers to be one of the 25 most biologically important on earth," says Peter Galvin, the group's 44-year-old cofounder and conservation director, "what can we save?"

On paper this scruffy outfit – a hodgepodge of 62 lawyers, biologists, activists, and ordinary folks – shouldn't have a prayer against the political, economic, and legal resources behind SimCity … Compared with operations like the Sierra Club, the center's $6.5 million budget is shoestring, but its biologists and attorneys are considered leaders in their fields … [D]uring the past 20 years, the Center for Biological Diversity has won close to 90 percent of its 500 cases …

Since the Endangered Species Act was passed in 1973, 70 percent of the plant and animal species given protection under the law have been listed because of efforts by the center. More than 100 million acres of wildlands have been preserved as habitats for these endangered species ... Their aggressive use of science and lawsuits to compel compliance with the Endangered Species Act and other environmental laws has defeated off-roaders and offshore oil drillers, developers and Detroit automakers, adversaries, and an alphabet soup of government agencies from Washington State to Washington, D.C., and as far away as Okinawa.

The center's work has transformed overgrazed, trampled, and befouled federal lands that had been all but left for dead into lush riparian forests. Thousands of miles of ocean waters nearly stripped of life have been made off-limits to dragnets, bringing endangered sea turtles and depleted fisheries back from the brink of extinction ... Its latest target is the most threatening source of environmental damage, extinctions, and habitat loss yet – global warming – and Tejon Ranch is ground zero.

... It argues that state and federal laws should force developers at Tejon – and elsewhere – to quantify their contribution to global warming and then do everything feasible to eliminate that impact, from installing solar roofs to mandating zero-emission vehicles for residents ...

Tejón is Spanish for "badger," a creature once plentiful near the ranch ... The land had long been coveted for its fertility, beauty, and strategic location. It was occupied by the Yokuts and several other Native American nations, was claimed by Mexico in the 19th century and carved up into four land-grant ranchos, then became U.S. terrain after the Mexican–American War and California's admission to the Union.

Fort Tejon was established in 1854 at the urging of a storied California military man, explorer, road builder, and land baron, Edward Fitzgerald Beale. Among many firsts, he surveyed for the transcontinental railroad [and] brought news to Washington that gold had been discovered in California ... As head of the Bureau of Indian Affairs (he was also lead Indian negotiator and surveyor general of California and Nevada), Beale helped manage reservation land for local tribes. He also snapped up the four ranchos to form the present-day boundaries of Tejon Ranch.

The Beale family kept the ranch for 57 years, then sold it for $3 million in 1912 to a consortium of investors led by Harry Chandler, who later became publisher of the *Los Angeles Times*. The Chandler family's Times Mirror Company converted the Tejon Ranch into a publicly traded corporation. In the 1970s, it was listed on the American Stock Exchange, where its stock prices soared to more than $600 a share in the mid-1980s as interest intensified in the company's plans for massive development ...

… In 1996, the current CEO, a San Diego developer named Bob Stine, took over, along with new board members who had similar real estate backgrounds and ambitions. Then Times Mirror sold its controlling interest, and Third Avenue Management entered the picture. Planning to transform the ranch into a city and resort began …

For those who own Tejon Ranch, the people who have invested in the vision of a new city and resort complex set amid windswept hills and oak groves, the issue is a simple question of property rights. They say they have bent over backward to set aside significant land for a nature preserve and open space. They have invited environmental groups to help oversee the conserved lands. What more must they do to satisfy the center? "The fundamental core values of the ranch from the get-go are conservation and good stewardship," says Barry Zoeller, vice president of corporate communications for the ranch.

Much of the Tejon Ranch project is to be in semirural Kern County, where the county seat is the city of Bakersfield. Civic leaders there have complained that the Center for Biological Diversity is going too far and should not try to block jobs and revenue in the region. A columnist with *The Bakersfield Californian*, Marylee Shrider – in an article reprinted on the Tejon Company's Web site – summed up these sentiments, deriding the center's "saber rattling" and "unwarranted sense of entitlement" as environmental extremism …

Early on, and despite its reputation for being uncompromising, the center had participated in meetings with the Tejon Ranch Company, the Wildlands Conservancy, the Sierra Club, Audubon California, the Natural Resources Defense Council, the Planning and Conservation League, the Endangered Habitats League, and others … [But the] center [eventually] parted company for good with its former allies. The Sierra Club, the NRDC, and the other groups have focused on what would be saved, its epic size and scope, on the notion that the deal serves the greater good. The center activists and attorneys argue that it is a grave mistake … to surrender the right to object to a development with such enormous potential to harm species and landscapes. No matter how much land is saved, Galvin maintains, it cannot make up for establishing Centennial in what is now grasslands and putting a resort in critical lakeside condor habitat. The endangered birds and other species will inevitably suffer, perhaps catastrophically, he argues, and the state will lose credibility as a champion of "smart growth" and a foe of climate-damaging, resource-hogging sprawl ...

A media event was held at the ranch in May 2008, featuring Governor Schwarzenegger and one environmental leader after another praising the deal. Reynolds described it as a "once-in-a-lifetime achievement." Bill Corcoran of the Sierra Club called it the "ecological equivalent of the Louisiana Purchase." The *Los Angeles Times* proclaimed that it "ends years of debate over the fate of an untrammeled tableau of mountains, wildflower fields, twisted oaks and Joshua trees."

Missing from the praise of the plan was that 23,000 homes as well as hotels, condos, golf courses, and an industrial center were going to be plopped down in the midst of the preserves. Absent also were the Sierra Club activists who lived near the area slated for development and who adamantly opposed it. They resigned from leadership in the local Sierra Club group so they could continue to voice opposition to the development ...

...

Third Avenue Management, a specialist in distressed properties (it recently acquired a $20 million share of LandSource Communities Development, the bankrupt owner of 15,000 acres in Newhall and Valencia), certainly sees the conservation agreement as a good investment. Michael Winer, a Third Avenue portfolio manager and Tejon board member, wrote in a quarterly letter to shareholders that the deal allows the company to avoid 50 years of litigation and to pack more development onto the ranch than it could ever have achieved had the environmental groups refused to bargain. "Such protracted litigation," he added, "would obviously have a devastating impact on the value of Tejon Ranch common stock."

... The uncertain economy and housing market woes will likely hold off the bulldozers for now, but activists fear that government agencies, particularly at the county level, may be more inclined than ever to issue permits in hope of providing an economic stimulus ...

For the Center for Biological Diversity, the stakes are just as high. If it can alter the course of the Tejon development, if the construction can be stopped or molded into something environmentally sound, if consideration of extinction and global warming can be made to trump money and sprawl here, on California's last frontier, then [the center] sees Tejon Ranch as the start of something big, something nationwide, a seismic shift. It will mean the United States is no longer stuck on the old questions of how and why we should take action against global warming and extinction. We will have moved on to the questions of how much and how fast we should act.

Source: Edward Humes, "The Last Frontier," *Los Angeles Magazine*, 54(6) (June 2009), pp. 94–97, 124. Reproduced by permission of Emmis Publishing Company. Reproduced by permission of Edward Humes.

Editor's note: *In April 2012, the 5th District Court of Appeals dismissed a challenge by opponents of the Tejon Mountain Village project, a proposed residential and resort community. The court ruled that the environmental impact report filed by Kern County was sufficient to permit groundbreaking. The Village is scheduled to include 3,450 homes, 160,000 square feet of commercial space, two golf courses, hiking trails, hotel facilities, and "various resort-style amenities." "The ranching lifestyle," report the developers, "will also be preserved by the community's design, and cattle grazing will continue within the preserved open space of the community."*

Questions for Discussion

1. Are American metropolitan regions more or less inclusive than they were 60 years ago?
2. How have the dynamics of city building changed in light of the following developments: the decline of American manufacturing and growth of service industries; changing patterns of immigration; the federal commitment articulated in civil rights legislation to protect all Americans against discriminatory treatment; the rise of the modern environmental movement?
3. Use clusters of sources and headnotes from this volume to reconstruct the modern history of one of the metropolitan regions listed below. What trends can you document? How does the history of a single American place relate to the history of *other* places and to powerful private and public institutions? For metropolitan New York City, see 1.1–4; 2.1–3; 3.1, 5; 4.1, 4–5; 5.1–4; 6.1, 4; 7.1–2, 4–6; 8.1, 3–4; 10.1–4; 11.1–4; 12.1–2, 4–5; 13.1–3; 14.2–3; for Los Angeles and Southern California, see 1.1–4; 3.1; 4.3; 6.4; 7.1–2, 5–6; 8.1; 9.1–2, 4; 10.1–4; 11.1–4; 12.1–2, 4–5; 13.4; 14.2–3, 5; for metropolitan Chicago, see 1.1–4; 3.1, 3; 4.4–5; 5.1, 4; 6.3–4; 7.2, 5–6; 8.1–2; 10.1–4; 11.1–4; 12.1–2, 4–5; 13.1; for Dallas–Fort Worth, see 1.1–4; 3.1; 4.3; 6.2, 4; 8.1, 6; 9.1–2; 10.1–4; 11.1–4; 12.1–2, 4–5; 14.2; for metropolitan Detroit, see 1.1–4; 3.1; 4.5; 5.1, 4; 6.4; 7.1–3, 5–6; 8.1; 9.1; 10.1–4; 11.1–4; 12.1–2, 4–6; 13.1, 5; 14.2.
4. What makes a place "urban," "suburban," or "rural"?

Further Reading

Listed here is a small sample of the work on which I drew to prepare this volume. Follow these authors' leads to identify the extensive scholarship and commentary as well as primary sources related to topics of interest.

General works

Chudacoff, Howard P., Judith E. Smith, and Peter C. Baldwin, *The Evolution of American Urban Society* (7th ed., Pearson, 2009).

Corey, Steven H. and Lisa Krissof Boehm, *The American Urban Reader: History and Theory* (Routledge, 2010).

Hayden, Dolores, *Building Suburbia: Green Fields and Urban Growth, 1820–2000* (Vintage, 2004).

Jackson, Kenneth T., *Crabgrass Frontier: The Suburbanization of the United States* (Oxford University Press, 1987).

Judd, Dennis R. and Todd Swanstrom, *City Politics* (8th ed., Pearson, 2011).

Lefebvre, Henri, *The Production of Space*, translated by Donald Nicholson-Smith (Blackwell, 1992).

Logan, John R. and Harvey L. Molotch, *Urban Fortunes: The Political Economy of Place* (20th anniversary ed., University of California Press, 2007).

Melosi, Martin V., *Urban Infrastructure in America from Colonial Times to the Present* (Johns Hopkins University Press, 1999).

The Modern American Metropolis: A Documentary Reader, First Edition.
Edited by David M. P. Freund.

Mohl, Raymond A. and Roger Biles (eds.), *The Making of Urban America* (rev. 3rd ed., Rowman & Littlefield, 2011).
Monkkonen, Eric H., *America Becomes Urban: The Development of U.S. Cities and Towns, 1780–1980* (University of California Press, 1990).
Nicolaides, Becky and Andrew Wiese (eds.), *The Suburb Reader* (Routledge, 2006).
Sies, Mary Corbin and Christopher Silver (eds.), *Planning the Twentieth-Century American City* (Johns Hopkins University Press, 1996).

Part I Cities and Hinterlands in Mid-Nineteenth-Century America

Bernstein, Iver, *The New York City Draft Riots: Their Significance for American Society and Politics in the Age of the Civil War* (Oxford University Press, 1990).
Cronon, William, *Nature's Metropolis: Chicago and the Great West* (Norton, 1992).
Dublin, Thomas, *Transforming Women's Work: New England Lives in the Industrial Revolution* (Cornell University Press, 1995).
Johnson, Walter, *River of Dark Dreams: Slavery and Empire in the Cotton Kingdom* (Harvard University Press, 2013).
Ryan, Mary, *Cradle of the Middle Class: The Family in Oneida County, New York, 1790–1865* (Cambridge University Press, 1983).
White, Richard, *"It's Your Misfortune and None of My Own": A New History of the American West* (University of Oklahoma Press, 1993).

Part II From Walking City to Industrial Metropolis, 1860–1920

Beckert, Sven, *The Monied Metropolis: New York City and the Consolidation of the American Bourgeoisie, 1850–1896* (Cambridge University Press, 2003).
Deutsch, Sarah, *Women and the City: Gender, Space, and Power in Boston, 1870–1940* (Oxford University Press, 2002).
Deverell, William, *Whitewashed Adobe: The Rise of Los Angeles and the Remaking of Its Mexican Past* (University of California Press, 2005).
Ethington, Phillip J., *The Public City: The Political Construction of Urban Life in San Francisco, 1850–1900* (new ed., University of California Press, 2001).
Gilfoyle, Timothy J., *A Pickpocket's Tale: The Underworld of Nineteenth-Century New York* (Norton, 2007).
Green, James, *Death In the Haymarket: A Story of Chicago, the First Labor Movement and the Bombing That Divided Gilded Age America* (Anchor, 2007).
Grossman, James R., *Land of Hope: Chicago, Black Southerners, and the Great Migration* (University of Chicago Press, 1991).
Hunter, Tera W., *To 'Joy My Freedom: Southern Black Women's Lives and Labors After the Civil War* (Harvard University Press, 1998).

Klingle, Matthew, *Emerald City: An Environmental History of Seattle* (Yale University Press, 2007).

Leach, William R., *Land of Desire: Merchants, Power, and the Rise of a New American Culture* (Vintage, 1994).

Lee, Erika, *At America's Gates: Chinese Immigration during the Exclusion Era, 1882–1943* (University of North Carolina Press, 2007).

Leuchtenberg, Alan, *The Incoporation of America: Culture and Society in the Gilded Age* (Hill & Wang, 2007).

Muncy, Robyn, *Creating a Female Dominion in American Reform, 1890–1935* (Oxford University Press, 1991).

Peiss, Kathy, *Cheap Amusements: Working Women and Leisure in Turn-of-the Century New York* (Temple University Press, 1996).

Peterson, Jon A., *The Birth of City Planning in the United States, 1840–1917* (Johns Hopkins University Press, 2003).

Revell, Keith D., *Building Gotham: Civic Culture and Public Policy in New York City, 1898–1938* (Johns Hopkins University Press, 2005).

Roediger, David R., *Working Toward Whiteness: How America's Immigrants Became White: The Strange Journey from Ellis Island to the Suburbs* (Basic Books, 2006).

Rosenzweig, Roy and Elizabeth Blackmar, *The Park and the People: A History of Central Park* (Cornell University Press, 1998).

Warner, Sam Bass, Jr., *Streetcar Suburbs: The Process of Growth in Boston, 1870–1900* (2nd ed., Harvard University Press, 1978).

Part III City and Suburb Ascendant, 1920–1945

Brooks, Charlotte, *Alien Neighbors, Foreign Friends: Asian Americans, Housing, and the Transformation of Urban California* (University of Chicago Press, 2009).

Calder, Lendol, *Financing the American Dream: A Cultural History of Consumer Credit* (Princeton University Press, 2001).

Chauncey, George, *Gay New York: Gender, Urban Culture, and the Making of the Gay Male World, 1890–1940* (Basic Books, 1995).

Cohen, Lizabeth, *Making a New Deal: Industrial Workers in Chicago, 1919–1939* (2nd ed., Cambridge University Press, 2008).

Drake, St. Clair and Horace R. Cayton, *Black Metropolis: A Study of Negro Life in a Northern City* (1945; University of Chicago Press, 1993).

Dumenil, Lynn, *The Modern Temper: American Culture and Society in the 1920s* (Hill & Wang, 1995).

Fogelson, Robert M., *Downtown: Its Rise and Fall, 1880–1950* (Yale University Press, 2001).

Gelfand, Mark I., *A Nation of Cities: The Federal Government and Urban America, 1933–1965* (Oxford University Press, 1975).

Gregory, James, *American Exodus: The Dust Bowl Migration and Okie Culture in California* (Oxford University Press, 1991).

Isenberg, Alison, *Downtown: A History of the Place and the People Who Made It* (University of Chicago Press, 2005).

Kurashige, Scott, *The Shifting Grounds of Race: Black and Japanese Americans in the Making of Multiethnic Los Angeles* (Princeton University Press, 2008).

Lewis, David Levering, *When Harlem Was in Vogue* (Penguin, 1997).

Lotchin, Roger W., *Fortress California, 1910–1961: From Warfare to Welfare* (University of Illinois Press, 2002).

Nicolaides, Becky M., *My Blue Heaven: Life and Politics in the Working-Class Suburbs of Los Angeles, 1920–1965* (University of Chicago Press, 2002).

Radford, Gail, *Modern Housing for America: Policy Struggles in the New Deal Era* (University of Chicago Press, 1997).

Sanchez, George J., *Becoming Mexican American: Ethnicity, Culture, and Identity in Chicano Los Angeles, 1900–1945* (Oxford University Press, 1993).

Ward, David and Oliver Zunz, *The Landscape of Modernity: New York City, 1900–1940* (Johns Hopkins University Press, 1997).

Wolcott, Victoria, *Remaking Respectability: African American Women in Interwar Detroit* (University of North Carolina Press, 2000).

Part IV Creating a Suburban Nation, 1945–1970s

Ballon, Hilary and Kenneth T. Jackson (eds.), *Robert Moses and the Modern City: The Transformation of New York* (Norton, 2008).

Biles, Roger, *The Fate of Cities: Urban America and the Federal Government, 1945–2000* (University Press of Kansas, 2011).

Cohen, Lizabeth, *A Consumer's Republic: The Politics of Mass Consumption in Postwar America* (Vintage, 2003).

Coontz, Stephanie, *The Way We Never Were: American Families and the Nostalgia Trap* (Basic Books, 1993).

Cowie, Jefferson, *Capital Moves: RCA's Seventy-Year Quest for Cheap Labor* (New Press, 2001).

Freund, David M. P., *Colored Property: State Policy and White Racial Politics in Suburban America* (University of Chicago Press, 2007).

Hirsch, Arnold R., *Making the Second Ghetto: Race and Housing in Chicago, 1940–1960* (University of Chicago Press, 1998).

Hoffung-Garskof, Jesse, *A Tale of Two Cities: Santo Domingo and New York after 1950* (Princeton University Press, 2010).

Kelley, Robin D. G., *Race Rebels: Culture, Politics, and the Black Working Class* (Free Press, 1996).

Kruse, Kevin, *White Flight: Atlanta and the Making of Modern Conservatism* (Princeton University Press, 2005).

Kwong, Peter, *The New Chinatown* (rev. ed., Hill & Wang, 1996).

Lassiter, Matthew D., *The Silent Majority: Suburban Politics in the Sunbelt South* (Princeton University Press, 2007).

Morris, Aldon, *The Origins of the Civil Rights Movement: Black Communities Organizing For Change* (Free Press, 1986).
Nickerson, Michelle and Darren Dochuk (eds.), *Sunbelt Rising: The Politics of Space, Place, and Region* (University of Pennsylvania Press, 2011).
Ransby, Barbara, *Ella Baker and the Black Freedom Movement: A Radical Democratic Vision* (University of North Carolina Press, 2005).
Rome, Adam, *The Bulldozer in the Countryside: Suburban Sprawl and the Rise of American Environmentalism* (Cambridge University Press, 2001).
Self, Robert O., *American Babylon: Race and the Struggle for Postwar Oakland* (Princeton University Press, 2003).
Schlosser, Eric, *Fast Food Nation: The Dark Side of the All-American Meal* (Mariner, 2012).
Schulman, Bruce J., *From Cotton Belt to Sunbelt: Federal Policy, Economic Development, and the Transformation of the South, 1938–1980* (Duke University Press, 1994).
Shilts, Randy, *The Mayor of Castro Street: The Life and Times of Harvey Milk* (St. Martin's, 2008).
Sugrue, Thomas J., *The Origins of the Urban Crisis: Race and Inequality in Postwar Detroit* (rev. ed., Princeton University Press, 2005).
Wiese, Andrew, *Places of Their Own: African American Suburbanization in the Twentieth Century* (University of Chicago Press, 2005).
Williams, Rhonda, *The Politics of Public Housing: Black Women's Struggles against Urban Inequality* (Oxford University Press, 2005).

Part V What Makes a City? The "Postindustrial" Metropolis

Alexander, Michelle, *The New Jim Crow: Mass Incarceration in the Age of Colorblindness* (New Press, 2012).
Angotti, Tom, *New York For Sale: Community Planning Confronts Global Real Estate* (MIT Press, 2008).
Bluestone, Barry and Bennett Harrison, *The Deindustrialization of America: Plant Closings, Community Abandonment, and the Dismantling of Basic Industry* (Basic Books, 1984).
Davila, Arlene, *Barrio Dreams: Puerto Ricans, Latinos, and the Neoliberal City* (University of California Press, 2004).
Davis, Mike and Robert Morrow, *City of Quartz: Excavating the Future in Los Angeles* (Verso, 1990).
Freeman, Lance, *There Goes the 'Hood: Views of Gentrification from the Ground Up* (Temple University Press, 2006).
Gillette, Howard, Jr., *Camden After the Fall: Decline and Renewal in a Post-Industrial City* (University of Pennsylvania Press, 2006).
Halle, David, *America's Working Man: Work, Home, and Politics among Blue Collar Property Owners* (University of Chicago Press, 1987).

Linkon, Sherry Lee and John Russo, *Steeltown U.S.A.: Work and Memory in Youngstown* (University Press of Kansas, 2002).
McKenzie, Evan, *Privatopia: Homeowners Associations and the Rise of Residential Private Government* (Yale University Press, 1994).
Mele, Christopher, *Selling the Lower East Side: Culture, Real Estate, and Resistance in New York City* (University of Minnesota Press, 2000).
Patillo-McCoy, Mary, *Black Picket Fences: Privilege and Peril among the Black Middle Class* (2nd ed., University of Chicago Press, 2013).
Sassen, Saskia, *Cities in a World Economy* (4th ed., Sage, 2012).
Stacey, Judith, *Brave New Families: Stories of Domestic Upheaval in Late Twentieth Century America* (University of California Press, 1990).

Index

Abernathy, Ralph 245, 247, 248
Addams, Jane 141–142
Agnes M. *see* M., Agnes
Aid for Families with Dependent Children (AFDC) 232, 281–282
Allen, Frederick Lewis 157
American Boy 161
American Can Company 271
American Federation of Labor (AFL) 148, 190
Appleby's 21
Area Redevelopment Administration (ARA) 232–235
Arbeiter Zeitung 84
Army Corps of Engineers 15, 71, 84, 299
Atlanta, GA 6, 46
Austria 39, 41
automobiles 8, 18, 35, 159, 160, *161*, 163, 165–170, 175, 177, 224, 227, 241, 246, 248–249, 254, 271, 280, 288, 289, 296, 297, 298, 303, 304

Baca, Judith Francisca 299–300
Baltimore, MD 19, 46, 160, 162
Baltimore Afro-American 160, *162*
Basquiat, Jean-Michel 298
Bessemer process 11
Black Panther Party 257–258
Black Power 257–263
boosterism 29–36, 84–85, 194–199, 254
Bosque County, TX 41–45
Boston, MA 18, 21, 36, 60–63, 75–80, 106, 108, 125, 130, 134, 236–240, 264, 266, 273
Brazil 46, 47
Brooklyn (New York City) 93, 96, 170–176, 273, 298
Brownsville (New York City) 93, 170–176
built environment (defined) 3
Burlington, MA 21
Butte, MT 96–97, *98–99*

C. H. McCormick & Co. 36–40, 80–84
see also McCormick, Cyrus

The Modern American Metropolis: A Documentary Reader, First Edition.
Edited by David M. P. Freund.

Canada 34, 85, 169
canals 12, 29, 31, 32, 71, 84, 139, 280
Carmichael, Stokely *see* Ture, Kwame
Cervantes, Henry 199–206
Chavez Ravine 299, *300*
Chicago 11, 18, 29–40, 80–84, 107, 108, 110–117, *119*, 122, 125, 130, 131, 141–147, 148–149, 179, 185, 224, 273
Chicago Defender 106, 110–117, 188–190
Chicago Urban League 111
Chicago World's Fair 125
China 97
Chinese Exclusion Act (1882) 97
Cincinnati, OH 21, 64
City Beautiful movement 125
Civil Rights Act (1968) 230
Civil War (US) 15, 45–46, 75
Cleveland, OH 18, 111, 125, 271–272
Colombia 13
see also Isthmus of Panama; New Granada
commuting 4, 7, 20, 24, 75–76, 79, 80, 106–110, *119*, 178, 206–208, 241, 244–250, 254, 283
Coney Island, NY 95, 96, 122, 123, 124, 125–129
Congress of Industrial Organizations (CIO) 190, 192
Congress of Racial Equality (CORE) 257, 258
Crónica, La 97, 100–106
Cuba 46, 190–193
CVS 20

Daily Democrat, The 29–36
Dallas-Fort Worth, TX 6, 41, 111, 139–141
Daughters of Bilitis 263
Dearborn, MI 160, 163, 165–170, 179, *180*, 181, 250–253
Democratic Party 140, 182, 233, 264, 266
Detroit, MI 111, 160, 163, 165–170, 251, 271, 286–288, 309
Dodge City, KS 300–305
"Double V" campaign 206
Douglas, Harlan Paul 175–176
Duwamish channel 84

Ebony 223–224, *225*
Edgewick, WA 84
El Salvador 305
electricity 2, 4, 24, 113, 118, 146, 198, 241, 305
Endangered Species Act (1973) 309
Engineering News 84–85
Erath, George Bernard 41–45
Esquire 226
Evanston, IL 179, 185
Executive Order 9066 208–213
see also Japanese internment
England 47, 48, 49, 54, 128, 130

Federal Housing Administration (FHA) 229–232, 285
Federal Housing Authority *see* Federal Housing Administration
Federal Interstate and Defense Act (1956) 254
see also Interstate System
Federal National Mortgage Association (FNMA) 229
Fifth Avenue Association 87–89
Flint, MI 272
Ford, Henry 163, 191, 271
Ford Motor Company 160, *161*, 163, 165–170, 271
Fort Tejon 209
see also Tejon Ranch
France 48, 122, 130
Frowne, Sadie 87, 90–96, 106, 122, 125

Garden City, KS 300–305
Garrity, Jr., Arthur 264
Gary, IN 223–226, *225*

Gans, Herbert 236
Gap, The 20
General Motors 158
gentrification 22, 273–281, 284, 286
Germany 122, 124, 130, 242
GI Bill 217–219, 229, 253–254
 see also Veterans Administration
Gillespie, C. B. 140
Gilmore, Georgia 245, 249–250
Good Housekeeping 106–107
Great Wall of Los Angeles 298–299, *299–300*
Greece 90
Guatemala 305

Hamilton, Charles V. 257–258
Hamilton, Cynthia 281–282
Hard Rock Cafe 20
Haring, Keith 298
Harlem (New York City) 123, 187–190, 258
Harlem Renaissance 187
Harper's Magazine 157
Harper's Weekly 130
Harrison, Thomas 41–43
Haymarket Square 80–84
Head Start 281–282
Hine, Lewis 80, 119, *120*
hinterlands (defined) 9
Hoboken, NJ 273–278, 280
Hoboken Reporter 273
homelessness 7, 8, 20, 21, 283, 285, 286
homeownership 4, 7, 20, 22, 75–76, 87, 107, 144, 191, 217–226, 229–232, 236, 250–253, 278–281, 283, 295–298
Homestead Act 51
Honduras 305
Housing Act (1949) 236
Houston, TX 6, 97
Houston, Jeanne Wakatsuki 208–209
How the Other Half Lives (1890) 119
Howells, William Dean 75–76
Hoxie, Robert Franklin 147–148
Hughes, Langston 187–188, 190
Humphrey, Hubert H. 232–235
Hull House 122, 141–147
Huneker, James 122, 125
Hunt's Merchants' Magazine and Commercial Review 45–46
Hurricane Katrina 5–6

immigration 15, 19, 55, 50–53, 90–92, 96–97, 100, 101, 102, 122–123, 160, 170, 199, 284, 292, 294, 300–305
immigration restriction 97, 100, 170
"Indian removal" 10, 15, 41–45, 73, 84, 209
International Harvester Corp. 38
 see also C. H. McCormick & Co.
Interstate System 3, 21, 236, 253–257, 259, 284, 308
 see also Federal Interstate and Defense Act (1956)
Ireland 50–53
Isthmus of Panama 13
 see also Colombia; New Granada
Italy 77, 90

Japan 209, 210, 212
Japanese internment 200, 208–213, 299
Jersey City, NJ 273, 278–281, *279*
Jim Crow 16, 110–117, 188, 200, 224, 244–250, 284
Johnson, Lyndon B. 253–257
Journal of Negro History 111

Kansas City, KS 19
Kansas City, MO 19, 21
Kazin, Alfred 170
Kenosha, WI 272
King, Coretta Scott 245, 248
King, Martin Luther, Jr. 245, 247, 248, 257
King, Rodney 282

"Kitchen Debate" 219–220
Knights of Labor 82, 96–97, 148
Khrushchev, Nikita 219–220
Ku Klux Klan 140, 192, 282

LA Weekly 281
Ladies' Home Journal 157–158, 160, *164*
Landsmark, Theodore 264, *265*
Lake Washington (Seattle) 84
Laredo, TX 97, 100–106
Las Vegas, NV 3, 296
Lee, Denver and Willa 223–226, *225*
Lewis, Rufus 248–249
Levitt, William 217–219
Levittowns 217–219
Life 160, *165*, 226–228
Ling Temco Vought 272
Long Beach, CA 209, 282
Long Island, NY 124, 134, 217–219
Lowell, MA 54, 59, 60
Los Angeles 9, 19, 21, 97, 160, *167*, 178, 194–199, 209–213, 232, 271–272, 273, 281–286, 298–299, *299–300*, 305–312
Los Angeles Chamber of Commerce 194–199
Lynn, MA 60–63

M., Agnes 122–125
McCormick, Cyrus 36, *37*, 38–40, 82
  see also C. H. McCormick & Co.
Manzanar 209, 213
Marblehead, MA 60–63
Martin, Trayvon 282
Mattachine Society 263–264, *265*
Memphis, TN 253–257
Merced, CA 295–298
Mexico 13, 100, 101, 205, 301–302, 305, 309
Mexico City 205
Miami, FL 3, 179
Minneapolis-St. Paul, MN 292–294
Minneapolis Star Tribune 292
Montgomery, AL 244–250
Montgomery Improvement Association 248
Moscow 219

NAACP (National Association for the Advancement of Colored People) 225, 246
Nashville, TN 21
Nashua, NH 60
Nation, The 179
National Municipal League 140
National Welfare Rights Organization (NWRO) 257
New Deal 182–183, *183–184*, 185–193, 253
New Granada 13
  see also Colombia; Isthmus of Panama
New Orleans, LA 5–6, 29, 36, 47, 116
New York City 3, 18, 29, 36, 46, 48–49, 50–53, 54, 58, 59, 87–89, 90–96, 106, 108, 111, 114, 119, *120–121*, 122–129, 130–134, 135–139, 170–175, 187–193, 218, 263–264, *265*, 266, 273, 278, 280, 298, 307
New York Independent 90–96, 122–125
New York Stock Exchange 46, 48–49
  see also Wall Street
New York Times 60–63, 87–89, 217–219, 262, 295–298, 308
Nixon, E. D. 245, 246–247, 248
Nixon, Richard 219–220, 285
Norfolk, VA 57–58, 59
Northwest Ordinance 41
Norway 41
Novi, MI 286–291

Oakland, CA 271–272
Oklahoma City, OK 6
Olmsted, Frederick Law 53–54

Oregon Trail 13
Oregon Trail, The 40–41
Orlando, FL 20
Overton Park 253–257

Pacific Railway Act (1862) 71–75
Panama Canal 84, 139
see also Isthmus of Panama
Panera Bread 21
Parks, Rosa 245–247
Patterson, NJ 60
Pearl Harbor 207, 209, 210, 211
Peru 195
Philadelphia, PA 29, 36, 106, 131, 178, 194, 206–208
Philadelphia Transportation Co. 206–208
Phoenix, AZ 97, 202
Pittsburgh, PA 271–272
Pittsburgh Courier 206
planning 41, 84–87, 87–88, 107, 125, 129–130, 230, 236–240, 240–241, 286–291, 306
Plunkitt, George Washington 135–139
Poland 91, 92
Primerica 271
Populist Party 72
public housing 5–6, 232, 251, 254, 281–282
Public Housing Administration (PHA) 232

railroads 11, 12, 13, 15, 16, 17, 29–36, 36, 41, 46, 54–56, 60, 71–75, 78, 84, 85, 93, 100, 107, 108, 109, 122, 131, 170–171, 178, 206–208, 244, 278, 280, 288, 298, 309
Randolph, A. Philip 206
Raskob, Jacob 157–159
Reading, MA 21
rent parties 187–190
renting 4, 8, 20, 64, 66, 88, 89, 91, 93, 102, 144, 145, 173, 177, 187–190, 191, 217, 224, 236–240, 250, 251, 259, 263, 274, 275, 276, 278, 284, 295–298, 305
Republican Party 71, 233, 266
Republic of Texas 97
Richmond, VA 55–56, 58, 59
Riis, Jacob 80, 119, 121
Riordin, William L. 136
Robinson, Jo Ann 245, 247–248
Roosevelt, Franklin Delano 182, 193, 198, 206, 207, 208, 213
Runnells, Hardin R. 41
Russia 48, 49, 90

San Diego, CA *184*, 196, 198, 310
San Fernando Valley (LA County) 21, 285, 299
Santa Monica, CA 208–213
Seattle, WA 19, 84–87
St. Louis, MO 18, 36, 111, 131
San Francisco, CA 13, 18, 63–67, 74, 125, 128, 197, 200, 273
Shelley v. Kraemer (1948) 251
Sierra Club 307, 310, 311
slavery 12, 14, 17, 24, 45–49, 53–59, 97, 100
"slum clearance" 84–87, 236–240, 281–286
see also urban renewal
Southern California Business 194–195
Southern Christian Leadership Council (SCLC) 244
Southwest Dearborn Civic Association (SDCA) 250–253
Spain 192
Spies, August Theodore 80–81
Sports Authority, The 21
Standard Metropolitan Area (defined) 22
Starr, Ellen Gates 141
Stoner, Anona 257
Stonewall Inn 263
Stonewall Riots 263–264, *265*

Student Nonviolent Coordinating Committee (SNCC) 257, 258
Suburban Life 107
Suburban Sketches 75–76
Sunset 219–220
Superstorm Sandy 6, 24–25

Tammany Hall 135–139, 142
Tampa, FL 190–193
Tejon Ranch 305–312
  see also Fort Tejon
Terkel, Studs 185
Treaty of Guadalupe Hidalgo 100, 101–102, 103
Ture, Kwame 257–258
Tuskegee, AL *183*

Underwriting Manual 229–230
US Bureau of the Census 22, 292
US Department of Defense 194–197, 234, 235
US News and World Report 240–241
US Steel 271–272
US Supreme Court 88, 251
Urban Outfitters 20, 298
urban renewal 19–20, 22, 236–240, 253–254, 259, 281–286
  see also "slum clearance"

Veterans Administration (VA) 217–219, 229, 253–254
  see also GI Bill
Villard, Henry S. 179

Wagner Act (1935) 190
Wall Street 137, 181, 277, 308
Washington, D.C. 1–8, 36, 54–55, *166*, 200, 254, 309
Williams, Albert 63–64
Williams, Harry 232–235
Woburn, MA 21
Women's Political Council 245, 247
Works Progress Administration (WPA) 182–183, *183–184*, 186, 193

Ybor City (Tampa, FL) 190–193
Yglesias, Jose 190
Yoder, Jane 185, 190
Youngstown, OH 271–272, *272*
Youth's Companion 160, 161

Zimmerman, George 282
Zimmerman, Louis 84–85
Zoot Suit riots 200, 299
Zoning 5, 14, 87–89, 223–224, 230–231, 250, 253, 259, 283, 284, 287, 289, 291